English / Korean
영어 / 한국어

THE OXFORD
Picture Dictionary

NORMA SHAPIRO AND JAYME ADELSON-GOLDSTEIN

Translated by Techno-Graphics & Translations, Inc.

Oxford University Press

Oxford University Press
198 Madison Avenue, New York, NY 10016 USA
Great Clarendon Street, Oxford OX2 6DP England

Oxford New York

Auckland Cape Town Dar es Salaam Hong Kong Karachi
Kuala Lumpur Madrid Melbourne Mexico City Nairobi
New Delhi Shanghai Taipei Toronto
With offices in
Argentina Austria Brazil Chile Czech Republic France Greece
Guatemala Hungary Italy Japan Poland Portugal Singapore
South Korea Switzerland Thailand Turkey Ukraine Vietnam

OXFORD is a trademark of Oxford University Press.

Library of Congress Cataloging-in-Publication Data

Shapiro, Norma.
    The Oxford picture dictionary: English–Korean/
Norma Shapiro and Jayme Adelson-Goldstein; translated
by Techno-Graphics and Translations, Inc.
        p.   cm.
    Includes biographical references and index.
    ISBN-13: 978 0 19 435191 1
    ISBN-10: 0 19 435191 2
    1. Picture dictionaries, Korean.   2. Picture dictionaries,
English.   3. Korean language—Dictionaries—English.
    4. English language—Dictionaries—Korean.
I. Adelson-Goldstein, Jayme.   II. Title.
PL939.S52   1998   98-10947
423'.947—DC21

No unauthorized photocopying.

Translation reviewed by: Cambridge Translation Resources
Editorial Manager: Susan Lanzano
Art Director: Lynn Luchetti
Senior Editor: Eliza Jensen
Senior Designer: Susan P. Brorein
Production Editor: Rita Chabot
Art Buyer: Tracy A. Hammond
Cover Design Production: Brett Sonnenschein
Production Services by: Techno-Graphics and Translations, Inc.
Production Manager: Abram Hall
Production Controller: Georgiann Baran
Pronunciation Editor: Sharon Goldstein
Cover design by Silver Editions

Printing (last digit): 10

Printed in China.

Illustrations by: David Aikins, Doug Archer, Craig Attebery,
Garin Baker, Sally Bensusen, Eliot Bergman, Mark Bischel, Dan
Brown / Artworks NY, Roy Douglas Buchman, George Burgos /
Larry Dodge, Carl Cassler, Mary Chandler, Robert Crawford, Jim
DeLapine, Judy Francis, Graphic Chart and Map Co., Dale
Gustafson, Biruta Akerbergs Hansen, Marcia Hartsock, C.M.I.,
David Hildebrand, The Ivy League of Artists, Inc. / Judy
Degraffenreid, The Ivy League of Artists, Inc. / Tom Powers, The
Ivy League of Artists, Inc. / John Rice, Pam Johnson, Ed
Kurtzman, Narda Lebo, Scott A. MacNeill / MACNEILL &
MACINTOSH, Andy Lendway / Deborah Wolfe Ltd., Jeffrey
Mangiat, Suzanne Mogensen, Mohammad Mansoor, Tom
Newsom, Melodye Benson Rosales, Stacey Schuett, Rob
Schuster, James Seward, Larry Taugher, Bill Thomson, Anna
Veltfort, Nina Wallace, Wendy Wassink- Ackison, Michael
Wepplo, Don Wieland
Thanks to Mike Mikos for his preliminary architectural sketches
of several pieces.

References
Boyer, Paul S., Clifford E. Clark, Jr., Joseph F. Kett, Thomas L.
Purvis, Harvard Sitkoff, Nancy Woloch *The Enduring Vision: A
History of the American People*, Lexington, Massachusetts:
D.C. Heath and Co., 1990.

Grun, Bernard, *The Timetables of History: A Horizontal Linkage
of People and Events*, (based on Werner Stein's Kulturfahrplan)
New York: A Touchstone Book, Simon and Schuster, 1946,
1963, 1975, 1979.

Statistical Abstract of the United States: 1996, 116th Edition,
Washington, DC: US Bureau of the Census, 1996.

The World Book Encyclopedia, Chicago: World Book Inc., a
Scott Fetzer Co., 1988 Edition.

Toff, Nancy, Editor-in-Chief, *The People of North America*
(Series), New York: Chelsea House Publishers, Main Line
Books, 1988.

Trager, James, *The People's Chronology, A Year-by-Year Record
of Human Events from Prehistory to the Present*, New York:
Henry Holt Reference Book, 1992.

Acknowledgments

The publisher and authors would like to thank the following people for reviewing the manuscript and/or participating in focus groups as the book was being developed:

Ana Maria Aguilera, Lubie Alatriste, Ann Albarelli, Margaret Albers, Sherry Allen, Fiona Armstrong, Ted Auerbach, Steve Austen, Jean Barlow, Sally Bates, Sharon Batson, Myra Baum, Mary Beauparlant, Gretchen Bitterlin, Margrajean Bonilla, Mike Bostwick, Shirley Brod, Lihn Brown, Trish Brys-Overeem, Lynn Bundy, Chris Bunn, Carol Carvel, Leslie Crucil, Robert Denheim, Joshua Denk, Kay Devonshire, Thomas Dougherty, Gudrun Draper, Sara Eisen, Lynda Elkins, Ed Ende, Michele Epstein, Beth Fatemi, Andra R. Fawcett, Alice Fiedler, Harriet Fisher, James Fitzgerald, Mary Fitzsimmons, Scott Ford, Barbara Gaines, Elizabeth Garcia Grenados, Maria T. Gerdes, Penny Giacalone, Elliott Glazer, Jill Gluck de la Llata, Javier Gomez, Pura Gonzales, Carole Goodman, Joyce Grabowski, Maggie Grennan, Joanie Griffin, Sally Hansen, Fotini Haritos, Alice Hartley, Fernando Herrera, Ann Hillborn, Mary Hopkins, Lori Howard, Leann Howard, Pamela Howard, Rebecca Hubner, Jan Jarrell, Vicki Johnson, Michele Kagan, Nanette Kafka, Gena Katsaros, Evelyn Kay, Greg Keech, Cliff Ker, Gwen Kerner-Mayer, Marilou Kessler, Patty King, Linda Kiperman, Joyce Klapp, Susan Knutson, Sandy Kobrine, Marinna Kolaitis, Donna Korol, Lorraine Krampe, Karen Kuser, Andrea Lang, Nancy Lebow, Tay Lesley, Gale Lichter, Sandie Linn, Rosario Lorenzano, Louise Louie, Cheryl Lucas, Ronna Magy, Juanita Maltese, Mary Marquardsen, Carmen Marques Rivera, Susan McDowell, Alma McGee, Jerry McLeroy, Kevin McLure, Joan Meier, Patsy Mills, Judy Montague, Vicki Moore, Eneida Morales, Glenn Nadelbach, Elizabeth Neblett, Kathleen Newton, Yvonne Nishio, Afra Nobay, Rosa Elena Ochoa, Jean Owensby, Jim Park, John Perkins, Jane Pers, Laura Peskin, Maria Pick, Percy Pleasant, Selma Porter, Kathy Quinones, Susan Ritter, Martha Robledo, Maureen Rooney, Jean Rose, David Ross, Julietta Ruppert, Lorraine Ruston, Susan Ryan, Frederico Salas, Leslie Salmon, Jim Sandifer, Linda Sasser, Lisa Schreiber, Mary Segovia, Abe Shames, Debra Shaw, Stephanie Shipp, Pat Singh, Mary Sklavos, Donna Stark, Claire Cocoran Stehling, Lynn Sweeden, Joy Tesh, Sue Thompson, Christine Tierney, Laura Topete, Carmen Villanueva, Laura Webber, Renée Weiss, Beth Winningham, Cindy Wislofsky, Judy Wood, Paula Yerman.

A special thanks to Marna Shulberg and the students of the Saticoy Branch of Van Nuys Community Adult School.

We would also like to thank the following individuals and organizations who provided their expertise:

Carl Abato, Alan Goldman, Dr. Larry Falk, Caroll Gray, Henry Haskell, Susan Haskell, Los Angeles Fire Department, Malcolm Loeb, Barbara Lozano, Lorne Dubin, United Farm Workers.

Authors' Acknowledgments

Throughout our careers as English language teachers, we have found inspiration in many places—in the classroom with our remarkable students, at schools, conferences, and workshops with our fellow teachers, and with our colleagues at the ESL Teacher Institute. We are grateful to be part of this international community.

We would like to sincerely thank and acknowledge Eliza Jensen, the project's Senior Editor. Without Eliza, this book would not have been possible. Her indomitable spirit, commitment to clarity, and unwavering advocacy allowed us to realize the book we envisioned.

Creating this dictionary was a collaborative effort and it has been our privilege to work with an exceptionally talented group of individuals who, along with Eliza Jensen, make up the Oxford Picture Dictionary team. We deeply appreciate the contributions of the following people:

Lynn Luchetti, Art Director, whose aesthetic sense and sensibility guided the art direction of this book,

Susan Brorein, Senior Designer, who carefully considered the design of each and every page,

Klaus Jekeli, Production Editor, who pored over both manuscript and art to ensure consistency and accuracy, and

Tracy Hammond, Art Buyer, who skillfully managed thousands of pieces of art and reference material.

We also want to thank Susan Mazer, the talented artist who was by our side for the initial problem-solving and Mary Chandler who also lent her expertise to the project.

We have learned much working with Marjorie Fuchs, Lori Howard, and Renée Weiss, authors of the dictionary's ancillary materials. We thank them for their on-going contributions to the dictionary program.

We must make special mention of Susan Lanzano, Editorial Manager, whose invaluable advice, insights, and queries were an integral part of the writing process.

This book is dedicated to my husband, Neil Reichline, who has encouraged me to take the road less traveled, and to my sons, Eli and Alex, who have allowed me to sit at their baseball games with my yellow notepad. —NS

This book is lovingly dedicated to my husband, Gary and my daughter, Emily Rose, both of whom hugged me tight and let me work into the night. —JAG

A Letter to the Teacher

Welcome to The Oxford Picture Dictionary.

This comprehensive vocabulary resource provides you and your students with over 3,700 words, each defined by engaging art and presented in a meaningful context. *The Oxford Picture Dictionary* enables your students to learn and use English in all aspects of their daily lives. The 140 key topics cover home and family, the workplace, the community, health care, and academic studies. The topics are organized into 12 thematic units that are based on the curriculum of beginning and low-intermediate level English language coursework. The word lists of the dictionary include both single word entries and verb phrases. Many of the prepositions and adjectives are presented in phrases as well, demonstrating the natural use of words in conjunction with one another.

The Oxford Picture Dictionary uses a variety of visual formats, each suited to the topic being represented. Where appropriate, word lists are categorized and pages are divided into sections, allowing you to focus your students' attention on one aspect of a topic at a time.

Within the word lists:

- nouns, adjectives, prepositions, and adverbs are numbered,
- verbs are bolded and identified by letters, and
- targeted prepositions and adjectives within phrases are bolded.

The dictionary includes a variety of exercises and self-access tools that will guide your students toward accurate and fluent use of the new words.

- Exercises at the bottom of the pages provide vocabulary development through pattern practice, application of the new language to other topics, and personalization questions.

- An alphabetical index assists students in locating all words and topics in the dictionary.

- A phonetic listing for each word in the index and a pronunciation guide give students the key to accurate pronunciation.

- A verb index of all the verbs presented in the dictionary provides students with information on the present, past, and past participle forms of the verbs.

The Oxford Picture Dictionary is the core of *The Oxford Picture Dictionary Program* which includes a *Dictionary Cassette,* a *Teacher's Book* and its companion *Focused Listening Cassette, Beginning* and *Intermediate Workbooks, Classic Classroom Activities* (a photocopiable activity book), *Overhead Transparencies,* and *Read All About It 1* and *2.* Bilingual editions of *The Oxford Picture Dictionary* are available in Spanish, Chinese, Vietnamese, and many other languages.

TEACHING THE VOCABULARY

Your students' needs and your own teaching philosophy will dictate how you use *The Oxford Picture Dictionary* with your students. The following general guidelines, however, may help you adapt the dictionary's pages to your particular course and students. (For topic-specific, step-by-step guidelines and activities for presenting and practicing the vocabulary on each dictionary page see the *Oxford Picture Dictionary Teacher's Book.*)

Preview the topic

A good way to begin any lesson is to talk with students to determine what they already know about the topic. Some different ways to do this are:

- Ask general questions related to the topic;

- Have students brainstorm a list of words they know from the topic; or

- Ask questions about the picture(s) on the page.

Present the vocabulary

Once you've discovered which words your students already know, you are ready to focus on presenting the words they need. Introducing 10–15 new words in a lesson allows students to really learn the new words. On pages where the word lists are longer, and students are unfamiliar with many of the words, you may wish to introduce the words by categories or sections, or simply choose the words you want in the lesson.

Here are four different presentation techniques. The techniques you choose will depend on the topic being studied and the level of your students.

- Say each new word and describe or define it within the context of the picture.

- Demonstrate verbs or verb sequences for the students, and have volunteers demonstrate the actions as you say them.

- Use Total Physical Response commands to build comprehension of the vocabulary: *Put the pencil on your book. Put it on your notebook. Put it on your desk.*

- Ask a series of questions to build comprehension and give students an opportunity to say the new words:

▶ Begin with *yes/no* questions. *Is #16 chalk?* (yes)

▶ Progress to *or* questions. *Is #16 chalk or a marker?* (chalk)

▶ Finally ask *Wh* questions.

What can I use to write on this paper? (a marker/ Use a marker.)

Check comprehension

Before moving on to the practice stage, it is helpful to be sure all students understand the target vocabulary. There are many different things you can do to check students' understanding. Here are two activities to try:

• Tell students to open their books and point to the items they hear you say. Call out target vocabulary at random as you walk around the room checking to see if students are pointing to the correct pictures.

• Make true/false statements about the target vocabulary. Have students hold up two fingers for true, three fingers for false. *You can write with a marker.* [two fingers] *You raise your notebook to talk to the teacher.* [three fingers]

Take a moment to review any words with which students are having difficulty before beginning the practice activities.

Practice the vocabulary

Guided practice activities give your students an opportunity to use the new vocabulary in meaningful communication. The exercises at the bottom of the pages are one source of guided practice activities.

• **Talk about...** This activity gives students an opportunity to practice the target vocabulary through sentence substitutions with meaningful topics.

e.g. **Talk about your feelings.**

I feel <u>happy</u> when I see my friends.

• **Practice...** This activity gives students practice using the vocabulary within common conversational functions such as making introductions, ordering food, making requests, etc.

e.g. **Practice asking for things in the dining room.**

Please pass <u>the platter</u>.

May I have <u>the creamer</u>?

Could I have <u>a fork</u>, please?

• **Use the new language.** This activity asks students to brainstorm words within various categories, or may

ask them to apply what they have learned to another topic in the dictionary. For example, on *Colors*, page 12, students are asked to look at *Clothing I*, pages 64–65, and name the colors of the clothing they see.

• **Share your answers.** These questions provide students with an opportunity to expand their use of the target vocabulary in personalized discussion. Students can ask and answer these questions in whole class discussions, pair or group work, or they can write the answers as journal entries.

Further guided and communicative practice can be found in the *Oxford Picture Dictionary Teacher's Book* and in *Classic Classroom Activities*. The *Oxford Picture Dictionary Beginning* and *Intermediate Workbooks* and *Read All About It 1* and *2* provide your students with controlled and communicative reading and writing practice.

We encourage you to adapt the materials to suit the needs of your classes, and we welcome your comments and ideas. Write to us at:

Oxford University Press
ESL Department
198 Madison Avenue
New York, NY 10016

Jayme Adelson-Goldstein

Norma Shapiro

A Letter to the Student

Dear Student of English,

Welcome to *The Oxford Picture Dictionary*. The more than 3,700 words in this book will help you as you study English.

Each page in this dictionary teaches about a specific topic. The topics are grouped together in units. All pages in a unit have the same color and symbol. For example, each page in the Food unit has this symbol:

On each page you will see pictures and words. The pictures have numbers or letters that match the numbers or letters in the word lists. Verbs (action words) are identified by letters and all other words are identified by numbers.

How to find words in this book

- Use the Table of Contents, pages ix–xi.
  Look up the general topic you want to learn about.

- Use the Index, pages 173–205.
  Look up individual words in alphabetical (A–Z) order.

- Go topic by topic.
  Look through the book until you find something that interests you.

How to use the Index

When you look for a word in the index this is what you will see:

the word   the number (or letter) in the word list

apples [ăp/əlz] **50**–4

the pronunciation   the page number

If the word is on one of the maps, pages 122–125, you will find it in the Geographical Index on pages 206–208.

How to use the Verb Guide

When you want to know the past form of a verb or its past participle form, look up the verb in the verb guide. The regular verbs and their spelling changes are listed on pages 170–171. The simple form, past form, and past participle form of irregular verbs are listed on page 172.

Workbooks

There are two workbooks to help you practice the new words:
The Oxford Picture Dictionary Beginning and *Intermediate Workbooks*.

As authors and teachers we both know how difficult English can be (and we're native speakers!). When we wrote this book, we asked teachers and students from the U.S. and other countries for their help and ideas. We hope their ideas and ours will help you. Please write to us with your comments or questions at:

Oxford University Press
ESL Department
198 Madison Avenue
New York, NY 10016

We wish you success!

Jayme Adelson-Goldstein   *Norma Shapiro*

학생들에게 드리는 편지

영어를 배우는 학생 여러분들에게,

옥스포드 그림 사전 (The Oxford Picture Dictionary) 을 사용해주셔서 감사합니다. 이 사전에 들어있는 3,700 개 이상의 단어들은 여러분이 영어를 공부하는 데 도움이 될 것입니다.

이 사전의 각 페이지는 특정한 주제를 다루고 있습니다. 주제들을 모아서 한 섹션으로 분류하였습니다. 한 섹션의 모든 페이지들은 같은 색깔과 심벌들을 갖고 있습니다. 예를 들어서 음식 섹션에는 이런 심벌을 사용합니다:

각 페이지에는 단어와 그림이 나와 있습니다. 그림에는 단어 차례의 숫자나 글자와 맞는 숫자나 글자가 있습니다. 동사(행동 단어)는 글자로 표시되어 있고 그밖의 모든 단어들은 숫자로 표시되어 있습니다.

이 사전에서 단어를 찾는 방법은

- 차례를 사용하십시오. ix-xi 페이지
  배우고자 하는 일반 주제를 찾아 보십시오.

- 색인을 사용하십시오. 173-205 페이지
  알파벳 (A-Z) 순서로 된 단어들을 찾아 보십시오.

- 주제별로 찾아 보십시오.
  흥미가 있는 주제가 나올 때까지 책을 쭉 들춰보십시오.

색인을 사용하는 방법

색인에서 단어를 찾을 때 이와 같은 것을 보게 될 것입니다:

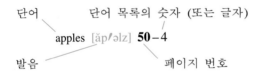

페이지 122-125 의 지도에 나오는 단어는 206-208 페이지에 나와 있는 지역 색인에서 찾을 수 있습니다.

동사 가이드를 사용하는 방법

어떤 동사의 과거형이나 과거분사형을 알고 싶으면, 동사 가이드에서 그 동사를 찾아 보십시오. 170-171 페이지에 규칙 동사와 그 스펠링의 변화가 실려있습니다. 불규칙 동사의 단순형, 과거형, 과거분사형은 172 페이지에 실려있습니다.

연습장

새 단어들을 사용하는 데 도움을 주는 2 개의 연습장이 있습니다: 옥스포드 그림 사전 (초급) (The Oxford Picture Dictionary Beginning) 과 중급 연습장 (Intermediate Workbooks) 입니다.

저자이며 교사인 저희 자신들은 영어가 모국어인데도 불구하고 영어가 얼마나 어려운지 잘 알고 있습니다. 저희들이 이 책을 쓸 때, 저희들은 미국과 다른 나라의 교사들과 학생들에게 자문과 아이디어를 구했습니다. 그들과 저희 아이디어가 여러분에게 도움이 될 것으로 믿습니다. 의견이나 문의가 있으시면 저희들에게 연락주시기 바랍니다:

Oxford University Press
ESL Department
198 Madison Avenue
New York, NY 10016

성공을 바랍니다!

Jayme Adelson-Goldstein   *Norma Shapiro*

Contents 차례

1. Everyday Language 생활 언어

A Classroom 교실	2–3
Personal Information 신상 정보	4
School 학교	5
Studying 공부하기	6–7
Everyday Conversation 일상 회화	8
The Telephone 전화	9
Weather 날씨	10
Describing Things 사물 묘사하기	11
Colors 색깔	12
Prepositions 전치사	13
Numbers and Measurements 숫자와 단위	14–15
Time 시간	16–17
The Calendar 달력	18–19
Money 화폐	20
Shopping 쇼핑	21

2. People 사람

Age and Physical Description 나이와 신체 묘사	22
Describing Hair 헤어스타일 묘사하기	23
Family 가족	24–25
Daily Routines 일과	26–27
Life Events 인생 경로	28–29
Feelings 느낌	30–31
A Graduation 졸업	32–33

3. Housing 주택

Places to Live 주거 장소	34
Finding a Home 집 구하기	35
Apartments 아파트	36–37
A House 주택	38
A Yard 뜰	39
A Kitchen 주방	40
A Dining Area 식당	41
A Living Room 거실	42
A Bathroom 욕실	43
A Bedroom 침실	44
A Children's Bedroom 어린이 침실	45
Housework 가사/집안일	46
Cleaning Supplies 청소 용구	47
Household Problems and Repairs 고장과 수리	48–49

4. Food 음식

Fruit 과일	50
Vegetables 야채	51
Meat and Poultry 고기류	52
Deli and Seafood 조제식품과 해산물	53
The Market 시장	54–55
Containers and Packaged Foods 용기와 포장식품	56
Weights and Measures 무게와 단위	57
Food Preparation 음식 준비	58
Kitchen Utensils 주방 용구	59

Contents 차례

Fast Food 패스트 푸드		60
A Coffee Shop Menu 커피 숍 메뉴		61
A Restaurant 식당		62–63

5. Clothing 의복

Clothing I 의복 I		64–65
Clothing II 의복 II		66
Clothing III 의복 III		67
Shoes and Accessories 신발과 액세서리		68–69
Describing Clothes 의복 묘사		70–71
Doing the Laundry 세탁하기		72
Sewing and Alterations 재봉 및 수선		73

6. Health 건강

The Body 신체		74–75
Personal Hygiene 개인 위생		76–77
Symptoms and Injuries 증상과 상해		78
Illnesses and Medical Conditions 질병과 건강상태		79
Health Care 건강 관리		80–81
Medical Emergencies 건강 위급 상황		82
First Aid 응급치료		83
Clinics 치료소 / 진료소		84
Medical and Dental Exams 건강진단과 치아검사		85
A Hospital 병원		86–87

7. Community 지역사회

City Streets 시가지		88–89
An Intersection 교차로		90–91
A Mall 쇼핑센터		92–93
A Childcare Center 탁아소		94–95
U.S. Mail 미국 우편		96
A Bank 은행		97
A Library 도서관		98
The Legal System 법제도		99
Crime 범죄		100
Public Safety 공중 안전		101
Emergencies and Natural Disasters 비상시와 천재지변		102–103

8. Transportation 교통

Public Transportation 대중교통		104
Prepositions of Motion 동작 관련 전치사		105
Cars and Trucks 자동차와 트럭		106
Directions and Traffic Signs 방향과 교통 표지판		107
Parts of a Car and Car Maintenance 자동차 부속과 자동차 정비		108–109
An Airport 공항		110
A Plane Trip 항공 여행		111

9. Areas of Study 학과

Types of Schools 학교 종류		112
English Composition 영작문		113
U.S. History 미국 역사		114–115

U.S. Government and Citizenship   미국 정부와 시민권   116
Geography   지리   117
Mathematics   수학   118
Science   과학   119
Music   음악   120
More School Subjects   기타 학교 과목   121
North America and Central America   북미주와 중미   122–123
The World   세계   124–125
Energy and the Environment   에너지와 환경   126
The Universe   우주   127

10. Plants and Animals   식물과 동물

Trees and Plants   나무와 화초   128
Flowers   꽃   129
Marine Life, Amphibians, and Reptiles   바다생물, 양서류   130–131
그리고 파충류
Birds, Insects, and Arachnids   새, 곤충 그리고 거미류   132
Domestic Animals and Rodents   가축과 설치류 동물   133
Mammals   포유동물   134–135

11. Work   일

Jobs and Occupations, A–H   직업 (A-H, 영어순)   136–137
Jobs and Occupations, H–W   직업 (H-W, 영어순)   138–139
Job Skills   직업 특기   140
Job Search   직업 찾기   141
An Office   사무실   142–143
Computers   컴퓨터   144
A Hotel   호텔   145
A Factory   공장   146
Job Safety   작업 안전   147
Farming and Ranching   농사일과 목장일   148
Construction   건축   149
Tools and Building Supplies   공구와 건물보수 용품   150–151

12. Recreation   레크리에이션

Places to Go   놀러가는 곳   152
The Park and Playground   공원과 놀이터   153
Outdoor Recreation   야외 활동   154
The Beach   해변   155
Sports Verbs   스포츠 동사   156–157
Team Sports   팀 스포츠   158
Individual Sports   개인 스포츠   159
Winter Sports and Water Sports   동계 스포츠와 수중 스포츠   160
Sports Equipment   운동기구   161
Hobbies and Games   취미와 게임   162–163
Electronics and Photography   전자제품과 사진   164–165
Entertainment   엔터테인먼트   166–167
Holidays   축제일   168
A Party   파티   169
Verb Guide   동사 가이드   170
Index   색인   173
Geographical Index   지리 색인   206
Korean Index   한글 색인   209

1. chalkboard
칠판

2. screen
화면

3. student
학생

4. overhead projector
오버헤드 프로젝터 (OHP)

5. teacher
선생

6. desk
책상

7. chair / seat
의자 / 좌석

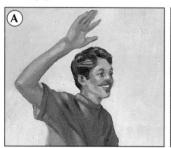

A. Raise your hand.
손을 올리세요.

B. Talk to the teacher.
선생님께 이야기하세요.

C. Listen to a cassette.
카세트를 들으세요.

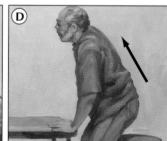

D. Stand up.
일어서세요.

E. Sit down. / Take a seat.
앉으세요. / 자리에 앉으세요.

F. Point to the picture.
그림을 가리키세요.

G. Write on the board.
칠판에 쓰세요.

H. Erase the board.
칠판을 지우세요.

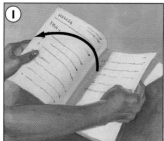

I. Open your book.
책을 펴세요.

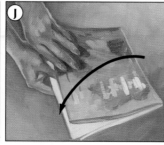

J. Close your book.
책을 덮으세요.

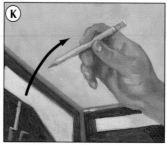

K. Take out your pencil.
연필을 꺼내세요.

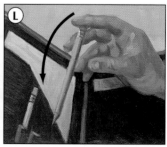

L. Put away your pencil.
연필을 치우세요.

8. bookcase
책장

9. globe
지구

10. clock
시계

11. cassette player
카세트 플레이어

12. map
지도

13. pencil sharpener
연필 깎이

14. bulletin board
게시판

15. computer
컴퓨터

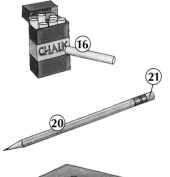

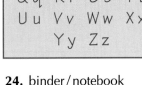

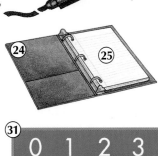

16. chalk
분필

17. chalkboard eraser
칠판 지우개

18. pen
펜

19. marker
마커

20. pencil
연필

21. pencil eraser
연필 지우개

22. textbook
교과서

23. workbook
연습장

24. binder / notebook
바인더 / 공책

25. notebook paper
공책 종이

26. spiral notebook
공책

27. ruler
자

28. dictionary
사전

29. picture dictionary
그림 사전

30. the alphabet
알파벳

31. numbers
숫자

Use the new language.

1. Name three things you can open.

2. Name three things you can put away.

3. Name three things you can write with.

Share your answers.

1. Do you like to raise your hand?

2. Do you ever listen to cassettes in class?

3. Do you ever write on the board?

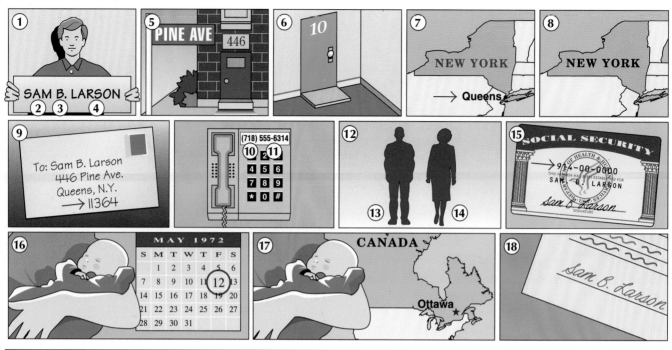

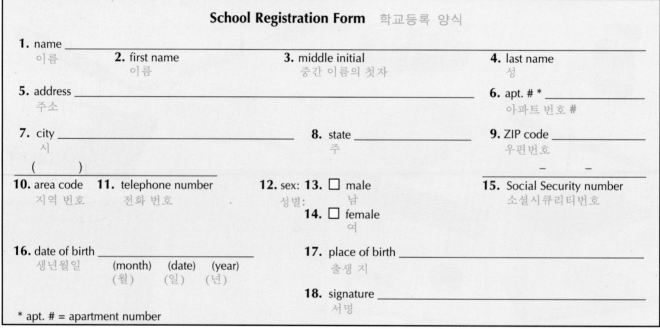

School Registration Form 학교등록 양식

1. name _____
   이름

2. first name
   이름

3. middle initial
   중간 이름의 첫자

4. last name
   성

5. address _____
   주소

6. apt. # * _____
   아파트 번호 #

7. city _____
   시

8. state _____
   주

9. ZIP code _____
   우편번호

( )
10. area code   11. telephone number
   지역 번호   전화 번호

12. sex: 13. ☐ male
성별: 남
         14. ☐ female
                여

15. Social Security number
   소셜시큐리티번호

16. date of birth _____
   생년월일   (month) (date) (year)
              (월)   (일)   (년)

17. place of birth _____
   출생 지

18. signature _____
   서명

* apt. # = apartment number

A. **Spell** your name.
이름의 철자를 쓰세요.

B. **Fill out** a form.
서식에 기입하세요.

C. **Print** your name.
이름을 정자로 쓰세요.

D. **Sign** your name.
서명하세요.

Talk about yourself.

My first name is Sam.

My last name is spelled L-A-R-S-O-N.

I come from Ottawa.

Share your answers.

1. Do you like your first name?

2. Is your last name from your mother? father? husband?

3. What is your middle name?

1. classroom 교실	**7.** lockers 사물함	**13.** principal's office 교장실
2. teacher 교사	**8.** rest rooms 화장실	**14.** principal 교장
3. auditorium 강당	**9.** gym 체육관	**15.** counselor's office 상담 교사실
4. cafeteria 카페테리아	**10.** bleachers 외야석	**16.** counselor 상담 교사
5. lunch benches 점심 벤치	**11.** track 경주로	**17.** main office 주 사무실
6. library 도서관	**12.** field 경기장	**18.** clerk 사무원

More vocabulary

instructor: teacher

coach: gym teacher

administrator: principal or other school supervisor

Share your answers.

1. Do you ever talk to the principal of your school?

2. Is there a place for you to eat at your school?

3. Does your school look the same as or different from the one in the picture?

Dictionary work 사전 공부

A. Look up a word.
단어를 찾아보세요.

B. Read the word.
단어를 읽으세요.

C. Say the word.
단어를 말하세요.

D. Repeat the word.
단어를 반복해 말하세요.

E. Spell the word.
단어의 철자를 쓰세요.

F. Copy the word.
단어를 베껴 쓰세요.

Work with a partner 짝과 함께 공부하기

G. Ask a question.
질문을 하세요.

H. Answer a question.
질문에 답하세요.

I. Share a book.
책을 같이 보세요.

J. Help your partner.
짝을 도와 주세요.

Work in a group 그룹으로 공부하기

K. Brainstorm a list.
목록을 같이
생각해 보세요.

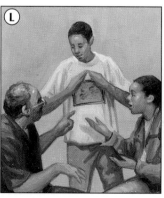

L. Discuss the list.
목록에 대해서
논의하세요.

M. Draw a picture.
그림을 그리세요.

N. Dictate a sentence.
문장을 받아 쓰세요.

Class work 수업 공부

O. Pass out the papers.
과제를 나누어 주세요.

P. Talk with each other.
서로 이야기하세요.

Q. Collect the papers.
과제를 모으세요.

Follow directions 지시를 따라하기

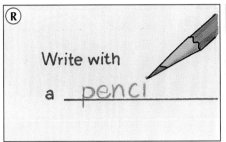

R. Fill in the blank.
빈 칸을 채우세요.

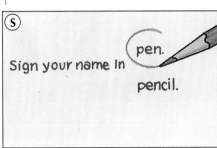

S. Circle the answer.
정답에 동그라미를 치세요.

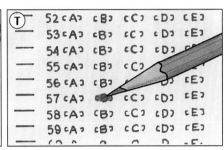

T. Mark the answer sheet.
답안지에 표시하세요.

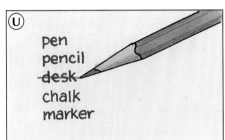

U. Cross out the word.
단어에 선을 그어 지우세요.

V. Underline the word.
단어에 밑줄을 치세요.

W. Put the words **in order.**
단어들을 순서대로 놓으세요.

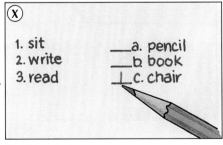

X. Match the items.
맞는 항목끼리 짝지우세요.

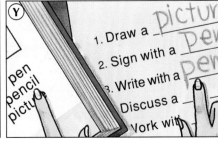

Y. Check your work.
한 것을 점검하세요.

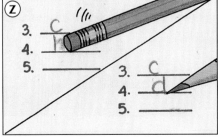

Z. Correct the mistake.
틀린 것을 고치세요.

Share your answers.

1. Do you like to work in groups?

2. Do you like to share books?

3. Do you like to answer questions?

4. Is it easy for you to talk with your classmates?

5. Do you always check your work?

6. Do you cross out your mistakes or erase them?

A. greet someone
누군가에게 인사하세요

B. begin a conversation
대화를 시작하세요

C. end the conversation
대화를 끝내세요

D. introduce yourself
자신을 소개하세요

E. make sure you **understand**
이해하고 있는지

F. introduce your friend
친구를 소개하세요

G. compliment your friend
친구를 칭찬하세요

H. thank your friend
친구에게 감사하세요

I. apologize
사과하세요

Practice introductions.

Hi, I'm <u>Sam Jones</u> and this is my friend, <u>Pat Green</u>.

  Nice to meet you. I'm <u>Tomas Garcia</u>.

Practice giving compliments.

That's a great <u>sweater</u>, <u>Tomas</u>.

  Thanks <u>Pat</u>. I like your <u>shoes</u>.

Look at **Clothing I**, pages **64–65** for more ideas.

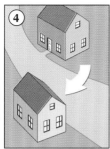

1. telephone/phone
   전화

2. receiver
   수화기

3. cord
   코드

4. local call
   시내 전화

5. long-distance call
   장거리 전화

6. international call
   국제 전화

7. operator
   교환수

8. directory assistance (411)
   전화번호 안내 서비스 (411)

9. emergency service (911)
   구급 서비스 (911)

10. phone card
    전화 카드

11. pay phone
    공중 전화

12. cordless phone
    무선 전화기

13. cellular phone
    세룰라폰

14. answering machine
    자동 응답기

15. telephone book
    전화 번호부

16. pager
    호출기

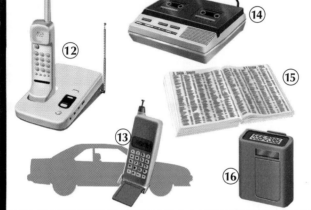

Using a pay phone 공중전화 사용

A. **Pick up** the receiver.
   수화기를 드세요.

B. **Listen** for the dial tone.
   발신음을 들으세요.

C. **Deposit** coins.
   동전을 넣으세요.

D. **Dial** the number.
   번호를 돌리세요.

E. **Leave** a message.
   메세지를 남기세요.

F. **Hang up** the receiver.
   수화기를 제자리에 놓으세요.

More vocabulary

When you get a person or place that you didn't want to call, we say you have the **wrong number.**

Share your answers.

1. What kinds of calls do you make?

2. How much does it cost to call your country?

3. Do you like to talk on the telephone?

Temperature
기온

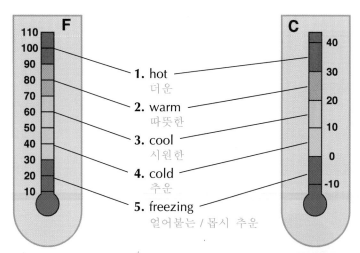

Degrees
Fahrenheit

Degrees
Celsius

1. hot
더운

2. warm
따뜻한

3. cool
시원한

4. cold
추운

5. freezing
얼어붙는 / 몹시 추운

6. sunny / clear
해가 비치는 / 맑게 갠

7. cloudy
구름낀

8. raining
비오는

9. snowing
눈오는

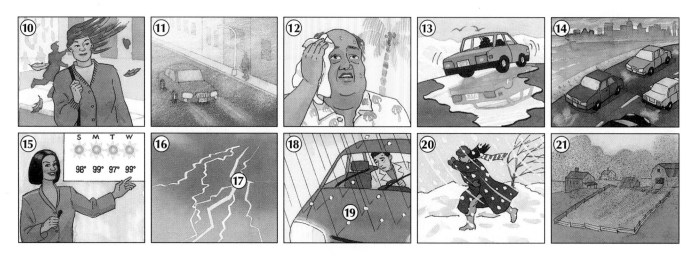

10. windy
바람부는

11. foggy
안개낀

12. humid
습한

13. icy
얼음이 덮인

14. smoggy
스모그가 많은

15. heat wave
혹서 / 열파

16. thunderstorm
뇌우

17. lightning
번개

18. hailstorm
우박 폭풍

19. hail
우박

20. snowstorm
눈보라

21. dust storm
모래 바람

Language note: *it is, there is*

For **1–14** we use,   *It's <u>cloudy</u>.*

For **15–21** we use,   *There's <u>a heat wave</u>.*
                        There's <u>lightning</u>.

Talk about the weather.

Today it's <u>hot</u>. It's <u>98 degrees</u>.

Yesterday it was <u>warm</u>. It was <u>85 degrees</u>.

1. **little** hand
   작은 손
2. **big** hand
   큰 손

3. **fast** driver
   빠른 운전사
4. **slow** driver
   느린 운전사

5. **hard** chair
   딱딱한 의자
6. **soft** chair
   부드러운 의자

7. **thick** book/
   fat book
   두꺼운 책
8. **thin** book
   얇은 책

9. **full** glass
   가득찬 잔
10. **empty** glass
    빈 잔

11. **noisy** children/
    loud children
    시끄러운 아이들
12. **quiet** children
    조용한 아이들

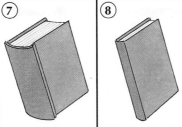

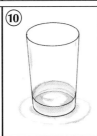

13. **heavy** box
    무거운 상자
14. **light** box
    가벼운 상자

15. **neat** closet
    잘 정리된 옷장
16. **messy** closet
    어질러진 옷장

17. **good** dog
    착한 개
18. **bad** dog
    나쁜 개

19. **expensive** ring
    비싼 반지
20. **cheap** ring
    싼 반지

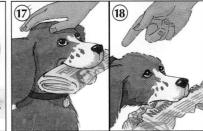

21. **beautiful** view
    아름다운 경치
22. **ugly** view
    보기 흉한 광경

23. **easy** problem
    쉬운 문제
24. **difficult** problem/
    hard problem
    어려운 문제

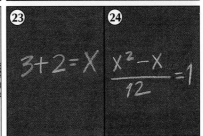

$3+2=X$ $\dfrac{X^2-X}{12}=1$

Use the new language.
1. Name three things that are thick.
2. Name three things that are soft.
3. Name three things that are heavy.

Share your answers.
1. Are you a slow driver or a fast driver?
2. Do you have a neat closet or a messy closet?
3. Do you like loud or quiet parties?

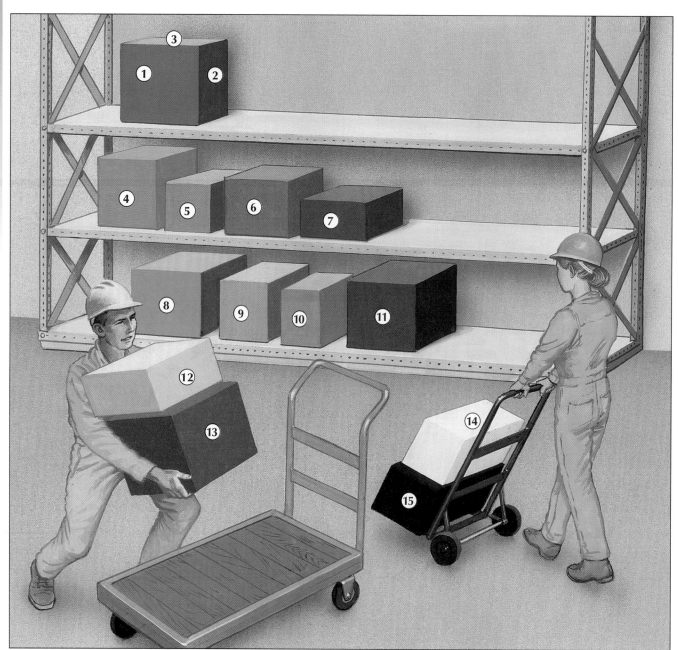

1. blue 파란색	**6.** orange 주황색	**11.** brown 갈색
2. dark blue 암청색	**7.** purple 보라색	**12.** yellow 노란색
3. light blue 하늘색	**8.** green 초록색	**13.** red 빨간색
4. turquoise 청록색	**9.** beige 베이지 색	**14.** white 흰색
5. gray 회색	**10.** pink 분홍색	**15.** black 검정 색

Use the new language.

Look at **Clothing I,** pages **64–65.**

Name the colors of the clothing you see.

That's a dark blue suit.

Share your answers.

1. What colors are you wearing today?

2. What colors do you like?

3. Is there a color you don't like? What is it?

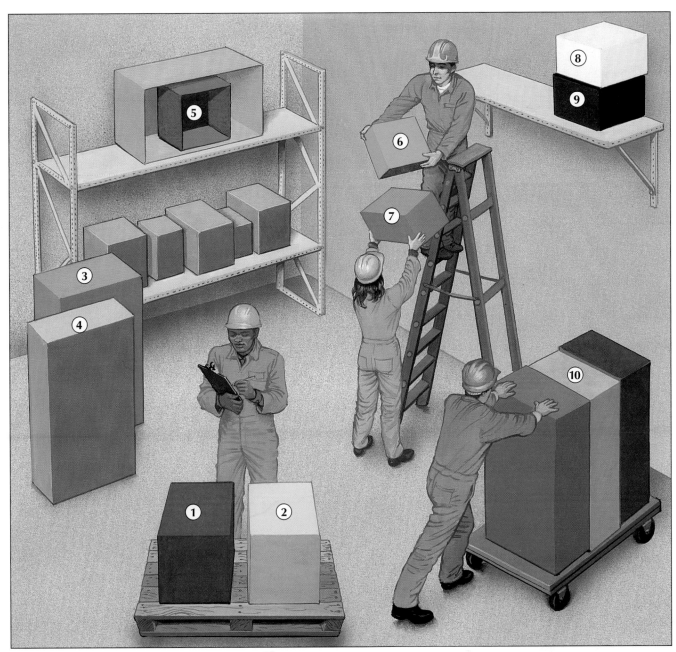

1. The red box is **next to** the yellow box, **on the left.**
빨간색 상자는 노란색 상자 옆, 왼쪽에 있습니다.

2. The yellow box is **next to** the red box, **on the right.**
노란색 상자는 빨간색 상자 옆, 오른쪽에 있습니다.

3. The turquoise box is **behind** the gray box.
청록색 상자는 회색 상자의 뒤에 있습니다.

4. The gray box is **in front of** the turquoise box.
회색 상자는 청록색 상자의 앞에 있습니다.

5. The dark blue box is **in** the beige box.
암청색 상자는 베이지색 상자 안에 있습니다.

6. The green box is **above** the orange box.
초록색 상자는 주황색 상자의 위에 있습니다.

7. The orange box is **below** the green box.
주황색 상자는 초록색 상장의 아래에 있습니다.

8. The white box is **on** the black box.
흰색 상자는 검정색 상자 위에 있습니다.

9. The black box is **under** the white box.
검정색 상자는 흰색 상자 아래에 있습니다.

10. The pink box is **between** the purple box and the brown box.
핑크색 상자는 보라색 상자와 갈색 상자 사이에 있습니다.

More vocabulary

near: in the same area
The white box is **near** the black box.

far from: not near
The red box is **far from** the black box.

HOME **1 8** VISITOR **2 2**

 SAN DIEGO 235 miles

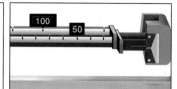

Cardinals 기수

0 zero 영	11 eleven 십일	21 twenty-one 이십일	101 one hundred one 백일
1 one 일	12 twelve 십이	22 twenty-two 이십이	1,000 one thousand 천
2 two 이	13 thirteen 십삼	30 thirty 삼십	1,001 one thousand one 천일
3 three 삼	14 fourteen 십사	40 forty 사십	10,000 ten thousand 만
4 four 사	15 fifteen 십오	50 fifty 오십	100,000 one hundred thousand 십만
5 five 오	16 sixteen 십육	60 sixty 육십	1,000,000 one million 백만
6 six 육	17 seventeen 십칠	70 seventy 칠십	1,000,000,000 one billion 십억
7 seven 칠	18 eighteen 십팔	80 eighty 팔십	
8 eight 팔	19 nineteen 십구	90 ninety 구십	
9 nine 구	20 twenty 이십	100 one hundred 백	
10 ten 십			

Ordinals 서수

1st first 첫째	8th eighth 여덟째	15th fifteenth 열다섯째
2nd second 둘째	9th ninth 아홉째	16th sixteenth 열여섯째
3rd third 셋째	10th tenth 열번째	17th seventeenth 열일곱째
4th fourth 넷째	11th eleventh 열한번째	18th eighteenth 열여덟째
5th fifth 다섯째	12th twelfth 열두째	19th nineteenth 열아홉째
6th sixth 여섯째	13th thirteenth 열셋째	20th twentieth 스무번째
7th seventh 일곱째	14th fourteenth 열넷째	

Roman numerals 로마 숫자

I = 1	VII = 7	XXX = 30
II = 2	VIII = 8	XL = 40
III = 3	IX = 9	L = 50
IV = 4	X = 10	C = 100
V = 5	XV = 15	D = 500
VI = 6	XX = 20	M = 1,000

Fractions 분수

1. 1/8 one-eighth
8분의 1

2. 1/4 one-fourth
4분의 1

3. 1/3 one-third
3분의 1

4. 1/2 one-half
2분의 1

5. 3/4 three-fourths
4분의 3

6. 1 whole
정수

1 cup
— 3/4
2/3 —
— 1/2
1/3 —
— 1/4

Percents 퍼센트

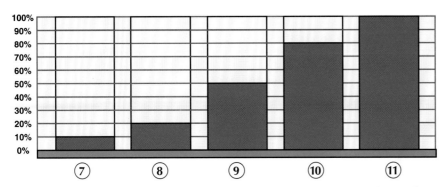

100%
90%
80%
70%
60%
50%
40%
30%
20%
10%
0%

⑦ ⑧ ⑨ ⑩ ⑪

7. 10% ten percent
10% 10 퍼센트

8. 20% twenty percent
20% 20 퍼센트

9. 50% fifty percent
50% 50 퍼센트

10. 80% eighty percent
80% 80 퍼센트

11. 100% one hundred percent
100% 100 퍼센트

Dimensions 수치

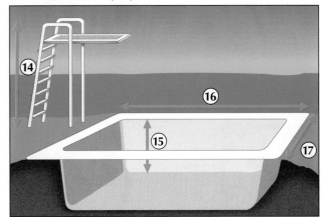

⑭ ⑯ ⑮ ⑰

Measurement 측정법

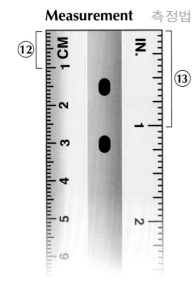

⑫ ⑬

1 CM IN.

12. centimeter [cm]
센티미터(cm)

13. inch [in.]
인치(in)

Equivalencies 환산율

1 inch	= 2.54 centimeters
1 yard	= .91 meters
1 mile	= 1.6 kilometers
12 inches	= 1 foot
3 feet	= 1 yard
1,760 yards	= 1 mile

14. height
높이

15. depth
깊이

16. length
길이

17. width
너비

More vocabulary

measure: to find the size or amount of something

count: to find the total number of something

Share your answers.

1. How many students are in class today?

2. Who was the first person in class today?

3. How far is it from your home to your school?

1. second
초

2. minute
분

3. hour
시

A.M.

P.M.

4. 1:00
one o'clock
한시

5. 1:05
one-oh-five
한시 오분
five after one
한시 오분

6. 1:10
one-ten
한시 십분
ten after one
한시 십분

7. 1:15
one-fifteen
한시 십오분
a quarter after one
한시 십오분

8. 1:20
one-twenty
한시 이십분
twenty after one
한시 이십분

9. 1:25
one twenty-five
한시 이십오분
twenty-five after one
한시 이십오분

10. 1:30
one-thirty
한시 삼십분
half past one
한시 삼십분

11. 1:35
one thirty-five
한시 삼십오분
twenty-five to two
한시 삼십오분

12. 1:40
one-forty
한시 사십분
twenty to two
한시 사십분

13. 1:45
one forty-five
한시 사십오분
a quarter to two
한시 사십오분

14. 1:50
one-fifty
한시 오십분
ten to two
한시 오십분

15. 1:55
one fifty-five
한시 오십오분
five to two
한시 오십오분

Talk about the time.

What time is it? It's <u>10:00 a.m.</u>

What time do you wake up on weekdays? At <u>6:30 a.m.</u>

What time do you wake up on weekends? At <u>9:30 a.m.</u>

Share your answers.

1. How many hours a day do you study English?
2. You are meeting friends at 1:00. How long will you wait for them if they are late?

16

16. morning
아침

17. noon
정오

18. afternoon
오후

19. evening
저녁

20. night
밤

21. midnight
자정

22. early
이른

23. late
늦은

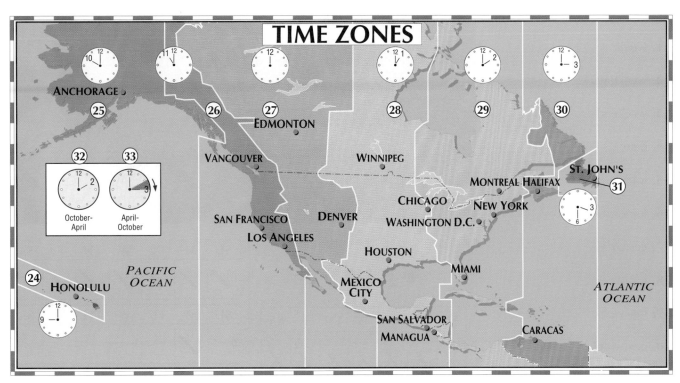

TIME ZONES

24. Hawaii-Aleutian time
하와이-알류트 표준시

25. Alaska time
알라스카 표준시

26. Pacific time
태평양 표준시

27. mountain time
산지 표준시

28. central time
중부 표준시

29. eastern time
동부 표준시

30. Atlantic time
대서양 표준시

31. Newfoundland time
뉴펀들랜드 표준시

32. standard time
표준시간

33. daylight saving time
일광절약시간 (서머타임)

More vocabulary

on time: not early and not late

*He's **on time.***

Share your answers.

1. When do you watch television? study?
do housework?

2. Do you come to class on time? early? late?

Days of the week
요일

1. Sunday
   일요일

2. Monday
   월요일

3. Tuesday
   화요일

4. Wednesday
   수요일

5. Thursday
   목요일

6. Friday
   금요일

7. Saturday
   토요일

8. year
   해(년)

9. month
   달(월)

10. day
    일

11. week
    주

12. weekdays
    평일

13. weekend
    주말

14. date
    날짜

15. today
    오늘(금일)

16. tomorrow
    내일

17. yesterday
    어제

18. last week
    지난 주

19. this week
    이번 주(금주)

20. next week
    다음 주

21. every day
    매일

22. once a week
    일 주에 한 번

23. twice a week
    일 주에 두 번

24. three times a week
    일 주에 세 번

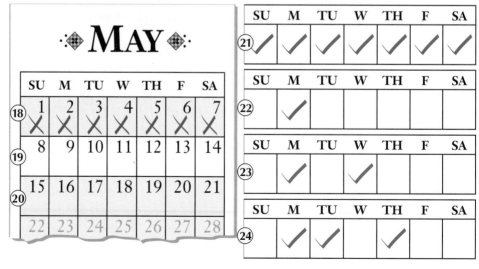

Talk about the calendar.

What's today's date? It's <u>March 10th</u>.

What day is it? It's <u>Tuesday</u>.

What day was yesterday? It was <u>Monday</u>.

Share your answers.

1. How often do you come to school?
2. How long have you been in this school?

18

2001

JAN (25)
SUN	MON	TUE	WED	THU	FRI	SAT
	1	2	3	4	5	6
7	8	9	10	11	12	13
14	15	16	17	18	19	20
21	22	23	24	25	26	27
28	29	30	31			

FEB (26)
SUN	MON	TUE	WED	THU	FRI	SAT
				1	2	3
4	5	6	7	8	9	10
11	12	13	14	15	16	17
18	19	20	21	22	23	24
25	26	27	28			

MAR (27)
SUN	MON	TUE	WED	THU	FRI	SAT
				1	2	3
4	5	6	7	8	9	10
11	12	13	14	15	16	17
18	19	20	21	22	23	24
25	26	27	28	29	30	31

APR (28)
SUN	MON	TUE	WED	THU	FRI	SAT
1	2	3	4	5	6	7
8	9	10	11	12	13	14
15	16	17	18	19	20	21
22	23	24	25	26	27	28
29	30					

MAY (29)
SUN	MON	TUE	WED	THU	FRI	SAT
		1	2	3	4	5
6	7	8	9	10	11	12
13	14	15	16	17	18	19
20	21	22	23	24	25	26
27	28	29	30	31		

JUN (30)
SUN	MON	TUE	WED	THU	FRI	SAT
					1	2
3	4	5	6	7	8	9
10	11	12	13	14	15	16
17	18	19	20	21	22	23
24	25	26	27	28	29	30

JUL (31)
SUN	MON	TUE	WED	THU	FRI	SAT
1	2	3	4	5	6	7
8	9	10	11	12	13	14
15	16	17	18	19	20	21
22	23	24	25	26	27	28
29	30	31				

AUG (32)
SUN	MON	TUE	WED	THU	FRI	SAT
			1	2	3	4
5	6	7	8	9	10	11
12	13	14	15	16	17	18
19	20	21	22	23	24	25
26	27	28	29	30	31	

SEP (33)
SUN	MON	TUE	WED	THU	FRI	SAT
						1
2	3	4	5	6	7	8
9	10	11	12	13	14	15
16	17	18	19	20	21	22
23/30	24	25	26	27	28	29

OCT (34)
SUN	MON	TUE	WED	THU	FRI	SAT
	1	2	3	4	5	6
7	8	9	10	11	12	13
14	15	16	17	18	19	20
21	22	23	24	25	26	27
28	29	30	31			

NOV (35)
SUN	MON	TUE	WED	THU	FRI	SAT
				1	2	3
4	5	6	7	8	9	10
11	12	13	14	15	16	17
18	19	20	21	22	23	24
25	26	27	28	29	30	

DEC (36)
SUN	MON	TUE	WED	THU	FRI	SAT
						1
2	3	4	5	6	7	8
9	10	11	12	13	14	15
16	17	18	19	20	21	22
23/30	24/31	25	26	27	28	29

MARCH 21

JUNE 21

SEPT. 21

DEC. 21

JUNE 5 — TIM!

MARCH 2 — ANNIVERSARY

JULY 4 — INDEPENDENCE DAY — STATE BANK — CLOSED—JULY 4

APRIL 4 — EASTER SUNDAY

MAY 17 — DOCTOR 4:30

AUGUST

Months of the year
월명

25. January
1월

26. February
2월

27. March
3월

28. April
4월

29. May
5월

30. June
6월

31. July
7월

32. August
8월

33. September
9월

34. October
10월

35. November
11월

36. December
12월

Seasons
계절

37. spring
봄

38. summer
여름

39. fall
가을

40. winter
겨울

41. birthday
생일

42. anniversary
기념일

43. legal holiday
법정 휴일

44. religious holiday
종교적 휴일

45. appointment
약속

46. vacation
휴가 / 방학

Use the new language.

Look at the **ordinal numbers** on page **14**.
Use ordinal numbers to say the date.
It's June 5th. It's the fifth.

Talk about your birthday.

My birthday is in the winter.
My birthday is in January.
My birthday is on January twenty-sixth.

Money   화폐

Coins   농전

1. $.01 = 1¢
a penny/1 cent
페니/1 센트

2. $.05 = 5¢
a nickel/5 cents
니켈/5 센트

3. $.10 = 10¢
a dime/10 cents
다임/10 센트

4. $.25 = 25¢
a quarter/25 cents
쿼터/25 센트

5. $.50 = 50¢
a half dollar
50센트 은화

6. $1.00
a silver dollar
1 달러 은화

Bills   지폐

7. $1.00
a dollar
1 달러

8. $5.00
five dollars
5 달러

9. $10.00
ten dollars
10 달러

10. $20.00
twenty dollars
20 달러

11. $50.00
fifty dollars
50 달러

12. $100.00
one hundred dollars
100 달러

Ways to pay   지불 방법

13. cash
현금

14. personal check
개인 수표

15. credit card
신용 카드

16. money order
송금환

17. traveler's check
여행자 수표

More vocabulary

borrow: to get money from someone and return it later
lend: to give money to someone and get it back later
pay back: to return the money that you borrowed

Other ways to talk about money:

a dollar bill or *a one*
a five-dollar bill or *a five*
a ten-dollar bill or *a ten*
a twenty-dollar bill or *a twenty*

20

A. shop for ~을/를 사려고 다니다	**E. keep** 가지고 있다	**2.** regular price 정상가	**6.** price/cost 가격/비용
B. sell 팔다	**F. return** 반환하다	**3.** sale price 특매가/세일가격	**7.** sales tax 판매세
C. pay for/**buy** 지불하다 / 사다	**G. exchange** 교환하다	**4.** bar code 판독용 기호	**8.** total 총액
D. give 주다	**1.** price tag 가격표	**5.** receipt 영수증	**9.** change 거스름돈

More vocabulary

When you use a credit card to shop, you get a **bill** in the mail. Bills list, in writing, the items you bought and the total you have to pay.

Share your answers.

1. Name three things you pay for every month.
2. Name one thing you will buy this week.
3. Where do you like to shop?

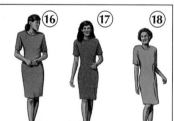
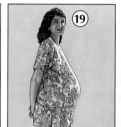

1. children
어린이

2. baby
아기

3. toddler
유아

4. 6-year-old boy
6세 소년

5. 10-year-old girl
10세 소녀

6. teenagers
10대 청소년

7. 13-year-old boy
13세 소년

8. 19-year-old girl
19세 소녀

9. adults
성인

10. woman
여자

11. man
남자

12. senior citizen
노인

13. young
젊은

14. middle-aged
중년의

15. elderly
나이 지긋한

16. tall
키가 큰

17. average height
평균 신장

18. short
키가 작은

19. pregnant
임신한

20. heavyset
체격이 큰

21. average weight
평균 체중

22. thin/slim
날씬한 / 호리호리한

23. attractive
예쁜

24. cute
귀여운

25. physically challenged
신체 부자유인

26. sight impaired/blind
시각 장애인 / 눈먼

27. hearing impaired/deaf
청각 장애인 / 귀먼

Talk about yourself and your teacher.

I am _young_, _average height_, and _average weight_.

My teacher is _a middle-aged_, _tall_, _thin_ man.

Use the new language.

Turn to **Hobbies and Games**, pages **162–163**.

Describe each person on the page.

He's _a heavyset_, _short_, _senior citizen_.

Trends Hair Salon
NO APPT. NECESSARY

SHAMPOO
BLOW DRY
CUT

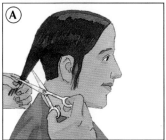

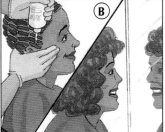

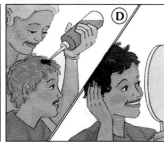

1. short hair
짧은 머리

2. shoulder-length hair
어깨 길이의 머리

3. long hair
긴 머리

4. part
가르마타다

5. mustache
콧수염

6. beard
턱수염

7. sideburns
짧은 구레나룻

8. bangs
앞머리

9. straight hair
곧은 머리

10. wavy hair
구불거리는 머리

11. curly hair
곱슬 머리

12. bald
대머리

13. gray hair
흰머리

14. red hair
빨강 머리

15. black hair
검은 머리

16. blond hair
금발 머리

17. brown hair
갈색 머리

18. brush
솔

19. scissors
가위

20. blow dryer
드라이어

21. rollers
롤러

22. comb
빗

A. cut hair
머리를 자르다

B. perm hair
머리를 파마하다

C. set hair
머리를 세트하다

D. color hair / **dye** hair
머리를 염색하다

More vocabulary

hair stylist: a person who cuts, sets, and perms hair

hair salon: the place where a hair stylist works

Talk about your hair.

My hair is <u>long</u>, <u>straight</u>, and <u>brown</u>.

I have <u>long</u>, <u>straight</u>, <u>brown</u> hair.

When I was a child my hair was <u>short</u>, <u>curly</u>, and <u>blond</u>.

23

Tom Lee's Family

1. grandparents
조부모

Min

Lu

2. grandmother
할머니 / 조모

3. grandfather
할아버지 / 조부

4. parents
부모

Rose

Chang

Helen

Daniel

5. mother
어머니

6. father
아버지

10. aunt
숙모/이모/고모

11. uncle
삼촌

Tom

Lily

Alex

Emily

8. sister
여자형제 /
여동생 / 누나

9. brother
남자형제 /
형/남동생

12. cousin
사촌

7. (Min and Lu's)
grandson
(민과 루) 손자

Berta

Mario

Ana Garcia's Family

Ana

13. mother-in-law
시어머니 / 장모

14. father-in-law
시아버지 / 장인

Marta

Carlos

Tito

20. (Tito's) wife
(티토의) 부인

15. sister-in-law
형수 / 시누이

16. brother-in-law
처남 / 매부

19. husband
남편

Alice

Eddie

Sara

Felix

17. niece
질녀 / 여자조카

18. nephew
조카

21. daughter
딸

22. son
아들

More vocabulary

Lily and Emily are Min and Lu's **granddaughters.**
Daniel is Min and Lu's **son-in-law.**
Ana is Berta and Mario's **daughter-in-law.**

Share your answers.

1. How many brothers and sisters do you have?
2. What number son or daughter are you?
3. Do you have any children?

Lisa Smith's Family

23. married
결혼하고 있다

24. divorced
이혼했다

Carol   *Dan*

Lisa

25. single mother
독신모

26. single father
독신부

Rick   *Carol*

27. remarried
재혼했다

Dan   *Sue*

Rick   *Carol*

Lisa

Dan   *Sue*

28. stepfather
의붓 아버지 / 계부

David   *Mary*

31. stepmother
의붓 어머니 / 계모

Kim   *Bill*

29. half brother
이복/이부 남자형제

30. half sister
이복/이부 여자형제

32. stepsister
의붓 여자형제

33. stepbrother
의붓 남자형제

More vocabulary

Carol is Dan's **former wife.**

Sue is Dan's **wife.**

Dan is Carol's **former husband.**

Rick is Carol's **husband.**

Lisa is the **stepdaughter** of both Rick and Sue.

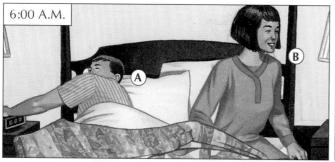

6:00 A.M.

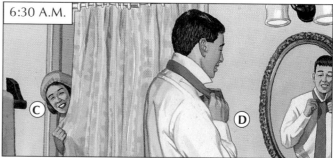

6:30 A.M.

7:00 A.M.

7:30 A.M.

8:00 A.M.

10:00 A.M.

4:30 P.M.

5:00 P.M.

A. **wake up**
잠에서 깨다

B. **get up**
일어나다

C. **take** a shower
샤워를 하다

D. **get dressed**
옷을 입다

E. **eat** breakfast
아침 식사를 하다

F. **make** lunch
점심을 만들다

G. **take** the children to school
자녀를 학교에 데려다 주다

H. **take** the bus to school
버스로 학교에 가다

I. **drive** to work / **go** to work
차로 출근하다

J. **be** in school
학교에서 공부하다

K. **work**
일하다

L. **go** to the market
시장에 가다

M. **leave** work
퇴근하다

Grammar point: 3rd person singular

For **he** and **she**, we add **-s** or **-es** to the verb.

He/She wakes up.

He/She watches TV.

These verbs are different (irregular):

be   *He/She **is** in school at 10:00 a.m.*

have   *He/She **has** dinner at 6:30 p.m.*

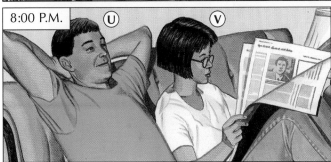

N. clean the house
집을 청소하다

O. pick up the children
자녀를 데려오다

P. cook dinner
저녁 식사를 요리하다

Q. come home/**get** home
집에 오다 / 집에 도착하다

R. have dinner
저녁 식사를 하다

S. watch TV
텔레비전을 보다

T. do homework
숙제를 하다

U. relax
쉬다

V. read the paper
신문을 읽다

W. exercise
운동하다

X. go to bed
잠자리에 들다 / 자다

Y. go to sleep
잠이 들다 / 자다

Talk about your daily routine.

I take a shower in the morning.

I go to school in the evening.

I go to bed at 11 o'clock.

Share your answers.

1. Who makes dinner in your family?
2. Who goes to the market?
3. Who goes to work?

Life Events 인생 경로

A. be born
태어나다

B. start school
학교를 다니기 시작하다

C. immigrate
이민하다

D. graduate
졸업하다

E. learn to drive
운전을 배우다

F. join the army
군에 입대하다

G. get a job
직장을 구하다

H. become a citizen
시민이 되다

I. rent an apartment
아파트를 임대하다

J. go to college
대학에 들어가다

K. fall in love
사랑에 빠지다

L. get married
결혼하다

Grammar point: past tense

start		immigrate		be	— was	have	— had
learn		graduate		get	— got	buy	— bought
join	+ed	move	+d	become	— became		
rent		retire		go	— went		
travel		die		fall	— fell		

 1960

 1967

M. have a baby
아기를 낳다

N. travel
여행하다

 1971

 1971

O. buy a house
집을 사다

P. move
이사하다

 1985

 1997

Q. have a grandchild
손자를 보다

R. die
죽다

1. birth certificate
출생 증명서

2. diploma
졸업 증서

3. Resident Alien card
영주권

  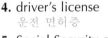

4. driver's license
운전 면허증

5. Social Security card
사회 보장 카드

6. Certificate of Naturalization
귀화 증명서

7. college degree
대학 학위

8. marriage license
결혼 증서

9. passport
여권

More vocabulary

When a husband dies, his wife becomes a **widow**.
When a wife dies, her husband becomes a **widower**.
When older people stop working, we say they **retire**.

Talk about yourself.

I was born in 1968.
I learned to drive in 1987.
I immigrated in 1990.

1. hot
더운

2. thirsty
목마른

3. sleepy
졸리는

4. cold
추운 / 찬

5. hungry
배고픈

6. full
배부른

7. comfortable
편안한

8. uncomfortable
불편한

9. disgusted
역겨운

10. calm
침착한

11. nervous
초조한

12. in pain
아픈

13. worried
염려되는

14. sick
병든

15. well
건강한 / 상태가 좋은

16. relieved
안도된

17. hurt
다친

18. lonely
외로운

19. in love
사랑에 빠진

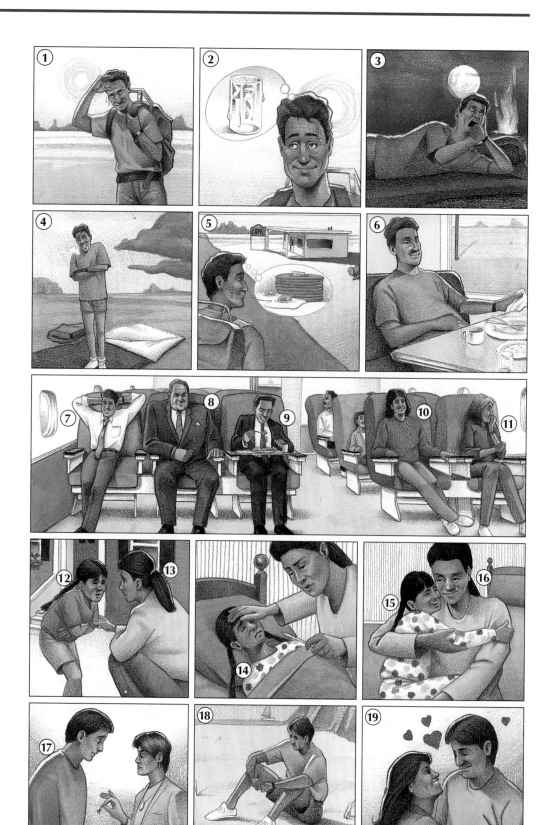

More vocabulary

furious: very angry
terrified: very scared
overjoyed: very happy

exhausted: very tired
starving: very hungry
humiliated: very embarrassed

Talk about your feelings.

I feel _happy_ when I see _my friends_.
I feel _homesick_ when I think about _my family_.

20. sad
슬픈

21. homesick
향수병에 걸린

22. proud
자랑스러운

23. excited
흥분된

24. scared
겁이 난

25. embarrassed
당황한

26. bored
지루한

27. confused
혼란된

28. frustrated
낙심한

29. angry
화난

30. upset
기분이 나쁜

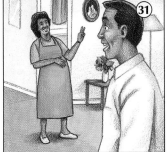

31. surprised
놀란

32. happy
행복한

33. tired
피곤한

Use the new language.

Look at **Clothing I,** page **64,** and answer the questions.

1. How does the runner feel?

2. How does the man at the bus stop feel?

3. How does the woman at the bus stop feel?

4. How do the teenagers feel?

5. How does the little boy feel?

A Graduation 졸업

The Ceremony

1. **graduating class**
   졸업반

2. **gown**
   졸업 가운

3. **cap**
   졸업모

4. **stage**
   무대

5. **podium**
   연단

6. **graduate**
   졸업생

7. **diploma**
   졸업 증서

8. **valedictorian**
   졸업생 대표

9. **guest speaker**
   초빙 연사

10. **audience**
    관객

11. **photographer**
    사진사

A. **graduate**
   졸업하다

B. **applaud / clap**
   박수치다 / 손뼉치다

C. **cry**
   울다

D. **take** a picture
   사진을 찍다

E. **give** a speech
   연설하다

Talk about what the people in the pictures are doing.

She is
- tak**ing** a picture.
- giv**ing** a speech.
- smil**ing**.
- laugh**ing**.

He is
- mak**ing** a toast.
- clap**ping**.

They are
- graduat**ing**.
- hug**ging**.
- kiss**ing**.
- applaud**ing**.

The Party

12. caterer 연회 요리 담당자	**15.** banner 기	**18.** gifts 선물	**H.** laugh 웃다
13. buffet 부페	**16.** dance floor 무도장	**F.** kiss 키스하다	**I.** make a toast 축배를 들다
14. guests 손님들	**17.** DJ (disc jockey) 디스크 자키 / DJ	**G.** hug 포옹하다	**J.** dance 춤추다

Share your answers.

1. Did you ever go to a graduation? Whose?

2. Did you ever give a speech? Where?

3. Did you ever hear a great speaker? Where?

4. Did you ever go to a graduation party?

5. What do you like to eat at parties?

6. Do you like to dance at parties?

Places to Live 주거 장소

1. the city / an urban area
도시 / 도회 지역

2. the suburbs
교외

3. a small town
작은 마을

4. the country / a rural area
시골 / 전원 지역

5. apartment building
아파트 건물

6. house
집 / 가옥

7. townhouse
연립 주택

8. mobile home
이동식 주택

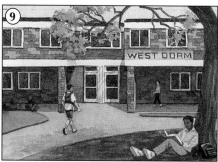

9. college dormitory
대학 기숙사

10. shelter
보호소

11. nursing home
양로원

12. ranch
목장

13. farm
농장

More vocabulary

duplex house: a house divided into two homes

condominium: an apartment building where each apartment is owned separately

co-op: an apartment building owned by the residents

Share your answers.

1. Do you like where you live?

2. Where did you live in your country?

3. What types of housing are there near your school?

34

Renting an apartment 아파트 임대하기

A. look for a new apartment
새 아파트를 찾아 보다

B. talk to the manager
매니저와 이야기하다

C. sign a rental agreement
임대 계약서에 서명하다

D. move in
입주하다

E. unpack
짐을 풀다

F. pay the rent
임대료를 지불하다

Buying a house 집을 사기

G. talk to the Realtor
부동산업자와 이야기하다

H. make an offer
값을 제의하다

I. get a loan
융자금을 얻다

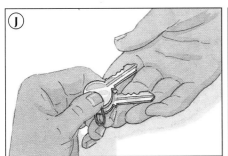

J. take ownership
집소유권을 얻다

K. arrange the furniture
가구를 배치하다

L. pay the mortgage
주택 융자금을 지불하다

More vocabulary

lease: a rental agreement for a specific period of time

utilities: gas, water, and electricity for the home

Practice talking to an apartment manager.

How much is the rent?

Are utilities included?

When can I move in?

35

1. first floor
1층

2. second floor
2층

3. third floor
3층

4. fourth floor
4층

5. roof garden
옥상 정원

6. playground
운동장

7. fire escape
비상구 계단

8. intercom / speaker
인터콤 / 스피커

9. security system
안보 장치

10. doorman
수위

11. vacancy sign
빈 방 광고문

12. manager / superintendent
지배인 / 관리인

13. security gate
보안용 문

14. storage locker
보관함

15. parking space
주차 공간

More vocabulary

rec room: a short way of saying **recreation room**

basement: the area below the street level of an apartment
or a house

Talk about where you live.

I live in Apartment 3 near the entrance.

*I live in Apartment 11 on the second floor near the fire
escape.*

16. swimming pool
수영장

17. balcony
발코니

18. courtyard
안뜰

19. air conditioner
냉난방 장치 / 에어콘

20. trash bin
쓰레기통

21. alley
골목

22. neighbor
이웃

23. fire exit
비상구

24. trash chute
쓰레기 낙하장치

25. smoke detector
연기 탐지기

26. stairway
계단

27. peephole
들여다 보는 구멍

28. door chain
문 사슬

29. dead-bolt lock
초강력 열쇠장치

30. doorknob
문 손잡이

31. key
열쇠

32. landlord
집주인

33. tenant
임대인

34. elevator
승강기

35. stairs
계단

36. mailboxes
우편함

Grammar point: *there is, there are*
singular: *there is*   plural: *there are*
There is *a fire exit in the hallway.*
There are *mailboxes in the lobby.*

Talk about apartments.
My apartment has <u>an elevator</u>, <u>a lobby</u>, and <u>a rec room</u>.
My apartment doesn't have <u>a pool</u> or <u>a garage</u>.
My apartment needs <u>air conditioning</u>.

1. floor plan
평면도

2. backyard
뒷마당

3. fence
울타리

4. mailbox
우편함

5. driveway
드라이브웨이

6. garage
차고

7. garage door
차고문

8. screen door
칸막이 문

9. porch light
현관등

10. doorbell
초인종

11. front door
앞문

12. storm door
유리 끼운 덧문

13. steps
층계

14. front walk
전방 통로

15. front yard
앞마당

16. deck
널찍한 주택 갑판

17. window
창문

18. shutter
겉문

19. gutter
홈통

20. roof
지붕

21. chimney
굴뚝

22. TV antenna
텔레비전 안테나

More vocabulary

two-story house: a house with two floors

downstairs: the bottom floor

upstairs: the part of a house above the bottom floor

Share your answers.

1. What do you like about this house?

2. What's something you don't like about the house?

3. Describe the perfect house.

1. hedge
헤지 울타리

2. hammock
해먹

3. garbage can
쓰레기통

4. leaf blower
강풍 낙엽 청소기

5. patio furniture
안뜰용 가구

6. patio
안뜰

7. barbecue grill
바베큐 석쇠

8. sprinkler
살수장치

9. hose
호스

10. compost pile
퇴비 더미

11. rake
갈퀴

12. hedge clippers
헤지 울타리 깎는 가위

13. shovel
삽

14. trowel
흙손

15. pruning shears
전정 가위

16. wheelbarrow
외바퀴 손수레

17. watering can
물뿌리개

18. flowerpot
화분

19. flower
화초

20. bush
관목

21. lawn
잔디 (밭)

22. lawn mower
잔디 깎는 기계

A. **weed** the flower bed
화단의 잡초를 뽑으세요

B. **water** the plants
식물에 물을 주세요

C. **mow** the lawn
잔디를 깎으세요

D. **plant** a tree
나무를 심으세요

E. **trim** the hedge
나무 울타리를 다듬으세요

F. **rake** the leaves
낙엽을 긁어 모으세요

Talk about your yard and gardening.

I like to plant trees.

I don't like to weed.

I like/don't like to work in the yard/garden.

Share your answers.

1. What flowers, trees, or plants do you see in the picture? (Look at **Trees, Plants, and Flowers,** pages **128–129** for help.)

2. Do you ever use a barbecue grill to cook?

A Kitchen 주방

1. cabinet
   찬장/캐비닛

2. paper towels
   종이 타월

3. dish drainer
   그릇 배수기

4. dishwasher
   식기세척기

5. garbage disposal
   음식찌꺼기처리기

6. sink
   싱크

7. toaster
   토스터

8. shelf
   선반

9. refrigerator
   냉장고

10. freezer
    냉동고

11. coffeemaker
    커피 메이커

12. blender
    요리용 믹서

13. microwave oven
    전자 렌지

14. electric can opener
    전기 깡통 따개

15. toaster oven
    오븐 토스터

16. pot
    냄비

17. teakettle
    차주전자

18. stove
    스토브

19. burner
    버너

20. oven
    오븐

21. broiler
    브로일러

22. counter
    조리대

23. drawer
    서랍

24. pan
    팬

25. electric mixer
    전기 믹서

26. food processor
    식품 가공기

27. cutting board
    도마

Talk about the location of kitchen items.

The toaster oven is *on the counter* *near the stove.*

The microwave is *above the stove.*

Share your answers.

1. Do you have a garbage disposal? a dishwasher? a microwave?

2. Do you eat in the kitchen?

1. china cabinet
자기그릇 캐비닛/찬장

2. set of dishes
식기 세트

3. platter
쟁반접시

4. ceiling fan
천장 팬

5. light fixture
조명 기구

6. serving dish
서빙 접시

7. candle
초

8. candlestick
촛대

9. vase
꽃병

10. tray
쟁반

11. teapot
차 주전자

12. sugar bowl
설탕 그릇

13. creamer
크림 그릇

14. saltshaker
소금통(식탁용)

15. pepper shaker
후추통(식탁용)

16. dining room chair
식탁 의자

17. dining room table
식탁

18. tablecloth
식탁보

19. napkin
냅킨

20. place mat
접시 받침

21. fork
포크

22. knife
칼

23. spoon
숟가락

24. plate
접시

25. bowl
사발

26. glass
유리컵

27. coffee cup
커피컵

28. mug
머그

Practice asking for things in the dining room.

Please pass <u>the platter</u>.

May I have <u>the creamer</u>?

Could I have <u>a fork</u>, please?

Share your answers.

1. What are the women in the picture saying?

2. In your home, where do you eat?

3. Do you like to make dinner for your friends?

1. bookcase 책장	**8.** mantel 벽로선반	**15.** floor lamp 플로어 램프	**22.** magazine holder 잡지 꽂이대
2. basket 바구니	**9.** fireplace 벽난로	**16.** drapes 커튼	**23.** coffee table 커피 탁자
3. track lighting 트랙 조명	**10.** fire 벽난로 불	**17.** window 창문	**24.** armchair/easy chair 안락의자
4. lightbulb 전구	**11.** fire screen 불꽃 가리개	**18.** plant 식물	**25.** love seat 2인용 소파
5. ceiling 천장	**12.** logs 장작	**19.** sofa/couch 소파	**26.** TV (television) 텔레비전
6. wall 벽	**13.** wall unit 벽장	**20.** throw pillow 쓰로우 필러	**27.** carpet 카페트
7. painting 그림	**14.** stereo system 스테레오 전축	**21.** end table 소파 옆 소탁자	

Use the new language.

Look at **Colors,** page **12,** and describe this room.

There is a gray sofa and a gray armchair.

Talk about your living room.

In my living room I have a sofa, two chairs, and a coffee table.

I don't have a fireplace or a wall unit.

1. hamper 빨래 바구니	**8. towel rack** 수건걸이	**15. toilet paper** 화장지	**22. sink** 세면대
2. bathtub 욕탕	**9. tile** 타일	**16. toilet brush** 변기 세척솔	**23. soap** 비누
3. rubber mat 고무 매트	**10. showerhead** 샤워기 앞부분	**17. toilet** 변기	**24. soap dish** 비누 접시
4. drain 배수구	**11. (mini)blinds** 블라인드	**18. mirror** 거울	**25. wastebasket** 쓰레기통
5. hot water 온수	**12. bath towel** 목욕용 큰 수건	**19. medicine cabinet** 약품 진열장	**26. scale** 저울
6. faucet 수도꼭지	**13. hand towel** 작은 수건	**20. toothbrush** 치솔	**27. bath mat** 욕실용 매트
7. cold water 냉수	**14. washcloth** 와시클로스	**21. toothbrush holder** 치솔통	

More vocabulary

half bath: a bathroom without a shower or bathtub

linen closet: a closet or cabinet for towels and sheets

stall shower: a shower without a bathtub

Share your answers.

1. Do you turn off the water when you brush your teeth? wash your hair? shave?

2. Does your bathroom have a bathtub or a stall shower?

1. mirror
거울

2. dresser/bureau
화장대

3. drawer
서랍

4. closet
옷장

5. curtains
커튼

6. window shade
차양

7. photograph
사진

8. bed
침대

9. pillow
베개

10. pillowcase
베갯잇

11. bedspread
침대 커버

12. blanket
담요

13. flat sheet
침대 이불 시트

14. fitted sheet
침대 매트레스 시트

15. headboard
(침대)머리판

16. clock radio
시계겸용 라디오

17. lamp
램프

18. lampshade
램프갓

19. light switch
전등 스위치

20. outlet
콘센트

21. night table
침대 곁 소탁자

22. dust ruffle
먼지 방지용 프릴

23. rug
양탄자

24. floor
방바닥

25. mattress
매트리스

26. box spring
침대 스프링

27. bed frame
침대틀

Use the new language.

Describe this room. (See **Describing Things**, page **11**, for help.)

I see a soft pillow and a beautiful bedspread.

Share your answers.

1. What is your favorite thing in your bedroom?

2. Do you have a clock in your bedroom? Where is it?

3. Do you have a mirror in your bedroom? Where is it?

1. bunk bed
2단 침대

2. comforter
이불

3. night-light
야간등

4. mobile
모빌

5. wallpaper
벽지

6. crib
소아용 침대

7. bumper pad
완충 패드

8. chest of drawers
서랍장

9. baby monitor
아기 모니터

10. teddy bear
곰인형

11. smoke detector
연기 탐지기

12. changing table
기저귀 갈이용 탁자

13. diaper pail
기저귀통

14. dollhouse
인형 집

15. blocks
쌓기 장난감

16. ball
공

17. picture book
그림책

18. doll
인형

19. cradle
요람

20. coloring book
색칠책

21. crayons
크레용

22. puzzle
퍼즐

23. stuffed animals
봉제 동물 완구

24. toy chest
장난감 상자

Talk about where items are in the room.

The dollhouse is near *the coloring book.*

The teddy bear is on *the chest of drawers.*

Share your answers.

1. Do you think this is a good room for children? Why?

2. What toys did you play with when you were a child?

3. What children's stories do you know?

A. **dust** the furniture
가구의 먼지를 털다

B. **recycle** the newspapers
신문을 재활용하다

C. **clean** the oven
오븐을 청소하다

D. **wash** the windows
창문을 닦다

E. **sweep** the floor
마루바닥을 쓸다

F. **empty** the wastebasket
쓰레기통을 비우다

G. **make** the bed
침대를 정돈하다

H. **put away** the toys
장난감들을 치우다

I. **vacuum** the carpet
카페트를 진공 청소하다

J. **mop** the floor
마루를 걸레질하다

K. **polish** the furniture
가구에 광을 내다

L. **scrub** the floor
마루바닥을 문질러 닦다

M. **wash** the dishes
그릇을 씻다

N. **dry** the dishes
그릇을 말리다

O. **wipe** the counter
조리대를 닦아내다

P. **change** the sheets
시트를 갈다

Q. **take out** the garbage
쓰레기를 내다놓다

Talk about yourself.

I wash <u>the dishes</u> every day.
I change <u>the sheets</u> every week.
I never <u>dry the dishes</u>.

Share your answers.

1. Who does the housework in your family?
2. What is your favorite cleaning job?
3. What is your least favorite cleaning job?

1. feather duster
깃털 총채

2. recycling bin
재활용 통

3. oven cleaner
오븐 클리너

4. rubber gloves
고무 장갑

5. steel-wool soap pads
강모 비누실 다발

6. rags
발깔개

7. stepladder
발판 사닥다리

8. glass cleaner
유리 클리너

9. squeegee
스퀴지

10. broom
빗자루

11. dustpan
쓰레받기

12. trash bags
쓰레기봉지

13. vacuum cleaner
진공 청소기

14. vacuum cleaner attachments
진공 청소기 부착물

15. vacuum cleaner bag
진공 청소기 안주머니

16. wet mop
물걸레

17. dust mop
자루 걸레

18. furniture polish
가구 광택제

19. scrub brush
수세미

20. bucket / pail
바켓 / 들통

21. dishwashing liquid
그릇 세척 용제

22. dish towel
그릇 말리는 수건

23. cleanser
세제

24. sponge
스폰지

Practice asking for the items.

I want to <u>wash the windows</u>.
Please hand me <u>the squeegee</u>.

I have to <u>sweep the floor</u>.
Can you get me <u>the broom</u>, please?

1. The water heater is **not working**.
   워터 히터가 고장났다.

2. The power is **out**.
   전원이 나갔다.

3. The roof is **leaking**.
   지붕이 새다.

4. The wall is **cracked**.
   벽에 금이갔다.

5. The window is **broken**.
   유리창이 깨졌다.

6. The lock is **broken**.
   자물쇠가 부서졌다.

7. The steps are **broken**.
   계단이 부서졌다.

8. roofer
   지붕 수리공

9. electrician
   전기공

10. repair person
    수리공

11. locksmith
    자물쇠 제조공

12. carpenter
    목수

13. fuse box
    두꺼비집-퓨즈 상자

14. gas meter
    가스미터 / 가스계량기

Use the new language.

Look at **Tools and Building Supplies**, pages **150–151**.

Name the tools you use for household repairs.

I use <u>a hammer and nails</u> to fix <u>a broken step</u>.

I use <u>a wrench</u> to repair <u>a dripping faucet</u>.

15. The furnace is **broken**.
보일러가 고장났다.

16. The faucet is **dripping**.
수도꼭지가 새다.

17. The sink is **overflowing**.
싱크물이 넘치다.

18. The toilet is **stopped up**.
변기가 막혔다.

19. The pipes are **frozen**.
파이프가 얼었다.

20. plumber
배관공

21. exterminator
해충 구제인

Household pests
가정 해충

22. termite(s)
흰 개미

23. flea(s)
벼룩

24. ant(s)
개미

25. cockroach(es)
바퀴벌레

26. mice*
생쥐

27. rat(s)
쥐 / 시궁쥐

*Note: *one mouse, two mice*

More vocabulary

fix: to repair something that is broken

exterminate: to kill household pests

pesticide: a chemical that is used to kill household pests

Share your answers.

1. Who does household repairs in your home?

2. What is the worst problem a home can have?

3. What is the most expensive problem a home can have?

49

1. grapes 포도	**9.** grapefruit 자몽	**17.** strawberries 딸기	**25.** dates 대추
2. pineapples 파인애플	**10.** oranges 오렌지	**18.** raspberries 나무딸기	**26.** prunes 서양 자두
3. bananas 바나나	**11.** lemons 레몬	**19.** blueberries 블루베리	**27.** raisins 건포도
4. apples 사과	**12.** limes 라임	**20.** papayas 파파야	**28.** not ripe 익지 않은
5. peaches 복숭아	**13.** tangerines 귤	**21.** mangoes 망고	**29.** ripe 익은
6. pears 배	**14.** avocadoes 아보카도	**22.** coconuts 코코야자 열매	**30.** rotten 썩은
7. apricots 살구	**15.** cantaloupes 멜론	**23.** nuts 견과류	
8. plums 자두	**16.** cherries 체리	**24.** watermelons 수박	

Language note: *a bunch of*

We say *a bunch of grapes* and *a bunch of bananas*.

Share your answers.

1. Which fruits do you put in a fruit salad?

2. Which fruits are sold in your area in the summer?

3. What fruits did you have in your country?

1. lettuce
상추

2. cabbage
양배추

3. carrots
당근

4. zucchini
서양호박

5. radishes
무

6. beets
근대

7. sweet peppers
피망

8. chili peppers
칠리고추

9. celery
셀러리

10. parsley
파슬리

11. spinach
시금치

12. cucumbers
오이

13. squash
호박

14. turnips
순무

15. broccoli
브로콜리

16. cauliflower
꽃양배추

17. scallions
부추

18. eggplants
가지

19. peas
완두콩

20. artichokes
아티초크

21. potatoes
감자

22. yams
고구마

23. tomatoes
토마토

24. asparagus
아스파라거스

25. string beans
깍지 강낭콩

26. mushrooms
버섯

27. corn
옥수수

28. onions
양파

29. garlic
마늘

Language note: *a bunch of, a head of*

We say *a bunch of carrots, a bunch of celery,* and *a bunch of spinach.*

We say *a head of lettuce, a head of cabbage,* and *a head of cauliflower.*

Share your answers.

1. Which vegetables do you eat raw? cooked?

2. Which vegetables need to be in the refrigerator?

3. Which vegetables don't need to be in the refrigerator?

MEAT

Beef 쇠고기

1. roast beef
로스트비프

2. steak
스테이크

3. stewing beef
스튜용 쇠고기

4. ground beef
다진 쇠고기

5. beef ribs
쇠갈비

6. veal cutlets
송아지 고기 카틀렛

7. liver
쇠간

8. tripe
소의 위

Pork 돼지고기

9. ham
햄

10. pork chops
돼지고기춉 / 돼지부분육

11. bacon
베이컨

12. sausage
소세지

Lamb 양고기

13. lamb shanks
양 정강이 살

14. leg of lamb
양 다리고기

15. lamb chops
양고기춉 / 양부분육

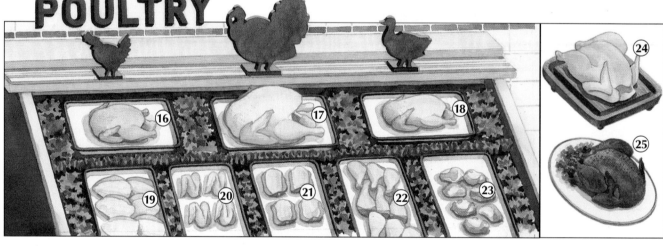

POULTRY

16. chicken
닭고기

17. turkey
칠면조 고기

18. duck
오리 고기

19. breasts
가슴

20. wings
날개

21. thighs
넓적다리

22. drumsticks
닭다리

23. gizzards
모래주머니

24. **raw** chicken
날 닭고기

25. **cooked** chicken
조리한 닭고기

More vocabulary

vegetarian: a person who doesn't eat meat
Meat and poultry without bones are called **boneless**.
Poultry without skin is called **skinless**.

Share your answers.

1. What kind of meat do you eat most often?
2. What kind of meat do you use in soup?
3. What part of the chicken do you like the most?

1. white bread
   흰 빵

2. wheat bread
   밀빵

3. rye bread
   호밀빵

4. smoked turkey
   훈제 칠면조

5. salami
   살라미

6. pastrami
   훈제 쇠고기

7. roast beef
   로스트 비프

8. corned beef
   콘드비프

9. American cheese
   아메리칸 치즈

10. cheddar cheese
    체다 치즈

11. Swiss cheese
    스위스 치즈

12. jack cheese
    잭 치즈

13. potato salad
    감자 샐러드

14. coleslaw
    양배추 샐러드

15. pasta salad
    파스타 샐러드

Fish 생선

16. trout
    송어

17. catfish
    메기

18. whole salmon
    연어 한 마리

19. salmon steak
    스테이크용 연어

20. halibut
    큰 넙치

21. filet of sole
    혀가자미필레 살

Shellfish 갑각류

22. crab
    게

23. lobster
    가재

24. shrimp
    새우

25. scallops
    가리비

26. mussels
    홍합

27. oysters
    굴

28. clams
    대합 조개

29. **fresh** fish
    신선한 생선

30. **frozen** fish
    냉동 생선

Practice ordering a sandwich.

I'd like roast beef and American cheese on rye bread.

Tell what you want on it.

Please put tomato, lettuce, onions, and mustard on it.

Share your answers.

1. Do you like to eat fish?

2. Do you buy fresh or frozen fish?

53

1. bottle return
병 회수

2. meat and poultry section
고기류

3. shopping cart
쇼핑 카트

4. canned goods
통조림된 식품

5. aisle
복도

6. baked goods
제과류

7. shopping basket
쇼핑 바구니

8. manager
지배인

9. dairy section
유제품

10. pet food
애완동물 식품

11. produce section
채소류

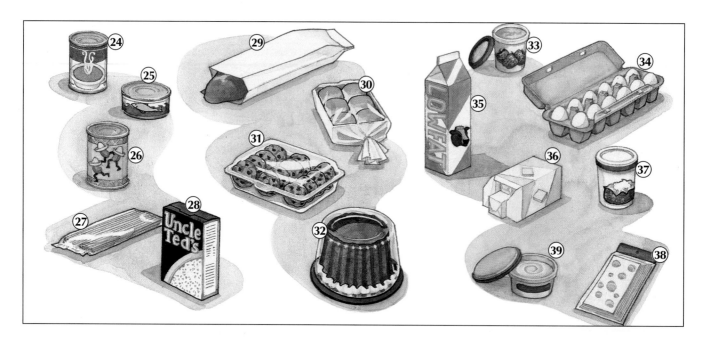

24. soup
수프

25. tuna
참치

26. beans
콩류

27. spaghetti
스파게티

28. rice
쌀

29. bread
빵

30. rolls
롤빵

31. cookies
쿠키

32. cake
케이크

33. yogurt
요구르트

34. eggs
달걀

35. milk
우유

36. butter
버터

37. sour cream
사워크림

38. cheese
치즈

39. margarine
마가린

12. frozen foods
냉동 식품

13. baking products
제과류

14. paper products
종이 제품

15. beverages
음료수

16. snack foods
간식

17. checkstand
계산대

18. cash register
금전 등록기

19. checker
현금 출납원

20. line
줄

21. bagger
물건 담아주는 사람

22. paper bag
종이 봉투

23. plastic bag
비닐 봉투

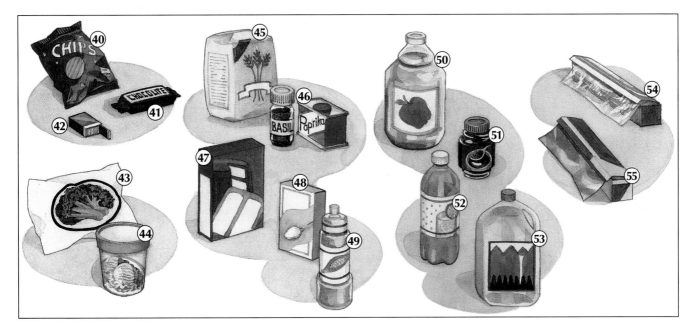

40. potato chips
감자 칩

41. candy bar
초콜릿 / 캔디바

42. gum
껌

43. frozen vegetables
냉동야채

44. ice cream
아이스크림

45. flour
밀가루

46. spices
양념류

47. cake mix
케익재료

48. sugar
설탕

49. oil
식용유

50. apple juice
사과 쥬스

51. instant coffee
인스턴트 커피

52. soda
탄산음료수 / 소다

53. bottled water
생수

54. plastic wrap
비닐랩

55. aluminum foil
알루미늄 포일

1. bottle
병

2. jar
병

3. can
캔

4. carton
카톤

5. container
용기

6. box
상자

7. bag
봉지

8. package
꾸러미

9. six-pack
6 개들이 팩

10. loaf
덩어리

11. roll
두루말이

12. tube
통 (튜브)

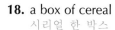

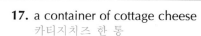
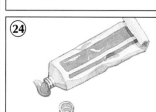

13. a bottle of soda
탄산음료수 한 병

14. a jar of jam
잼 한 병

15. a can of soup
수프 한 캔

16. a carton of eggs
달걀 한 카톤

17. a container of cottage cheese
카티지치즈 한 통

18. a box of cereal
시리얼 한 박스

19. a bag of flour
밀가루 한 봉지

20. a package of cookies
쿠키 한 봉지

21. a six-pack of soda
탄산음료수 6 개들이 팩

22. a loaf of bread
빵 한 덩어리

23. a roll of paper towels
종이타월 두루말이 하나

24. a tube of toothpaste
치약 튜브 하나

Grammar point: *How much? How many?*
Some foods can be counted: *one apple, two apples.*
How many apples do you need? I need ***two*** apples.

Some foods cannot be counted, like liquids, grains, spices, or dairy foods. For these, count containers: *one box of rice, two boxes of rice.*
How much rice do you need? I need ***two boxes.***

1 cup = 237 milliliters

A. Measure the ingredients.
재료를 측량하다.

B. Weigh the food.
음식 무게를 달다.

C. Convert the measurements.
측량치를 환산하다.

Liquid measures   액량

① 1 fl. oz.

② 1 c.

③ 1 pt.

④ 1 qt.

⑤ 1 gal.

Dry measures   건량

⑥ 1 tsp.

⑦ 1 TBS.

⑧ 1/4 c.

⑨ 1/2 c.

⑩ 1 c.

Weight   중량

⑪ .06 lb.

⑫ 1.00 lb.

1. a fluid ounce of water
   물 1 온스

2. a cup of oil
   기름 한 컵

3. a pint of yogurt
   요구르트 1 파인트

4. a quart of milk
   우유 1 쿼트

5. a gallon of apple juice
   사과 쥬스 1 갤런

6. a teaspoon of salt
   소금 티스푼 하나

7. a tablespoon of sugar
   설탕 테이블스푼 하나

8. a 1/4 cup of brown sugar
   흑설탕 4분의 1 컵

9. a 1/2 cup of raisins
   건포도 2분의 1 컵

10. a cup of flour
    밀가루 한 컵

11. an ounce of cheese
    치즈 1 온스

12. a pound of roast beef
    로스트 비프 1 파운드

VOLUME
1 fl. oz. = 30 milliliters (ml.)
1 c. = 237 ml.
1 pt. = .47 liters (l.)
1 qt. = .95 l.
1 gal. = 3.79 l.

EQUIVALENCIES	
3 tsp. = 1 TBS.	2 c. = 1 pt.
2 TBS. = 1 fl. oz.	2 pt. = 1 qt.
8 fl. oz. = 1 c.	4 qt. = 1 gal.

WEIGHT
1 oz. = 28.35 grams (g.)
1 lb. = 453.6 g.
2.205 lbs. = 1 kilogram
1 lb. = 16 oz.

Scrambled eggs 스크램블드 달걀

A. Break 3 eggs.
달걀 3개를
깨뜨린다.

B. Beat well.
잘 휘젓는다.

C. Grease the pan.
팬에 기름칠을
한다.

D. Pour the eggs into
the pan.
달걀을 팬에 붓는다.

E. Stir.
젓는다.

F. Cook until done.
다 될 때까지
익힌다.

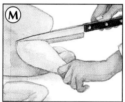

Vegetable casserole 야채 찜냄비 요리

G. Chop the onions.
양파를 잘게 썬다.

H. Sauté the onions.
양파를 살짝 기름에
익힌다.

I. Steam the broccoli.
브로콜리를 찐다.

J. Grate the cheese.
치즈를 간다.

K. Mix the ingredients.
재료를 섞는다.

L. Bake at 350° for
45 minutes.
350°에서 45분간
굽는다.

Chicken soup 닭고기 수프

M. Cut up the chicken.
닭고기를 자른다

N. Peel the carrots.
당근 껍질을 벗긴다.

O. Slice the carrots.
당근을 얇게 썬다.

P. Boil the chicken.
닭고기를 삶는다.

Q. Add the vegetables.
야채를 첨가한다.

R. Simmer for 1 hour.
1시간동안 약한
불에 끓인다.

Five ways to cook chicken 다섯 가지 닭고기 요리법

S. fry
튀긴다

T. barbecue / grill
바베큐하다

U. roast
로스트하다

V. broil
굽는다

W. stir-fry
센불에 볶는다

Talk about the way you prepare these foods.

I _fry_ eggs.

I _bake_ potatoes.

Share your answers.

1. What are popular ways in your country to make rice?
vegetables? meat?

2. What is your favorite way to cook chicken?

1. can opener
깡통 따개

2. grater
강판

3. plastic storage container
플라스틱 저장용기

4. steamer
찜통

5. frying pan
후라이팬

6. pot
냄비

7. ladle
국자

8. double boiler
이중 냄비

9. wooden spoon
나무 숟가락

10. garlic press
마늘 압착기

11. casserole dish
뚜껑있는 찜냄비

12. carving knife
써는 칼

13. roasting pan
굽기용 팬

14. roasting rack
굽기용 쇠선반

15. vegetable peeler
야채 껍질 제거기

16. paring knife
과도

17. colander
여과기

18. kitchen timer
부엌용 타이머

19. spatula
주걱

20. eggbeater
달걀 교반기

21. whisk
거품기

22. strainer
체

23. tongs
집게

24. lid
뚜껑

25. saucepan
소스 냄비

26. cake pan
케이크팬

27. cookie sheet
쿠키 판

28. pie pan
파이 팬

29. pot holders
냄비 집게

30. rolling pin
밀방망이

31. mixing bowl
믹스용 그릇

Talk about how to use the utensils.

You use a peeler to peel potatoes.

You use a pot to cook soup.

Use the new language.

Look at **Food Preparation**, page **58**.

Name the different utensils you see.

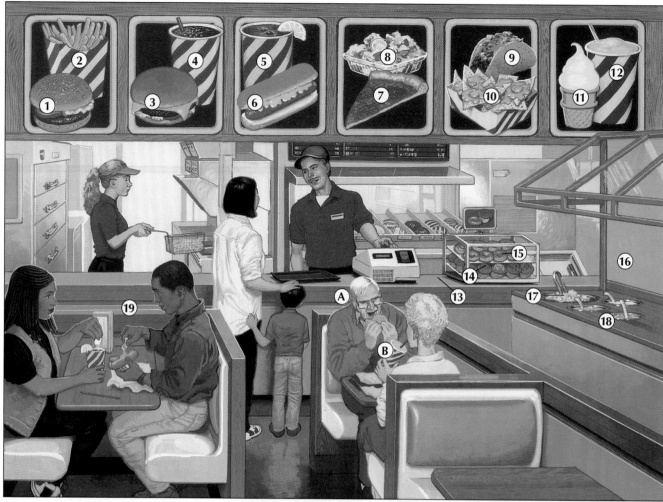

1. hamburger
햄버거

2. french fries
감자 튀김

3. cheeseburger
치즈버거

4. soda
탄산음료수

5. iced tea
냉차

6. hot dog
핫도그

7. pizza
피자

8. green salad
야채 샐러드

9. taco
타코

10. nachos
나쵸

11. frozen yogurt
냉동 요구르트

12. milk shake
밀크 쉐이크

13. counter
계산대

14. muffin
머핀

15. doughnut
도너츠

16. salad bar
샐러드 바

17. lettuce
상추

18. salad dressing
샐러드 드레싱

19. booth
칸막은 좌석

20. straw
빨대

21. sugar
설탕

22. sugar substitute
설탕 대체품

23. ketchup
케첩

24. mustard
겨자 소스

25. mayonnaise
마요네즈

26. relish
양념

A. eat
먹다

B. drink
마시다

More vocabulary

donut: doughnut (spelling variation)

condiments: relish, mustard, ketchup, mayonnaise, etc.

Share your answers.

1. What would you order at this restaurant?

2. Which fast foods are popular in your country?

3. How often do you eat fast food? Why?

Breakfast

Lunch

Dinner

Beverages

Desserts

1. scrambled eggs
   스크램블드 에그

2. sausage
   소세지

3. toast
   토스트

4. waffles
   와플

5. syrup
   시럽

6. pancakes
   팬케이크

7. bacon
   베이컨

8. grilled cheese sandwich
   그릴 치즈 샌드위치

9. chef's salad
   주방장 샐러드

10. soup of the day
    오늘의 수프

11. mashed potatoes
    매시포테이토

12. roast chicken
    구운 닭고기

13. steak
    스테이크

14. baked potato
    구운 감자

15. pasta
    파스타

16. garlic bread
    마늘빵

17. fried fish
    생선 튀김

18. rice pilaf
    밥 필레프

19. cake
    케이크

20. pudding
    푸딩

21. pie
    파이

22. coffee
    커피

23. decaf coffee
    무카페인 커피

24. tea
    차

Practice ordering from the menu.

I'd like <u>a grilled cheese sandwich</u> *and* <u>some soup</u>.

I'll have <u>the chef's salad</u> *and* <u>a cup of decaf coffee</u>.

Use the new language.

Look at **Fruit,** page **50.**

Order a slice of pie using the different fruit flavors.

Please give me a slice of <u>apple</u> *pie.*

1. hostess
호스테스

2. dining room
다이닝룸

3. menu
메뉴

4. server/waiter
종업원 / 웨이터

5. patron/diner
손님 / 식당

A. set the table
식탁을 차리다

B. seat the customer
손님을 앉히다

C. pour the water
물을 따르다

D. order from the menu
메뉴보고 주문하다

E. take the order
주문을 받다

F. serve the meal
음식을 서브하다

G. clear the table
식탁을 치우다

H. carry the tray
쟁반을 나르다

I. pay the check
계산서를 물다

J. leave a tip
팁을 놓다

More vocabulary

eat out: to go to a restaurant to eat

take out: to buy food at a restaurant and take it home to eat

Practice giving commands.

Please <u>set the table</u>.

I'd like you to <u>clear the table</u>.

It's time to <u>serve the meal</u>.

6. server / waitress
서버 / 웨이트레스

7. dessert tray
디저트 쟁반

8. bread basket
빵바구니

9. busperson
빈그릇 운반인

10. kitchen
주방

11. chef
주방장

12. dishroom
식기 세척실

13. dishwasher
식기 세척기

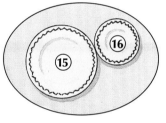

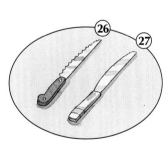

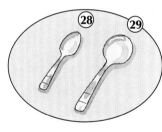

14. place setting
접시 놓기

15. dinner plate
디너 접시

16. bread-and-butter plate
빵과 버터 접시

17. salad plate
샐러드 접시

18. soup bowl
수프용 그릇

19. water glass
물잔

20. wine glass
포도주 잔

21. cup
컵

22. saucer
받침 접시

23. napkin
냅킨

24. salad fork
샐러드 포크

25. dinner fork
디너 포크

26. steak knife
스테이크용 나이프

27. knife
나이프

28. teaspoon
티스푼

29. soupspoon
수프스푼

Talk about how you set the table in your home.

The glass is on the right.

The fork goes on the left.

The napkin is next to the plate.

Share your answers.

1. Do you know anyone who works in a restaurant? What does he or she do?

2. In your opinion, which restaurant jobs are hard? Why?

Clothing I 의복 I

1. three-piece suit
스리피스 정장

2. suit
정장

3. dress
드레스

4. shirt
셔츠

5. jeans
청바지

6. sports coat
스포츠 코트

7. turtleneck
터틀네크 스웨터

8. slacks / pants
평상복 바지

9. blouse
블라우스

10. skirt
치마

11. pullover sweater
풀오버 스웨터

12. T-shirt
티셔츠

13. shorts
반바지

14. sweatshirt
트레이닝 윗도리

15. sweatpants
트레이닝 바지

More vocabulary:

outfit: clothes that look nice together

When clothes are popular, they are **in fashion.**

Talk about what you're wearing today and what you wore yesterday.

I'm wearing <u>a gray sweater</u>, <u>a red T-shirt</u>, and <u>blue jeans</u>.

Yesterday I wore <u>a green pullover sweater</u>, <u>a white shirt</u>, and <u>black slacks</u>.

16. jumpsuit
점프수트

17. uniform
유니폼

18. jumper
소매없는 원피스

19. maternity dress
임산부용 드레스

20. knit shirt
니트 셔츠

21. overalls
오버롤

22. tunic
긴 상의

23. leggings
레깅

24. vest
조끼

25. split skirt
갈라진 스커트

26. sports shirt
스포츠 셔츠

27. cardigan sweater
카디건 스웨터

28. tuxedo
턱시도

29. evening gown
이브닝 가운

Use the new language.

Look at **A Graduation**, pages **32–33.**

Name the clothes you see.

The man at the podium is wearing a suit.

Share your answers.

1. Which clothes in this picture are in fashion now?

2. Who is the best-dressed person in this line? Why?

3. What do you wear when you go to the movies?

1. hat
모자

5. gloves
장갑

2. overcoat
외투

6. cap
모자

3. leather jacket
가죽 자켓

7. jacket
자켓

4. wool scarf/muffler
울 스카프

8. parka
파카

12. earmuffs
귀마개

9. mittens
벙어리 장갑

13. down vest
오리털 조끼

10. ski cap
스키 모자

14. ski mask
스키 마스크

11. tights
타이츠

15. down jacket
오리털 자켓

16. umbrella
우산

20. trench coat
트렌치 코트

24. windbreaker
스포츠용 잠바

17. raincoat
비옷

21. sunglasses
선글라스

25. cover-up
비치 가운(걸쳐 입는 옷)

18. poncho
판초

22. swimming trunks
수영 팬츠

26. swimsuit/bathing suit
수영복

19. rain boots
장화

23. straw hat
밀짚모자

27. baseball cap
야구 모자

Use the new language.

Look at **Weather**, page **10**.

Name the clothing for each weather condition.

Wear a jacket when it's windy.

Share your answers.

1. Which is better in the rain, an umbrella or a poncho?

2. Which is better in the cold, a parka or a down jacket?

3. Do you have more summer clothes or winter clothes?

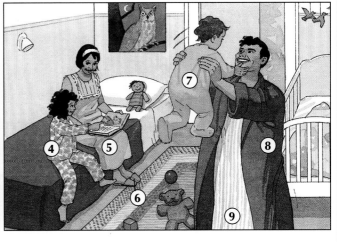

1. leotard
무용 타이츠

2. tank top
소매없는 짧은 상의

3. bike shorts
자전거 타기용 반바지

4. pajamas
파자마

5. nightgown
잠옷

6. slippers
슬리퍼

7. blanket sleeper
담요 잠옷

8. bathrobe
목욕가운

9. nightshirt
남자용 긴 잠옷

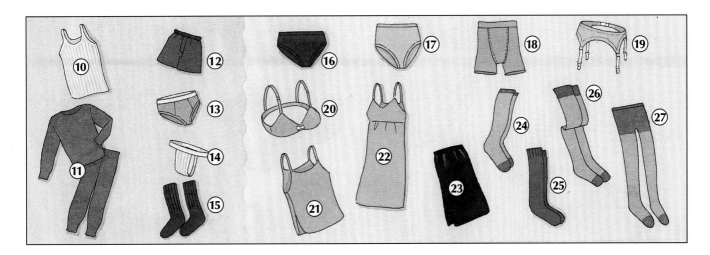

10. undershirt
속셔츠

11. long underwear
긴 내의

12. boxer shorts
사각 팬티

13. briefs
남자 팬티

14. athletic supporter / jockstrap
운동경기용 서포터

15. socks
양말

16. (bikini) panties
비키니

17. briefs / underpants
여자 팬티

18. girdle
거들

19. garter belt
(여성용) 양말 대님

20. bra
브라자

21. camisole
캐미솔

22. full slip
전신용 슬립

23. half slip
하의용 슬립

24. knee-highs
반 양말

25. kneesocks
무릎 양말

26. stockings
스타킹

27. pantyhose
팬티스타킹

More vocabulary

lingerie: underwear or sleepwear for women

loungewear: clothing (sometimes sleepwear) people wear around the home

Share your answers.

1. What do you wear when you exercise?

2. What kind of clothing do you wear for sleeping?

Shoes and Accessories 신발과 액세서리

1. salesclerk
   점원
2. suspenders
   멜빵
3. shoe department
   신발류
4. silk scarves*
   실크 스카프
5. hats
   모자

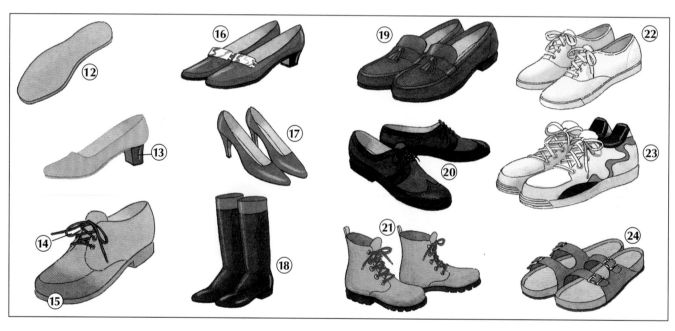

12. sole
    신발밑창
13. heel
    구두굽
14. shoelace
    구두끈
15. toe
    구두 앞 편자
16. pumps
    끈없는 가벼운 구두
17. high heels
    하이힐
18. boots
    부츠
19. loafers
    간편화
20. oxfords
    옥스포드화
21. hiking boots
    등산화
22. tennis shoes
    테니스화
23. athletic shoes
    운동화
24. sandals
    샌들

*Note: one scarf, two scarves

Talk about the shoes you're wearing today.

I'm wearing a pair of <u>white sandals</u>.

Practice asking a salesperson for help.

Could I try on these <u>sandals</u> in size <u>10</u>?

Do you have any <u>silk scarves</u>?

Where are <u>the hats</u>?

6. purses / handbags
핸드백

7. display case
진열장

8. jewelry
보석류

9. necklaces
목걸이

10. ties
넥타이

11. belts
벨트

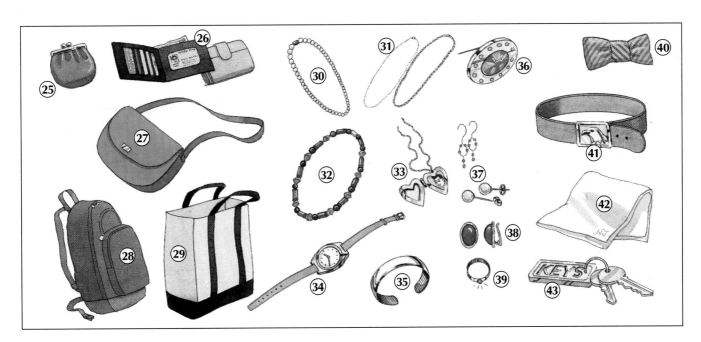

25. change purse
동전 지갑

26. wallet
남자 지갑

27. shoulder bag
숄더 백

28. backpack / bookbag
백 팩 / 책가방

29. tote bag
대형 핸드백

30. string of pearls
진주 목걸이

31. chain
목걸이 줄

32. beads
구슬 목걸이

33. locket
로켓

34. (wrist)watch
(손목) 시계

35. bracelet
팔찌

36. pin
장식핀

37. pierced earrings
삽입형 귀고리

38. clip-on earrings
클립형 귀고리

39. ring
반지

40. bow tie
나비 넥타이

41. belt buckle
벨트 버클

42. handkerchief
손수건

43. key chain
열쇠고리

Share your answers.

1. Which of these accessories are usually worn by women? by men?

2. Which of these do you wear every day?

3. Which of these would you wear to a job interview? Why?

4. Which accessory would you like to receive as a present? Why?

Describing Clothes 의복 묘사

Sizes 사이즈

1. extra small
특소

2. small
소

3. medium
중

4. large
대

5. extra large
특대

Patterns 무늬

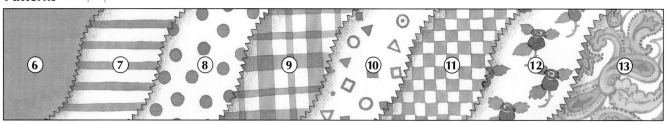

6. solid green
무지 초록색

7. striped
줄무늬

8. polka-dotted
물방울

9. plaid
격자 무늬

10. print
프린트무늬

11. checked
체크 무늬

12. floral
꽃무늬

13. paisley
페이즐리 무늬

Types of material 천 종류

14. wool sweater
울 스웨터

15. silk scarf
실크 스카프

16. cotton T-shirt
면 티셔츠

17. linen jacket
리넨 자켓

18. leather boots
가죽 부츠

19. nylon stockings*
나일론 스타킹

Problems 문제점들

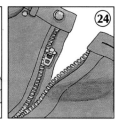

20. too small
너무 작은

21. too big
너무 큰

22. stain
얼룩

23. rip/tear
찢어진

24. broken zipper
고장난 지퍼

25. missing button
떨어진 단추

*Note: Nylon, polyester, rayon, and plastic are synthetic materials.

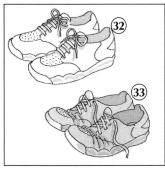

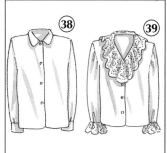

26. **crewneck** sweater
크루넥 스웨터

27. **V-neck** sweater
브이넥 스웨터

28. **turtleneck** sweater
터틀넥 스웨터

29. **sleeveless** shirt
소매없는 셔츠

30. **short-sleeved** shirt
반소매 셔츠

31. **long-sleeved** shirt
긴소매 셔츠

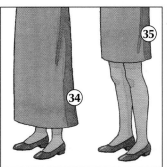

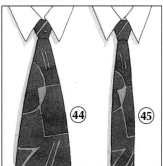

32. **new** shoes
새 신발

33. **old** shoes
헌 신발

34. **long** skirt
긴 치마

35. **short** skirt
짧은 치마

36. **formal** dress
정장 드레스

37. **casual** dress
캐주얼 드레스

38. **plain** blouse
평범한 블라우스

39. **fancy** blouse
화려한 블라우스

40. **light** jacket
얇은 자켓

41. **heavy** jacket
두꺼운 자켓

42. **loose** pants / **baggy** pants
헐거운 바지 / 헐렁한 바지

43. **tight** pants
꼭끼는 바지

44. **wide** tie
넓은 넥타이

45. **narrow** tie
좁은 넥타이

46. **low** heels
낮은 굽

47. **high** heels
높은 굽 구두

Talk about yourself.

I like _long-sleeved_ shirts and _baggy_ pants.

I like _short skirts_ and _high heels_.

I usually wear _plain_ clothes.

Share your answers.

1. What type of material do you usually wear in the summer? in the winter?

2. What patterns do you see around you?

3. Are you wearing casual or formal clothes?

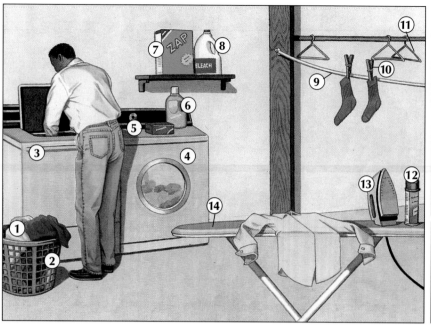

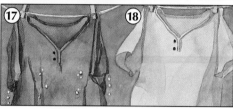

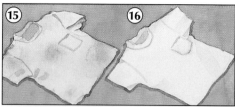

1. laundry
   빨래

2. laundry basket
   빨래통

3. washer
   세탁기

4. dryer
   건조기

5. dryer sheets
   건조기에 넣는 종이 소
   프너

6. fabric softener
   옷감 소프너

7. laundry detergent
   세제

8. bleach
   표백제

9. clothesline
   빨랫줄

10. clothespin
    빨래 집게

11. hanger
    옷걸이

12. spray starch
    풀 뿌리개

13. iron
    다리미

14. ironing board
    다리미판

15. **dirty** T-shirt
    더러운 티셔츠

16. **clean** T-shirt
    깨끗한 티셔츠

17. **wet** T-shirt
    젖은 티셔츠

18. **dry** T-shirt
    마른 티셔츠

19. **wrinkled** shirt
    구겨진 셔츠

20. **ironed** shirt
    다린 셔츠

A. **Sort** the laundry.
   빨래를 분류하다.

B. **Add** the detergent.
   세제를 넣다.

C. **Load** the washer.
   세탁기에 빨래를 넣다.

D. **Clean** the lint trap.
   보풀 트랩을 제거하다.

E. **Unload** the dryer.
   건조기에서 옷을 꺼내다.

F. **Fold** the laundry.
   빨래를 개다.

G. **Iron** the clothes.
   옷을 다리미질하다.

H. **Hang up** the clothes.
   옷을 걸다.

More vocabulary

dry cleaners: a business that cleans clothes using chemicals, not water and detergent

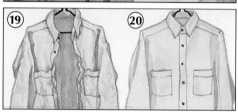 wash in cold water only

 no bleach

 line dry

 dry-clean only, do not wash

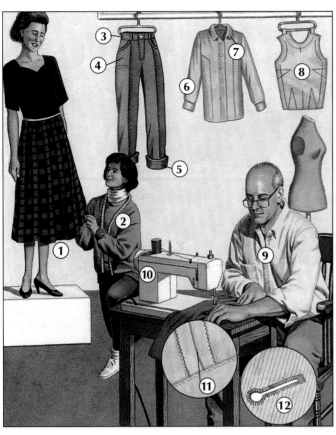

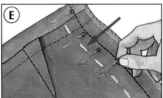

A. **sew** by hand
손으로 바느질하다

B. **sew** by machine
재봉틀로 바느질하다

C. **lengthen**
기장을 늘이다

D. **shorten**
기장을 줄이다

E. **take in**
옆선을 줄여 넣다

F. **let out**
옆선을 늘여 내다

1. hemline
   옷단의 안선
2. dressmaker
   양재사
3. waistband
   허리띠

4. pocket
   호주머니
5. cuff
   소맷부리
6. sleeve
   소매

7. collar
   칼라
8. pattern
   패턴
9. tailor
   재단사

10. sewing machine
    재봉틀
11. seam
    솔기
12. buttonhole
    단추구멍

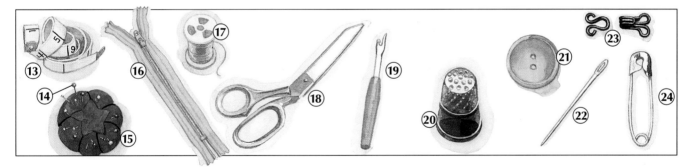

13. tape measure
    줄자
14. pin
    핀
15. pin cushion
    바늘겨레

16. zipper
    지퍼
17. spool of thread
    실패
18. (pair of) scissors
    가위

19. seam ripper
    솔기 터는 기구
20. thimble
    골무
21. button
    단추

22. needle
    바늘
23. hook and eye
    훅단추
24. safety pin
    안전핀

More vocabulary

pattern maker: a person who makes patterns

garment worker: a person who works in a clothing factory

fashion designer: a person who makes original clothes

Share your answers.

1. Do you know how to use a sewing machine?
2. Can you sew by hand?

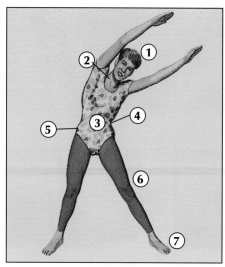

1. head
머리

2. neck
목

3. abdomen
배

4. waist
허리

5. hip
히프

6. leg
다리

7. foot
발

8. hand
손

9. arm
팔

10. shoulder
어깨

11. back
등

12. buttocks
엉덩이

13. chest
가슴

14. breast
유방

15. elbow
팔꿈치

16. thigh
허벅지

17. knee
무릎

18. calf
종아리

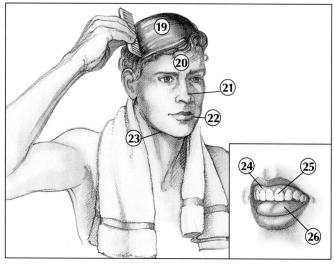
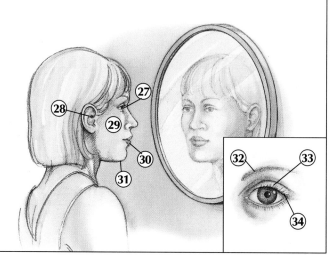

The face
얼굴

19. hair
머리카락

20. forehead
이마

21. nose
코

22. mouth
입

23. jaw
아래턱

24. gums
잇몸

25. teeth
이

26. tongue
혀

27. eye
눈

28. ear
귀

29. cheek
볼

30. lip
입술

31. chin
턱끝

32. eyebrow
눈썹

33. eyelid
눈꺼풀

34. eyelashes
속눈썹

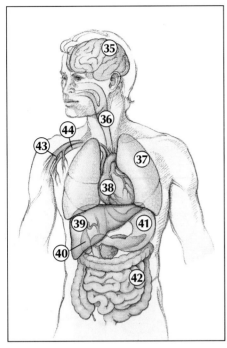

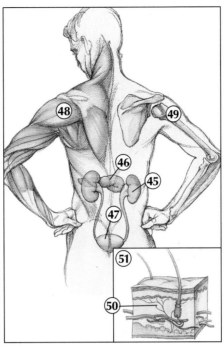

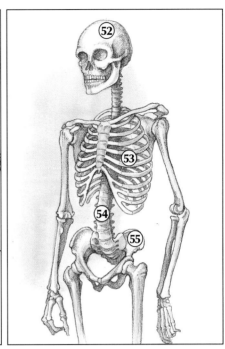

Inside the body
신체 내부

35. brain
뇌

36. throat
목구멍(인후)

37. lung
허파

38. heart
심장

39. liver
간

40. gallbladder
쓸개

41. stomach
위

42. intestines
장

43. artery
동맥

44. vein
정맥

45. kidney
신장

46. pancreas
췌장

47. bladder
방광

48. muscle
근육

49. bone
뼈

50. nerve
신경

51. skin
피부

The skeleton
골격

52. skull
두개골

53. rib cage
흉곽

54. spinal column
척추

55. pelvis
골반

The Hand	The Foot	The Senses

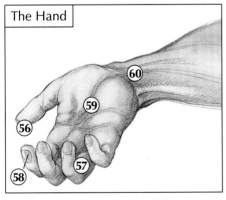

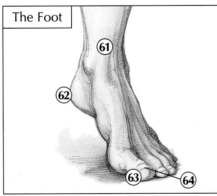

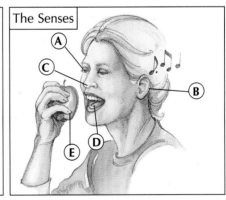

56. thumb
엄지 손가락

57. fingers
손가락

58. fingernail
손톱

59. palm
손바닥

60. wrist
손목

61. ankle
발목

62. heel
발꿈치

63. toe
발가락

64. toenail
발톱

A. see
보다

B. hear
듣다

C. smell
냄새 맡다

D. taste
맛보다

E. touch
만지다

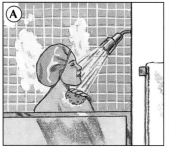

A. take a shower
샤워하다

B. bathe / take a bath
목욕하다

C. use deodorant
탈취제를 사용하다

D. put on sunscreen
선스크린을 바르다

1. shower cap
   샤워캡

2. soap
   비누

3. bath powder / talcum powder
   목욕 파우더 / 텔컴 파우더

4. deodorant
   탈취제

5. perfume / cologne
   향수 / 콜롱

6. sunscreen
   선스크린 / 태양 광선 차단제

7. body lotion
   바디 로숀

8. moisturizer
   보습제

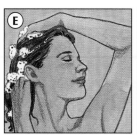
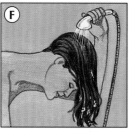
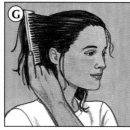

E. wash…hair
머리를 감다

F. rinse…hair
머리를 헹구다

G. comb…hair
머리를 빗다

H. dry…hair
머리를 말리다

I. brush…hair
머리를 빗다

9. shampoo
   샴푸

10. conditioner
    컨디셔너

11. hair gel
    헤어젤

12. hair spray
    헤어 스프레이

13. comb
    빗

14. brush
    솔빗

15. curling iron
    고대기

16. blow dryer
    헤어 드라이기

17. hair clip
    헤어 클립

18. barrette
    머리핀

19. bobby pins
    실핀

J. brush…teeth
이를 닦다

K. floss…teeth
이를 플로스하다

L. gargle
양치질하다

M. shave
면도하다

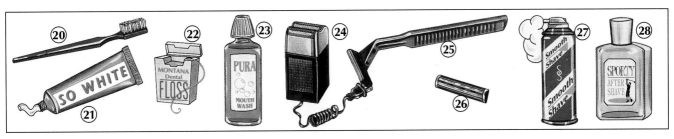

20. toothbrush
치솔

21. toothpaste
치약

22. dental floss
플로스

23. mouthwash
양치수

24. electric shaver
전기 면도기

25. razor
면도칼

26. razor blade
면도날

27. shaving cream
면도용 크림

28. aftershave
아프터쉐이브

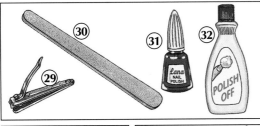

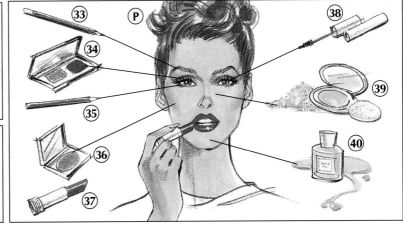

N. cut…nails
손톱을 깎다

O. polish…nails
손톱에 매니큐어
칠하다

P. put on…makeup
화장을 하다

29. nail clipper
손톱 깎기

30. emery board
손톱줄

31. nail polish
손톱 광택제(매니큐어)

32. nail polish remover
매니큐어 제거제

33. eyebrow pencil
눈썹그리는 연필

34. eye shadow
아이새도우

35. eyeliner
아이라이너

36. blush / rouge
볼연지 / 루즈

37. lipstick
립스틱

38. mascara
마스카라

39. face powder
화장분

40. foundation
파운데이션

More vocabulary

A product without perfume or scent is **unscented.**

A product that is better for people with allergies is **hypoallergenic.**

Share your answers.

1. What is your morning routine if you stay home?
   if you go out?

2. Do women in your culture wear makeup? How old
   are they when they begin to use it?

1. headache
두통

2. toothache
치통

3. earache
귀앓이

4. stomachache
복통

5. backache
요통

6. sore throat
목아픔

7. nasal congestion
코막힘

8. fever/temperature
열 / 온도

9. chills
오한

10. rash
발진

A. **cough**
기침하다

B. **sneeze**
재채기하다

C. **feel** dizzy
어지럽다

D. **feel** nauseous
메스껍다

E. **throw up/vomit**
구토하다 / 토하다

     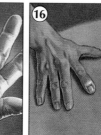  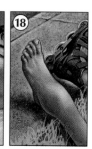

11. insect bite
벌레에게 물린 상처

12. bruise
멍

13. cut
베인 상처

14. sunburn
햇볕에 탐

15. blister
물집

16. **swollen** finger
부어오른 손가락

17. **bloody** nose
코피가 나다

18. **sprained** ankle
발목을 삐다

Use the new language.
Look at **Health Care**, pages **80–81**.

Tell what medication or treatment you would use for each health problem.

Share your answers.

1. For which problems would you go to a doctor? use medication? do nothing?

2. What do you do for a sunburn? for a headache?

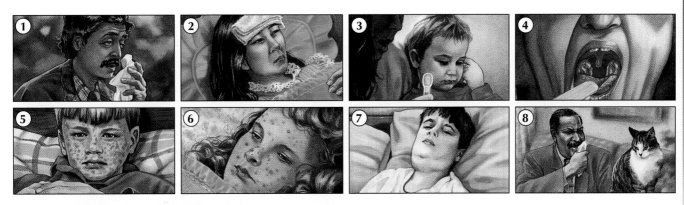

Common illnesses and childhood diseases 흔한 병 및 어린이 질병

1. cold
감기

2. flu
유행성 감기

3. ear infection
이염

4. strep throat
후두염

5. measles
홍역

6. chicken pox
수두

7. mumps
이하선염

8. allergies
알레르기

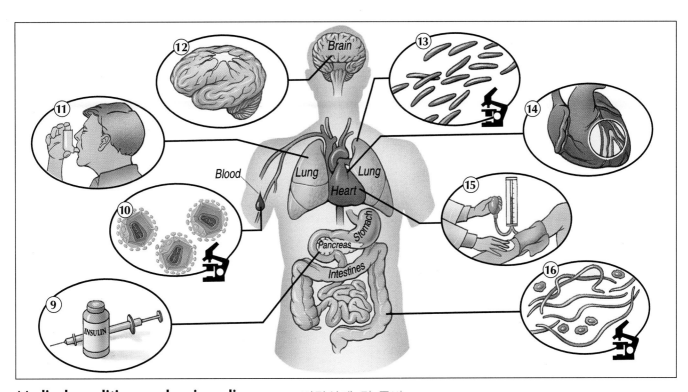

Medical conditions and serious diseases 건강상태 및 중병

9. diabetes
당뇨병

10. HIV (human immunodeficiency virus)
HIV (인체 면역 결핍 바이러스)

11. asthma
천식

12. brain cancer
뇌암

13. TB (tuberculosis)
결핵

14. heart disease
심장병

15. high blood pressure
고혈압

16. intestinal parasites
장내 기생충

More vocabulary

AIDS (acquired immunodeficiency syndrome): a medical condition that results from contracting the HIV virus

influenza: flu

hypertension: high blood pressure

infectious disease: a disease that is spread through air or water

Share your answers.

Which diseases on this page are infectious?

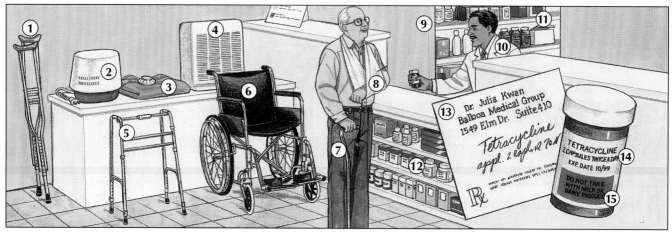

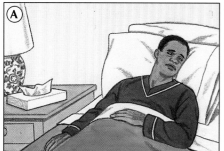

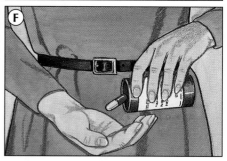

1. crutches
   목발

2. humidifier
   가습기

3. heating pad
   보온 패드

4. air purifier
   공기 정화기

5. walker
   보행보조기

6. wheelchair
   휠체어

7. cane
   지팡이

8. sling
   삼각 붕대

9. pharmacy
   약국

10. pharmacist
    약제사

11. prescription medication
    처방약

12. over-the-counter medication
    비처방약

13. prescription
    처방

14. prescription label
    처방표

15. warning label
    경고문

A. **Get** bed rest.
   침상에서 요양하다.

B. **Drink** fluids.
   액체류를 마시다.

C. **Change** your diet.
   식사습관을 바꾸다.

D. **Exercise.**
   운동하다.

E. **Get** an injection.
   주사 맞다.

F. **Take** medicine.
   약을 먹다.

More vocabulary

dosage: how much medicine you take and how many times a day you take it

expiration date: the last day the medicine can be used

treatment: something you do to get better

Staying in bed, drinking fluids, and getting physical therapy are treatments.

An injection that stops a person from getting a serious disease is called **an immunization** or **a vaccination**.

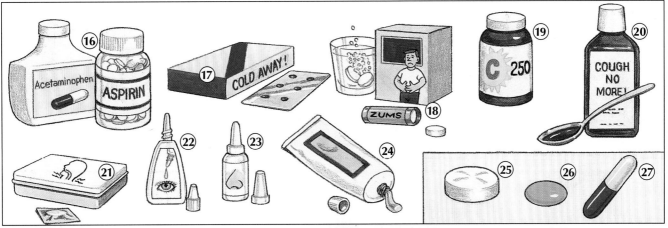

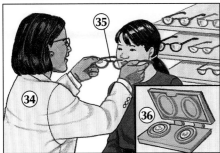

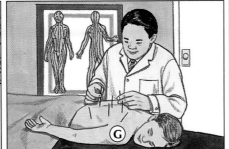

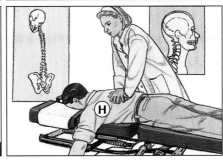

16. pain reliever
진통제

17. cold tablets
감기용 정제약

18. antacid
제산제

19. vitamins
비타민

20. cough syrup
기침시럽

21. throat lozenges
목알약

22. eyedrops
눈약

23. nasal spray
코 스프레이

24. ointment
연고

25. tablet
정제약

26. pill
알약

27. capsule
캡슐약

28. orthopedist
정형외과 의사

29. cast
석고붕대

30. physical therapist
물리치료사

31. brace
브레이스

32. audiologist
청력 전문의

33. hearing aid
보청기

34. optometrist
검안사

35. (eye)glasses
안경

36. contact lenses
콘택트 렌즈

G. Get acupuncture.
침을 맞다.

H. Go to a chiropractor.
척추 지압사에게 가다.

Share your answers.

1. What's the best treatment for a headache? a sore throat? a stomachache? a fever?

2. Do you think vitamins are important? Why or why not?

3. What treatments are popular in your culture?

A. **be** injured / **be** hurt
다치다

B. **be** unconscious
의식을 잃다

C. **be** in shock
쇼크 상태에 있다

D. **have** a heart attack
심장마비를 일으키다

E. **have** an allergic reaction
알레르기 반응을 보이다

F. **get** an electric shock
전기 충격을 받다

G. **get** frostbite
동상을 입다

H. **burn** (your)self
화상을 입다

I. **drown**
물에 빠지다

J. **swallow** poison
독약을 삼키다

K. **overdose** on drugs
약을 과량복용하다

L. **choke**
질식되다

M. **bleed**
출혈하다

N. **can't breathe**
숨을 못쉬다

O. **fall**
떨어지다

P. **break** a bone
뼈가 부러지다

Grammar point: past tense

burn	—	burned	choke	—	choked	bleed — bled
drown	—	drowned	be	—	was, were	can't — couldn't
swallow	—	swallowed	have	—	had	fall — fell
overdose	—	overdosed	get	—	got	break — broke

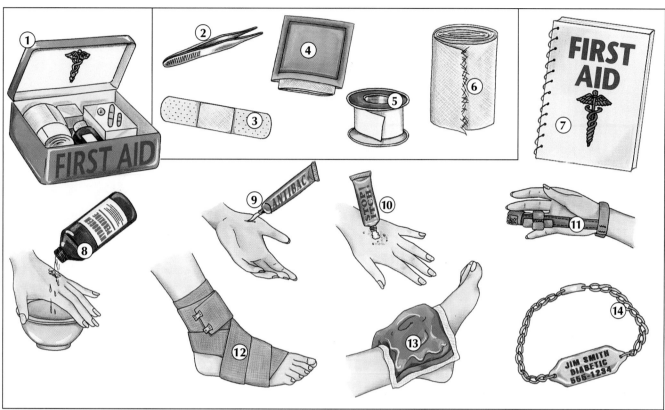

1. **first aid kit**
   응급 치료 상자

2. **tweezers**
   핀셋

3. **adhesive bandage**
   반창고

4. **sterile pad**
   무균 패드

5. **tape**
   테입

6. **gauze**
   가제

7. **first aid manual**
   응급 치료 설명서

8. **hydrogen peroxide**
   과산화수소

9. **antibacterial ointment**
   항생연고제

10. **antihistamine cream**
    항히스타민 연고제

11. **splint**
    부목

12. **elastic bandage**
    탄력 붕대

13. **ice pack**
    얼음찜질팩

14. **medical emergency bracelet**
    응급환자식별 팔찌

15. **stitches**
    봉합 바늘

16. **rescue breathing**
    응급 호흡법

17. **CPR (cardiopulmonary resuscitation)**
    CPR (심폐기능 소생법)

18. **Heimlich maneuver**
    심폐기능 소생법

Important Note: Only people who are properly trained should give stitches or do CPR.

Share your answers.

1. Do you have a First Aid kit in your home? Where can you buy one?

2. When do you use hydrogen peroxide? an elastic support bandage? antihistamine cream?

3. Do you know first aid? Where did you learn it?

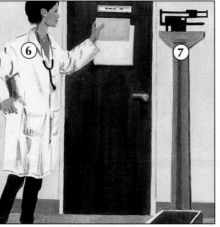
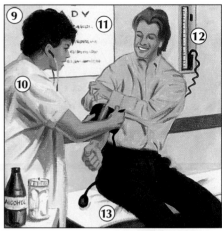

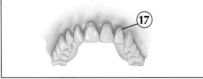
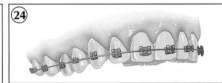

Medical clinic 치료소 / 진료소

1. **waiting room**
   대기실

2. **receptionist**
   접수원

3. **patient**
   환자

4. **insurance card**
   보험 카드

5. **insurance form**
   보험양식

6. **doctor**
   의사

7. **scale**
   저울

8. **stethoscope**
   청진기

9. **examining room**
   진찰실

10. **nurse**
    간호사

11. **eye chart**
    시력 검사표

12. **blood pressure gauge**
    혈압계

13. **examination table**
    진료대

14. **syringe**
    주사

15. **thermometer**
    체온계

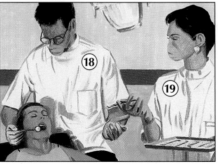
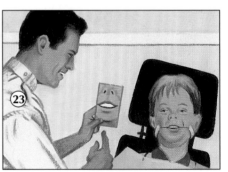

Dental clinic 치과 병원

16. **dental hygienist**
    구강 위생사

17. **tartar**
    치석

18. **dentist**
    치과의사

19. **dental assistant**
    치과 보조원

20. **cavity**
    충치

21. **drill**
    드릴

22. **filling**
    충전재

23. **orthodontist**
    교정치과의

24. **braces**
    치아 교정기

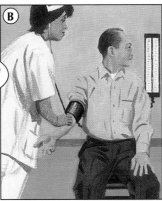

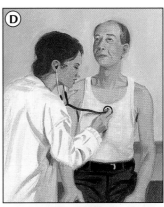

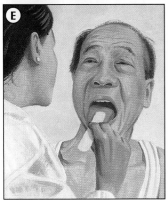

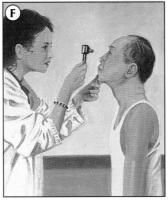

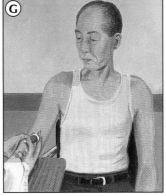

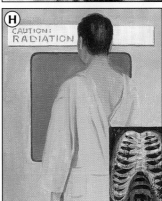

A. make an appointment
예약을 하다

B. check...blood pressure
혈압을 재다

C. take...temperature
체온을 재다

D. listen to...heart
심장 박동을 듣다

E. look in...throat
목안을 검사하다

F. examine...eyes
눈을 검사하다

G. draw...blood
피를 뽑다

H. get an X ray
엑스레이를 찍다

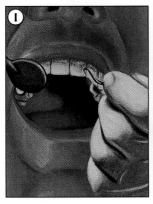

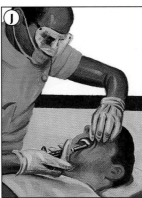

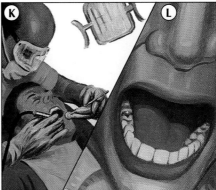

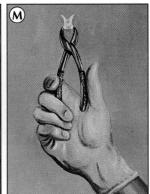

I. clean...teeth
이를 클린하다

J. give...a shot of anesthetic
마취제 주사를 놓다

K. drill a tooth
이를 드릴하다

L. fill a cavity
충치 구멍을 메꾸다

M. pull a tooth
이를 뽑다

More vocabulary

get a checkup: to go for a medical exam

extract a tooth: to pull out a tooth

Share your answers.

1. What is the average cost of a medical exam in your area?

2. Some people are nervous at the dentist's office. What can they do to relax?

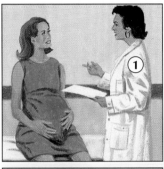
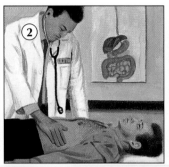

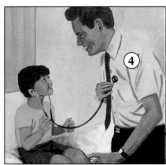
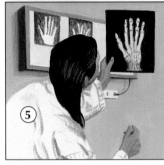

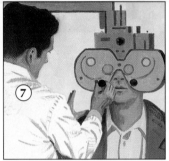
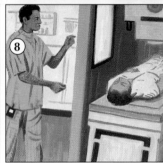

Hospital staff 병원 의료진

1. obstetrician
산과의사

2. internist
내과 의사

3. cardiologist
심장병 전문의

4. pediatrician
소아과 의사

5. radiologist
방사선과 의사

6. psychiatrist
정신과 의사

7. ophthalmologist
안과 의사

8. X-ray technician
엑스레이 기사

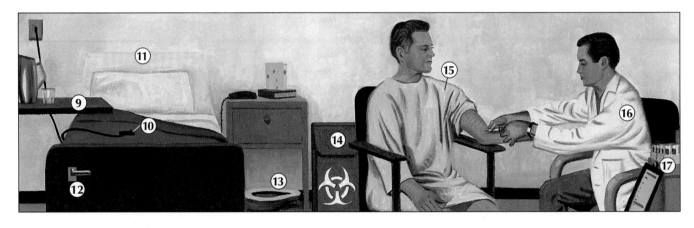

Patient's room 환자실

9. bed table
침대 옆 작은 탁자

10. call button
호출 단추

11. hospital bed
병원 침대

12. bed control
침대 조절기

13. bedpan
환자용 변기

14. medical waste disposal
의료 폐기물 처리기

15. hospital gown
병원가운

16. lab technician
실험실 기사

17. blood work/blood test
혈액 검사

More vocabulary

nurse practitioner: a nurse licensed to give medical exams

specialist: a doctor who only treats specific medical problems

gynecologist: a specialist who examines and treats women

nurse midwife: a nurse practitioner who examines pregnant women and delivers babies

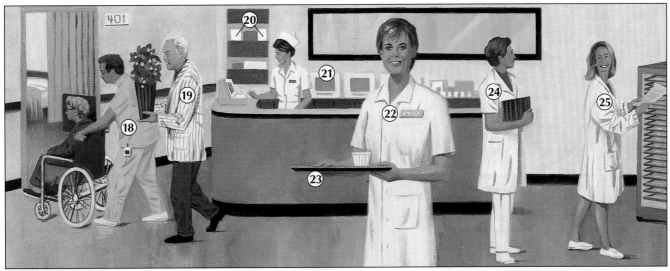

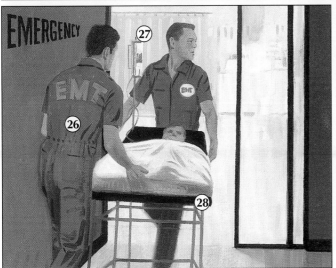

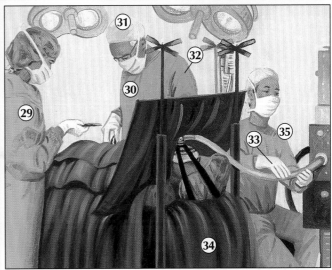

Nurse's station
간호원실

18. orderly
보조원

19. volunteer
자원 봉사자

20. medical charts
병원 건강 기록부

21. vital signs monitor
생명 징후 검사기

22. RN (registered nurse)
공인 간호사

23. medication tray
약 접시

24. LPN (licensed practical nurse)/
LVN (licensed vocational nurse)
허가받은 직업 간호사

25. dietician
영양사

Emergency room
응급실

26. emergency medical technician
(EMT)
응급 의료 테크니션

27. IV (intravenous drip)
정맥 영양 주사

28. stretcher/gurney
바퀴 달린 들것

Operating room
수술실

29. surgical nurse
수술실 간호원

30. surgeon
외과 의사

31. surgical cap
수술용 캡

32. surgical gown
수술용 가운

33. latex gloves
수술용 고무 장갑

34. operating table
수술대

35. anesthesiologist
마취사

Practice asking for the hospital staff.

Please get <u>the nurse</u>. I have a question for <u>her</u>.
Where's <u>the anesthesiologist</u>? I need to talk to <u>her</u>.
I'm looking for <u>the lab technician</u>. Have you seen <u>him</u>?

Share your answers.

1. Have you ever been to an emergency room? Who helped you?
2. Have you ever been in the hospital? How long did you stay?

City Streets 시가지

1. fire station
   소방서

2. coffee shop
   커피 숍

3. bank
   은행

4. car dealership
   자동차 딜러

5. hotel
   호텔

6. church
   교회

7. hospital
   병원

8. park
   공원

9. synagogue
   유대회당

10. theater
    극장

11. movie theater
    극장

12. gas station
    주유소

13. furniture store
    가구점

14. hardware store
    철물점

15. barber shop
    이발소

More vocabulary

skyscraper: a very tall office building

downtown/city center: the area in a city with the city hall, courts, and businesses

Practice giving your destination.

I'm going to go <u>downtown</u>.

I have to go to <u>the post office</u>.

16. bakery
제과점

17. city hall
시청

18. courthouse
법원

19. police station
경찰서

20. market
시장

21. health club
헬스클럽

22. motel
모텔

23. mosque
회교사원

24. office building
사무실 빌딩

25. high-rise building
고층 건물

26. parking garage
주차장 (옥내)

27. school
학교

28. library
도서관

29. post office
우체국

Practice asking for and giving the locations of buildings.

Where's the post office?

It's on Oak Street.

Share your answers.

1. Which of the places in this picture do you go to every week?

2. Is it good to live in a city? Why or why not?

3. What famous cities do you know?

89

1. Laundromat
빨래방

2. drugstore / pharmacy
약국

3. convenience store
편의점

4. photo shop
사진 현상소

5. parking space
주차 공간

6. traffic light
신호등

7. pedestrian
보행자

8. crosswalk
횡단 보도

9. street
거리

10. curb
연석

11. newsstand
신문매점

12. mailbox
우편함

13. drive-thru window
드라이브 스루 윈도우

14. fast food restaurant
패스트 푸드 식당

15. bus
버스

A. **cross** the street
길을 건너시오

B. **wait** for the light
신호등을 기다리시오

C. **drive** a car
자동차를 운전하시오

More vocabulary

neighborhood: the area close to your home

do errands: to make a short trip from your home to buy or pick up something

Talk about where to buy things.

You can buy <u>newspapers</u> at <u>a newsstand</u>.

You can buy <u>donuts</u> at <u>a donut shop</u>.

You can buy <u>food</u> at <u>a convenience store</u>.

16. bus stop
버스 정류장

17. corner
모퉁이

18. parking meter
주차 미터

19. motorcycle
오토바이

20. donut shop
도너츠 가게

21. public telephone
공중전화

22. copy center / print shop
복사센터 / 인쇄소

23. streetlight
신호등

24. dry cleaners
세탁소

25. nail salon
네일 살롱

26. sidewalk
보도

27. garbage truck
쓰레기차

28. fire hydrant
소화전

29. sign
표지판

30. street vendor
행상인

31. cart
카트

D. **park** the car
자동차를 주차하십시오

E. **ride** a bicycle
자전거를 타십시오

Share your answers.

1. Do you like to do errands?

2. Do you always like to go to the same stores?

3. Which businesses in the picture are also in your neighborhood?

4. Do you know someone who has a small business? What kind?

5. What things can you buy from a street vendor?

1. music store
   뮤직 스토어

2. jewelry store
   보석상

3. candy store
   캔디 가게

4. bookstore
   서점

5. toy store
   장난감 가게

6. pet store
   애완동물 가게

7. card store
   카드 가게

8. optician
   안경점

9. travel agency
   여행사

10. shoe store
    신발 가게

11. fountain
    분수

12. florist
    꽃가게

More vocabulary

beauty shop: hair salon

men's store: a store that sells men's clothing

dress shop: a store that sells women's clothing

Talk about where you want to shop in this mall.

Let's go to the card store.

I need to buy a card for Maggie's birthday.

13. department store
백화점

14. food court
식당 구역

15. video store
비디오 가게

16. hair salon
미장원

17. maternity shop
임산부 옷가게

18. electronics store
전자제품 가게

19. directory
안내판

20. ice cream stand
아이스크림 판매대

21. escalator
에스컬레이터

22. information booth
안내소

Practice asking for and giving the location of different shops.

Where's <u>the maternity shop</u>?

   It's on <u>the first floor</u>, next to <u>the hair salon</u>.

Share your answers.

1. Do you like shopping malls? Why or why not?

2. Some people don't go to the mall to shop.
Name some other things you can do in a mall.

93

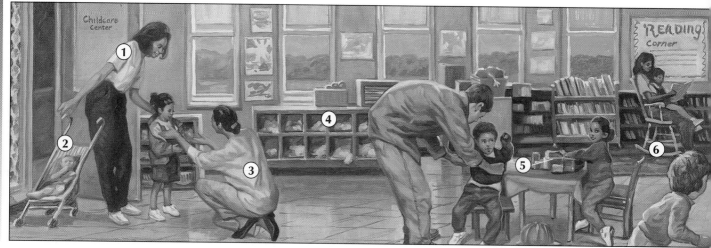

1. parent
부모

2. stroller
유모차

3. childcare worker
탁아소 직원

4. cubby
아늑한 곳

5. toys
장난감

6. rocking chair
록킹 의자

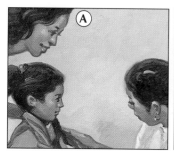 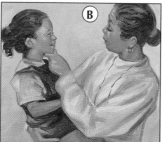  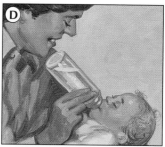

A. drop off
내려주다

B. hold
잡다

C. nurse
젖먹이다

D. feed
음식을 먹이다

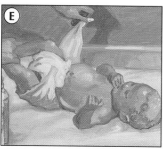   

E. change diapers
기저귀를 갈아주다

F. read a story
이야기책을 읽어주다

G. pick up
피컵하다 / 맡긴 사람 /
물건을 받아 오다

H. rock
흔들다

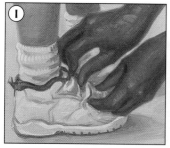   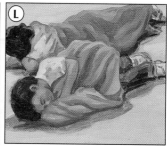

I. tie shoes
신발끈을 매다

J. dress
옷을 입다

K. play
놀다

L. take a nap
낮잠을 자다

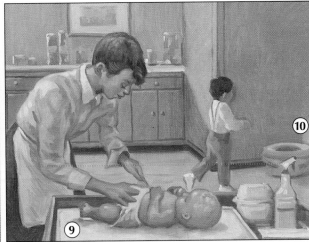

7. high chair
높은 의자

8. bib
턱받이

9. changing table
떼어낼 수 있는 테이블

10. potty seat
어린이용 변기

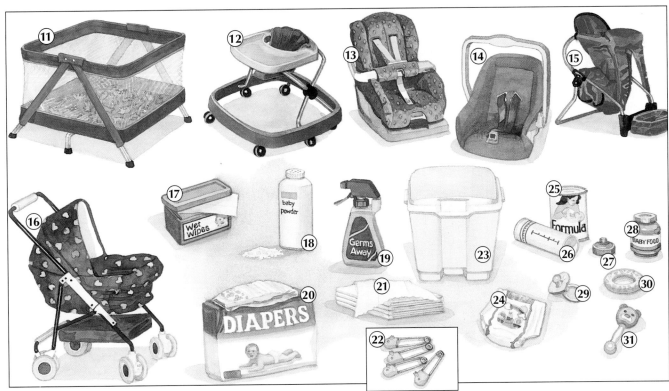

11. playpen
아기 보호망 / 보호펜

12. walker
보행기

13. car safety seat
어린이 안전 시트

14. baby carrier
아기 캐리어

15. baby backpack
아기 백팩

16. carriage
유모차

17. wipes
젖은 티슈

18. baby powder
베이비 파우더

19. disinfectant
살균제

20. disposable diapers
일회용 기저귀

21. cloth diapers
헝겊 기저귀

22. diaper pins
기저귀 핀

23. diaper pail
기저귀 통

24. training pants
기저귀 바지

25. formula
유아용 유동식

26. bottle
젖병

27. nipple
젖꼭지

28. baby food
이유식

29. pacifier
패시파이어 (타월, 고무 젖꼭지 등)

30. teething ring
고리 모양의 물리개

31. rattle
딸랑이

1. envelope
봉투

2. letter
편지

3. postcard
엽서

4. greeting card
축하 카드

5. package
수화물

6. letter carrier
우체부

7. return address
반송 주소

8. mailing address
우편 주소

9. postmark
우체국 소인

10. stamp / postage
우표

11. certified mail
등기 우편

12. priority mail
속달 우편

13. air letter / aerogramme
항공 편지

14. ground post /
parcel post
육상 우편 / 소포 우편

15. Express Mail /
overnight mail
특송 우편

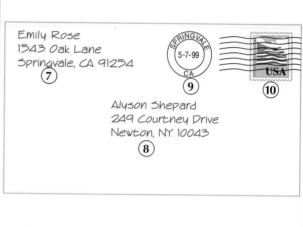

Emily Rose
1543 Oak Lane
Springvale, CA 91254

SPRINGVALE
5-7-99
CA

USA

Alyson Shepard
249 Courtney Drive
Newton, NY 10043

FRAGILE

EXPRESS MAIL
UNITED STATES POSTAL SERVICE

A. **address** a postcard
엽서에 주소를 쓰십시오

B. **send** it / **mail** it
우편으로 보내십시오

C. **deliver** it
배달하십시오

D. **receive** it
받으십시오

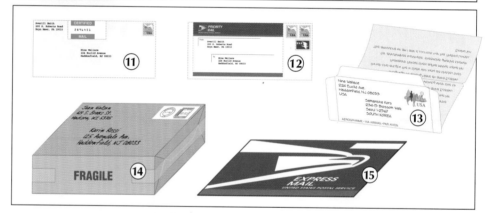

1. teller
   창구 계원

2. vault
   금고

3. ATM (automated teller machine)
   ATM (자동현금인출기)

4. security guard
   경비원

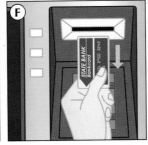

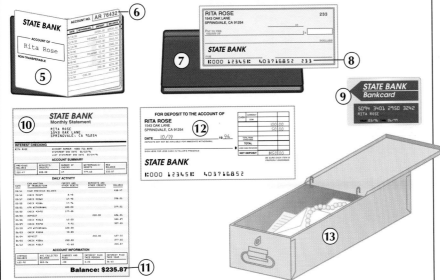

Balance: $235.87

5. passbook
   통장

6. savings account number
   저축예금 계좌번호

7. checkbook
   수표책

8. checking account number
   당좌예금구좌번호

9. ATM card
   ATM 카드

10. monthly statement
    월 계산서

11. balance
    잔액

12. deposit slip
    입금용지

13. safe-deposit box
    귀중품 보관함

Using the ATM machine ATM (자동 현금 인출기) 사용방법

A. **Insert** your ATM card.
   ATM 카드를 넣으십시오.

B. **Enter** your PIN number.*
   PIN 번호를 입력하십시오.

C. **Make** a deposit.
   입금을 하십시오.

D. **Withdraw** cash.
   현금 인출.

E. **Transfer** funds.
   자금 이체.

F. **Remove** your ATM card.
   ATM 카드를 빼십시오.

*PIN: personal identification number

More vocabulary

overdrawn account: When there is not enough money in an account to pay a check, we say the account is overdrawn.

Share your answers.

1. Do you use a bank?
2. Do you use an ATM card?
3. Name some things you can put in a safe-deposit box.

1. **reference librarian**
   참고도서 사서

2. **reference desk**
   참고도서부

3. **atlas**
   지도책

4. **microfilm reader**
   마이크로필름 판독기

5. **microfilm**
   마이크로필름

6. **periodical section**
   정기간행물 섹션

7. **magazine**
   잡지

8. **newspaper**
   신문

9. **online catalog**
   온라인 카탈로그

10. **card catalog**
    카드 카탈로그

11. **media section**
    미디어 섹션

12. **audiocassette**
    오디오 테이프

13. **videocassette**
    비디오 테이프

14. **CD (compact disc)**
    CD 컴팩트 디스크

15. **record**
    레코드

16. **checkout desk**
    체크아웃 데스크

17. **library clerk**
    도서관 서기

18. **encyclopedia**
    백과사전

19. **library card**
    도서관 카드

20. **library book**
    도서관 책

21. **title**
    제목

22. **author**
    저자

More vocabulary

check a book out: to borrow a book from the library

nonfiction: real information, history or true stories

fiction: stories from the author's imagination

Share your answers.

1. Do you have a library card?

2. Do you prefer to buy books or borrow them from the library?

You have the right to remain silent...

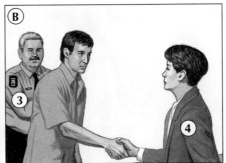

Bail is set at $20,000.

A. arrest a suspect
용의자를 체포하다
1. police officer
경찰관
2. handcuffs
수갑

B. hire a lawyer/**hire** an attorney
변호사를 고용하다
3. guard
경비원
4. defense attorney
피고측 변호사

C. appear in court
법정에 출두하다
5. defendant
피고
6. judge
재판관

D. stand trial
재판을 받다
7. courtroom
법정

8. jury
배심원
9. evidence
증거

10. prosecuting attorney
검사
11. witness
증인

12. court reporter
법원 속기사
13. bailiff
법정 간수

Guilty.

7 years.

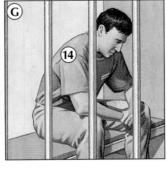

E. give the verdict*
평결을 내리다

F. sentence the defendant
피고에게 언도를 내리다

G. go to jail/**go** to prison
감옥으로 가다
14. convict
죄수

H. be released
석방되다

*Note: There are two possible verdicts, "guilty" and "not guilty."

Share your answers.

1. What are some differences between the legal system in the United States and the one in your country?

2. Do you want to be on a jury? Why or why not?

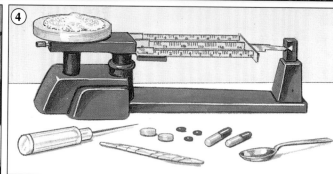

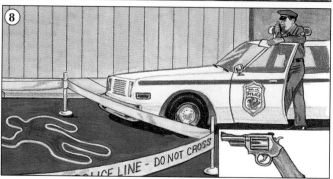

1. **vandalism**
   파괴 행위
2. **gang violence**
   갱 폭력
3. **drunk driving**
   음주 운전

4. **illegal drugs**
   불법 마약
5. **mugging**
   폭력 강도
6. **burglary**
   강도

7. **assault**
   폭행
8. **murder**
   살인
9. **gun**
   총

More vocabulary

commit a crime: to do something illegal

criminal: someone who commits a crime

victim: someone who is hurt or killed by someone else

Share your answers.

1. Is there too much crime on TV? in the movies?
2. Do you think people become criminals from watching crime on TV?

A. **Walk** with a friend.
친구와 같이 걸으십시오.

B. **Stay** on well-lit streets.
불이 환한 거리로만 가십시오.

C. **Hold** your purse close to your body.
핸드백을 몸에 꼭 대십시오.

D. **Protect** your wallet.
지갑을 보호하십시오.

E. **Lock** your doors.
문을 잠그십시오.

F. **Don't open** your door to strangers.
모르는 사람에게 문을 열어주지 마십시오.

G. **Don't drink** and **drive**.
음주 운전하지 마십시오.

H. **Report** crimes to the police.
범죄를 보면 경찰에 보고하십시오.

More vocabulary

Neighborhood Watch: a group of neighbors who watch for criminals in their neighborhood

designated drivers: people who don't drink alcoholic beverages so that they can drive drinkers home

Share your answers.

1. Do you feel safe in your neighborhood?

2. Look at the pictures. Which of these things do you do?

3. What other things do you do to stay safe?

1. lost child
미아

2. car accident
자동차 사고

3. airplane crash
비행기 추락

4. explosion
폭발

5. earthquake
지진

6. mudslide
진흙 사태

7. fire
화재

8. firefighter
소방수

9. fire truck
소방차

Practice reporting a fire.

This is <u>Lisa Broad</u>. There is a fire.

The address is <u>323 Oak Street</u>.

Please send someone quickly.

Share your answers.

1. Can you give directions to your home if there is a fire?

2. What information do you give to the other driver if you are in a car accident?

10. drought
가뭄

11. blizzard
눈보라

12. hurricane
허리케인 / 태풍

13. tornado
토네이도

14. volcanic eruption
화산 폭발

15. tidal wave
해일

16. flood
홍수

17. search and rescue team
수색구조팀

Share your answers.

1. Which disasters are common in your area? Which never happen?

2. What can you do to prepare for emergencies?

3. Do you have emergency numbers near your telephone?

4. What organizations will help you in an emergency?

1. bus stop 버스 정류장	**7.** passenger 승객	**13.** train station 전철역	**19.** taxi stand 택시 승차장
2. route 노선	**8.** bus driver 버스 운전사	**14.** ticket 승차권	**20.** taxi driver 택시 운전사
3. schedule 일정표	**9.** subway 지하철	**15.** platform 플랫폼	**21.** meter 미터
4. bus 버스	**10.** track 철로	**16.** conductor 차장	**22.** taxi license 택시 면허
5. fare 요금	**11.** token 토큰	**17.** train 전철	**23.** ferry 페리
6. transfer 환승	**12.** fare card 요금 카드	**18.** taxi/cab 택시	

More vocabulary

hail a taxi: to get a taxi driver's attention by raising your hand

miss the bus: to arrive at the bus stop late

Talk about how you and your friends come to school.

I take _the bus_ to school.　　He _drives_ to school.
You take _the train_.　　She _walks_ to school.
We take _the subway_.　　They _ride_ bikes.

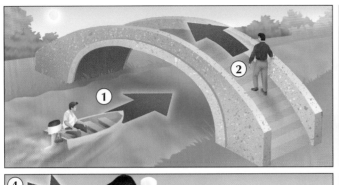

1. **under** the bridge
   다리 아래

2. **over** the bridge
   다리 위

3. **across** the water
   물 건너

4. **into** the taxi
   택시 안으로

5. **out of** the taxi
   택시 밖으로

6. **onto** the highway
   고속도로 위로

7. **off** the highway
   프리웨이를 벗어나서

8. **down** the stairs
   층계 아래

9. **up** the stairs
   층계 위

10. **around** the corner
    모퉁이 주위

11. **through** the tunnel
    터널을 통하여

Grammar point: *into, out of, on, off*

We say, *get **into** a taxi or a car.*

But we say, *get **on** a bus, a train, or a plane.*

We say, *get **out of** a taxi or a car.*

But we say, *get **off** a bus, a train, or a plane.*

Cars and Trucks 자동차와 트럭

1. subcompact
초소형 차

2. compact
소형 차

3. midsize car
중형 차

4. full-size car
대형 차

5. convertible
컨버터블

6. sports car
스포츠 카

7. pickup truck
픽업 트럭

8. station wagon
스테이션 웨곤

9. SUV (sports utility vehicle)
SUV (스포츠 유틸리티 카)

10. minivan
미니밴

11. camper
캠퍼

12. dump truck
덤프 트럭

13. tow truck
견인차

14. moving van
이삿짐 트럭

15. tractor trailer/semi
세미 트랙터 트레일러

16. cab
캡

17. trailer
트레일러

More vocabulary

make: the name of the company that makes the car

model: the style of car

Share your answers.

1. What is your favorite kind of car?

2. What kind of car is good for a big family? for a single person?

Directions 방향

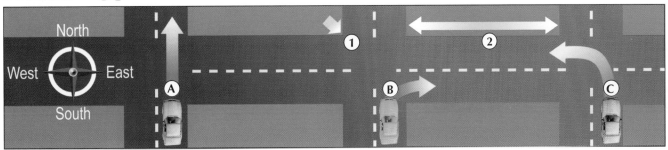

A. go straight
직행하시오

B. turn right
우회전 하시오

C. turn left
좌회전 하시오

1. corner
모퉁이

2. block
블록

Signs 표지판

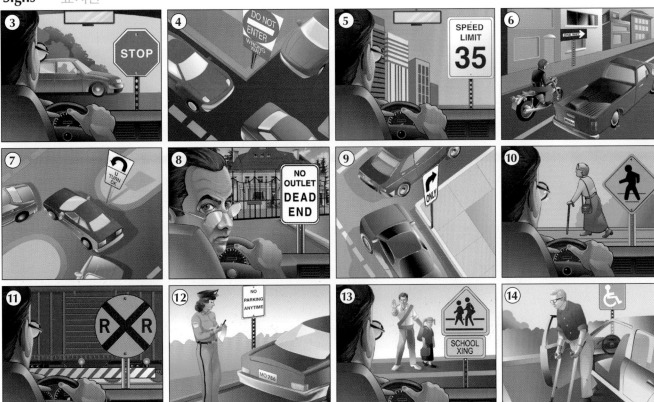

3. stop
정지

4. do not enter/wrong way
통행금지

5. speed limit
제한 속도

6. one way
일방통행

7. U-turn OK
U 회전 허용

8. no outlet/dead end
출구 없음 / 막다른 길

9. right turn only
우회전만 허용

10. pedestrian crossing
횡단보도

11. railroad crossing
철도 건널목

12. no parking
주차금지

13. school crossing
학교 횡단보도

14. handicapped parking
신체장애자 주차

More vocabulary

right-of-way: the right to go first

yield: to give another person or car the right-of-way

Share your answers.

1. Which traffic signs are the same in your country?

2. Do pedestrians have the right-of-way in your city?

3. What is the speed limit in front of your school? your home?

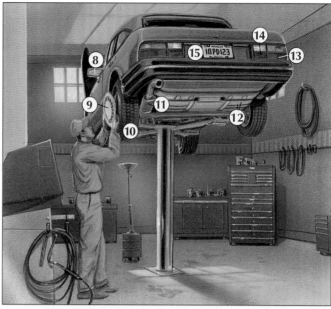

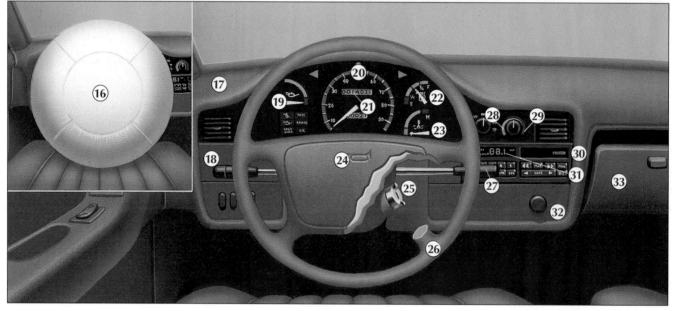

1. rearview mirror
백미러

2. windshield
앞유리

3. windshield wipers
앞유리 와이퍼

4. turn signal
방향 지시등

5. headlight
전조등

6. hood
보닛

7. bumper
범퍼

8. sideview mirror
사이드 미러

9. hubcap
휠캡

10. tire
타이어

11. muffler
머플러

12. gas tank
연료 탱크

13. brake light
제동등

14. taillight
미등

15. license plate
번호판

16. air bag
에어백

17. dashboard
계기판

18. turn signal
방향 지시등

19. oil gauge
유량계

20. speedometer
속도 계기

21. odometer
주행 기록계

22. gas gauge
연료 계기

23. temperature gauge
온도 계기

24. horn
경적

25. ignition
점화장치

26. steering wheel
핸들

27. gearshift
기어 전환장치

28. air conditioning
에어컨

29. heater
히터

30. tape deck
테이프 덱

31. radio
라디오

32. cigarette lighter
담배 라이터

33. glove compartment
사물함

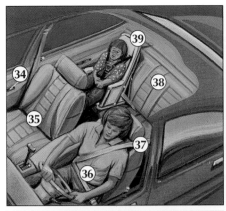

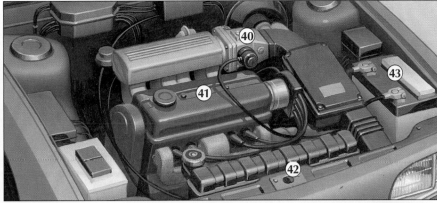

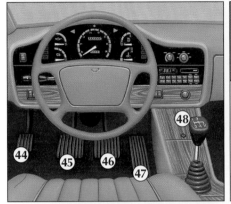

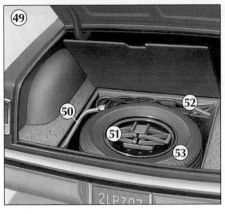

34. lock
잠금장치

35. front seat
앞좌석

36. seat belt
안전 벨트

37. shoulder harness
어깨 벨트

38. backseat
뒷좌석

39. child safety seat
어린이 카 시트

40. fuel injection system
연료분사 장치

41. engine
엔진

42. radiator
라디에이터

43. battery
배터리

44. emergency brake
비상 브레이크

45. clutch*
클러치

46. brake pedal
브레이크 페달

47. accelerator/gas pedal
액셀러레이터 / 페달

48. stick shift
수동 변속 레버

49. trunk
트렁크

50. lug wrench
러그렌치

51. jack
잭

52. jumper cables
점퍼 케이블

53. spare tire
예비 타이어

54. The car needs **gas**.
이 자동차는 휘발유가 필요하다.

55. The car needs **oil**.
이 자동차는 오일이 필요하다.

56. The radiator needs **coolant**.
이 라디에이터는 냉각수가 필요하다.

57. The car needs **a smog check**.
이 자동차는 스모그 검사
가 필요하다.

58. The battery needs **recharging**.
이 배터리는 재충전이 필요하다.

59. The tires need **air**.
이 타이어는 공기가 필요하다.

***Note:** Standard transmission cars have a clutch; automatic transmission cars do not.

1. airline terminal
공항 터미널

2. airline representative
공항 직원

3. check-in counter
체크인 카운터

4. arrival and departure monitors
이착륙 모니터

5. gate
게이트 / 탑승구

6. boarding area
탑승 구역

7. control tower
관제탑

8. helicopter
헬기

9. airplane
비행기

10. overhead compartment
머리위 짐칸

11. cockpit
조종실

12. pilot
조종사

13. flight attendant
승무원

14. oxygen mask
산소 마스크

15. airsickness bag
멀미 봉투

16. tray table
트레이 테이블

17. baggage claim area
수화물 찾는 곳

18. carousel
원형 컨베이어

19. luggage carrier
수화물 캐리어

20. customs
세관

21. customs officer
세관직원

22. declaration form
신고서

23. passenger
승객

A. **buy** your ticket
항공권을 사십시오

B. **check** your bags
짐을 체크하십시오

C. **go through** security
보안검사를 통과하십시오

D. **check in** at the gate
게이트에서 체크인 하십시오

E. **get** your boarding pass
탑승권을 받으십시오

F. **board** the plane
비행기에 탑승하십시오

G. **find** your seat
좌석을 찾으십시오

H. **stow** your carry-on bag
기내휴대물을 보관함에 넣으십시오

I. **fasten** your seat belt
안전 벨트를 매십시오

J. **look for** the emergency exit
비상구를 찾으십시오

K. **look at** the emergency card
비상 카드를 보십시오

L. **take off / leave**
이륙 / 출발

M. **request** a blanket
담요를 달라고 하십시오

N. **experience** turbulence
흔들림을 경험하다

O. **land / arrive**
착륙 / 도착

P. **claim** your baggage
수화물을 찾으십시오

More vocabulary

destination: the place the passenger is going

departure time: the time the plane takes off

arrival time: the time the plane lands

direct flight: a plane trip between two cities with no stops

stopover: a stop before reaching the destination, sometimes to change planes

1. public school
공립학교

2. private school
사립학교

3. parochial school
카톨릭 학교

4. preschool
유치원

5. elementary school
초등학교

**6. middle school/
junior high school**
중학교

7. high school
고등학교

8. adult school
성인학교

9. vocational school/trade school
직업학교

10. college/university
대학교

Note: In the U.S. most children begin school at age 5 (in kindergarten) and graduate from high school at 17 or 18.

More vocabulary

When students graduate from a college or university they receive a **degree**:

Bachelor's degree—usually 4 years of study

Master's degree—an additional 1–3 years of study

Doctorate—an additional 3–5 years of study

community college: a two-year college where students can get an Associate of Arts degree

graduate school: a school in a university where students study for their master's degrees and doctorates

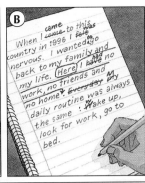

1. writing assignment
작문 숙제

A. Write a first draft.
초안을 쓰다.

B. Edit your paper.
작문을 수정하다.

C. Get feedback.
다른 사람의 평을 받다.

D. Rewrite your paper.
작문을 다시 쓰다.

E. Turn in your paper.
작문을 제출하다.

2. paper / composition
작문

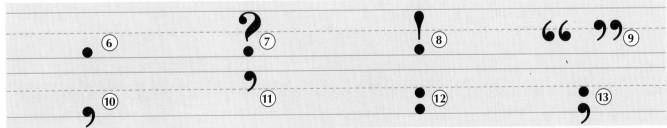

③ **My life in the U.S.**

④ I arrived in this country in 1996. My family did not come with me. I was homesick, nervous, and a little excited. I had no job and no friends here. I lived with my aunt and my daily routine ⑤ was always the same: get up, look for a job, go to bed. At night I remembered my mother's words to me, "Son, you can always come home!" I was homesick and scared, but I did not go home.

I started to study English at night. English is a difficult language and many times I was too tired to study. One teacher, Mrs. Armstrong, was very kind to me. She showed me many

3. title
제목

4. sentence
문장

5. paragraph
문단

Punctuation 발음

● ⑥	? ⑦	! ⑧	" " ⑨
, ⑩	' ⑪	: ⑫	; ⑬

6. period
마침표

7. question mark
물음표

8. exclamation mark
느낌표

9. quotation marks
따옴표

10. comma
쉼표

11. apostrophe
아포스트로피

12. colon
콜론

13. semicolon
세미콜론

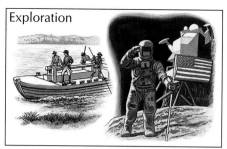

Exploration

War

Immigration

| **Historical and Political Events** 역사적 및 정치적 사건 | **1492 →** French, Spanish, English explorers 프랑스, 스페인, 영국 탐험가들 | **1607–1750** Colonies along Atlantic coast founded by Northern Europeans 북유럽인들이 대서양 연안에 설립한 식민지들 | **1619** 1st African slave sold in Virginia 버지니아에서 최초로 아프리카 노예 **1653** 1st Indian reservation in Virginia 버지니아에 최초로 세운 인디언 보호구역 |

Before 1700   1700

| **Immigration*** 이민 | **1607** 1st English in Virginia 버지니아에 최초 영국인 | **1610** Spanish at Santa Fe 산타페의 스페인 사람들 | |

Population** 인구   Before 1700: Native American: 1,000,000+   1700: colonists: 250,000
미국 인디언: 1,000,000+   식민지 주민: 250,000

| **1803** Louisiana Purchase 루이지애나 구입지 | **1812** War of 1812 1812년 전쟁 | **1820** Missouri Compromise 미주리 타협 | **1830** Indian Removal Act 인디언 제거 법안 | **1835–1838** Cherokee Trail of Tears 체로키족의 눈물의 산길 | **1846–1848** U.S. war with Mexico 멕시코와 미국과의전쟁 |

1800   1810   1820   1830   1840

1815 → Irish 아일랜드인

1800: citizens and free blacks: 5,300,000   slaves: 450,000
미국시민과 해방된 노예들: 5,300,00   노예: 450,000

| **1903** 1st *Model A* Ford car 포드 자동차 최초 모델   1st air flight 첫 번째 비행 | **1927** 1st sound pictures 최초 사운드 필름 | **1929** stock market crashes 증권시장 폭락 | **1939–1945** World War II 이차세계대전 | **1945** United Nations 국제연합 |

| **1914–1918** World War I 일차세계대전 | **1920** women get vote 여성 참정권 | **1930–1940** The Depression 대공황 | **1945** 1st atomic bomb 최초 원자탄 | **1948–1985** The Cold War 냉전 |

1900   1910   1920   1930   1940

1910 → Mexicans 맥시칸

1924 U.S. closes borders 미국 국경 차단

1942–1945 Japanese internment 일본인 강제수용

1945 → Puerto Ricans 푸에르토 리칸

1948 WW II refugees immigrate 이차세계대전 피난민 이민

1900: 75,994,000

*Immigration dates indicate a time when large numbers of that group first began to immigrate to the U.S.
**All population figures before 1790 are estimates. Figures after 1790 are based on the official U.S. census.

Movement

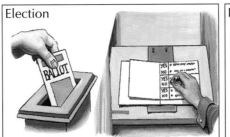

Election

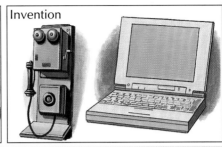

Invention

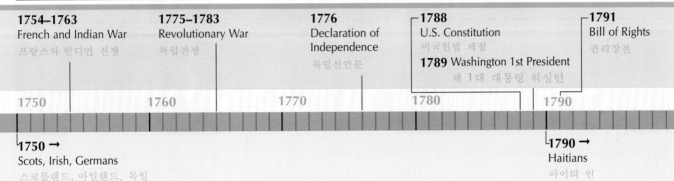

1754–1763
French and Indian War
프랑스와 인디언 전쟁

1775–1783
Revolutionary War
독립전쟁

1776
Declaration of Independence
독립선언문

1788
U.S. Constitution
미국헌법 제정

1789 Washington 1st President
제 1 대 대통령 워싱턴

1791
Bill of Rights
권리장전

1750   1760   1770   1780   1790

1750 →
Scots, Irish, Germans
스코틀랜드, 아일랜드, 독일

1790 →
Haitians
아이티 인

1750: Native American: 1,000,000 +
미국 인디언: 1,000,000 +

colonists and free blacks: 1,171,000
식민지 거주자들과 비노예 흑인: 1,171,000

slaves: 200,000
노예: 200,000

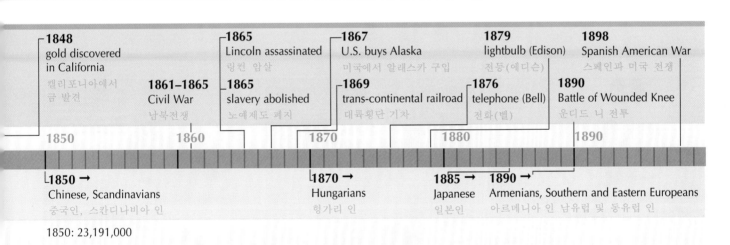

1848
gold discovered in California
캘리포니아에서 금 발견

1865
Lincoln assassinated
링컨 암살

1865
slavery abolished
노예제도 폐지

1867
U.S. buys Alaska
미국에서 알래스카 구입

1869
trans-continental railroad
대륙횡단 기차

1879
lightbulb (Edison)
전등(에디슨)

1876
telephone (Bell)
전화(벨)

1898
Spanish American War
스페인과 미국 전쟁

1890
Battle of Wounded Knee
운디드 니 전투

1861–1865
Civil War
남북전쟁

1850   1860   1870   1880   1890

1850 →
Chinese, Scandinavians
중국인, 스칸디나비아 인

1870 →
Hungarians
헝가리 인

1885 →
Japanese
일본인

1890 →
Armenians, Southern and Eastern Europeans
아르메니아 인 남유럽 및 동유럽 인

1850: 23,191,000

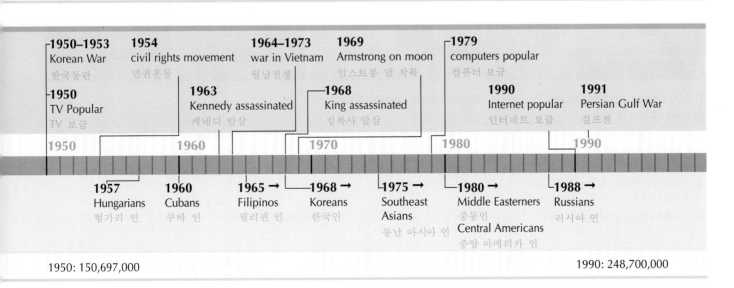

1950–1953
Korean War
한국동란

1954
civil rights movement
민권운동

1964–1973
war in Vietnam
월남전쟁

1969
Armstrong on moon
암스트롱 달 착륙

1979
computers popular
컴퓨터 보급

1950
TV Popular
TV 보급

1963
Kennedy assassinated
케네디 암살

1968
King assassinated
킹목사 암살

1990
Internet popular
인터넷 보급

1991
Persian Gulf War
걸프전

1950   1960   1970   1980   1990

1957
Hungarians
헝가리 인

1960
Cubans
쿠바 인

1965 →
Filipinos
필리핀 인

1968 →
Koreans
한국인

1975 →
Southeast Asians
동남 아시아 인

1980 →
Middle Easterners
중동인
Central Americans
중앙 아메리카 인

1988 →
Russians
러시아 인

1950: 150,697,000

1990: 248,700,000

115

BRANCHES OF GOVERNMENT

Legislative

Executive

Judicial

1. The House of Representatives
하원

2. congresswoman / congressman
하원의원

3. The Senate
상원

4. senator
상원의원

5. The White House
백악관

6. president
대통령

7. vice president
부통령

8. The Supreme Court
대법원

9. chief justice
대법원장

10. justices
대법관

Citizenship application requirements
시민권 신청 자격

A. **be** 18 years old
18세가 되다

B. **live** in the U.S. for five years
미국에서 5년동안 살다

C. **take** a citizenship test
시민권 시험을 보다

Rights and responsibilities
권리와 의무

D. **vote**
투표하다

E. **pay** taxes
세금을 내다

F. **register** with Selective Service*
선발 징병제에 등록하다

G. **serve** on a jury
배심원 임무를 수행하다

H. **obey** the law
법을 지키다

*Note: All males 18 to 26 who live in the U.S. are required to register with Selective Service.

1. rain forest
다우림

2. waterfall
폭포

3. river
강

4. desert
사막

5. sand dune
모래 언덕

6. ocean
바다

7. peninsula
반도

8. island
섬

9. bay
만

10. beach
해변

11. forest
숲

12. shore
해안

13. lake
호수

14. mountain peak
산봉우리

15. mountain range
산맥

16. hills
언덕

17. canyon
협곡

18. valley
계곡

19. plains
평원

20. meadow
초원

21. pond
연못

More vocabulary

a body of water: a river, lake, or ocean
stream/creek: a very small river

Talk about where you live and where you like to go.

I live in <u>a valley</u>. There is <u>a lake</u> <u>nearby</u>.
I like to go to <u>the beach</u>.

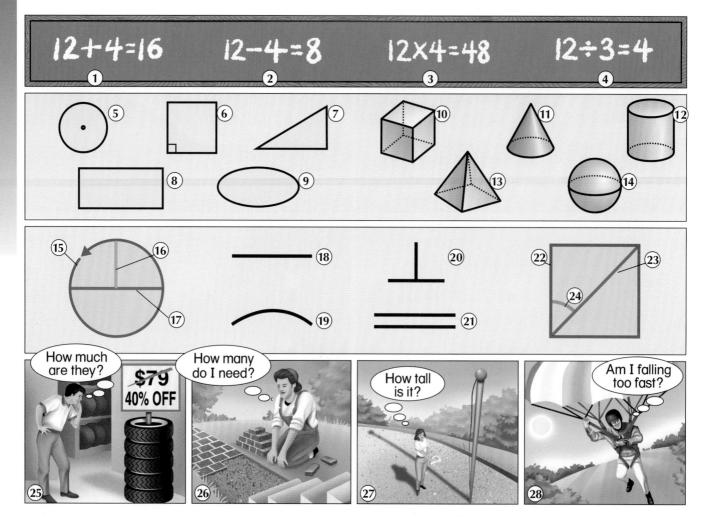

Operations
연산

1. addition
더하기

2. subtraction
빼기

3. multiplication
곱하기

4. division
나누기

Shapes
모양

5. circle
동그라미

6. square
정사각형

7. triangle
삼각형

8. rectangle
직사각형 / 구형

9. oval/ellipse
타원

Solids
입체

10. cube
입방체

11. cone
원추형

12. cylinder
원통

13. pyramid
피라미드

14. sphere
구체

Parts of a circle
원의 부분

15. circumference
원주

16. radius
반지름

17. diameter
지름

Lines
선

18. straight
직선

19. curved
곡선

20. perpendicular
수직

21. parallel
평행

Parts of a square
정사각형의 부분

22. side
면

23. diagonal
대각선

24. angle
각도

Types of math
수학의 종류

25. algebra
대수

26. geometry
기하

27. trigonometry
삼각법

28. calculus
미적분

More vocabulary

total: the answer to an addition problem

difference: the answer to a subtraction problem

product: the answer to a multiplication problem

quotient: the answer to a division problem

pi (π): the number when you divide the circumference of a circle by its diameter (approximately = 3.14)

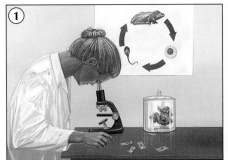

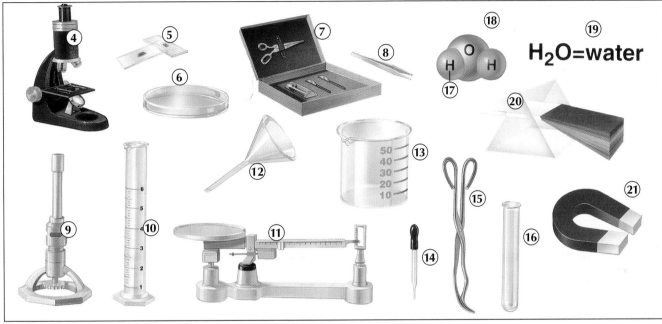

H₂O=water

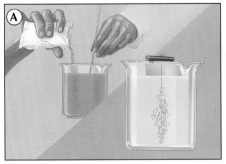

1. biology
생물

2. chemistry
화학

3. physics
물리

4. microscope
현미경

5. slide
슬라이드

6. petri dish
페트리 접시

7. dissection kit
해부 키트

8. forceps
핀셋

9. Bunsen burner
분젠 가스 버너

10. graduated cylinder
눈금새긴 윈통

11. balance
저울

12. funnel
깔때기

13. beaker
비커

14. dropper
점적기

15. crucible tongs
도가니 집게

16. test tube
시험관

17. atom
원자

18. molecule
분자

19. formula
공식

20. prism
프리즘

21. magnet
자석

A. **do** an experiment
실험하다

B. **observe**
관찰하다

C. **record** results
결과를 기록하다

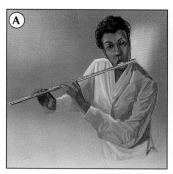

A. play an instrument
악기를 연주하다

B. sing a song
노래를 부르다

1. orchestra
오케스트라

2. rock band
록 밴드

Woodwinds

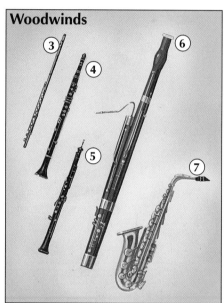

Strings

Brass

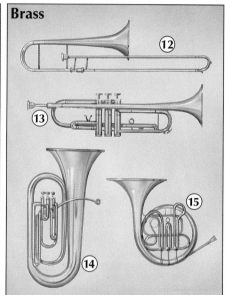

Percussion

Other Instruments

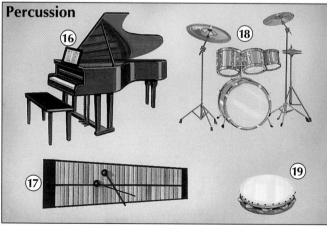

3. flute
플루트

4. clarinet
클라리넷

5. oboe
오보에

6. bassoon
바순

7. saxophone
색소폰

8. violin
바이올린

9. cello
첼로

10. bass
바스

11. guitar
기타

12. trombone
트롬본

13. trumpet / horn
트럼벳 / 혼

14. tuba
투바

15. French horn
프렌치 혼

16. piano
피아노

17. xylophone
실로폰

18. drums
드럼

19. tambourine
탬버린

20. electric keyboard
전자 키보드

21. accordion
아코디언

22. organ
오르간

1. art
미술

2. business education
상업교육

3. chorus
합창

4. computer science
전산학

5. driver's education
운전교육

6. economics
경제학

7. English as a second language
영어 제2외국어

8. foreign language
외국어

9. home economics
가정학

10. industrial arts/shop
산업미술 / 실습

11. PE (physical education)
체육

12. theater arts
연극예술

More vocabulary

core course: a subject students have to take

elective: a subject students choose to take

Share your answers.

1. What are your favorite subjects?

2. In your opinion, what subjects are most important? Why?

3. What foreign languages are taught in your school?

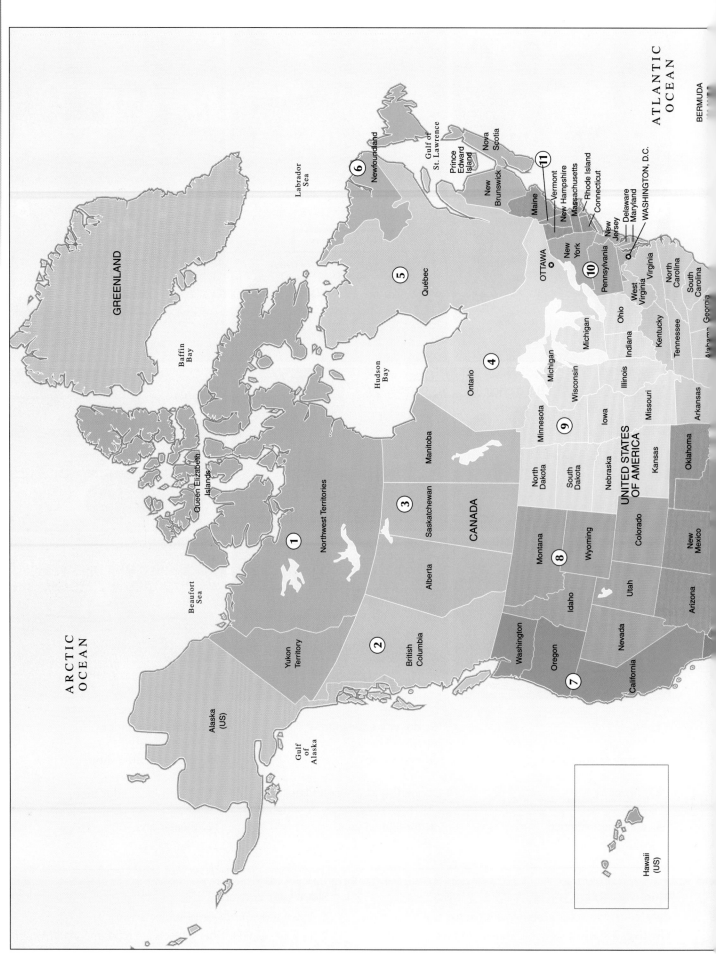

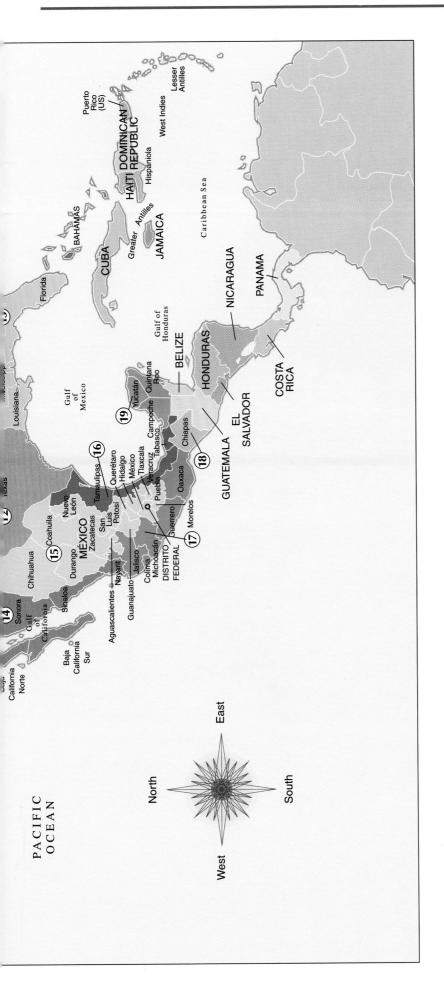

Regions of Canada
캐나다 지역

1. Northern Canada
   북 캐나다
2. British Columbia
   브리티시 콜럼비아
3. The Prairie Provinces
   프레리 프로빈스
4. Ontario
   온타리오
5. Québec
   퀘벡
6. The Atlantic Provinces
   애틀랜틱 프로빈스

Regions of the United States
미국 지역

7. The Pacific States/the West Coast
   태평양 연안주/서해안
8. The Rocky Mountain States
   록키 산주
9. The Midwest
   중기부
10. The Mid-Atlantic States
    미드 애틀랜틱 주
11. New England
    뉴잉글랜드
12. The Southwest
    남서부
13. The Southeast/the South
    남동부/남부

Regions of Mexico
멕시코 지역

14. The Pacific Northwest
    태평양 북서부
15. The Plateau of Mexico
    멕시코 고원
16. The Gulf Coastal Plain
    걸프 해안 평원
17. The Southern Uplands
    남부 고원
18. The Chiapas Highlands
    치아파스 고지
19. The Yucatan Peninsula
    유카탄 반도

The World 세계

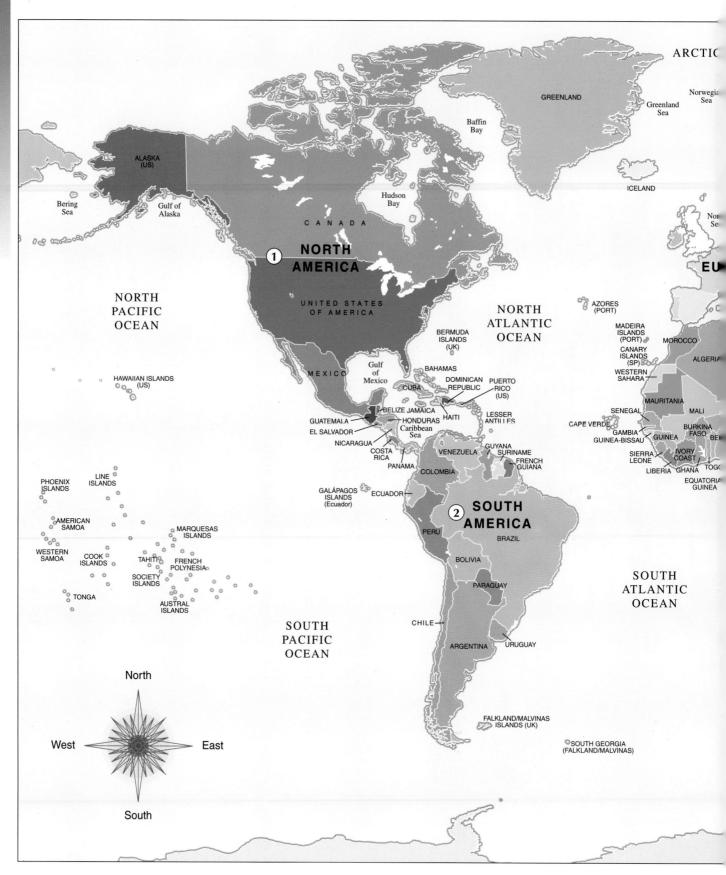

Continents
대륙

1. North America
북미

2. South America
남미

OCEAN

SVALBARD
(NORWAY)

FRANZ JOSEF LAND
(RUSSIA)

Barents Sea

R U S S I A

④ ASIA

Sea of
Okhotsk

Bering
Sea

ALEUTIAN ISLANDS
(US)

③

KAZAKHSTAN

MONGOLIA

NORTH
PACIFIC
OCEAN

PE

Caspian
Sea

Black Sea GEORGIA
AZERBAIJAN
ARMENIA
TURKEY   TURKMENISTAN

UZBEKISTAN KYRGYZSTAN

TAJIKISTAN

NORTH
KOREA

SOUTH
KOREA

Sea of
Japan

JAPAN

Cyprus SYRIA
Mediterranean Sea LEBANON
ISRAEL
JORDAN KUWAIT
IRAQ

IRAN

AFGHANISTAN

CHINA

East
China
Sea

LIBYA

EGYPT

BAHRAIN
Persian
Gulf QATAR
UNITED
ARAB
EMIRATES
OMAN

PAKISTAN

NEPAL BHUTAN

BANGLADESH
MYANMAR

LAOS

HONG
KONG

TAIWAN

VOLCANO
ISLANDS

DAITO
ISLANDS
(JAPAN)

PARECE
VELA
(JAPAN)

WAKE ISLAND
(US)

SAUDI
ARABIA

Red
Sea

INDIA

NIGER

⑤

CHAD

ERITREA

YEMEN

Arabian
Sea

THAILAND

HAINAN

VIETNAM

CAMBODIA

PHILIPPINES

South
China
Sea

Philippine
Sea

YAP
ISLANDS

GUAM
(US)

NORTHERN
MARIANA
ISLANDS
(US)

MARSHALL
ISLANDS

AFRICA

SUDAN

DJIBOUTI SOMALIA

SOCOTRA
(YEMEN)

NICOBAR
ISLANDS
(INDIA)

BRUNEI

PALAU

FEDERATED STATE
OF MICRONESIA

CENTRAL
AFRICAN
REPUBLIC

CAMEROON

ETHIOPIA

UGANDA

MALDIVE
ISLANDS

SRI
LANKA

ANDAMAN
ISLANDS
(INDIA)

MALAYSIA
SINGAPORE

BORNEO

CELEBES

NAURU

KIRIBATI

CONGO
GABON

KENYA

SUMATRA

DEMOCRATIC
REPUBLIC
OF THE
CONGO

RWANDA
BURUNDI

TANZANIA

ZANZIBAR

CHAGOS ARCHIPELAGO

JAVA

INDONESIA

NEW GUINEA
PAPUA
NEW
GUINEA

SOLOMON
ISLANDS

TUVALU

SEYCHELLES

INDIAN
OCEAN

Coral
Sea

VANUATU

ANGOLA
ZAMBIA MALAWI

COMOROS

MAURITIUS

CORAL SEA
ISLANDS
TERRITORY
(AUSTRALIA)

FIJI

ZIMBABWE
MOZAMBIQUE

NAMIBIA
BOTSWANA

MADAGASCAR

⑥ AUSTRALIA

NEW
CALEDONIA

SOUTH
PACIFIC
OCEAN

SWAZILAND

LESOTHO

SOUTH
AFRICA

ICELAND

FINLAND

NORWAY

SWEDEN

North
Sea

Baltic
Sea

ESTONIA

LATVIA
LITHUANIA

RUSSIA

NORTH
ISLAND

NEW
ZEALAND

TASMANIA
(AUSTRALIA)

SOUTH
ISLAND

DENMARK
NETHER-
LANDS

RUSSIA

BELARUS

IRELAND UNITED
KINGDOM

GERMANY

POLAND

BELGIUM
LUXEMBOURG
LIECHTENSTEIN

CZECH
REPUBLIC
AUSTRIA SLOVAKIA

UKRAINE

SWITZER-
LAND SLOVENIA

HUNGARY

MOLDOVA

FRANCE

CROATIA
BOSNIA
HERZEGOVINA
MONTENEGRO

ROMANIA
SERBIA

SOUTHERN
OCEAN

ANDORRA

CORSICA
(FR)

MONACO

BULGARIA Black Sea

SPAIN

ITALY

MACEDONIA
ALBANIA

PORTUGAL

BALEARIC
ISLANDS
(SP)

SARDINIA
(IT)

SICILY (IT)

GREECE

ANTARCTICA ⑦

MALTA

CRETE CYPRUS

Mediterranean Sea

3. Europe
유럽

4. Asia
아시아

5. Africa
아프리카

6. Australia
호주

7. Antarctica
남극대륙

125

Energy resources 에너지 자원

1. solar energy
태양 에너지

2. wind
바람

3. natural gas
천연가스

4. coal
석탄

5. hydroelectric power
수력발전

6. oil / petroleum
오일 / 석유

7. geothermal energy
지열 에너지

8. nuclear energy
원자력 에너지

Pollution 공해

9. hazardous waste
위험 폐기물

10. air pollution / smog
공해 / 스모그

11. acid rain
산성 비

12. water pollution
수질 오염

13. radiation
방사능

14. pesticide poisoning
살충제 중독

15. oil spill
석유 유출

Conservation 보존

A. **recycle**
재활용

B. **save** water / **conserve** water
물 절약 / 보존

C. **save** energy / **conserve** energy
에너지 절약 / 보존

Share your answers.

1. How do you heat your home?

2. Do you have a gas stove or an electric stove?

3. What are some ways you can save energy when it's cold?

4. Do you recycle? What products do you recycle?

5. Does your market have recycling bins?

The Solar System

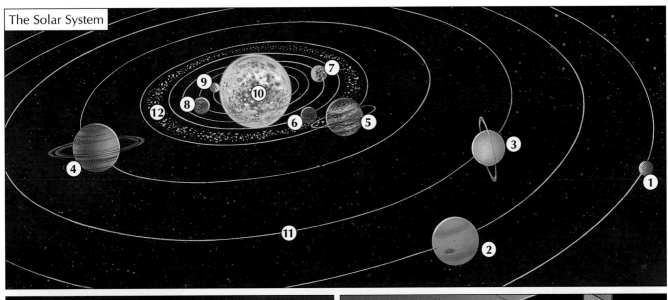

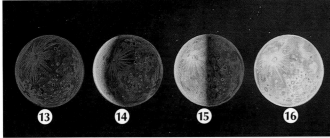

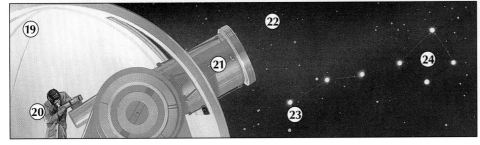

The planets
행성

1. Pluto
   명왕성

2. Neptune
   해왕성

3. Uranus
   천왕성

4. Saturn
   토성

5. Jupiter
   목성

6. Mars
   화성

7. Earth
   지구

8. Venus
   금성

9. Mercury
   수성

10. sun
    태양

11. orbit
    궤도

12. asteroid belt
    우주

13. new moon
    신월

14. crescent moon
    초승달

15. quarter moon
    하현달

16. full moon
    만월 / 보름달

17. astronaut
    우주 비행사

18. space station
    우주 정류장

19. observatory
    관측소

20. astronomer
    천문학자

21. telescope
    망원경

22. space
    우주

23. star
    별

24. constellation
    별자리

25. comet
    혜성

26. galaxy
    은하계

More vocabulary

lunar eclipse: when the earth is between the sun and the moon

solar eclipse: when the moon is between the earth and the sun

Share your answers.

1. Do you know the names of any constellations?
2. How do you feel when you look up at the night sky?
3. Is the night sky in the U.S. the same as in your country?

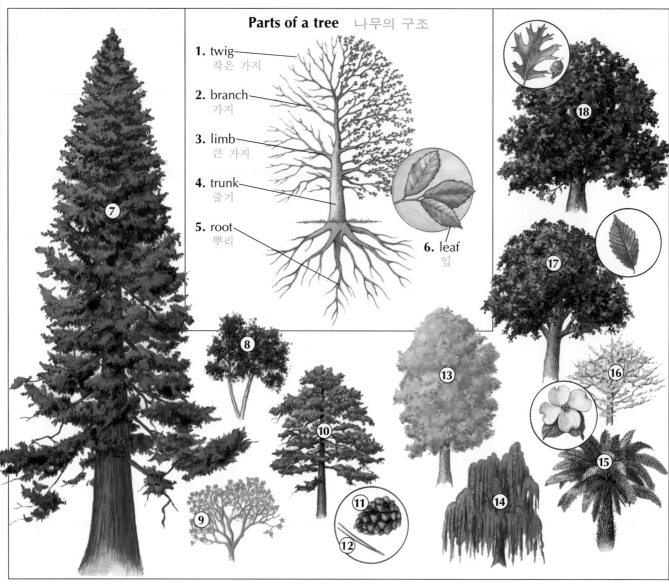

Parts of a tree 나무의 구조

1. twig
작은 가지

2. branch
가지

3. limb
큰 가지

4. trunk
줄기

5. root
뿌리

6. leaf
잎

7. redwood 아메리카삼나무	**10.** pine 소나무	**13.** maple 단풍나무	**16.** dogwood 충충나무
8. birch 자작나무	**11.** pinecone 솔방울	**14.** willow 버드나무	**17.** elm 느릅나무
9. magnolia 태산목	**12.** needle 침엽	**15.** palm 종려	**18.** oak 오크

Plants 화초

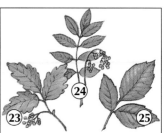

19. holly 서양호랑가시나무	**21.** cactus 선인장	**23.** poison oak 독있는 오크	**25.** poison ivy 덩굴옻나무
20. berries 장과	**22.** vine 포도나무	**24.** poison sumac 독있는 옻나무	

Parts of a flower 꽃의 부분 명칭

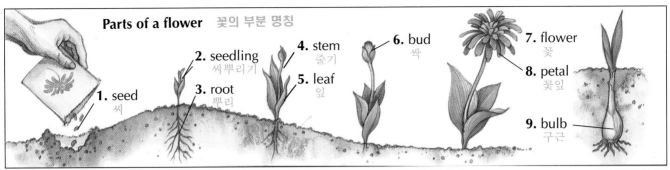

1. seed
씨

2. seedling
씨뿌리기

3. root
뿌리

4. stem
줄기

5. leaf
잎

6. bud
싹

7. flower
꽃

8. petal
꽃잎

9. bulb
구근

10. sunflower
해바라기

11. tulip
튤립

12. hibiscus
하이비스커스

13. marigold
금잔화

14. daisy
데이지

15. rose
장미

16. gardenia
치자나무

17. orchid
난초

18. carnation
카네이션

19. chrysanthemum
국화

20. iris
홍채

21. jasmine
재스민

22. violet
제비꽃

23. poinsettia
포인세티아

24. lily
백합

25. crocus
크로커스

26. daffodil
수선화

27. bouquet
꽃다발

28. thorn
가시

29. houseplant
실내 화초

Marine Life, Amphibians, and Reptiles 바다생물, 양서류 그리고 파충류

Parts of a fish 물고기의 부분

Sea animals 바다 동물

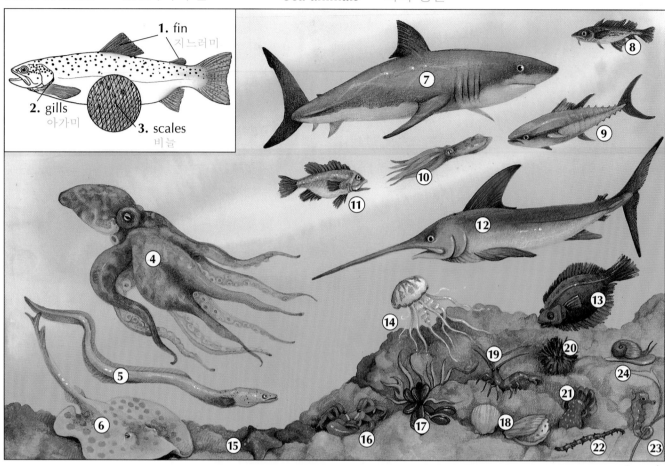

1. fin
지느러미

2. gills
아가미

3. scales
비늘

4. octopus 문어	**11.** bass 바스	**18.** scallop 가리비
5. eel 뱀장어	**12.** swordfish 황새치	**19.** shrimp 새우
6. ray 가오리	**13.** flounder 가자미	**20.** sea urchin 섬게
7. shark 상어	**14.** jellyfish 해파리	**21.** sea anemone 말미잘
8. cod 대구	**15.** starfish 불가사리	**22.** worm 벌레
9. tuna 참치	**16.** crab 게	**23.** sea horse 해마
10. squid 오징어	**17.** mussel 홍합	**24.** snail 달팽이

Amphibians 양서류

25. frog
개구리

26. newt
영원

27. salamander
도룡뇽

28. toad
두꺼비

Sea mammals 바다 포유동물

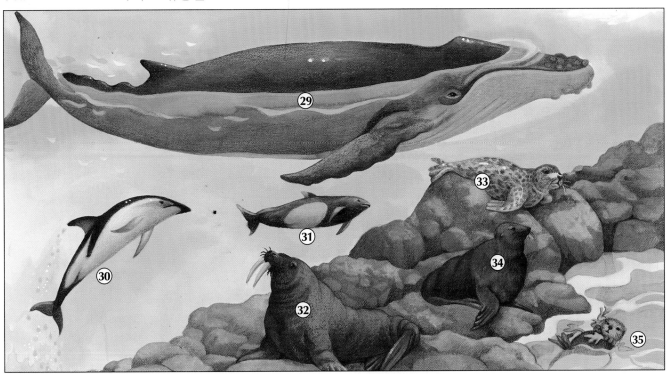

29. whale 고래	**31.** porpoise 돌고래 무리	**33.** seal 물개	**35.** otter 수달
30. dolphin 돌고래	**32.** walrus 해마	**34.** sea lion 바다 사자	

Reptiles 파충류

36. alligator 악어	**38.** rattlesnake 방울뱀	**40.** cobra 코브라	**42.** turtle 자라
37. crocodile 크로코다일	**39.** garter snake 누룩뱀	**41.** lizard 도마뱀	

Parts of a bird 새의 부분 명칭

1. beak / bill
   부리
2. wing
   날개
3. nest 둥우리
4. claw
   발톱
5. feather
   깃털

6. owl 올빼미	**9.** woodpecker 딱따구리	**12.** penguin 펭귄	**15.** peacock 공작
7. blue jay 큰어치	**10.** eagle 독수리	**13.** duck 오리	**16.** pigeon 비둘기
8. sparrow 참새	**11.** hummingbird 벌새	**14.** goose 거위	**17.** robin 로빈

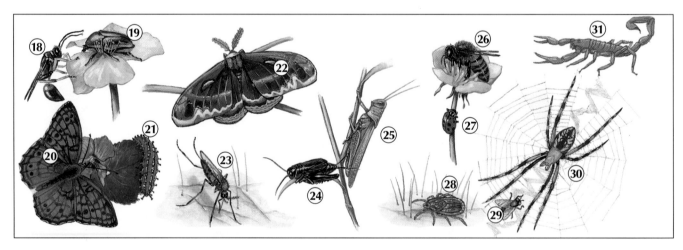

18. wasp 말벌	**22.** moth 나방	**26.** honeybee 꿀벌	**30.** spider 거미
19. beetle 딱정벌레	**23.** mosquito 모기	**27.** ladybug 무당벌레	**31.** scorpion 전갈
20. butterfly 나비	**24.** cricket 귀뚜라미	**28.** tick 진드기	
21. caterpillar 모충	**25.** grasshopper 메뚜기	**29.** fly 파리	

Farm animals 농장 동물

1. goat
염소

2. donkey
당나귀

3. cow
젖소

4. horse
말

5. hen
암탉

6. rooster
수탉

7. sheep
양

8. pig
돼지

Pets 애완동물

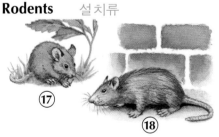

9. cat
고양이

10. kitten
새끼 고양이

11. dog
개

12. puppy
강아지

13. rabbit
토끼

14. guinea pig
기니피그 (쥐의 일종)

15. parakeet
잉꼬

16. goldfish
금붕어

Rodents 설치류

17. mouse
생쥐

18. rat
쥐

19. gopher
들쥐

20. chipmunk
얼룩 다람쥐

21. squirrel
다람쥐

22. prairie dog
프레리 도그

More vocabulary

Wild animals live, eat, and raise their young away from people, in the forests, mountains, plains, etc.

Domesticated animals work for people or live with them.

Share your answers.

1. Do you have any pets? any farm animals?

2. Which of these animals are in your neighborhood? Which are not?

1. moose 무스	**5.** wolf 늑대	**9.** beaver 비버	**13.** raccoon 너구리
2. mountain lion 쿠거	**6.** buffalo/bison 들소	**10.** porcupine 고슴도치	**14.** deer 사슴
3. coyote 코요테	**7.** bat 박쥐	**11.** bear 곰	**15.** fox 여우
4. opossum 주머니 쥐	**8.** armadillo 아르마딜로	**12.** skunk 스컹크	

16. antler 사슴뿔	**18.** whiskers 수염	**20.** paw 발	**22.** tail 꼬리
17. hoof 발굽	**19.** coat/fur 가죽	**21.** horn 뿔	**23.** quill 깃대

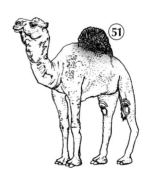

24. anteater
개미 핥기

25. leopard
표범

26. llama
라마

27. monkey
원숭이

28. chimpanzee
침판지

29. rhinoceros
코뿔소

30. gorilla
고릴라

31. hyena
하이에나

32. baboon
개코원숭이

33. giraffe
기린

34. zebra
얼룩말

35. antelope
영양

36. lion
사자

37. tiger
호랑이

38. camel
낙타

39. panther
표범

40. orangutan
오랑우탄

41. panda
팬더 곰

42. elephant
코끼리

43. hippopotamus
하마

44. kangaroo
캥거루

45. koala
코알라 곰

46. platypus
오리 너구리

47. trunk
코끼리 코

48. tusk
앞니

49. mane
갈기

50. pouch
주머니

51. hump
혹

Jobs and Occupations, A–H 직업 (A–H, 영어순)

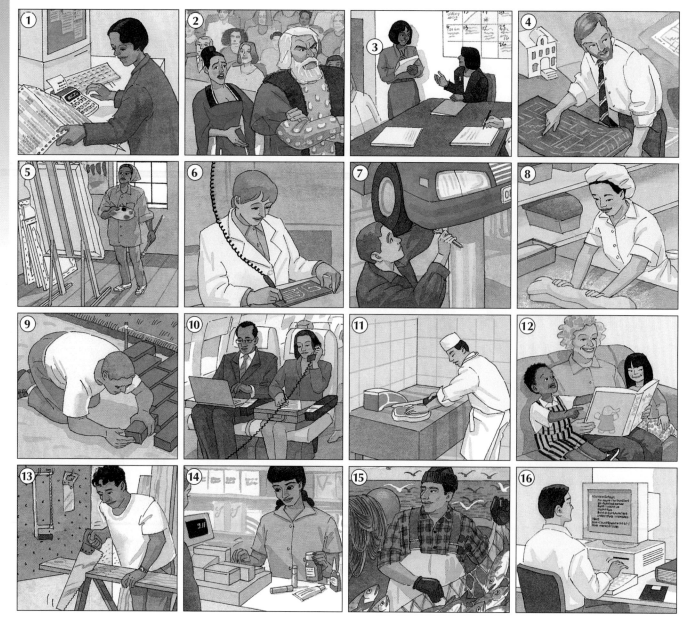

1. accountant
   회계사

2. actor
   배우

3. administrative assistant
   사무원

4. architect
   건축가

5. artist
   예술가

6. assembler
   조립공

7. auto mechanic
   자동차 기술자

8. baker
   제과 기술자

9. bricklayer
   벽돌공

10. businessman / businesswoman
    사업가

11. butcher
    푸주한

12. caregiver / baby-sitter
    아기 돌보는 사람

13. carpenter
    목수

14. cashier
    계산원

15. commercial fisher
    어부

16. computer programmer
    컴퓨터 프로그래머

Use the new language.

1. Who works outside?

2. Who works inside?

3. Who makes things?

4. Who uses a computer?

5. Who wears a uniform?

6. Who sells things?

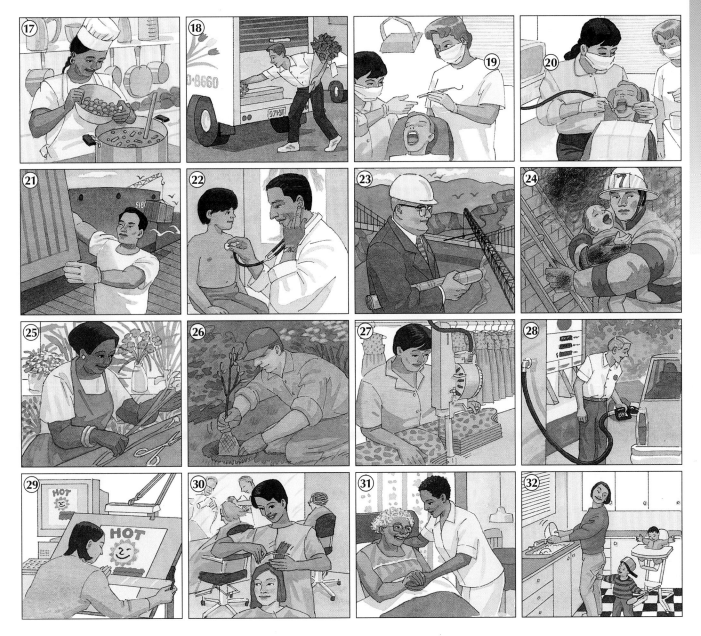

17. cook
요리사

18. delivery person
배달원

19. dental assistant
치과 보조원

20. dentist
치과의사

21. dockworker
부두 근로자

22. doctor
의사

23. engineer
엔지니어

24. firefighter
소방원

25. florist
화초 재배자

26. gardener
정원사

27. garment worker
재봉사

28. gas station attendant
주유소 종업원

29. graphic artist
그래픽 아티스트

30. hairdresser
미용사

31. home attendant
가사 보조원

32. homemaker
주부

Share your answers.

1. Do you know people who have some of these jobs? What do they say about their work?

2. Which of these jobs are available in your city?

3. For which of these jobs do you need special training?

33. housekeeper
가정부

34. interpreter / translator
통역사 / 번역사

35. janitor / custodian
건물 관리인

36. lawyer
변호사

37. machine operator
기계 작동자

38. messenger / courier
탁배원

39. model
모델

40. mover
이삿짐 배달원

41. musician
음악가

42. nurse
간호사

43. painter
화가

44. police officer
경찰

45. postal worker
우편 집배원

46. printer
인쇄 기술자

47. receptionist
접수원

48. repair person
수리공

Talk about each of the jobs or occupations.

She's a housekeeper. She works in a hotel.
He's an interpreter. He works for the government.

She's a nurse. She works with patients.

49. reporter
신문기자

50. salesclerk / salesperson
판매원

51. sanitation worker
환경미화원

52. secretary
비서

53. server
웨이터

54. serviceman / servicewoman
서비스 요원

55. stock clerk
창고원

56. store owner
상점 주인

57. student
학생

58. teacher / instructor
교사

59. telemarketer
텔레마케터

60. travel agent
여행사 직원

61. truck driver
트럭 기사r

62. veterinarian
수의사

63. welder
용접공

64. writer / author
작가

Talk about your job or the job you want.

What do you do?

  I'm a salesclerk. I work in a store.

What do you want to do?

  I want to be a veterinarian. I want to work with animals.

A. **assemble** components
부품을 조립하다

B. **assist** medical patients
환자를 보조하다

C. **cook**
요리하다

D. **do** manual labor
육체 노동을 하다

E. **drive** a truck
트럭을 운전하다

F. **operate** heavy machinery
중장비를 운전하다

G. **repair** appliances
가전제품을 수리하다

H. **sell** cars
자동차를 팔다

I. **sew** clothes
옷을 바느질하다

J. **speak** another language
외국어를 말하다

K. **supervise** people
사람을 관리하다

L. **take care** of children
어린이를 돌보다

M. **type**
타이핑하다

N. **use** a cash register
금전 등록기를 사용하다

O. **wait on** customers
손님 접대하다

P. **work** on a computer
컴퓨터를 사용하다

More vocabulary

act: to perform in a play, movie, or TV show

fly: to pilot an airplane

teach: to instruct, to show how to do something

Share your answers.

1. What job skills do you have? Where did you learn them?

2. What job skills do you want to learn?

A. **talk** to friends
친구들에게 말하다

B. **look** at a job board
직업 게시판을 보다

C. **look** for a help wanted sign
구인 광고 사인을 찾아보다

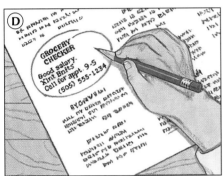

D. **look** in the classifieds
광고란을 보다

E. **call** for information
전화를 걸어 문의하다

F. **ask** about the hours
근무시간을 물어보다

G. **fill out** an application
취업원서를 작성하다

H. **go** on an interview
면담을 하다

I. **talk** about your experience
경험을 말하다

J. **ask** about benefits
복지후생에 대하여 물어보다

K. **inquire** about the salary
급료를 물어보다

L. **get hired**
고용이 되다

1. **desk**
   책상

2. **typewriter**
   타이프라이터

3. **secretary**
   비서

4. **microcassette transcriber**
   마이크로카셋 녹음기

5. **stacking tray**
   스태킹 트레이

6. **desk calendar**
   탁상용 달력

7. **desk pad**
   책상 깔개

8. **calculator**
   계산기

9. **electric pencil sharpener**
   전기 연필깍개

10. **file cabinet**
    서류함

11. **file folder**
    파일 폴더

12. **file clerk**
    사무 보조원

13. **supply cabinet**
    비품 보관함

14. **photocopier**
    복사기

A. **take** a message
   메시지를 받다

B. **fax** a letter
   편지를 팩스로 보내다

C. **transcribe** notes
   메시지를 적다

D. **type** a letter
   편지를 타자치다

E. **make** copies
   복사를 하다

F. **collate** papers
   용지 순서를 맞추다

G. **staple**
   스테이플러로 찍다

H. **file** papers
   서류를 파일에 넣다

Practice taking messages.

Hello. My name is <u>Sara Scott</u>. Is <u>Mr. Lee</u> in?

Not yet. Would you like to leave a message?

Yes. Please ask <u>him</u> to call me at <u>555-4859</u>.

Share your answers.

1. Which office equipment do you know how to use?
2. Which jobs does a file clerk do?
3. Which jobs does a secretary do?

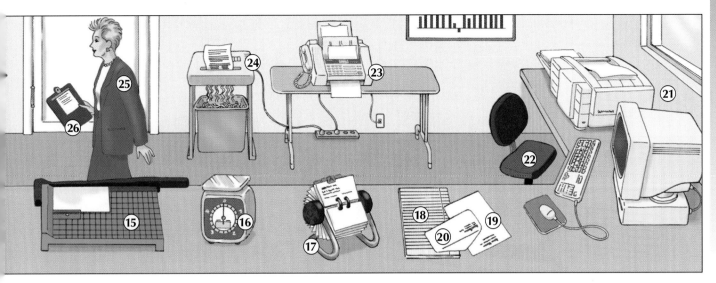

15. paper cutter
종이 재단기

16. postal scale
우편물 저울

17. rotary card file
회전 카드 파일

18. legal pad
리걸 패드

19. letterhead paper
레터헤드 편지지 (회사명이 들어 있는)

20. envelope
봉투

21. computer workstation
컴퓨터 웍스테이션

22. swivel chair
회전의자

23. fax machine
팩스기

24. paper shredder
페이퍼 쉬레더

25. office manager
사무실 매니저

26. clipboard
클립보드

27. appointment book
예약일지

28. stapler
스테이플러

29. staple
스테이플

30. organizer
오거나이저

31. typewriter cartridge
타자기 카트리지

32. mailer
메일러

33. correction fluid
오자 교정액

34. Post-it notes
포스트 잇 노트

35. label
레이블

36. notepad
노트북

37. glue
풀

38. rubber cement
고무풀

39. clear tape
투명 테이프

40. rubber stamp
고무 도장

41. ink pad
잉크 스탬프 패드

42. packing tape
포장 테이프

43. pushpin
압핀

44. paper clip
페이퍼 클립

45. rubber band
고무 밴드

Use the new language.

1. Which items keep things together?

2. Which items are used to mail packages?

3. Which items are made of paper?

Share your answers.

1. Which office supplies do students use?

2. Where can you buy them?

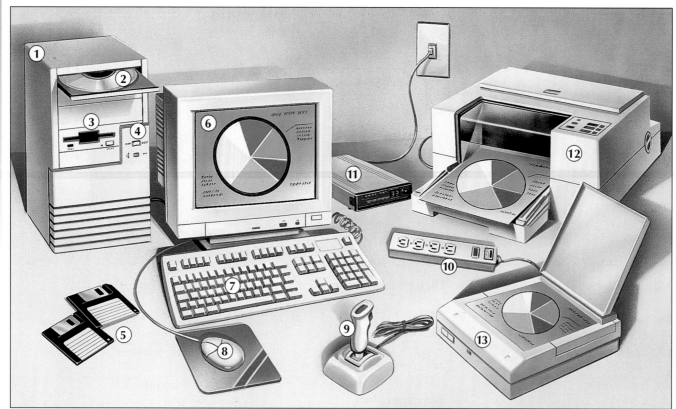

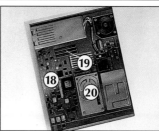

Hardware
하드웨어

1. CPU (central processing unit)
   CPU (중앙 처리 장치)

2. CD-ROM disc
   CD ROM 디스크

3. disk·drive
   디스크 드라이브

4. power switch
   전원 스위치

5. disk/floppy
   플로피 디스크

6. monitor/screen
   모니터 / 화면

7. keyboard
   키보드

8. mouse
   마우스

9. joystick
   조이스틱

10. surge protector
    서지 보호기

11. modem
    모뎀

12. printer
    프린터

13. scanner
    스캐너

14. laptop
    랩톱

15. trackball
    트랙볼

16. cable
    케이블

17. port
    포트

18. motherboard
    본체 기판

19. slot
    슬롯

20. hard disk drive
    하드디스크 드라이브

Software
소프트웨어

21. program/application
    응용 프로그램

22. user's manual
    사용 설명서

More vocabulary

data: information that a computer can read

memory: how much data a computer can hold

speed: how fast a computer can work with data

Share your answers.

1. Can you use a computer?

2. How did you learn? in school? from a book? by yourself?

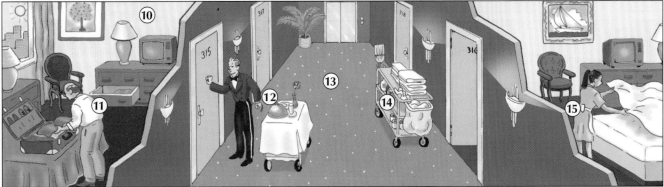

1. valet parking
관리인이 있는 주차장

2. doorman
도어맨

3. lobby
로비

4. bell captain
벨 캡틴

5. bellhop
호텔 도어맨

6. luggage cart
가방 카트

7. gift shop
선물가게

8. front desk
프런트 데스크

9. desk clerk
데스크 직원

10. guest room
객실

11. guest
손님

12. room service
룸 서비스

13. hall
홀

14. housekeeping cart
청소 카트

15. housekeeper
청소부

16. pool
수영장

17. pool service
수영장 서비스

18. ice machine
제빙기

19. meeting room
회의실

20. ballroom
볼룸

More vocabulary

concierge: the hotel worker who helps guests find restaurants and interesting places to go

service elevator: an elevator for hotel workers

Share your answers.

1. Does this look like a hotel in your city? Which one?

2. Which hotel job is the most difficult?

3. How much does it cost to stay in a hotel in your city?

1. front office
   프런트 오피스

2. factory owner
   공장 주인

3. designer
   디자이너

4. time clock
   타임 클록

5. line supervisor
   라인 조장

6. factory worker
   공장 근로자

7. parts
   부품

8. assembly line
   조립 라인

9. warehouse
   창고

10. order puller
    주문 담당자

11. hand truck
    핸드트럭

12. conveyor belt
    컨베이어 벨트

13. packer
    포장하는 사람

14. forklift
    지게차

15. shipping clerk
    출하담당 계원

16. loading dock
    적재 도크

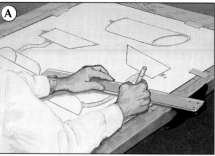

A. design
   디자인하다

B. manufacture
   제조하다

C. ship
   수송하다

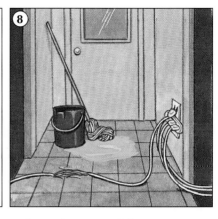

1. electrical hazard
전기 위험

2. flammable
인화물질

3. poison
독성

4. corrosive
부식성

5. biohazard
생물학적 위험

6. radioactive
방사능

7. hazardous materials
위험물질

8. dangerous situation
위험한 상황

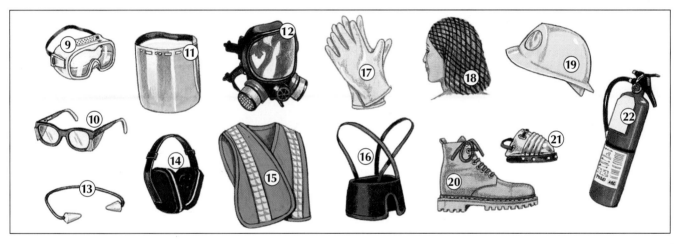

9. safety goggles
보호 안경

10. safety glasses
보호 안경

11. safety visor
안전 마스크

12. respirator
호흡 마스크

13. earplugs
귀마개

14. safety earmuffs
안전 귀가리개

15. safety vest
안전 조끼

16. back support
허리 보호

17. latex gloves
고무 장갑

18. hair net
헤어 네트

19. hard hat
안전모

20. safety boot
안전 장화

21. toe guard
발가락 보호

22. fire extinguisher
소화기

23. careless
부주의한

24. careful
조심스러운

Crops 농작물

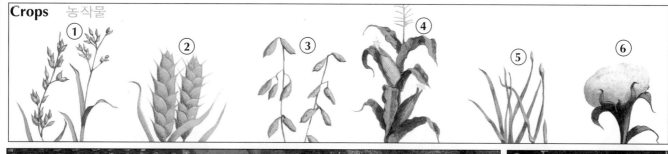

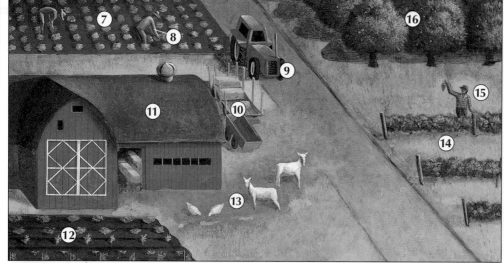

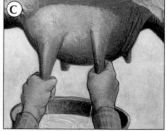

1. rice 쌀	**8.** farmworker 농사꾼	**15.** farmer / grower 농부 / 농산물 재배자	**22.** rancher 목장주
2. wheat 밀	**9.** tractor 트랙터	**16.** orchard 과수원	**A.** **plant** 화초
3. soybeans 콩	**10.** farm equipment 농기구	**17.** corral 가축 우리	**B.** **harvest** 추수
4. corn 옥수수	**11.** barn 헛간	**18.** hay 건초	**C.** **milk** 우유
5. alfalfa 알파파	**12.** vegetable garden 채소밭	**19.** fence 울타리	**D.** **feed** 사료
6. cotton 목화	**13.** livestock 가축	**20.** hired hand 일꾼	
7. field 밭	**14.** vineyard 포도원	**21.** steers / cattle 수송아지	

1. construction worker
건설 작업자

2. ladder
사닥다리

3. I beam / girder
들보 / 대들보

4. scaffolding
발판

5. cherry picker
체리 피커

6. bulldozer
불도저

7. crane
크레인

8. backhoe
백호

9. jackhammer / pneumatic drill
잭해머 / 압축공기 드릴

10. concrete
콘크리트

11. bricks
벽돌

12. trowel
흙손

13. insulation
단열재

14. stucco
치장 벽토

15. window pane
창유리

16. plywood
베니어판

17. wood / lumber
목재

18. drywall
드라이월

19. shingles
지붕널

20. pickax
곡괭이

21. shovel
삽

22. sledgehammer
큰 쇠망치

A. **paint**
페인트칠하다

B. **lay** bricks
벽돌을 쌓다

C. **measure**
측정하다

D. **hammer**
망치질하다

1. hammer
망치

2. mallet
나무메

3. ax
도끼

4. handsaw
핸드소 / 한손잡이 나무 톱

5. hacksaw
핵소 / 궁형 톱 (금속판 절단용)

6. C-clamp
C-클램프

7. pliers
펜치

8. electric drill
전동 드릴

9. power sander
전동 샌더

10. circular saw
원형 톱

11. blade
톱날

12. router
루터

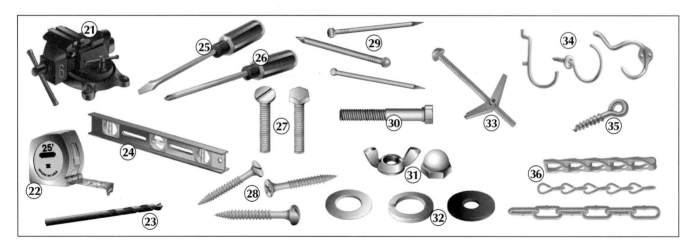

21. vise
바이스

22. tape measure
줄자

23. drill bit
드릴 비트

24. level
수준기

25. screwdriver
드라이버

26. Phillips screwdriver
십자 드라이버

27. machine screw
기계 나사

28. wood screw
나무 나사

29. nail
못

30. bolt
볼트

31. nut
너트

32. washer
와셔

33. toggle bolt
토글 볼트

34. hook
훅

35. eye hook
고리 나사

36. chain
쇠사슬

Use the new language.

1. Which tools are used for plumbing?

2. Which tools are used for painting?

3. Which tools are used for electrical work?

4. Which tools are used for working with wood?

13. wire
전선

14. extension cord
연결 코드

15. yardstick
야드 자

16. pipe
파이프

17. fittings
피팅

18. wood
목재

19. spray gun
스프레이 건

20. paint
페인트

37. wire stripper
와이어 스트리퍼

38. electrical tape
전기 테이프

39. flashlight
플래시라이트

40. battery
배터리

41. outlet
콘센트

42. pipe wrench
파이프 렌치

43. wrench
렌치

44. plunger
플런저

45. paint pan
페인트 팬

46. paint roller
페인트 롤러

47. paintbrush
페인트 브러시

48. scraper
스크레이퍼

49. masking tape
마스킹 테이프

50. sandpaper
샌드페이퍼

51. chisel
끌

52. plane
대패

Use the new language.

Look at **Household Problems and Repairs,**
pages **48–49.**

Name the tools you use to fix the problems you see.

Share your answers.

1. Which tools do you have in your home?

2. Which tools can be dangerous to use?

Places to Go 놀러가는 곳

1. zoo 동물원	**10.** the movies 영화	**19.** county fair 카운티 페어
2. animals 동물	**11.** seat 좌석	**20.** first place/first prize 일등상
3. zookeeper 동물 사육자	**12.** screen 화면	**21.** exhibition 전시회
4. botanical gardens 식물원	**13.** amusement park 유원지	**22.** swap meet/flea market 스왑미트 / 플리마켓 / 중고품시장 / 벼룩시장
5. greenhouse 온실	**14.** puppet show 인형극	**23.** booth 판매대
6. gardener 정원사	**15.** roller coaster 롤러코스터	**24.** merchandise 상품
7. art museum 미술관	**16.** carnival 카니발	**25.** baseball game 야구 게임
8. painting 그림	**17.** rides 탈 것	**26.** stadium 경기장
9. sculpture 조각품	**18.** game 게임	**27.** announcer 아나운서

Talk about the places you like to go.

I like <u>animals</u>, so I go to <u>the zoo</u>.

I like <u>rides</u>, so I go to <u>carnivals</u>.

Share your answers.

1. Which of these places is interesting to you?

2. Which rides do you like at an amusement park?

3. What are some famous places to go to in your country?

1. ball field
공놀이터

2. bike path
자전거 길

3. cyclist
자전거 타는 사람

4. bicycle/bike
자전거(두바퀴)

5. jump rope
줄넘기 줄

6. duck pond
오리 연못

7. tennis court
테니스 코트

8. picnic table
피크닉 테이블

9. tricycle
세발 자전거

10. bench
벤치

11. water fountain
음료수 대

12. swings
그네

13. slide
미끄럼틀

14. climbing apparatus
기어오르는 놀이 기구

15. sandbox
모래 놀이통

16. seesaw
시소

A. **pull** the wagon
웨곤을 잡아당기다

B. **push** the swing
그네를 밀다

C. **climb** on the bars
놀이 틀 위를 기어오르다

D. **picnic/have** a picnic
피크닉/피크닉을 갖다

1. camping
캠핑

2. boating
뱃놀이

3. canoeing
카누 타기

4. rafting
래프팅

5. fishing
낚시

6. hiking
하이킹

7. backpacking
배낭메고 걷기

8. mountain biking
산악 자전거 타기

9. horseback riding
말타기

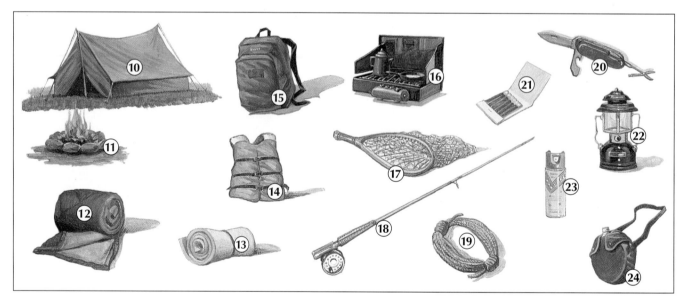

10. tent
텐트

11. campfire
캠프파이어

12. sleeping bag
슬리핑백

13. foam pad
폼 패드

14. life vest
구명 조끼

15. backpack
배낭

16. camping stove
캠핑 스토브

17. fishing net
고기잡이 그물

18. fishing pole
낚싯대

19. rope
로프

20. multi-use knife
다용도 칼

21. matches
성냥

22. lantern
등불

23. insect repellent
방충제

24. canteen
수통

1. ocean/water
대양 / 물

2. fins
핀

3. diving mask
다이빙 마스크

4. sailboat
요트

5. surfboard
서프보드

6. wave
파도

7. wet suit
잠수복

8. scuba tank
스쿠버 탱크

9. beach umbrella
비치 파라솔

10. sand castle
모래성

11. cooler
아이스 박스

12. shade
그늘

13. sunscreen/sunblock
선스크린 / 선블록

14. beach chair
해변용 의자

15. beach towel
비치 타월

16. pier
부두

17. sunbather
일광욕하는 사람

18. lifeguard
구조대원

19. lifesaving device
인명구조 기구

20. lifeguard station
구조대원실

21. seashell
조개

22. pail/bucket
버킷

23. sand
모래

24. rock
바위

More vocabulary

seaweed: a plant that grows in the ocean

tide: the level of the ocean. The tide goes in and out every twelve hours.

Share your answers.

1. Are there any beaches near your home?

2. Do you prefer to spend more time on the sand or in the water?

3. Where are some of the world's best beaches?

A. walk
걷다

B. jog
조깅하다

C. run
뛰다

D. throw
던지다

E. catch
받다

F. pitch
던지다

G. hit
치다

H. pass
패스하다

I. shoot
슈트하다

J. jump
점프하다

K. dribble / bounce
드리블하다 / 바운드
시키다

L. kick
차다

M. tackle
태클하다

Practice talking about what you can do.

I can <u>swim</u>, but I can't <u>dive</u>.

I can <u>pass the ball</u> well, but I can't <u>shoot</u> too well.

Use the new language.

Look at **Individual Sports,** page **159.**

Name the actions you see people doing.

The man in number 18 is riding a horse.

N. serve
서브하다

O. swing
스윙하다

P. exercise / work out
운동하다

Q. stretch
스트레치하다

R. bend
구부리다

S. dive
다이빙하다

T. swim
수영하다

U. ski
스키를 타다

V. skate
스케이트 타다

W. ride
타다

X. start
출발하다

Y. race
경주하다

Z. finish
결승점에 닿다

Share your answers.

1. What do you like to do?

2. What do you have difficulty doing?

3. How often do you exercise? Once a week? Two or three times a week? More? Never?

4. Which is more difficult, throwing a ball or catching it?

1. score
   점수 / 득점
2. coach
   코치
3. team
   팀
4. fan
   팬
5. player
   선수
6. official / referee
   심판 / 레프리
7. basketball court
   농구 코트

8. basketball
   농구
9. baseball
   야구
10. softball
    소프트볼
11. football
    미식 축구
12. soccer
    축구
13. ice hockey
    아이스 하키
14. volleyball
    배구
15. water polo
    수구

More vocabulary

captain: the team leader

umpire: in baseball, the name for referee

Little League: a baseball league for children

win: to have the best score

lose: the opposite of win

tie: to have the same score as the other team

1. archery
   양궁

2. billiards / pool
   당구 / 포켓볼

3. bowling
   볼링

4. cycling / biking
   사이클링

5. fencing
   펜싱

6. flying disc*
   프리즈비

7. golf
   골프

8. gymnastics
   체조

9. inline skating
   롤러 스케이팅

10. martial arts
    무술

11. racquetball
    라켓볼

12. skateboarding
    스케이트보딩

13. table tennis /
    Ping-Pong™
    탁구

14. tennis
    테니스

15. weightlifting
    역도

16. wrestling
    레슬링

17. track and field
    육상 경기

18. horse racing
    경마

*Note: one brand is Frisbee®
(Mattel, Inc.)

Talk about sports.

Which sports do you like?

I like <u>tennis</u> but I don't like <u>golf</u>.

Share your answers.

1. Which sports are good for children to learn? Why?
2. Which sport is the most difficult to learn? Why?
3. Which sport is the most dangerous? Why?

1. downhill skiing
활강 스킹

2. snowboarding
스노보딩

3. cross-country skiing
크로스컨트리 스킹

4. ice skating
아이스 스케이팅

5. figure skating
피겨 스케이팅

6. sledding
썰매타기

7. waterskiing
수상스키

8. sailing
요트 경기

9. surfing
서핑

10. sailboarding
세일보딩

11. snorkeling
스노클링

12. scuba diving
스쿠버 다이빙

Use the new language.

Look at **The Beach**, page 155.

Name the sports you see.

Share your answers.

1. Which sports are in the Winter Olympics?

2. Which sports do you think are the most exciting
to watch?

1. golf club 골프 채	**8.** target 과녁	**15.** catcher's mask 캐처 마스크	**22.** football 미식축구 공
2. tennis racket 테니스 라켓	**9.** ice skates 아이스 스케이트	**16.** uniform 유니폼	**23.** snowboard 스노보드
3. volleyball 배구공	**10.** inline skates 롤러 스케이트	**17.** glove 글러브	**24.** skis 스키
4. basketball 농구공	**11.** hockey stick 하키 스틱	**18.** baseball 야구공	**25.** ski poles 스키 폴
5. bowling ball 볼링 볼	**12.** soccer ball 축구공	**19.** weights 역기	**26.** ski boots 스키화
6. bow 활	**13.** shin guards 무릎 가드	**20.** football helmet 축구 헬멧	**27.** flying disc* 프리즈비
7. arrow 화살	**14.** baseball bat 야구 방망이	**21.** shoulder pads 어깨 패드	

***Note:** one brand is Frisbee®
(Mattel, Inc.)

Share your answers.

1. Which sports equipment is used for safety reasons?

2. Which sports equipment is heavy?

3. What sports equipment do you have at home?

Use the new language.

Look at **Individual Sports**, page **159**.

Name the sports equipment you see.

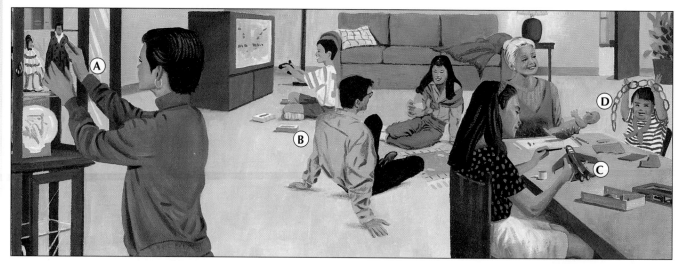

A. collect things
물건을 수집하다

B. play games
게임을 하다

C. build models
모형을 만들다

D. do crafts
공예를 하다

1. video game system
   비디오 게임

2. cartridge
   카트리지

3. board game
   보드게임

4. dice
   주사위

5. checkers
   체커스

6. chess
   체스 / 서양 장기

7. model kit
   모형 키트

8. glue
   풀

9. acrylic paint
   아크릴 페인트

10. figurine
    작은 입상

11. baseball card
    야구 카드

12. stamp collection
    우표 수집

13. coin collection
    동전 수집

14. clay
    점토

15. doll making kit
    인형 만드는 키트

16. woodworking kit
    목공 키트

Talk about how much time you spend on your hobbies.

I _do crafts_ all the time.

I _play chess_ sometimes.

I never _build models_.

Share your answers.

1. How often do you play video games? Often? Sometimes? Never?

2. What board games do you know?

3. Do you collect anything? What?

E. paint 그림 그리다	**F. knit** 짜다	**G. pretend** 흉내놀이를 하다	**H. play** cards 카드놀이를 하다

17. yarn
뜨개실

18. knitting needles
뜨개 바늘

19. embroidery
자수

20. crochet
크로셰

21. easel
이젤

22. canvas
캔버스

23. paintbrush
그림 붓

24. oil paint
유화

25. watercolor
수채화 물감

26. clubs
클럽

27. diamonds
다이아몬드

28. spades
스페이드

29. hearts
하트

30. paper doll
종이 인형

31. action figure
액션 인물

32. model trains
모델 기차

Share your answers.

1. Do you like to play cards? Which games?

2. Did you pretend a lot when you were a child? What did you pretend to be?

3. Is it important to have hobbies? Why or why not?

4. What's your favorite game?

5. What's your hobby?

1. clock radio
   시계 라디오

2. portable radio-cassette player
   휴대용 라디오 / 카세트 플레이어

3. cassette recorder
   카세트 녹음기

4. microphone
   마이크

5. shortwave radio
   단파 라디오

6. TV (television)
   텔레비전

7. portable TV
   휴대용 TV

8. VCR (videocassette recorder)
   VCR / 비디오 카세트 레코더

9. remote control
   리모콘

10. videocassette
    비디오 카세트

11. speakers
    스피커

12. turntable
    턴테이블

13. tuner
    튜너

14. CD player
    CD 플레이어

15. personal radio-cassette player
    소형 라디오 / 카세트 플레이어

16. headphones
    헤드폰

17. adapter
    어댑터

18. plug
    플러그

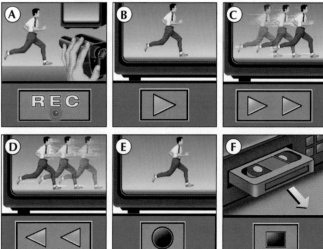

19. video camera 비디오 카메라	**27.** camera case 카메라 케이스	**35.** underexposed 노출 부족
20. tripod 삼발이	**28.** screen 스크린	**A.** **record** 녹음하다
21. camcorder 캠코더	**29.** carousel slide projector 캐로셀 슬라이드 프로젝터	**B.** **play** 재생하다
22. battery pack 배터리 팩	**30.** slide tray 슬라이드 트레이	**C.** **fast forward** 고속 앞으로
23. battery charger 배터리 충전기	**31.** slides 슬라이드	**D.** **rewind** 되감기
24. 35 mm camera 35mm 카메라	**32.** photo album 사진 앨범	**E.** **pause** 중단
25. zoom lens 줌 렌즈	**33.** out of focus 초점이 안맞다	**F.** **stop** and **eject** 정지 및 방출
26. film 필름	**34.** overexposed 노출 초과	

Entertainment 엔터테인먼트

Types of entertainment 엔터테인먼트의 종류

1. film/movie
영화

2. play
연극

3. television program
텔레비전 프로그램

4. radio program
라디오 프로그램

5. stand-up comedy
스탠드업 코메디

6. concert
콘서트

7. ballet
발레

8. opera
오페라

Types of stories 스토리 종류

9. western
서부영화

10. comedy
코메디

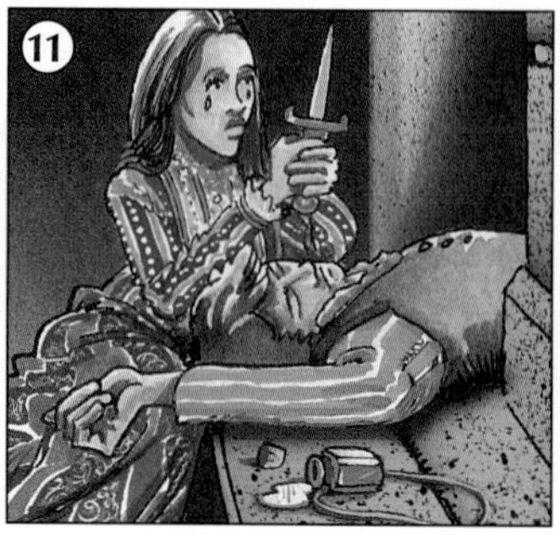

11. tragedy
비극

12. science fiction story
공상과학

13. action story/
adventure story
액션 / 모험

14. horror story
공포

15. mystery
추리

16. romance
로맨스

Types of TV programs   TV 프로그램 종류

17. news
뉴스

18. sitcom (situation comedy)
연속 코메디

19. cartoon
만화

20. talk show
토크 쇼

21. soap opera
멜로 드라마

22. nature program
자연 프로그램

23. game show/quiz show
게임 쇼 / 퀴즈 쇼

24. children's program
어린이 프로그램

25. shopping program
쇼핑 프로그램

26. serious book
심각한 책

27. funny book
재미있는 책

28. sad book
슬픈 책

29. boring book
지루한 책

30. interesting book
흥미있는 책

1. New Year's Day
정월 초하루

2. parade
퍼레이드

3. confetti
색종이 조각

4. Valentine's Day
밸런타인스 데이

5. card
카드

6. heart
하트

7. Independence Day / 4th of July
독립기념일 / 7월 4일

8. fireworks
불꽃 놀이

9. flag
국기

10. Halloween
할로윈

11. jack-o'-lantern
잭-오-랜턴

12. mask
가면

13. costume
가면 복장

14. candy
캔디

15. Thanksgiving
추수감사절

16. feast
잔치

17. turkey
칠면조

18. Christmas
크리스마스

19. ornament
장식

20. Christmas tree
크리스마스 트리

A. plan a party
파티를 계획하다

B. invite the guests
손님들을 초대하다

C. decorate the house
집을 치장하다

D. wrap a gift
선물을 싸다

E. hide
감춰놓다

F. answer the door
문을 열다

G. shout "surprise!"
"서프라이즈"하고 고함치다

H. light the candles
촛불을 켜다

I. sing "Happy Birthday"
"생일 축하합니다" 노래를 부르다

J. make a wish
소원을 말하다 (속으로)

K. blow out the candles
촛불을 불어 끄다

L. open the presents
선물을 뜯어보다

Practice inviting friends to a party.

I'd love for you to come to my party <u>next week</u>.

Could <u>you and your friend</u> come to my party?

Would <u>your friend</u> like to come to a party I'm giving?

Share your answers.

1. Do you celebrate birthdays? What do you do?

2. Are there birthdays you celebrate in a special way?

3. Is there a special birthday song in your country?

Verb Guide

Verbs in English are either regular or irregular in the past tense and past participle forms.

Regular Verbs

The regular verbs below are marked 1, 2, 3, or 4 according to four different spelling patterns. (See page 172 for the **irregular verbs** which do not follow any of these patterns.)

Spelling Patterns for the Past and the Past Participle		*Example*		
1. Add **-ed** to the end of the verb.		**ASK**	→	**ASKED**
2. Add **-d** to the end of the verb.		**LIVE**	→	**LIVED**
3. Double the final consonant and add **-ed** to the end of the verb.		**DROP**	→	**DROPPED**
4. Drop the final y and add **-ied** to the end of the verb.		**CRY**	→	**CRIED**

The Oxford Picture Dictionary List of Regular Verbs

act (1)
add (1)
address (1)
answer (1)
apologize (2)
appear (1)
applaud (1)
arrange (2)
arrest (1)
arrive (2)
ask (1)
assemble (2)
assist (1)
bake (2)
barbecue (2)
bathe (2)
board (1)
boil (1)
borrow (1)
bounce (2)
brainstorm (1)
breathe (2)
broil (1)
brush (1)
burn (1)
call (1)
carry (4)
change (2)
check (1)
choke (2)
chop (3)
circle (2)
claim (1)
clap (3)
clean (1)
clear (1)
climb (1)
close (2)
collate (2)

collect (1)
color (1)
comb (1)
commit (3)
compliment (1)
conserve (2)
convert (1)
cook (1)
copy (4)
correct (1)
cough (1)
count (1)
cross (1)
cry (4)
dance (2)
design (1)
deposit (1)
deliver (1)
dial (1)
dictate (2)
die (2)
discuss (1)
dive (2)
dress (1)
dribble (2)
drill (1)
drop (3)
drown (1)
dry (4)
dust (1)
dye (2)
edit (1)
eject (1)
empty (4)
end (1)
enter (1)
erase (2)
examine (2)
exchange (2)

exercise (2)
experience (2)
exterminate (2)
fasten (1)
fax (1)
file (2)
fill (1)
finish (1)
fix (1)
floss (1)
fold (1)
fry (4)
gargle (2)
graduate (2)
grate (2)
grease (2)
greet (1)
grill (1)
hail (1)
hammer (1)
harvest (1)
help (1)
hire (2)
hug (3)
immigrate (2)
inquire (2)
insert (1)
introduce (2)
invite (2)
iron (1)
jog (3)
join (1)
jump (1)
kick (1)
kiss (1)
knit (3)
land (1)
laugh (1)
learn (1)

lengthen (1)
listen (1)
live (2)
load (1)
lock (1)
look (1)
mail (1)
manufacture (2)
mark (1)
match (1)
measure (2)
milk (1)
miss (1)
mix (1)
mop (3)
move (2)
mow (1)
need (1)
nurse (2)
obey (1)
observe (2)
open (1)
operate (2)
order (1)
overdose (2)
paint (1)
park (1)
pass (1)
pause (2)
peel (1)
perm (1)
pick (1)
pitch (1)
plan (3)
plant (1)
play (1)
point (1)
polish (1)
pour (1)
pretend (1)
print (1)
protect (1)

pull (1)
push (1)
race (2)
raise (2)
rake (2)
receive (2)
record (1)
recycle (2)
register (1)
relax (1)
remove (2)
rent (1)
repair (1)
repeat (1)
report (1)
request (1)
return (1)
rinse (2)
roast (1)
rock (1)
sauté (2)
save (2)
scrub (3)
seat (1)
sentence (2)
serve (2)
share (2)
shave (2)
ship (3)
shop (3)
shorten (1)
shout (1)
sign (1)
simmer (1)
skate (2)
ski (1)
slice (2)
smell (1)
sneeze (2)
sort (1)
spell (1)
staple (2)

start (1)
stay (1)
steam (1)
stir (3)
stir-fry (4)
stop (3)
stow (1)
stretch (1)
supervise (2)
swallow (1)
tackle (2)
talk (1)
taste (2)
thank (1)
tie (2)
touch (1)
transcribe (2)
transfer (3)
travel (1)
trim (3)
turn (1)
type (2)
underline (2)
unload (1)
unpack (1)
use (2)
vacuum (1)
vomit (1)
vote (2)
wait (1)
walk (1)
wash (1)
watch (1)
water (1)
weed (1)
weigh (1)
wipe (2)
work (1)
wrap (3)
yield (1)

Verb Guide

Irregular Verbs

These verbs have irregular endings in the past and/or the past participle.

The Oxford Picture Dictionary List of Irregular Verbs

simple	past	past participle	simple	past	past participle
be	was	been	leave	left	left
beat	beat	beaten	lend	lent	lent
become	became	become	let	let	let
begin	began	begun	light	lit	lit
bend	bent	bent	make	made	made
bleed	bled	bled	pay	paid	paid
blow	blew	blown	picnic	picnicked	picnicked
break	broke	broken	put	put	put
build	built	built	read	read	read
buy	bought	bought	rewind	rewound	rewound
catch	caught	caught	rewrite	rewrote	rewritten
come	came	come	ride	rode	ridden
cut	cut	cut	run	ran	run
do	did	done	say	said	said
draw	drew	drawn	see	saw	seen
drink	drank	drunk	sell	sold	sold
drive	drove	driven	send	sent	sent
eat	ate	eaten	set	set	set
fall	fell	fallen	sew	sewed	sewn
feed	fed	fed	shoot	shot	shot
feel	felt	felt	sing	sang	sung
find	found	found	sit	sat	sat
fly	flew	flown	speak	spoke	spoken
get	got	gotten	stand	stood	stood
give	gave	given	sweep	swept	swept
go	went	gone	swim	swam	swum
hang	hung	hung	swing	swung	swung
have	had	had	take	took	taken
hear	heard	heard	teach	taught	taught
hide	hid	hidden	throw	threw	thrown
hit	hit	hit	wake	woke	woken
hold	held	held	wear	wore	worn
keep	kept	kept	withdraw	withdrew	withdrawn
lay	laid	laid	write	wrote	written

Index

Two numbers are shown after words in the index: the first refers to the page where the word is illustrated and the second refers to the item number of the word on that page. For example, cool [kōol] **10**-3 means that the word *cool* is item number 3 on page 10. If only the bold page number appears, then that word is part of the unit title or subtitle, or is found somewhere else on the page. A bold number followed by ✦ means the word can be found in the exercise space at the bottom of that page.

Words or combinations of words that appear in **bold** type are used as verbs or verb phrases. Words used as other parts of speech are shown in ordinary type. So, for example, **file** (in bold type) is the verb *file*, while file (in ordinary type) is the noun *file*. Words or phrases in small capital letters (for example, HOLIDAYS) form unit titles.

Phrases and other words that form combinations with an individual word entry are often listed underneath it. Rather than repeating the word each time it occurs in combination with what is listed under it, the word is replaced by three dots (...), called an ellipsis. For example, under the word *bus*, you will find ...driver and ...stop meaning *bus driver* and *bus stop*. Under the word *store* you will find shoe... and toy..., meaning *shoe store* and *toy store*.

Pronunciation Guide

The index includes a pronunciation guide for all the words and phrases illustrated in the book. This guide uses symbols commonly found in dictionaries for native speakers. These symbols, unlike those used in pronunciation systems such as the International Phonetic Alphabet, tend to use English spelling patterns and so should help you to become more aware of the connections between written English and spoken English.

Consonants

[b] as in back [băk]

[ch] as in cheek [chēk]

[d] as in date [dāt]

[dh] as in this [dhĭs]

[f] as in face [fās]

[g] as in gas [găs]

[h] as in half [hăf]

[j] as in jam [jăm]

[k] as in key [kē]

[l] as in leaf [lēf]

[m] as in match [măch]

[n] as in neck [něk]

[ng] as in ring [rĭng]

[p] as in park [pärk]

[r] as in rice [rīs]

[s] as in sand [sănd]

[sh] as in shoe [shōo]

[t] as in tape [tāp]

[th] as in three [thrē]

[v] as in vine [vīn]

[w] as in wait [wāt]

[y] as in yams [yămz]

[z] as in zoo [zōo]

[zh] as in measure [mĕzh/ər]

Vowels

[ā] as in bake [bāk]

[ă] as in back [băk]

[ä] as in car [kär] or box [bäks]

[ē] as in beat [bēt]

[ĕ] as in bed [bĕd]

[ë] as in bear [bër]

[ī] as in line [līn]

[ĭ] as in lip [lĭp]

[ï] as in near [nïr]

[ō] as in cold [kōld]

[ö] as in short [shört]

 or claw [klö]

[ōo] as in cool [kōol]

[ŏo] as in cook [kŏok]

[ow] as in cow [kow]

[oy] as in boy [boy]

[ŭ] as in cut [kŭt]

[ü] as in curb [kürb]

[ə] as in above [ə bŭv/]

All the pronunciation symbols used are alphabetical except for the schwa [ə]. The schwa is the most frequent vowel sound in English. If you use the schwa appropriately in unstressed syllables, your pronunciation will sound more natural.

Vowels before [r] are shown with the symbol [¨] to call attention to the special quality that vowels have before [r]. (Note that the symbols [ä] and [ö] are also used for vowels not followed by [r], as in *box* or *claw*.) You should listen carefully to native speakers to discover how these vowels actually sound.

Stress

This index follows the system for marking stress used in many dictionaries for native speakers.

1. Stress is not marked if a word consisting of a single syllable occurs by itself.

2. Where stress is marked, two levels are distinguished:

a bold accent [/] is placed after each syllable with primary (or strong) stress, a light accent [/] is placed after each syllable with secondary (or weaker) stress.

In phrases and other combinations of words, stress is indicated for each word as it would be pronounced within the whole phrase or other unit. If a word consisting of a single syllable is stressed in the combinations listed below it, the accent mark indicating the degree of stress it has in the phrases (primary or secondary) is shown in parentheses. A hyphen replaces any part of a word or phrase that is omitted. For example, bus [bŭs(/–)] shows that the word *bus* is said with primary stress in the combinations shown below it. The word ...driver [–drī/vər], listed under *bus*, shows that *driver* has secondary stress in the combination *bus driver*: [bŭs/ drī/vər].

Syllable Boundaries

Syllable boundaries are indicated by a single space or by a stress mark.

Note: The pronunciations shown in this index are based on patterns of American English. There has been no attempt to represent all of the varieties of American English. Students should listen to native speakers to hear how the language actually sounds in a particular region.

Index

abdomen [ăb/də mən] **74**–3
above [ə bŭv/] **13**–6
accelerator [ĭk sĕl/ə rā/tər] **109**–47
ACCESSORIES [ĭk sĕs/ə rēz] **68–69**
accident [ăk/sə dənt] **102**–2
accordion [ə kör/dē ən] **120**–21
accountant [ə kown/tnt] **136**–1
acid rain [ăs/əd rān/] **126**–11
across [ə krös/] **105**–3
acrylic paint [ə krĭl/ĭk pānt/] **162**–9
act [ăkt] **140** ✦
action [ăk/shən]
   ...figure [–fĭg/yər] **163**–31
   ...story [–stör/ē] **166**–13
actor [ăk/tər] **136**–2
acupuncture [ăk/yə pŭngk/chər] **81**–G
adapter [ə dăp/tər] **164**–17
add [ăd] **58**–Q, **72**–B
addition [ə dĭsh/ən] **118**–1
address [ə drĕs/] **96**–A
address [ə drĕs, ă/drĕs] **4**–5, **96**–7,8
adhesive bandage [əd hē/sĭv băn/dĭj] **83**–3
administrative assistant [əd mĭn/ə strā/tĭv ə sĭs/tənt] **136**–3
administrator [əd mĭn/ə strā/tər] **5** ✦
adults [ə dŭlts/, ăd/ŭlts] **22**–9
adult school [ə dŭlt/ skōōl/, ăd/ŭlt–] **112**–8
adventure story [əd vĕn/chər stör/ē] **166**–13
aerogramme [ĕr/ə grăm/] **96**–13
afternoon [ăf/tər nōōn/] **17**–18
aftershave [ăf/tər shāv/] **77**–28
AGE AND PHYSICAL DESCRIPTION [āj/ ən fĭz/ĭ kəl dĭ skrĭp/shən] **22**
AIDS (acquired immunodeficiency syndrome) [ādz] **79** ✦
air [ĕr(/–)] **109**–59
   ...bag [–băg/] **108**–16
   ...conditioner [–kən dĭsh/ə nər] **37**–19
   ...conditioning [–kən dĭsh/ə nĭng] **108**–28
   ...letter [–lĕt/ər] **96**–13
   ...pollution [–pə lōō/shən] **126**–10
   ...purifier [–pyōōr/ə fī ər] **80**–4
airline [ĕr/līn/]
   ...representative [–rĕp rĭ zĕn/tə tĭv] **110**–2
   ...terminal [–tür/mə nəl] **110**–1
airplane [ĕr/plān/] **110**–9
   ...crash [–krăsh/] **102**–3
AIRPORT [ĕr/pört/] **110**
airsickness bag [ĕr/sĭk/nəs băg/] **110**–15
aisle [īl] **54**–5
Alaska time [ə lăs/kə tīm/] **17**–25
alfalfa [ăl făl/fə] **148**–5
algebra [ăl/jə brə] **118**–25
allergies [ăl/ər jēz] **79**–8
alley [ăl/ē] **37**–21
alligator [ăl/ə gā/tər] **131**–36
alphabet [ăl/fə bĕt/] **3**–30
ALTERATIONS [öl/tə rā/shənz] **73**
aluminum foil [ə lōō/mə nəm foyl/] **55**–55
a.m. [ā/ĕm/] **16** ✦
American cheese [ə mĕr/ə kən chēz/] **53**–9
AMPHIBIANS [ăm fĭb/ē ənz] **130–131**
amusement park [ə myōōz/mənt pärk/] **152**–13
anesthesiologist [ăn/əs thē/zē ăl/ə jĭst] **87**–35
angle [ăng/gəl] **118**–24
angry [ăng/grē] **31**–29
animals [ăn/ə məlz] **152**–2
ANIMALS, DOMESTIC [də mĕs/tĭk ăn/ə məlz] **133**

ankle [ăng/kəl] **75**–61, **78**–18
anniversary [ăn/ə vür/sə rē] **19**–42
announcer [ə nown/sər] **152**–27
answer [ăn/sər]
   ...a question [–ə kwĕs/chən] **6**–H
   ...the door [–dhə dör/] **169**–F
answering machine [ăn/sə rĭng mə shēn/] **9**–14
answer sheet [ăn/sər shēt/] **7**–T
antacid [ănt ăs/əd] **81**–18
anteater [ănt/ē/tər] **135**–24
antelope [ăn/tə lōp/] **135**–35
antibacterial ointment [ăn/tē băk tîr/ē əl oynt/mənt] **83**–9
antihistamine cream [ăn/tĭ hĭs/tə mēn krēm/] **83**–10
antler [ănt/lər] **134**–16
ants [ănts] **49**–24
apartment [ə pärt/mənt]
   ...building [–bĭl/dĭng] **34**–5
   ...number [–nŭm/bər] **4**–6
APARTMENTS [ə pärt/mənts] **36–37**
apologize [ə päl/ə jīz/] **8**–I
apostrophe [ə päs/trə fē] **113**–11
appear in court [ə pîr/ ĭn kört/] **99**–C
applaud [ə plöd/] **32**–B
apple juice [ăp/əl jōōs/] **55**–50, **57**–5
apples [ăp/əlz] **50**–4
application [ăp/lə kā/shən] **144**–21
appointment [ə poynt/mənt] **19**–45, **85**
   ...book [–bōōk/] **143**–27
apricots [ăp/rə kăts/] **50**–7
April [ā/prəl] **19**–28
archery [är/chə rē] **159**–1
architect [är/kə tĕkt/] **136**–4
area [ĕr/ē ə] **34**–(1, 4)
area code [ĕr/ē ə kōd/] **4**–10
arm [ärm] **74**–9
armadillo [är/mə dĭl/ō] **134**–8
armchair [ärm/chër/] **42**–24
around [ə rownd/] **105**–10
arrange [ə rānj/] **35**–K
arrest [ə rĕst/] **99**–A
arrival and departure monitors [ə rī/vəl ən dĭ pär/chər män/ə tərz] **110**–4
arrival time [ə rī/vəl tīm/] **111** ✦
arrive [ə rīv/] **111**–O
arrow [ăr/ō] **161**–7
art [ärt] **121**–1
artery [är/tə rē] **75**–43
artichokes [är/tə chōks/] **51**–20
artist [är/tĭst] **136**–5
art museum [ärt/ myōō zē/əm] **152**–7
ask [ăsk(/–)]
   ...about benefits [–ə bowt/ bĕn/ə fĭts] **141**–J
   ...about the hours [–ə bowt/ dhē ow/ərz] **141**–F
   ...a question [–ə kwĕs/chən] **6**–G
asparagus [ə spăr/ə gəs] **51**–24
assault [ə sölt/] **100**–7
assemble [ə sĕm/bəl] **140**–A
assembler [ə sĕm/blər] **136**–6
assembly line [ə sĕm/blē līn/] **146**–8
assist [ə sĭst/] **140**–B
Associate of Arts (AA) [ə sō/shē ĭt əv ärts/, –sē ĭt–] / [ā/ā/] **112** ✦
asteroid belt [ăs/tə royd bĕlt/] **127**–12
asthma [ăz/mə] **79**–11
astronaut [ăs/trə nöt/] **127**–17
astronomer [ə strän/ə mər] **127**–20

athletic [ăth lĕt/ĭk]
...shoes [–sho͞oz/] **68**–23
...supporter [–sə pör/tər] **67**–14
Atlantic time [ət lăn/tĭk tīm/] **17**–30
atlas [ăt/ləs] **98**–3
ATM (automated teller machine) [ā/tē/ĕm/] **97**–3
ATM card [ā/tē/ĕm/ kärd/] **97**–9
atom [ăt/əm] **119**–17
attorney [ə tür/nē] **99**–4
attractive [ə trăk/tĭv] **22**–23
audience [ö/dē əns] **32**–10
audiocassette [ö/dē ō kə sĕt/] **98**–12
audiologist [ö/dē äl/ə jĭst] **81**–32
auditorium [ö/də tör/ē əm] **5**–3
August [ö/gəst] **19**–32
aunt [ănt] **24**–10
author [ö/thər] **98**–22, **139**–64
automatic transmission
    [ö/tə măt/ĭk trănz mĭsh/ən, –trăns–] **109**
auto mechanic [ö/tō mə kăn/ĭk] **136**–7
average [ăv/rĭj]
    ...height [–hīt/] **22**–17
    ...weight [–wāt/] **22**–21
avocadoes [ä/və kä/dōz, ăv/ə–] **50**–14
ax [ăks] **150**–3
baboon [bă bo͞on/] **135**–32
baby [bā/bē] **22**–2
    ...backpack [–băk/păk/] **95**–15
    ...carrier [–kăr/ē ər] **95**–14
    ...food [–fo͞od/] **95**–28
    ...monitor [–măn/ə tər] **45**–9
    ...powder [–pow/dər] **95**–18
baby-sitter [bā/bē sĭt/ər] **136**–12
Bachelor's degree [băch/lərz də grē/] **112** ✦
back [băk(/–)] **74**–11
    ...support [–sə pört/] **147**–16
backache [băk/āk/] **78**–5
backhoe [băk/hō/] **149**–8
backpack [băk/păk/] **69**–28, **95**–15, **154**–15
backpacking [băk/păk/ĭng] **154**–7
backseat [băk/sēt/] **109**–38
backyard [băk/yärd/] **38**–2
bacon [bā/kən] **52**–11, **61**–7
bad [băd] **11**–18
bag [băg] (market) **55**–22, 23, **56**–7, 19 (purse) **69**–27, 28, 29
baggage claim area [băg/ĭj klām/ ër/ē ə] **110**–17
bagger [băg/ər] **55**–21
baggy [băg/ē] **71**–42
bag of flour [băg/ əv flow/ər] **56**–19
bags (luggage) [băgz] **111**–B
bailiff [bā/ləf] **99**–13
bake [bāk] **58**–L
baked [bākt(/–)]
    ...goods [–go͞odz/] **54**–6
    ...potato [–pə tā/tō] **61**–14
baker [bā/kər] **136**–8
bakery [bā/kə rē] **89**–16
baking products [bā/kĭng prăd/ŭkts] **55**–13
balance [băl/əns] (bank) **97**–11, (science) **119**–11
balcony [băl/kə nē] **37**–17
bald [böld] **23**–12
ball [böl] **45**–16, **161**–3, 4, 5, 12, 18, 22
ballet [bă lā/] **166**–7
ball field [böl/ fēld/] **153**–1
ballroom [böl/ro͞om/] **145**–20

bananas [bə năn/əz] **50**–3
bandage [băn/dĭj] **83**–3, 12
bangs [băngz] **23**–8
BANK [băngk] **97**
bank [băngk] **88**–3
banner [băn/ər] **33**–15
barbecue [bär/bĭ kyo͞o/] **58**–T
barbecue grill [bär/bĭ kyo͞o grĭl/] **39**–7
barber shop [bär/bər shäp/] **88**–15
bar code [bär/ kōd/] **21**–4
barn [bärn] **148**–11
barrette [bə rĕt/] **76**–18
baseball [bās/böl/] **158**–9, **161**–18
    ...bat [–băt/] **161**–14
    ...cap [–kăp/] **66**–27
    ...card [–kärd/] **162**–11
    ...game [–gām/] **152**–25
basement [bās/mənt] **36** ✦
basket [băs/kət] **42**–2
basketball [băs/kət böl/] **158**–8, **161**–4
    ...court [–kört/] **158**–7
bass (fish) [băs] **130**–11
bass (instrument) [bās] **120**–10
bassoon [bə so͞on/] **120**–6
bat [băt] (animal) **134**–7, (baseball) **161**–14
bath [băth(/–)]
    ...mat [–măt/] **43**–27
    ...powder [–pow/dər] **76**–3
    ...towel [–tow/əl] **43**–12
bathe [bādh] **76**–B
bathing suit [bā/dhĭng so͞ot/] **66**–26
bathrobe [băth/rōb/] **67**–8
BATHROOM [băth/ro͞om/] **43**
bathtub [băth/tŭb/] **43**–2
battery [băt/ə rē] (car) **109**–43, (flashlight) **151**–40
    ...charger [–chär/jər] **165**–23
    ...pack [–păk/] **165**–22
bay [bā] **117**–9
be [bē]
    ...18 years old [–ā/tēn/ yïrz/ öld/] **116**–A
    ...**born** [–börn/] **28**–A
    ...**hurt** [–hürt/] **82**–A
    ...**injured** [–ĭn/jərd] **82**–A
    ...in school [–ĭn sko͞ol/] **26**–J
    ...in shock [–ĭn shäk/] **82**–C
    ...released [–rī lēst/] **99**–H
    ...unconscious [–ŭn kän/shəs] **82**–B
BEACH [bēch] **155**
beach [bēch(/–)] **117**–10
    ...chair [–chër/] **155**–14
    ...towel [–tow/əl] **155**–15
    ...umbrella [–ŭm brĕl/ə] **155**–9
beads [bēdz] **69**–32
beak [bēk] **132**–1
beaker [bē/kər] **119**–13
beam [bēm] **149**–3
beans [bēnz] **51**–25, **54**–26
bear [bër] **134**–11
beard [bïrd] **23**–6
beat [bēt] **58**–B
beautiful [byo͞o/tə fəl] **11**–21
beauty shop [byo͞o/tē shäp/] **92** ✦
beaver [bē/vər] **134**–9
become a citizen [bĭ kŭm/ ə sĭt/ə zən] **28**–H
bed [bĕd(/–)] **44**–8

...control [–kən trōl/] **86**–12
...frame [–frām/] **44**–27
...table [–tā/bəl] **86**–9
bedpan [bĕd/păn/] **86**–13
BEDROOM [bĕd/rōōm/] **44**
bedspread [bĕd/sprĕd/] **44**–11
Beef [bēf] **52**
beef ribs [bēf/ rĭbz/] **52**–5
beetle [bēt/l] **132**–19
beets [bēts] **51**–6
begin [bĭ gĭn/] **8**–B
behind [bĭ hīnd/] **13**–3
beige [bāzh] **12**–9
bell captain [bĕl/ kăp/tən] **145**–4
bellhop [bĕl/häp/] **145**–5
below [bĭ lō/] **13**–7
belt buckle [bĕlt/ bŭk/əl] **69**–41
belts [bĕlts] **69**–11
bench [bĕnch] **153**–10
bend [bĕnd] **157**–R
berries [bĕr/ēz] **128**–20
between [bĭ twēn/] **13**–10
beverages [bĕv/rə jəz] **55**–15, **61**
bib [bĭb] **95**–8
bicycle [bī/sĭ kəl] **153**–4
big [bĭg] **11**–2
bike [bīk(/–)] **153**–4
...path [–păth/] **153**–2
...shorts [–shörts/] **67**–3
biking [bī/kĭng] **159**–4
bikini panties [bə kē/nē păn/tēz] **67**–16
bill (bird) [bĭl] **132**–1
bill (invoice) [bĭl] **21** ✦
billiards [bĭl/yərdz] **159**–2
billion [bĭl/yən] **14**
bills (paper money) [bĭlz] **20, 20** ✦
bin [bĭn] **37**–20
binder [bīn/dər] **3**–24
biohazard [bī/ō hăz/ərd] **147**–5
biology [bī äl/ə jē] **119**–1
birch [bürch] **128**–8
BIRDS, INSECTS, AND ARACHNIDS
    [bürdz/ ĭn/sĕkts ən ə răk/nĭdz] **132**
birth certificate [bürth/ sər tĭf/ə kət] **29**–1
birthday [bürth/dā/] **19**–41, **169**–I
bison [bī/sən] **134**–6
black [blăk(/–)] **12**–15
...hair [–hĕr/] **23**–15
bladder [blăd/ər] **75**–47
blade [blād] **150**–11
blanket [blăng/kət] **44**–12
...sleeper [–slē/pər] **67**–7
bleach [blēch] **72**–8
bleachers [blē/chərz] **5**–10
bleed [blēd] **82**–M
blender [blĕn/dər] **40**–12
blind [blīnd] **22**–26
blinds [blīndz] **43**–11
blister [blĭs/tər] **78**–15
blizzard [blĭz/ərd] **103**–11
block [bläk] **107**–2
blocks [bläks] **45**–15
blond [bländ] **23**–16
blood [blŭd(/–)] **79**–15
...pressure gauge [–prĕsh/ər gāj/] **84**–12

...test [–tĕst/] **86**–17
...work [–würk/] **86**–17
bloody nose [blŭd/ē nōz/] **78**–17
blouse [blows] **64**–9
blow dryer [blō/ drī/ər] **23**–20, **76**–16
blow out [blō/ owt/] **169**–K
blue [blōō] **12**–1
blueberries [blōō/bĕr/ēz] **50**–19
blue jay [blōō/ jā/] **132**–7
blush [blŭsh] **77**–36
board game [börd/ gām/] **162**–3
boarding area [bör/dĭng ĕr/ē ə] **110**–6
board the plane [börd/ dhə plān/] **111**–F
boating [bō/tĭng] **154**–2
bobby pins [bäb/ē pĭnz/] **76**–19
BODY [bäd/ē] **74**–**75**
body lotion [bäd/ē lō/shən] **76**–7
body of water [bäd/ē əv wö/tər] **117** ✦
boil [boyl] **58**–P
bolt [bōlt] **37**–29, **150**–30, 33
bone [bōn] (body) **75**–49, (broken) **82**–P
boneless [bōn/ləs] **52** ✦
bookbag [bŏŏk/băg/] **69**–28
bookcase [bŏŏk/kās/] **3**–8, **42**–1
bookstore [bŏŏk/stör/] **92**–4
booth [bŏŏth] **60**–19, **152**–23
boots [bŏŏts] **68**–18
bored [börd] **31**–26
boring [bör/ĭng] **167**–29
borrow [bär/ō, bör/ō] **20** ✦
botanical gardens [bə tăn/ĭ kəl gär/dnz] **152**–4
bottle [bät/l] **56**–1, **95**–26
...of soda [–əv sō/də] **56**–13
bottled water [bät/ld wö/tər] **55**–53
bottle return [bät/l rĭ türn/] **54**–1
bounce [bowns] **156**–K
bouquet [bō kā/, bōō–] **129**–27
bow [bō] **161**–6
bowl [bōl] **41**–25
bowling [bō/lĭng] **159**–3
...ball [–böl/] **161**–5
bow tie [bō/ tī/] **69**–40
box [bäks(/–)] **56**–6
...of cereal [–əv sĭr/ē əl] **56**–18
...spring [–sprĭng/] **44**–26
boxer shorts [bäk/sər shörts/] **67**–12
boy [boy] **22**–4, 7
bra [brä] **67**–20
brace [brās] **81**–31
bracelet [brās/lət] **69**–35, **83**–14
braces [brā/səz] **84**–24
brain [brān(/–)] **75**–35
...cancer [–kăn/sər] **79**–12
brainstorm [brān/störm/] **6**–K
brake [brāk(/–)]
...light [–līt/] **108**–13
...pedal [–pĕd/l] **109**–46
branch [brănch] **128**–2
Branches of government [brăn/chəz əv gŭv/ər mənt] **116**
Brass [brăs] **120**
bread [brĕd(/–)] **53**–1, 2, 3, **54**–29
...basket [–băs/kət] **63**–8
bread-and-butter plate [brĕd/ n bŭt/ər plāt/] **63**–16
break [brāk(/–)]
...a bone [–ə bōn/] **82**–P

...three eggs [–thrē/ ĕgz/] **58**–A
Breakfast [brĕk/fəst] **61**
breast (body) [brĕst] **74**–14
breasts (chicken) [brĕsts] **52**–19
bricklayer [brĭk/lā/ər] **136**–9
bricks [brĭks] **149**–11
bridge [brĭj] **105**–2
briefs [brēfs] **67**–13, 17
broccoli [bräk/ə lē] **51**–15, **58**–I
broil [broyl] **58**–V
broiler [broy/lər] **40**–21
broken [brō/kən] **48**–5, 6, 7, **49**–15, **70**–24
broom [broom] **47**–10
brother [brŭdh/ər] / [–brŭdh/ər] **24**–9
    half... [hăf/–] **25**–29
brother-in-law [brŭdh/ər ĭn lö/] **24**–16
brown [brown(/–)] **12**–11
    ...hair [–hër/] **23**–17
bruise [brooz] **78**–12
brush [brŭsh(/–)]
    ...hair [–hër/] **76**–I
    ...teeth [–tēth/] **77**–J
brush [(–)brŭsh(/)] **23**–18, **76**–14
    paint... [pānt/–] **151**–47, **163**–23
    scrub... [skrŭb/–] **47**–19
    toilet... [toy/lət–] **43**–16
bucket [bŭk/ət] **47**–20, **155**–22
buckle [bŭk/əl] **69**–41
bud [bŭd] **129**–6
buffalo [bŭf/ə lō] **134**–6
buffet [bə fā/] **33**–13
building [bĭl/dĭng] **34**–5
BUILDING SUPPLIES [bĭl/dĭng sə plīz/] **150–151**
build models [bĭld/ mäd/lz] **162**–C
bulb [bŭlb] **129**–9
bulldozer [bool/dō/zər] **149**–6
bulletin board [bool/ə tn börd/] **3**–14
bumper [bŭm/pər] **108**–7
bumper pad [bŭm/pər păd/] **45**–7
bunk [bŭngk] **45**–1
Bunsen burner [bŭn/sən bür/nər] **119**–9
bureau [byoor/ō] **44**–2
burglary [bür/glə rē] **100**–6
burner [bür/nər] **40**–19
burn (your)self [bürn/ (yər)sĕlf/] **82**–H
bus [bŭs(/–)] **90**–15, **104**–4
    ...driver [–drī/vər] **104**–8
    ...stop [–stäp/] **91**–16, **104**–1
bush [boosh] **39**–20
business education [bĭz/nəs ĕj ə kā/shən] **121**–2
businessman [bĭz/nəs măn/] **136**–10
businesswoman [bĭz/nəs woom/ən] **136**–10
busperson [bŭs/pür/sən] **63**–9
butcher [booch/ər] **136**–11
butter [bŭt/ər] **54**–36
butterfly [bŭt/ər flī/] **132**–20
buttocks [bŭt/əks] **74**–12
button [bŭt/n] **73**–21
buttonhole [bŭt/n hōl/] **73**–12
buy [bī(/–)] **21**–C
    ...a house [–ə hows/] **29**–O
    ...your ticket [–yər tĭk/ət] **111**–A
Buying a house [bī/ĭng ə hows/] **35**
cab [kăb] **104**–18, **106**–16
cabbage [kăb/ĭj] **51**–2

cabinet [kăb/ə nət] **40**–1
cable [kā/bəl] **144**–16
cactus [kăk/təs] **128**–21
cafeteria [kăf/ə tïr/ē ə] **5**–4
cake [kāk(/–)] **54**–32, **61**–19
    ...mix [–mĭks/] **55**–47
    ...pan [–păn/] **59**–26
calculator [kăl/kyə lā/tər] **142**–8
calculus [kăl/kyə ləs] **118**–28
CALENDAR [kăl/ən dər] **18–19**
calf [kăf] **74**–18
call [köl] **141**–E
call button [köl/ bŭt/n] **86**–10
calm [käm] **30**–10
camcorder [kăm/kör/dər] **165**–21
camel [kăm/əl] **135**–38
camera [kăm/rə] **165**–19, 24, 27
    ...case [–kās/] **165**–27
camisole [kăm/ə sōl/] **67**–21
camper [kăm/pər] **106**–11
campfire [kămp/fïr/] **154**–11
camping [kăm/pĭng] **154**–1
    ...stove [–stōv/] **154**–16
can [kăn(/–)] **56**–3
    ...of soup [–əv soop/] **56**–15
    ...opener [–ō/pə nər] **40**–14, **59**–1
cancer [kăn/sər] **79**–12
candle [kăn/dl] **41**–7
candles [kăn/dlz] **169**–H, K
candlestick [kăn/dl stĭk/] **41**–8
candy [kăn/dē] **55**–41, **168**–14
    ...bar [–bär/] **55**–41
    ...store [–stör/] **92**–3
cane [kān] **80**–7
canned goods [kănd/ goodz/] **54**–4
canoeing [kə noo/ĭng] **154**–3
cantaloupes [kăn/tə lōps/] **50**–15
can't breathe [kănt/ brēdh/] **82**–N
canteen [kăn tēn/] **154**–24
canvas [kăn/vəs] **163**–22
canyon [kăn/yən] **117**–17
cap [kăp] (graduation) **32**–3, (clothing) **66**–6
capsule [kăp/səl] **81**–27
captain [kăp/tən] **158** ✦
car [kär(/–)]
    ...accident [–ăk/sə dənt] **102**–2
    ...dealership [–dē/lər shĭp] **88**–4
    ...safety seat [–sāf/tē sēt/] **95**–13
card [kärd(/–)] **96**–4, **168**–5
    ...catalog [–kăt/l ög, –äg] **98**–10
    ...store [–stör/] **92**–7
cardigan sweater [kär/də gən swĕt/ər] **65**–27
Cardinals [kärd/nəlz] **14**
cardiologist [kär/dē äl/ə jĭst] **86**–3
cards [kärdz] **163**–H
careful [kër/fəl] **147**–24
caregiver [kër/gĭv/ər] **136**–12
careless [kër/ləs] **147**–23
CAR MAINTENANCE [kär/ mān/tn əns] **108–109**
carnation [kär nā/shən] **129**–18
carnival [kär/nə vəl] **152**–16
carousel [kär/ə sĕl/] **110**–18
carousel slide projector [kär/ə sĕl/ slīd/ prə jĕk/tər] **165**–29
carpenter [kär/pən tər] **48**–12, **136**–13
carpet [kär/pət] **42**–27

Index

carriage [kăr**/**ĭj] **95**–16
carrots [kăr**/**əts] **51**–3
carry [kăr**/**ē] **62**–H
carry-on bag [kăr**/**ē ăn băg**/**, –ŏn–] **111**–H
CARS AND TRUCKS [kärz**/** ən trŭks**/**] **106**
cart [kärt] **54**–3, **91**–31
carton [kär**/**tn] **56**–4
 ...of eggs [–əv ĕgz**/**] **56**–16
cartoon [kär tōōn**/**] **167**–19
cartridge [kär**/**trĭj] / [–kär**/**trĭj] **162**–2
 typewriter... [tīp**/**rī**/**tər–] **143**–31
carving knife [kär**/**vĭng nīf**/**] **59**–12
cash [kăsh(**/**–)] **20**–13, **97**–D
 ...register [–rĕj**/**ə stər] **55**–18, **140**–N
cashier [kă shïr**/**] **136**–14
casserole dish [kăs**/**ə rōl dĭsh**/**] **59**–11
cassette [kə sĕt**/**]
 ...player [–plā**/**ər] **3**–11, **164**–2, 15
 ...recorder [–rĭ kör**/**dər] **164**–3
cast [kăst] **81**–29
casual [kăzh**/**ōō əl] **71**–37
cat [kăt] **133**–9
catch [kăch] **156**–E
catcher's mask [kăch**/**ərz măsk**/**] **161**–15
caterer [kā**/**tər ər] **33**–12
caterpillar [kăt**/**ə pĭl**/**ər, kăt**/**ər–] **132**–21
catfish [kăt**/**fĭsh**/**] **53**–17
cattle [kăt**/**l] **148**–21
cauliflower [kö**/**lĭ flow**/**ər, kä**/**–] **51**–16
cavity [kăv**/**ə tē] **84**–20
C-clamp [sē**/**klămp**/**] **150**–6
CD (compact disc) [sē**/**dē**/**] **98**–14
 ...player [–plā**/**ər] **164**–14
 ...ROM disc [–räm**/** dĭsk**/**] **144**–2
ceiling [sē**/**lĭng] **42**–5
 ...fan [–făn**/**] **41**–4
celery [sĕl**/**ə rē] **51**–9
cello [chĕl**/**ō] **120**–9
cellular phone [sĕl**/**yə lər fōn**/**] **9**–13
Celsius [sĕl**/**sē əs] **10**
cent [sĕnt] **20**–1
centimeter (cm) [sĕn**/**tə mē**/**tər] **15**–12
CENTRAL AMERICA [sĕn**/**trəl ə mĕr**/**ə kə] **122**–123
central time [sĕn**/**trəl tīm**/**] **17**–28
cents [sĕnts] **20**–2, 3, 4
cereal [sïr**/**ē əl] **56**–18
Ceremony [sĕr**/**ə mō**/**nē] **32**
Certificate of Naturalization
 [sər tĭf**/**ə kət əv năch**/**rə lə zā**/**shən] **29**–6
certified mail [sür**/**tə fīd**/** māl] **96**–11
chain [chān] (hardware) **37**–28, **150**–36, (jewelry) **69**–31
chair [(–)chër(**/**)] **2**–7
 dining room... [dī**/**nĭng rōōm**/**–] **41**–16
 easy... [ē**/**zē–] **42**–24
 high... [hī**/**–] **95**–7
 rocking... [räk**/**ĭng–] **94**–6
 swivel... [swĭv**/**əl–] **143**–22
chalk [chök] **3**–16
chalkboard [chök**/**börd**/**] **2**–1
 ...eraser [–ĭ rā**/**sər] **3**–17
change [chānj(**/**–)] **21**–9
 ...purse [–pürs**/**] **69**–25
change [chānj(**/**–)]
 ...diapers [–dī**/**pərz] **94**–E
 ...the sheets [–dhə shēts**/**] **46**–P

...your diet [–yər dī**/**ət] **80**–C
changing table [chān**/**jĭng tā**/**bəl] **45**–12, **95**–9
cheap [chēp] **11**–20
check [chĕk(**/**–)]
 ...blood pressure [–blŭd**/** prĕsh**/**ər] **85**–B
 ...your bags [–yər băgz**/**] **111**–B
 ...your work [–yər würk**/**] **7**–Y
checkbook [chĕk**/**bŏŏk**/**] **97**–7
checked [chĕkt] **70**–11
checker [chĕk**/**ər] **55**–19
checkers [chĕk**/**ərz] **162**–5
check in [chĕk**/** ĭn] **111**–D
check-in counter [chĕk**/**ĭn kown**/**tər] **110**–3
checking account number [chĕk**/**ĭng ə kownt**/** nŭm**/**bər] **97**–8
check out [chĕk**/** owt**/**] **98** ✦
checkout desk [chĕk**/**owt dĕsk**/**] **98**–16
checkstand [chĕk**/**stănd**/**] **55**–17
cheddar cheese [chĕd**/**ər chēz**/**] **53**–10
cheek [chēk] **74**–29
cheese [chēz] **53**–9, 10, 11, 12, **54**–38
cheeseburger [chēz**/**bür**/**gər] **60**–3
chef [shĕf] **63**–11
chef's salad [shĕfs**/** săl**/**əd] **61**–9
chemistry [kĕm**/**ə strē] **119**–2
cherries [chĕr**/**ēz] **50**–16
cherry picker [chĕr**/**ē pĭk**/**ər] **149**–5
chess [chĕs] **162**–6
chest (body) [chĕst] **74**–13
chest of drawers [chĕst**/** əv drörz**/**] **45**–8
chicken [chĭk**/**ən] **52**–16, **61**–12
 ...soup [–sōōp**/**] **58**
chicken pox [chĭk**/**ən päks**/**] **79**–6
Chief Justice [chēf**/** jŭs**/**təs] **116**–9
CHILDCARE CENTER [chīld**/**kër sĕn**/**tər] **94**–95
childcare worker [chīld**/**kër wür**/**kər] **94**–3
Childhood diseases [chīld**/**hŏŏd dĭ zē**/**zəz] **79**
children [chĭl**/**drən] **11**–11, 12, **22**–1
CHILDREN'S BEDROOM [chĭl**/**drənz bĕd**/**rōōm] **45**
children's program [chĭl**/**drənz prō**/**grăm] **167**–24
child safety seat [chīld**/** sāf**/**tē sēt**/**] **109**–39
chili peppers [chĭl**/**ē pĕp**/**ərz] **51**–8
chills [chĭlz] **78**–9
chimney [chĭm**/**nē] **38**–21
chimpanzee [chĭm**/**păn zē**/**] **135**–28
chin [chĭn] **74**–31
china cabinet [chī**/**nə kăb**/**ə nət] **41**–1
chipmunk [chĭp**/**mŭngk**/**] **133**–20
chiropractor [kī**/**rə prăk**/**tər] **81**–H
chisel [chĭz**/**əl] **151**–51
choke [chōk] **82**–L
chop [chäp] **58**–G
chorus [kör**/**əs] **121**–3
Christmas [krĭs**/**məs] **168**–18
 ...tree [–trē**/**] **168**–20
chrysanthemum [krĭ săn**/**thə məm] **129**–19
church [chürch] **88**–6
cigarette lighter [sĭg**/**ə rĕt**/** lī**/**tər, sĭg**/**ə rĕt–] **108**–32
circle [sür**/**kəl] **7**–5
circle [sür**/**kəl] **118**–5
circular saw [sür**/**kyə lər sö**/**] **150**–10
circumference [sər kŭm**/**frəns] **118**–15
Citizen application requirements
 [sĭt**/**ə zən ăp**/**lə kā**/**shən rĭ kwīr**/**mənts] **116**
CITIZENSHIP [sĭt**/**ə zən shĭp**/**] **116**
city [sĭt**/**ē] **4**–7, **34**–1

...center [–sĕn/tər] **88** ✦
...hall [–höl/] **89**–17
CITY STREETS [sĭt/ē strēts/] **88**–**89**
claim your baggage [klām/ yər băg/ĭj] **111**–P
clams [klămz] **53**–28
clap [klăp] **32**–B
clarinet [klăr/ə nĕt/] **120**–4
CLASSROOM [klăs/rōōm/] **2**–**3**
classroom [klăs/rōōm/] **5**–1
Class work [klăs/ würk/] **7**
claw [klö] **132**–4
clay [klā] **162**–14
clean [klēn] (household) **27**–N, **46**–C, **72**–D, (teeth) **85**–I
clean [klēn] **72**–16
CLEANING SUPPLIES [klē/nĭng sə plīz/] **47**
cleanser [klĕn/zər] **47**–23
clear [klïr(/–)] **10**–6
...tape [–tāp/] **143**–39
clear [klïr] **62**–G
clear [klïr] **10**–6
clerk [(–)klürk(/)] **5**–18
desk... [dĕsk/–] **145**–8
file... [fīl/–] **142**–12
library... [lī/brĕr ē–] **98**–17
shipping... [shĭp/ĭng–] **146**–15
stock... [stäk/–] **139**–55
climb [klīm] **153**–C
climbing apparatus [klī/mĭng ăp ə răt/əs] **153**–14
CLINICS [klĭn/ĭks] **84**
clipboard [klĭp/börd/] **143**–26
clip-on earrings [klĭp/än ïr/ĭngz, –ön–] **69**–38
clock [kläk(/–)] **3**–10
...radio [–rā/dē ō] **44**–16, **164**–1
close [klōz] **2**–J
closet [kläz/ət] **11**–15, 16, **43** ✦, **44**–4
cloth diapers [klöth/ dī/pərz] **95**–21
clothesline [klōz/līn/] **72**–9
clothespin [klōz/pĭn/] **72**–10
CLOTHING I, II, III [klō/dhĭng] **64**–**67**
cloudy [klow/dē] **10**–7
clubs [klŭbz] **163**–26
clutch [klŭch] **109**–45
coach [kōch] **5** ✦, **158**–2
coal [kōl] **126**–4
coat [kōt] (clothing) **66**, (animal) **134**–19
cobra [kō/brə] **131**–40
cockpit [käk/pĭt/] **110**–11
cockroaches [käk/rō/chəz] **49**–25
coconuts [kō/kə nŭts/] **50**–22
cod [käd] **130**–8
coffee [kö/fē] **55**–51, **61**–22
...cup [–kŭp/] **41**–27
...shop [–shäp/] **88**–2
...table [–tā/bəl] **42**–23
instant... [ĭn/stənt–] **55**–51
coffeemaker [kö/fē mā/kər] **40**–11
COFFEE SHOP MENU [kö/fē shäp/ mĕn/yōō] **61**
coin collection [koyn/ kə lĕk/shən] **162**–13
Coins [koynz] **20**
colander [käl/ən dər] **59**–17
cold [kōld] (weather) **10**–4, (feeling) **30**–4
cold (illness) [kōld(/–)] **79**–1
...tablets [–tăb/ləts] **81**–17
cold water [kōld/ wö/tər] **43**–7
coleslaw [kōl/slö/] **53**–14

collar [käl/ər] **73**–7
collate [kō/lāt/, kə lāt/] **142**–F
collect [kə lĕkt/]
...the papers [–dhə pā/pərz] **7**–Q
...things [–thĭngz/] **162**–A
collection [kə lĕk/shən] **162**–12, 13
college [käl/ĭj] **112**–10
...degree [–də grē/] **29**–7
...dormitory [–dör/mə tör/ē] **34**–9
community... [kə myōō/nə tē–] **112** ✦
cologne [kə lōn/] **76**–5
colon [kō/lən] **113**–12
color hair [kŭl/ər hër/] **23**–D
coloring book [kŭl/ə rĭng bōōk/] **45**–20
COLORS [kŭl/ərz] **12**
comb...hair [kōm/ hër/] **76**–G
comb [kōm] **23**–22, **76**–13
comedy [käm/ə dē] **166**–10
come home [kŭm/ hōm/] **27**–Q
comet [käm/ət] **127**–25
comfortable [kŭmf/tə bəl, –tər–] **30**–7
comforter [kŭm/fər tər] **45**–2
comma [käm/ə] **113**–10
commercial fisher [kə mür/shəl fĭsh/ər] **136**–15
commit a crime [kə mĭt/ ə krīm/] **100** ✦
Common illnesses and childhood diseases
[käm/ən ĭl/nə səz ən chīld/hōōd dĭ zē/zəz] **79**
community college [kə myōō/nə tē käl/ĭj] **112** ✦
compact [käm/păkt] **106**–2
compact disc (CD) [käm/păkt dĭsk/] **98**–14
compliment [käm/plə mĕnt/] **8**–G
components [kəm pō/nənts] **140**–A
composition [käm/pə zĭsh/ən] **113**–2
compost pile [käm/pōst pīl/] **39**–10
computer [kəm pyōō/tər] **3**–15
...programmer [–prō/grăm ər] **136**–16
...science [–sī/əns] **121**–4
...workstation [–würk/stā/shən] **143**–21
COMPUTERS [kəm pyōō/tərz] **144**
concert [kän/sərt] **166**–6
concierge [kän/sē ërzh/, kōn/–] **145** ✦
concrete [käng/krēt, kän krēt/] **149**–10
condiments [kän/də mənts] **60** ✦
conditioner [kən dĭsh/ə nər] **76**–10
condominium [kän/də mĭn/ē əm] **34** ✦
conductor [kən dŭk/tər] **104**–16
cone [kōn] **118**–11
confetti [kən fĕt/ē] **168**–3
confused [kən fyōōzd/] **31**–27
congestion [kən jĕs/chən] **78**–7
Congressman [käng/grəs mən] **116**–2
Congresswoman [käng/grəs wōōm/ən] **116**–2
Conservation [kän/sər vā/shən] **126**
conserve [kən sürv/] **126**–B, C
constellation [kän/stə lā/shən] **127**–24
CONSTRUCTION [kən strŭk/shən] **149**
construction worker [kən strŭk/shən wür/kər] **149**–1
contact lenses [kän/tăkt lĕn/zəz] **81**–36
container [kən tā/nər] **56**–5, **59**–3
...of cottage cheese [–əv kät/ĭj chēz/] **56**–17
CONTAINERS AND PACKAGED FOODS
[kən tā/nərz ən păk/ĭjd fōōdz/] **56**
Continents [kän/tə nənts] **124**
control tower [kən trōl/ tow/ər] **110**–7
convenience store [kən vēn/yəns stör/] **90**–3

Index

CONVERSATION, EVERYDAY [ĕv/rē dā/ kän/vər sā/shən] **8**
convertible [kən vür/tə bəl] **106**–5
convert the measurements
　[kən vürt/ dhə mĕzh/ər mənts] **57**–C
conveyor belt [kən vā/ər bĕlt/] **146**–12
convict [kən vĭkt/] **99**–14
cook [ko͝ok] **27**–P, **58**–F, **140**–C
cook [ko͝ok] **137**–17
cooked chicken [ko͝okt/ chĭk/ən] **52**–25
cookies [ko͝ok/ēz] **54**–31, **56**–20
cookie sheet [ko͝ok/ē shēt/] **59**–27
cool [ko͞ol] **10**–3
coolant [ko͞o/lənt] **109**–56
cooler [ko͞o/lər] **155**–11
co-op [kō/äp/] **34** ✦
copy [käp/ē] **6**–F
copy center [käp/ē sĕn/tər] **91**–22
cord [körd] **9**–3, **151**–14
cordless phone [körd/ləs fōn/] **9**–12
core course [kör/ körs/] **121** ✦
corn [körn] **51**–27, **148**–4
corned beef [körnd/ bēf/] **53**–8
corner [kör/nər] **91**–17, **105**–10, **107**–1
corral [kə răl/] **148**–17
correct [kə rĕkt/] **7**–Z
correction fluid [kə rĕk/shən flo͞o/əd] **143**–33
corrosive [kə rō/sĭv] **147**–4
cost [köst] **21**–6
costume [käs/to͞om] **168**–13
cottage cheese [kät/ĭj chēz/] **56**–17
cotton [kät/n] **70**–16, **148**–6
couch [kowch] **42**–19
cough [köf] **78**–A
cough syrup [köf/ sĭr/əp, –sür/–] **81**–20
counselor [kown/slər] **5**–16
counselor's office [kown/slərz ö/fəs] **5**–15
count [kownt] **15** ✦
counter [kown/tər] **40**–22, **46**–O, **60**–13, **80**–12, **110**–3
country [kŭn/trē] **34**–4
county fair [kown/tē fër/] **152**–19
courier [kür/ē ər, ko͝or/–] **138**–38
court [kört(/–)] **99**–C
　...reporter [–rĭ pör/tər] **99**–12
courthouse [kört/hows/] **89**–18
courtroom [kört/ro͞om/] **99**–7
courtyard [kört/yärd/] **37**–18
cousin [kŭz/ən] **24**–12
cover-up [kŭv/ər ŭp/] **66**–25
cow [kow] **133**–3
coyote [kī ō/tē, kī/ōt/] **134**–3
CPR (cardiopulmonary resuscitation) [sē/pē/är/] **83**–17
CPU (central processing unit) [sē/pē/yo͞o/] **144**–1
crab [krăb] **53**–22, **130**–16
cracked [krăkt] **48**–4
cradle [krād/l] **45**–19
crane [krān] **149**–7
crash [krăsh] **102**–3
crayons [krā/änz] **45**–21
creamer [krē/mər] **41**–13
credit card [krĕd/ət kärd/] **20**–15
creek [krēk, krĭk] **117** ✦
crescent moon [krĕs/ənt mo͞on/] **127**–14
crewneck sweater [kro͞o/nĕk/ swĕt/ər] **71**–26
crib [krĭb] **45**–6
cricket [krĭk/ət] **132**–24

CRIME [krīm] **100**
criminal [krĭm/ə nəl] **100** ✦
crochet [krō shā/] **163**–20
crocodile [kräk/ə dīl/] **131**–37
crocus [krō/kəs] **129**–25
Crops [kräps] **148**
cross-country skiing [krös/kŭn/trē skē/ĭng] **160**–3
cross out [krös/ owt/] **7**–U
cross the street [krös/ dhə strēt/] **90**–A
crosswalk [krös/wök/] **90**–8
crucible tongs [kro͞o/sə bəl tängz/, –töngz/] **119**–15
crutches [krŭch/əz] **80**–1
cry [krī] **32**–C
cubby [kŭb/ē] **94**–4
cube [kyo͞ob] **118**–10
cucumbers [kyo͞o/kŭm bərz] **51**–12
cuff [kŭf] **73**–5
cup [kŭp(/–)] **63**–21
　...of flour [–əv flow/ər] **57**–10
　...of oil [–əv oyl/] **57**–2
curb [kürb] **90**–10
curling iron [kür/lĭng ī/ərn] **76**–15
curly [kür/lē] **23**–11
curtains [kür/tnz] **44**–5
curved [kürvd] **118**–19
custodian [kŭ stō/dē ən] **138**–35
customs [kŭs/təmz] **110**–20
　...officer [–ö/fə sər] **110**–21
cut [kŭt] **23**–A, **77**–N
cut [kŭt] **78**–13
cute [kyo͞ot] **22**–24
cutting board [kŭt/ĭng börd/] **40**–27
cut up [kŭt/ ŭp/] **58**–M
cycling [sī/klĭng] **159**–4
cyclist [sī/klĭst] **153**–3
cylinder [sĭl/ən dər] **118**–12
daffodil [dăf/ə dĭl/] **129**–26
DAILY ROUTINES [dā/lē ro͞o tēnz/] **26**–27
dairy section [dër/ē sĕk/shən] **54**–9
daisy [dā/zē] **129**–14
dance [dăns] **33**–J
dance floor [dăns/ flör/] **33**–16
dangerous situation [dān/jər əs sĭch/o͞o ā/shən] **147**–8
dark blue [därk/ blo͞o/] **12**–2
dashboard [dăsh/börd/] **108**–17
data [dā/tə, dăt/ə] **144** ✦
date [dāt(/–)] **18**–14
　...of birth [–əv bürth/] **4**–16
dates (fruit) [dāts] **50**–25
daughter [dö/tər] **24**–21
daughter-in-law [dö/tər ĭn lö/] **24** ✦
day [dā] **18**–10
daylight saving time [dā/līt/ sā/vĭng tīm/] **17**–33
Days of the week [dāz/ əv dhə wēk/] **18**
dead-bolt lock [dĕd/bōlt/ läk/] **37**–29
dead end [dĕd/ĕnd/] **107**–8
deaf [dĕf] **22**–27
decaf coffee [dē/kăf/ kö/fē] **61**–23
December [dĭ sĕm/bər] **19**–36
deck [dĕk] **38**–16
declaration form [dĕk/lə rā/shən förm/] **110**–22
decorate [dĕk/ə rāt/] **169**–C
deer [dïr] **134**–14
defendant [dĭ fĕn/dənt] **99**–5
defense attorney [dĭ fĕns/ ə tür/nē] **99**–4

degree [də grē/] **29**–7, **112** ✦
degrees [də grēz/]
...Celsius [–sĕl/sē əs] **10**
...Fahrenheit [–făr/ən hīt/] **10**
DELI AND SEAFOOD [dĕl/ē ən sē/fōōd/] **53**
deliver [də lĭv/ər] **96**–C
delivery person [də lĭv/ə rē pür/sən] **137**–18
dental [dĕn/təl]
...assistant [–ə sĭs/tənt] **84**–19, **137**–19
...floss [–flös/, –fläs/] **77**–22
...hygienist [–hī jē/nĭst, –jĕn/ĭst] **84**–16
Dental clinic [dĕn/təl klĭn/ĭk] **84**
DENTAL EXAMS [dĕn/təl ĭg zămz/] **85**
dentist [dĕn/tĭst] **84**–18, **137**–20
deodorant [dē ō/dər ənt] **76**–4
department store [dĭ pärt/mənt stör/] **93**–13
departure time [dĭ pär/chər tīm/] **111** ✦
deposit [dĭ päz/ət] **9**–C
deposit [dĭ päz/ət] **97**–C
...slip [–slĭp/] **97**–12
depth [dĕpth] **15**–15
DESCRIBING CLOTHES [dĭ skrī/bĭng klōz/] **70**–71
DESCRIBING HAIR [dĭ skrī/bĭng hër/] **23**
DESCRIBING THINGS [dĭ skrī/bĭng thĭngz/] **11**
desert [dĕz/ərt] **117**–4
design [dĭ zīn/] **146**–A
designated drivers [dĕz/ĭg nā/təd drī/vərz] **101** ✦
designer [dĭ zī/nər] **146**–3
desk [dĕsk(/–)] **2**–6, **142**–1
...calendar [–kăl/ən dər] **142**–6
...clerk [–klürk/] **145**–9
...pad [–păd/] **142**–7
dessert tray [dĭ zürt/ trā/] **63**–7
destination [dĕs/tə nā/shən] **111** ✦
diabetes [dī/ə bē/tēz, –təs] **79**–9
diagonal [dī ăg/ə nəl, –ăg/nəl] **118**–23
dial [dī/əl] **9**–D
dial tone [dī/əl tōn/] **9**–B
diameter [dī ăm/ə tər] **118**–17
diamonds [dī/məndz] **163**–27
diaper [dī/pər]
...pail [–pāl/] **45**–13, **95**–23
...pins [–pĭnz/] **95**–22
dice [dīs] **162**–4
dictate [dĭk/tāt] **6**–N
dictionary [dĭk/shə nër/ē] **3**–28
Dictionary work [dĭk/shə nër ē würk/] **6**
die [dī] **29**–R
dietician [dī/ə tĭsh/ən] **87**–25
difference [dĭf/rəns] **118** ✦
difficult [dĭf/ĭ kŭlt/] **11**–24
dime [dīm] **20**–3
Dimensions [də mĕn/shənz] **15**
diner [dī/nər] **62**–5
DINING AREA [dī/nĭng ër/ē ə] **41**
dining room [dī/nĭng rōōm/] **62**–2
...chair [–chër/] **41**–16
...table [–tā/bəl] **41**–17
dinner [dĭn/ər]
...fork [–förk/] **63**–25
...plate [–plāt/] **63**–15
diploma [də plō/mə] **29**–2, **32**–7
direct flight [də rĕkt/ flīt/, dī–] **111** ✦
Directions [də rĕk/shənz, dī–] **107**

DIRECTIONS AND TRAFFIC SIGNS
[də rĕk/shənz ən trăf/ĭk sīnz/, dī–] **107**
directory [də rĕk/tə rē, dī–] **9**–8, **93**–19
directory assistance (411) [də rĕk/tə rē ə sĭs/təns, dī–] **9**–8
dirty [dür/tē] **72**–15
discuss [dĭ skŭs/] **6**–L
disgusted [dĭ skŭs/təd] **30**–9
dish [dĭsh(/–)]
...drainer [–drā/nər] **40**–3
...towel [–tow/əl] **47**–22
dishroom [dĭsh/rōōm/] **63**–12
dishwasher [dĭsh/wä/shər, –wö/–] (machine) **40**–4, (person) **63**–13
dishwashing liquid [dĭsh/wä/shĭng lĭk/wəd, –wö/–] **47**–21
disinfectant [dĭs/ən fĕk/tənt] **95**–19
disk [dĭsk(/–)] **144**–5
...drive [–drīv/] **144**–3
display case [dĭ splā/ kās/] **69**–7
disposable diapers [dĭ spō/zə bəl dī/pərz] **95**–20
dissection kit [dĭ sĕk/shən kĭt/, dī–] **119**–7
dive [dīv] **157**–5
diving mask [dī/vĭng măsk/] **155**–3
division [də vĭzh/ən] **118**–4
divorced [də vörst/] **25**–24
DJ (disc jockey) [dē/jā/] / [dĭsk/ jäk/ē] **33**–17
do [dōō(/–)]
...an experiment [–ən ĭk spër/ə mənt] **119**–A
...crafts [–krăfts/] **162**–A
...errands [–ër/əndz] **90** ✦
...homework [–hōm/würk/] **27**–T
...manual labor [–măn/yōō əl lā/bər] **140**–D
dockworker [däk/wür/kər] **137**–21
doctor [däk/tər] **84**–6, **137**–22
Doctorate [däk/tər ət] **112** ✦
dog [dög] **11**–17, 18, **133**–11
dogwood [dög/wōōd/] **128**–16
DOING THE LAUNDRY [dōō/ĭng dhə lön/drē] **72**–2
doll [däl] **45**–18
dollar [däl/ər] **20**–7
dollhouse [däl/hows/] **45**–14
doll making kit [däl/ mā/kĭng kĭt/] **162**–15
dolphin [däl/fən, döl/–] **131**–30
DOMESTIC ANIMALS AND RODENTS
[də mĕs/tĭk ăn/ə məlz ən rōd/nts] **133**
domesticated animals [də mĕs/tə kā/təd ăn/ə məlz] **133** ✦
donkey [däng/kē, dŭng/–, döng/–] **133**–2
do not enter [dōō/ nät/ ĕn/tər] **107**–4
do not wash [dōō/ nät/ wäsh/, –wösh/] **72** ✦
don't [dōnt(/–)]
...**drink and drive** [–drĭngk/ ən drīv/] **101**–G
...**open** [–ō/pən] **101**–F
donut shop [dō/nŭt shäp/] **91**–20
doorbell [dör/bĕl/] **38**–10
door chain [dör/ chān/] **37**–28
doorknob [dör/näb/] **37**–30
doorman [dör/măn/] **36**–10, **145**–2
dosage [dō/sĭj] **80** ✦
double boiler [dŭb/əl boy/lər] **59**–8
doughnut [dō/nŭt] **60**–15, **60** ✦
down (feathers) [down(/–)]
...jacket [–jăk/ət] **66**–15
...vest [–vĕst/] **66**–13
down (preposition) [down] **105**–8
downhill skiing [down/hĭl/ skē/ĭng] **160**–1
downstairs [down/stërz/] **38** ✦

Index

downtown [down/town/] **88** ✦
drain [drān] **43**–4
drapes [drāps] **42**–16
draw a picture [drö/ ə pĭk/chər] **6**–M
draw blood [drö/ blŭd/] **85**–G
drawer [drör] **40**–23, **44**–3
dress [(–)drĕs(/)] **64**–3
　maternity... [mə tür/nə tē–] **65**–19
dress [drĕs] **94**–J
dresser [drĕs/ər] **44**–2
dressmaker [drĕs/mā/kər] **73**–2
dress shop [drĕs/ shäp/] **92** ✦
dribble [drĭb/əl] **156**–K
drill [drĭl(/–)] **84**–21, **150**–8, 23
　...bit [–bĭt/] **150**–23
drill a tooth [drĭl/ ə tooth/] **85**–K
drink [drĭngk(/–)] / [–drĭngk/] **60**–B
　...fluids [–floo/ədz] **80**–B
　don't... [dōnt/–] **101**–G
dripping [drĭp/ĭng] **49**–16
drive [drīv] **26**–I, **90**–C, **140**–E
drive (computer) [drīv] **144**–3, 20
driver's [drī/vərz]
　...education [–ĕj/ə kā/shən] **121**–5
　...license [–lī/səns] **29**–4
drive-thru window [drīv/throo/ wĭn/dō] **90**–13
driveway [drīv/wā/] **38**–5
drop off [dräp/ öf/] **94**–A
dropper [dräp/ər] **119**–14
drought [drowt] **103**–10
drown [drown] **82**–I
drugs [drŭgz] **100**–4
drugstore [drŭg/stör/] **90**–2
drums [drŭmz] **120**–18
drumsticks [drŭm/stĭks/] **52**–22
drunk driving [drŭngk/ drī/vĭng] **100**–3
dry [drī(/–)]
　...hair [–hër/] **76**–H
　...the dishes [–dhə dĭsh/əz] **46**–N
dry [drī] **72**–18
dry-clean [drī/klēn/] **72** ✦
dry cleaners [drī/ klē/nərz] **72** ✦, **91**–24
dryer [drī/ər] **72**–4
　...sheets [–shēts/] **72**–5
Dry measures [drī/ mĕzh/ərz] **57**
drywall [drī/wöl/] **149**–18
duck [dŭk(/–)] **52**–18, **132**–13
　...pond [–pänd/] **153**–6
dump truck [dŭmp/ trŭk/] **106**–12
duplex house [doo/plĕks hows/] **34** ✦
dust [dŭst] **46**–A
dust [dŭst(/–)]
　...mop [–mäp/] **47**–17
　...ruffle [–rŭf/əl] **44**–22
　...storm [–störm/] **10**–21
dustpan [dŭst/pän/] **47**–11
dye hair [dī/ hër/] **23**–D
eagle [ē/gəl] **132**–10
ear [ïr(/–)] **74**–28
　...infection [–ĭn fĕk/shən] **79**–3
earache [ïr/āk/] **78**–3
early [ür/lē] **17**–22
earmuffs [ïr/mŭfs/] (outdoor) **66**–12, (safety) **147**–14
earplugs [ïr/plŭgz/] **147**–13
earrings [ïr/ĭngz] **69**–37

Earth [ürth] **127**–7
earthquake [ürth/kwāk/] **102**–5
easel [ē/zəl] **163**–21
east [ēst] **107, 123, 124**
eastern time [ē/stərn tīm/] **17**–29
easy [ē/zē] **11**–23
　...chair [–chër/] **42**–24
eat [ēt(/–)] **60**–B
　...breakfast [–brĕk/fəst] **26**–E
eat out [ēt/ owt/] **62** ✦
eclipse [ĭ klĭps/]
　lunar... [loo/nər–] **127** ✦
　solar... [sō/lər–] **127** ✦
economics [ĕk/ə näm/ĭks, ē/kə–] **121**–6
edit [ĕd/ət] **113**–B
eel [ēl] **130**–5
eggbeater [ĕg/bē/tər] **59**–20
eggplants [ĕg/plänts/] **51**–18
eggs [(–)ĕgz(/)] **54**–34
　scrambled... [skrăm/bəld–] **61**–1
eight [āt] **14**
eighteen [ā/tēn/] **14**
eighteenth [ā/tēnth/] **14**
eighth [ātth, āth] **14, 15**–1
eighty [ā/tē] **14, 15**–10
eject [ĭ jĕkt/] **165**–F
elastic bandage [ĭ lăs/tĭk băn/dĭj] **83**–12
elbow [ĕl/bō] **74**–15
elderly [ĕl/dər lē] **22**–15
Election [ĭ lĕk/shən] **115**
elective [ĭ lĕk/tĭv] **121** ✦
electric [ĭ lĕk/trĭk]
　...can opener [–kăn/ ō/pə nər] **40**–14
　...drill [–drĭl/] **150**–8
　...keyboard [–kē/börd/] **120**–20
　...mixer [–mĭk/sər] **40**–25
　...pencil sharpener [–pĕn/səl shär/pə nər] **142**–9
　...shaver [–shā/vər] **77**–24
electrical [ĭ lĕk/trĭ kəl] **151**–38
　...hazard [–hăz/ərd] **147**–1
　...tape [–tāp/] **151**–38
electrician [ĭ lĕk trĭsh/ən] **48**–9
ELECTRONICS AND PHOTOGRAPHY
　[ĭ lĕk trän/ĭks ən fə täg/rə fē] **164**–**165**
electronics store [ĭ lĕk trän/ĭks stör/] **93**–18
elementary school [ĕl/ə mĕn/trē skool/] **112**–5
elephant [ĕl/ə fənt] **135**–42
elevator [ĕl/ə vā/tər] **37**–34, **145** ✦
eleven [ĭ lĕv/ən] **14**
eleventh [ĭ lĕv/ənth] **14**
ellipse [ĭ lĭps/] **118**–9
elm [ĕlm] **128**–17
embarrassed [ĭm băr/əst] **31**–25
embroidery [ĭm broy/də rē] **163**–19
EMERGENCIES AND NATURAL DISASTERS [ĭ mür/jən sēz ən năch/rəl dĭ zăs/tərz, –năch/ər əl–] **102**–**103**
emergency [ĭ mür/jən sē]
　...brake [–brāk/] **109**–44
　...card [–kärd/] **111**–K
　...exit [–ĕg/zət, –ĕk/sət] **111**–J
　...medical technician (EMT)
　　[–mĕd/ĭ kəl tĕk nĭsh/ən] / [ē/ĕm/tē/] **87**–26
　...service (911) [–sür/vəs] **9**–9
Emergency room [ĭ mür/jən sē room/] **87**
emery board [ĕm/ə rē börd/, ĕm/rē–] **77**–30

empty [ĕmp/tē] **46**–F
empty [ĕmp/tē] **11**–10
encyclopedia [ĭn sī/klə pē/dē ə] **98**–18
end table [ĕnd/ tā/bəl] **42**–21
end the conversation [ĕnd/ dhə kän/vər sā/shən] **8**–C
ENERGY AND THE ENVIRONMENT
   [ĕn/ər jē ən dhē ĭn vī/rən mənt, –vī/ərn–] **126**
Energy resources [ĕn/ər jē rē/sör səz, –rĭ sör/səz] **126**
engine [ĕn/jən] **109**–41
engineer [ĕn/jə nïr/] **137**–23
English as a second language
   [ĭng/glĭsh əz ə sĕk/ənd lăng/gwĭj] **121**–7
ENGLISH COMPOSITION [ĭng/glĭsh käm/pə zĭsh/ən] **113**
ENTERTAINMENT [ĕn/tər tān/mənt] **166–167**
enter your PIN number [ĕn/tər yər pĭn/ nŭm/bər] **97**–B
entrance [ĕn/trəns] **36** ✦
Entryway [ĕn/trē wā/] **37**
envelope [ĕn/və lōp/] **96**–1, **143**–20
ENVIRONMENT [ĭn vī/rən mənt, –vī/ərn–] **126**
Equivalents [ĭ kwĭv/ə lənts] **15**
erase [ĭ rās/] **2**–H
eraser [ĭ rā/sər] **3**–21
escalator [ĕs/kə lā/tər] **93**–21
evening [ēv/nĭng] **17**–19
   ...gown [–gown/] **65**–29
every day [ĕv/rē dā/] **18**–21
EVERYDAY CONVERSATION [ĕv/rē dā/ kän/vər sā/shən] **8**
evidence [ĕv/ə dəns] **99**–9
examination table [ĭg zăm/ə nā/shən tā/bəl] **84**–13
examine [ĭg zăm/ən] **85**–F
examining room [ĭg zăm/ə nĭng rōōm/] **84**–9
exchange [ĭks chānj/] **21**–G
excited [ĭk sī/təd] **31**–23
exclamation mark [ĕk/sklə mā/shən märk/] **113**–8
Excuse me. [ĭk skyōōz/ mē] **8**
Executive [ĭg zĕk/yə tĭv] **116**
exercise [ĕk/sər sīz/] **27**–W, **80**–D, **157**–P
exhausted [ĭg zö/stəd] **30** ✦
exhibition [ĕk/sə bĭsh/ən] **152**–21
expensive [ĭk spĕn/sĭv] **11**–19
experience turbulence [ĭk spïr/ē əns tür/byə ləns] **111**–N
expiration date [ĕk/spə rā/shən dāt/] **80** ✦
Exploration [ĕk/splə rā/shən] **114**
explosion [ĭk splō/zhən] **102**–4
Express Mail [ĭk sprĕs/ māl/] **96**–15
extension cord [ĭk stĕn/shən körd/] **151**–14
exterminate [ĭk stür/mə nāt/] **49** ✦
exterminator [ĭk stür/mə nā/tər] **49**–21
extra [ĕk/strə]
   ...large [–lärj/] **70**–5
   ...small [–smöl/] **70**–1
extract a tooth [ĭk străkt/ ə tōōth/] **85** ✦
eye [ī(/–)] / [–ī/] **73**–23, **74**–27
   ...chart [–chärt/] **84**–11
   ...glasses [–glăs/əz] **81**–35
   ...hook [–hōōk/] **150**–35
   ...shadow [–shăd/ō] **77**–34
   hook and... [hōōk/ ən–] **73**–23
eyebrow [ī/brow/] **74**–32
   ...pencil [–pĕn/səl] **77**–33
eyedrops [ī/dräps/] **81**–22
eyelashes [ī/lăsh/əz] **74**–34
eyelid [ī/lĭd/] **74**–33
eyeliner [ī/lī/nər] **77**–35
fabric softener [făb/rĭk sö/fə nər] **72**–6

Face [fās] **74, 77**
face powder [fās/ pow/dər] **77**–39
FACTORY [făk/tə rē, –trē] **146**
factory [făk/tə rē, –trē]
   ...owner [–ō/nər] **146**–2
   ...worker [–wür/kər] **146**–6
fall [föl] **82**–O
fall [föl] **19**–39
fall in love [föl/ ĭn lŭv/] **28**–K
FAMILY [făm/lē, făm/ə lē] **24–25**
fan [făn] (appliance) **41**–4, (person) **158**–4
fancy [făn/sē] **71**–39
fare [fër(/–)] **104**–5
   ...card [–kärd/] **104**–12
far from [fär frŭm/, –frəm] **13** ✦
farm [färm(/–)] **34**–13
   ...equipment [–ī kwĭp/mənt] **148**–10
Farm animals [färm/ ăn/ə məlz] **133**
farmer [fär/mər] **148**–15
FARMING AND RANCHING [fär/mĭng ən răn/chĭng] **148**
farmworker [färm/wür/kər] **148**–8
fashion designer [făsh/ən dĭ zī/nər] **73** ✦
fast [făst] **11**–3
fasten your seat belt [făs/ən yər sēt/ bĕlt/] **111**–I
FAST FOOD [făst/ fōōd/] **60**
fast food restaurant [făst/ fōōd/ rĕs/tə rənt, –ränt] **90**–14
fast forward [făst/ för/wərd] **165**–C
fat [făt] **11**–7
father [fä/dhər] **24**–6, **25**–26
father-in-law [fä/dhər ĭn lö/] **24**–14
faucet [fö/sət] **43**–6, **49**–16
fax [făks] **142**–B
fax machine [făks/ mə shēn/] **143**–23
feast [fēst] **168**–16
feather [fĕdh/ər] **132**–5
   ...duster [–dŭs/tər] **47**–1
February [fĕb/yōō ër/ē, fĕb/rōō–] **19**–26
feed [fēd] **94**–D, **148**–D
feel [fēl(/–)]
   ...dizzy [–dĭz/ē] **78**–C
   ...nauseous [–nö/shəs, –zē əs] **78**–D
FEELINGS [fē/lĭngz] **30–31**
feet [fēt] **15** ✦
female [fē/māl/] **4**–14
fence [fĕns] **38**–3, **148**–19
fencing [fĕn/sĭng] **159**–5
ferry [fĕr/ē] **104**–23
fever [fē/vər] **78**–8
fiction [fĭk/shən] **98, 166**
field [fēld] (school) **5**–12, (farm) **148**–7, (sports) **159**–17
fifteen [fĭf/tēn/] **14**
fifteenth [fĭf/tēnth/] **14**
fifth [fĭfth] **14**
fifty [fĭf/tē] **14**
   ...dollars [–däl/ərz] **20**–11
   ...percent [–pər sĕnt/] **15**–9
figure skating [fĭg/yər skā/tĭng] **160**–5
figurine [fĭg/yə rēn/] **162**–10
file [fīl] **142**–H
file [fīl(/–)]
   ...cabinet [–kăb/ə nət] **142**–10
   ...clerk [–klürk/] **142**–12
   ...folder [–fōl/dər] **142**–11
filet of sole [fĭ lā/ əv sōl/] **53**–21
fill a cavity [fĭl/ ə kăv/ə tē] **85**–L

fill in the blank [fĭl′ ĭn dhə blăngk′] 7–R
fill out [fĭl′ owt′] / [fĭl′ owt′–]
　…a form [–ə förm′] 4–B
　…an application [–ən ăp/lə kā′/shən] 141–G
filling [fĭl′ĭng] 84–22
film [fĭlm] (camera) 165–26, (movie) 166–1
fin [fĭn] 130–1
find your seat [fīnd′ yər sēt′] 111–G
FINDING A HOME [fīn′dĭng ə hōm′] 35
fingernail [fĭng′gər nāl′] 75–58
fingers [fĭng′gərz] 75–57
finish [fĭn′ĭsh] 157–Z
fins [fĭnz] 155–2
fire [fīr(′–)] 42–10, 102–7
　…escape [–ĭ skāp′] 36–7
　…exit [–ĕg′zət, –ĕk/sət] 37–23
　…extinguisher [–ĭk stĭng′gwĭ shər] 147–22
　…hydrant [–hī/drənt] 91–28
　…screen [–skrēn′] 42–11
　…station [–stā′shən] 88–1
　…truck [–trŭk′] 102–9
firefighter [fīr′fī′tər] 102–8, 137–24
fireplace [fīr′plās′] 42–9
fireworks [fīr′würks′] 168–8
first [fürst(′–)] 14
　…draft [–drăft′] 113–A
　…floor [–flör′] 36–1
　…name [–nām′] 4–2
　…place [–plās′] 152–20
　…prize [–prīz′] 152–20
FIRST AID [fürst′ ād′] 83
first aid [fürst′ ād′]
　…kit [–kĭt′] 83–1
　…manual [–măn′yōō əl] 83–7
Fish [fĭsh] 53
fish [fĭsh] 61–17, 130–12, 14, 15
fishing [fĭsh′ĭng] 154–5
　…net [–nĕt′] 154–17
　…pole [–pōl′] 154–18
fitted sheet [fĭt′əd shēt′] 44–14
fittings [fĭt′ĭngz] 151–17
five [fīv(′–)] 14–5, 20
　…after one [–ăf′tər wŭn′] 16–5
　…to two [tə tōō′] 16–15
Five ways to cook chicken [fīv′ wāz′ tə kōōk′ chĭk′ən] 58
fix [fĭks] 49 ✦
flag [flăg] 168–9
flammable [flăm′ə bəl] 147–2
flashlight [flăsh′līt′] 151–39
flat sheet [flăt′ shēt′] 44–13
flea market [flē′ mär′kət] 152–22
fleas [flēz] 49–23
flight attendant [flīt′ ə tĕn′dənt] 110–13
flood [flŭd] 103–16
floor [flör(′–)] / [–flör′] 44–24
　…lamp [–lămp′] 42–15
　…plan [–plăn′] 38–1
　dance… [dăns′–] 33–16
floppy [fläp′ē] 144–5
floral [flör′əl] 70–12
florist [flör′ĭst] 92–12, 137–25
floss [flös, fläs] 77–K
flounder [flown′dər] 130–13
flour [flow′ər] 55–45, 57–10
flower [flow′ər] 39–19, 129–7

…bed [–bĕd′] 39–A
…pot [–pät′] 39–18
　Parts of a… [pärts′ əv ə–] 129
FLOWERS [flow′ərz] 129
flu [flōō] 79–2
fluid ounce [flōō′əd owns′] 57–1
flute [flōōt] 120–3
fly [flī] 140 ✦
fly [flī] 132–29
flying disc [flī′ĭng dĭsk′] 159–6, 161–27
foam pad [fōm′ păd′] 154–13
foggy [fö′gē, fäg′ē–] 10–11
fold [fōld] 72–F
Follow directions [fäl′ō də rek′shənz, –dī–] 7
food [fōōd(′–)]
　…court [–kört′] 93–14
　…processor [–prä′sĕ sər] 40–26
FOOD PREPARATION [fōōd′ prĕp ə rā′shən] 58
Foot [fōōt] 75
foot [fōōt] (measurement) 15 ✦, (body) 74–7
football [fōōt′böl′] 158–11, 161–22
　…helmet [–hĕl′mət] 161–20
forceps [för′səps, –sĕps] 119–8
forehead [för′əd, –hĕd′, fär′–] 74–20
foreign language [för′ən lăng′gwĭj, fär′–] 121–8
forest [för′əst, fär′–] 117–11
fork [förk] 41–21, 63–24, 25, ✦
forklift [förk′lĭft′] 146–14
form [(–)förm(′)]
　declaration… [dĕk′lə rā′shən–] 110–22
　registration… [rĕj′ə strā′shən–] 4
formal [för′məl] 71–36
former husband [för′mər hŭz′bənd] 25 ✦
former wife [för′mər wīf′] 25 ✦
formula [för′myə lə] 95–25, 119–19
forty [för′tē] 14, 16–12
foundation [fown dā′shən] 77–40
fountain [fown′tn] / [–fown′tn] 92–11
　water… [wö′tər–] 153–11
four [för] 14
fourteen [för′tēn′] 14
fourteenth [för′tēnth′] 14
fourth [förth(′–)] 14, 15–2
　…floor [–flör′] 36–4
fox [fäks] 134–15
Fractions [frăk′shənz] 15
freezer [frē′zər] 40–10
freezing [frē′zĭng] 10–5
french fries [frĕnch′ frīz′] 60–2
French horn [frĕnch′ hörn′] 120–15
fresh [frĕsh] 53–29
Friday [frī′dā, –dē] 18–6
fried [frīd] 61–17
frog [frög, fräg] 130–25
front… [frŭnt(′–)]
　…desk [–dĕsk′] 145–8
　…door [–dör′] 38–11
　…office [–ö′fəs] 146–1
　…seat [–sēt′] 109–35
　…walk [–wök′] 38–14
　…yard [–yärd′] 38–15
frozen [frō′zən]
　…fish [–fĭsh′] 53–30
　…foods [–fōōdz′] 55–12
　…vegetables [–vĕj′tə bəlz] 55–43

...yogurt [–yō/gərt] **60**–11
FRUIT [froot] **50**
frustrated [frŭs/trā/təd] **31**–28
fry [frī] **58**–5
frying pan [frī/ĭng păn/] **59**–5
fuel injection system [fyoo/əl ĭn jĕk/shən sĭs/təm] **109**–40
full [fool] (not empty) **11**–9, (satisfied) **30**–6
full [fool(/–)]
  ...moon [–moon/] **127**–16
  ...slip [–slĭp/] **67**–22
full-size car [fool/sīz/ kär/] **106**–4
funnel [fŭn/əl] **119**–12
funny [fŭn/ē] **167**–27
fur [für] **134**–19
furious [fyoor/ē əs] **30** ✦
furniture [für/nĭ chər] / [–für/nĭ chər] **35**–K
  ...polish [–päl/ĭsh] **47**–18
  ...store [–stör/] **88**–13
  patio... [păt/ē ō–] **39**–5
fuse box [fyooz/ bäks/] **48**–13
galaxy [găl/ək sē] **127**–26
gallbladder [göl/blăd/ər] **75**–40
gallon [găl/ən] **57**–5
game [gām(/–)] **152**–18
  ...show [–shō/] **167**–23
GAMES [gām(/–)] **162**–163
gang violence [găng/ vī/ə ləns] **100**–2
garage [gə räzh/, –räj/] / [–gə räzh/, –räj/] **36, 38**–6
  ...door [–dör/] **38**–7
garbage [gär/bĭj] **46**–Q
  ...can [–kăn/] **39**–3
  ...disposal [–dĭ spō/zəl] **40**–5
  ...truck [–trŭk/] **91**–27
garden [gär/dn] (vegetable) **148**–12, (botanical) **152**–4
gardener [gärd/nər, gär/dn ər] **137**–26, **152**–6
gardenia [gär dēn/yə] **129**–16
gargle [gär/gəl] **77**–L
garlic [gär/lĭk] **51**–29
  ...bread [–brĕd/] **61**–16
  ...press [–prĕs/] **59**–10
garment worker [gär/mənt wür/kər] **73** ✦, **137**–27
garter belt [gär/tər bĕlt/] **67**–19
garter snake [gär/tər snāk/] **131**–39
gas [găs(/–)] / [–găs/] **109**–54
  ...gauge [–gāj/] **108**–22
  ...meter [–mē/tər] **48**–14
  ...pedal [–pĕd/l] **109**–47
  ...station [–stā/shən] **88**–12, **137**–28
  ...station attendant [–stā/shən ə tĕn/dənt] **137**–28
  ...tank [–tăngk/] **108**–12
  natural... [năch/rəl–, năch/ər əl–] **126**–3
gate [gāt] (garage) **36**, (airport) **110**–5, **111**–D
gauge [gāj] **84**–12, **108**–19, 22, 23
gauze [göz] **83**–6
gearshift [gïr/shĭft/] **108**–27
GEOGRAPHY [jē äg/rə fē] **117**
geometry [jē äm/ə trē] **118**–26
geothermal energy [jē/ō thür/məl ĕn/ər jē] **126**–7
get [gĕt(/–)]
  ...a checkup [–ə chĕk/ŭp/] **85** ✦
  ...acupuncture [–ăk/yə pŭngk/chər] **81**–G
  ...a job [–ə jäb/] **28**–G
  ...a loan [–ə lōn/] **35**–I
  ...an electric shock [–ən ĭ lĕk/trĭk shäk/] **82**–F
  ...an injection [–ən ĭn jĕk/shən] **80**–E

  ...an X ray [–ən ĕks/ rā/] **85**–H
  ...bed rest [–bĕd/ rĕst/] **80**–A
  ...feedback [–fēd/băk/] **113**–C
  ...frostbite [–fröst/bīt/] **82**–G
  ...home [–hōm/] **27**–Q
  ...your boarding pass [–yər bör/dĭng păs/] **111**–E
get dressed [gĕt/ drĕst/] **26**–D
get hired [gĕt/ hīrd/] **141**–L
get married [gĕt/ măr/ēd] **28**–L
get up [gĕt/ ŭp/] **26**–B
gift [gĭft(/–)] **169**–D
  ...shop [–shäp/] **145**–7
gifts [gĭfts] **33**–18
gills [gĭlz] **130**–2
giraffe [jə răf/] **135**–33
girder [gür/dər] **149**–3
girdle [gür/dl] **67**–18
girl [gürl] **22**–5, 8
give [gĭv(/–)] **21**–D
  ...a shot of anesthetic [–ə shät/ əv ăn/əs thet/ĭk] **85**–J
  ...a speech [–ə spēch/] **32**–E
  ...the verdict [–dhə vür/dĭkt] **99**–E
gizzards [gĭz/ərdz] **52**–23
glass [glăs(/–)] **11**–9, 10, **41**–26, **63**–19, 20, ✦
  ...cleaner [–klē/nər] **47**–8
glasses [glăs/əz] **81**–35
globe [glōb] **3**–9
glove [glŭv(/–)] **161**–17
  ...compartment [–kəm pärt/mənt] **108**–33
gloves [glŭvz] **66**–5
glue [gloo] **143**–37, **162**–8
go [gō(/–)]
  ...on an interview [–än ən ĭn/tər vyoo/, –ön–] **141**–H
  ...straight [–strāt/] **107**–A
  ...through security [–throo sĭ kyoor/ə tē] **111**–C
  ...to a chiropractor [–too ə kī/rə präk/tər] **81**–H
  ...to bed [–tə bĕd/] **27**–X
  ...to college [–tə käl/ĭj] **28**–J
  ...to jail [–tə jāl/] **99**–G
  ...to prison [–tə prĭz/ən] **99**–G
  ...to sleep [–tə slēp/] **27**–Y
  ...to the market [–tə dhə mär/kət] **26**–L
  ...to work [–tə würk/] **26**–I
goat [gōt] **133**–1
goggles [gäg/əlz] **147**–9
goldfish [gōld/fĭsh/] **133**–16
golf [gälf(/–), gölf(/–)] **159**–7
  ...club [–klŭb/] **161**–1
good [good] **11**–17
good-bye [good bī/, gə–] **8**
goose [goos] **132**–14
gopher [gō/fər] **133**–19
gorilla [gə rĭl/ə] **135**–30
gown [gown] **32**–2, **65**–29
graduate [grăj/oo āt/] **28**–D, **32**–A
graduate [grăj/oo ət] **32**–6
  ...school [–skool/] **112** ✦
graduated cylinder [grăj/oo ā/təd sĭl/ən dər] **119**–10
graduating class [grăj/oo ā/tĭng klăs/] **32**–1
GRADUATION [grăj/oo ā/shən] **32**–33
grams [grămz] **57** ✦
grandchild [grăn/chīld/, grănd/–] **29**–Q
granddaughters [grăn/dö/tərz] **24** ✦
grandfather [grăn/fä/dhər, grănd/–] **24**–3
grandmother [grăn/mŭdh/ər, grănd/–] **24**–2

grandparents [grăn/pĕr/ənts, grănd/–] **24**–1
grandson [grăn/sŭn/, grănd/–] **24**–7
grapefruit [grāp/froot/] **50**–9
grapes [grāps] **50**–1
graphic artist [grăf/ĭk är/tĭst] **137**–29
grasshopper [grăs/häp/ər] **132**–25
grate [grāt] **58**–J
grater [grā/tər] **59**–2
gray [grā/–)] **12**–5
   ...hair [–hër/] **23**–13
grease [grēs] **58**–C
green [grēn] **12**–8
greenhouse [grēn/hows/] **152**–5
green salad [grēn/ săl/əd] **60**–8
greeting card [grē/tĭng kärd/] **96**–4
greet someone [grēt/ sŭm/wŭn] **8**–A
grill [grĭl] **58**–T
grilled cheese sandwich [grĭld/ chēz/ săn/wĭch, –sănd/–] **61**–8
ground beef [grownd/ bēf/] **52**–4
ground post [grownd/ pōst/] **96**–14
grower [grō/ər] **148**–15
guard [gärd] **97**–4, **99**–3
guest [gĕst(/–)] **32**–9, **145**–11
   ...room [–room/] **145**–10
   ...speaker [–spē/kər] **32**–9
guests [gĕsts] **33**–14, **169**–B
guilty [gĭl/tē] **99**
guinea pig [gĭn/ē pĭg/] **133**–14
guitar [gĭ tär/] **120**–11
gum [gŭm] **55**–42
gums [gŭmz] **74**–24
gun [gŭn] **100**–9
gurney [gür/nē] **87**–28
gutter [gŭt/ər] **38**–19
gym [jĭm] **5**–9
gymnastics [jĭm năs/tĭks] **159**–8
gynecologist [gī/nə käl/ə jĭst] **86** ✦
hacksaw [hăk/sö/] **150**–5
hail [hāl] **10**–19
hail a taxi [hāl/ ə tăk/sē] **104** ✦
hailstorm [hāl/störm/] **10**–18
hair [hër(/–)] **23**, **74**–19
   ...clip [–klĭp/] **76**–17
   ...gel [–jĕl/] **76**–11
   ...net [–nĕt/] **147**–18
   ...salon [–sə län/] **23** ✦, **93**–16
   ...spray [–sprā/] **76**–12
   ...stylist [–stī/lĭst] **23** ✦
hairdresser [hër/drĕs/ər] **137**–30
half [hăf(/–)] **15**–4, **16**–10, **20**–5
   ...bath [–băth/] **43** ✦
   ...brother [–brŭdh/ər] **25**–29
   ...cup of raisins [–kŭp/ əv rā/zənz] **57**–9
   ...past one [–păst/ wŭn/] **16**
   ...sister [–sĭs/tər] **25**–30
   ...slip [–slĭp/] **67**–23
halibut [hăl/ə bət] **53**–20
hall [höl] **89**–17, **145**–13
Halloween [hăl/ə wēn/, häl/–] **168**–10
Hallway [höl/wā/] **37**
ham [hăm] **52**–9
hamburger [hăm/bür/gər] **60**–1
hammer [hăm/ər] **149**–D
hammer [hăm/ər] **150**–1
hammock [hăm/ək] **39**–2

hamper [hăm/pər] **43**–1
Hand [hănd] **75**
hand [hănd(/–)] **2**, **11**, **74**–8
   ...towel [–tow/əl] **43**–13
   ...truck [–trŭk/] **146**–11
handbags [hănd/băgz/] **69**–6
handcuffs [hănd/kŭfs/] **99**–2
handicapped parking [hăn/dē kăpt pär/kĭng] **107**–14
handkerchief [hăng/kər chĭf, –chēf/] **69**–42
handsaw [hănd/sö/] **150**–4
hanger [hăng/ər] **72**–11
hang up [hăng/ ŭp/] / [hăng/ ŭp/–]
   ...the clothes [–dhə klōz/] **72**–H
   ...the receiver [–dhə rĭ sē/vər] **9**–F
happy [hăp/ē] **31**–32
Happy Birthday [hăp/ē bürth/dā] **169**
hard [härd] (surface) **11**–5, (difficult) **11**–24
hard [härd(/–)]
   ...disk drive [–dĭsk/ drīv/] **144**–20
   ...hat [–hăt/] **147**–19
Hardware [härd/wër/] **144**
hardware [härd/wër/] **150**
   ...store [–stör/] **88**–14
harvest [här/vəst] **148**–B
hat [hăt] **66**–1
hats [hăts] **68**–5
have [hăv(/–)]
   ...a baby [–ə bā/bē] **29**–M
   ...a grandchild [–ə grăn/chīld/, grănd/–] **29**–Q
   ...a heart attack [–ə härt/ ə tăk/] **82**–D
   ...an allergic reaction [–ən ə lür/jĭk rē ăk/shən] **82**–E
   ...a picnic [–ə pĭk/nĭk] **153**–D
   ...dinner [–dĭn/ər] **27**–R
Hawaii-Aleutian time [hə wī/ē ə loo/shən tīm/] **17**–24
hay [hā] **148**–18
hazardous [hăz/ər dəs]
   ...materials [–mə tïr/ē əlz] **147**–7
   ...waste [–wāst/] **126**–9
head [hĕd] **74**–1
headache [hĕd/āk/] **78**–1
headboard [hĕd/börd/] **44**–15
headlight [hĕd/līt/] **108**–5
headphones [hĕd/fōnz/] **164**–16
HEALTH CARE [hĕlth/ kër/] **80**–81
health [hĕlth(/–)]
   ...club [–klŭb/] **89**–21
   ...insurance card [–ĭn shoor/əns kärd/] **84**
hear [hïr] **75**–B
hearing aid [hïr/ĭng ād/] **81**–33
hearing impaired [hïr/ĭng ĭm përd/] **22**–27
heart (symbol) [härt] **168**–6
heart (body) [härt(/–)] **75**–38, **79**–14
   ...disease [–dĭ zēz/] **79**–14
listen to... [lĭs/ən tə–] **85**–D
hearts [härts] **163**–29
heater [hē/tər] **48**–1, **108**–29
heating pad [hē/tĭng păd/] **80**–3
heat wave [hēt/ wāv/] **10**–15
heavy [hĕv/ē] **11**–13, **71**–41
   ...machinery [–mə shē/nə rē] **140**–F
heavyset [hĕv/ē sĕt/] **22**–20
hedge [hĕj(/–)] **39**–1
   ...clippers [–klĭp/ərz] **39**–12
heel [hēl] (shoe) **68**–13, (foot) **75**–62
height [hīt] **15**–14, **22**

Heimlich maneuver [hīm/lǐk mə noo/vər] **83**–18
helicopter [hĕl/ə kăp/tər] **110**–8
hello [hə lō/, hĕ–] **8**
help [hĕlp] **6**–J
help wanted sign [hĕlp/ wän/təd sīn/, –wön/–] **141**–C
hemline [hĕm/līn/] **73**–1
hen [hĕn] **133**–5
Hi! [hī] **8**
hibiscus [hī bǐs/kəs, hǐ–] **129**–12
hide [hīd] **169**–E
high [hī(/–)]
   ...chair [–chër/] **95**–7
   ...heels [–hēlz/] **68**–17, **71**–47
high blood pressure [hī/ blŭd/ prĕsh/ər] **79**–15
high-rise building [hī/rīz/ bǐl/dǐng] **89**–25
high school [hī/ skool/] **112**–7
hiking [hī/kǐng] **154**–6
   ...boots [–boots/] **68**–21
hills [hǐlz] **117**–16
hip [hǐp] **74**–5
hippopotamus [hǐp/ə pät/ə məs] **135**–43
hire [hīr] **99**–B
hired hand [hīrd/ hănd/] **148**–20
hit [hǐt] **156**–G
HIV (human immunodeficiency virus) [āch/ī/vē/]
   [hyoo/mən ǐm/yə nō dǐ fǐsh/ən sē vī/rəs] **79**–10
HOBBIES AND GAMES [häb/ēz ən gāmz/] **162**–**163**
hockey stick [häk/ē stǐk/] **161**–11
hold [hōld] **94**–B, **101**–C
holiday [häl/ə dā/] **19**–43, 44
HOLIDAYS [häl/ə dāz/] **168**
holly [häl/ē] **128**–19
home [hōm(/–)]
   ...attendant [–ə tĕn/dənt] **137**–31
   ...economics [–ĕk/ə näm/ǐks, –ē/kə–] **121**–9
homemaker [hōm/mā/kər] **137**–32
homesick [hōm/sǐk/] **31**–21
honeybee [hŭn/ē bē/] **132**–26
hood [hood] **108**–6
hoof [hoof] **134**–17
hook [hook(/–)] **150**–34, 35
   ...and eye [–ən ī/] **73**–23
horn [hörn] (car) **108**–24, (music) **120**–13, (animal) **134**–21
horror story [hör/ər stör/ē, här/–] **166**–14
horse [hörs(/–)] **133**–4
   ...racing [–rā/sǐng] **159**–18
horseback riding [hörs/băk rī/dǐng] **154**–9
hose [hōz] **39**–9
HOSPITAL [häs/pǐ tl] **86**–**87**
hospital [häs/pǐ tl] **88**–7
   ...bed [–bĕd/] **86**–11
   ...gown [–gown/] **86**–15
Hospital staff [häs/pǐ tl stăf/] **86**
hostess [hō/stəs] **62**–1
hot [hät] (weather) **10**–1, (feeling) **30**–1
hot dog [hät/ dög/] **60**–6
HOTEL [hō tĕl/] **145**
hotel [hō tĕl/] **88**–5
hot water [hät/ wö/tər] **43**–5
hour [ow/ər] **16**–3
HOUSE [hows] **38**
house [(–)hows(/)] **34**–6
   buy a... [bī/ ə–] **29**–O
   clean the... [klēn/ dhə–] **27**–N
Household Pests [hows/hōld/ pĕsts/] **49**

HOUSEHOLD PROBLEMS AND REPAIRS
   [hows/hōld/ präb/ləmz ən rǐ përz/] **48**–**49**
housekeeper [hows/kē/pər] **138**–33, **145**–15
housekeeping cart [hows/kē/pǐng kärt/] **145**–14
House of Representatives [hows/ əv rĕp/rǐ zĕn/tə tǐvz] **116**–1
houseplant [hows/plănt/] **129**–29
HOUSEWORK [hows/würk/] **46**
hubcap [hŭb/kăp/] **108**–9
hug [hŭg] **33**–G
humid [hyoo/məd] **10**–12
humidifier [hyoo mǐd/ə fī/ər] **80**–2
humiliated [hyoo mǐl/ē ā/təd] **30** ✦
hummingbird [hŭm/ǐng bürd/] **132**–11
hump [hŭmp] **135**–51
hundred [hŭn/drəd] **14**
hungry [hŭng/grē] **30**–5
hurricane [hür/ə kān/] **103**–12
hurt [hürt] (feeling) **30**–17, (medical) **82**–A
husband [hŭz/bənd] **24**–19
hydrant [hī/drənt] **91**–28
hydroelectric power [hī/drō ǐ lĕk/trǐk pow/ər] **126**–5
hydrogen peroxide [hī/drə jən pə räk/sīd] **83**–8
hyena [hī ē/nə] **135**–31
hygienist [hī jē/nǐst, –jĕn/ǐst] **84**–16
hypertension [hī/pər tĕn/shən] **79** ✦
hypoallergenic [hī/pō ăl/ər jĕn/ǐk] **77** ✦
I beam [ī/ bēm/] **149**–3
ice [īs(/–)]
   ...hockey [–häk/ē] **158**–13
   ...machine [–mə shēn/] **145**–18
   ...pack [–păk/] **83**–13
   ...skates [–skāts/] **161**–9
   ...skating [–skā/tǐng] **160**–4
ice cream [īs/ krēm/] **55**–44
ice cream stand [īs/ krēm stănd/] **93**–20
iced tea [īst/ tē/] **60**–5
icy [ī/sē] **10**–13
ignition [ǐg nǐsh/ən] **108**–25
illegal drugs [ǐ lē/gəl drŭgz/] **100**–4
ILLNESSES AND MEDICAL CONDITIONS
   [ǐl/nə səz ən mĕd/ǐ kəl kən dǐsh/ənz] **79**
immigrate [ǐm/ə grāt/] **28**–C
Immigration [ǐm/ə grā/shən] **114**
immunization [ǐm/yə nə zā/shən] **80** ✦
in [ǐn] **13**–5
   ...fashion [–făsh/ən] **64** ✦
   ...front of [–frŭnt/ əv] **13**–4
   ...love [–lŭv/] **28**–K, **30**–19
   ...pain [–pān/] **30**–12
   ...shock [–shäk/] **82**
inch (in.) [ǐnch] **15**–13
Independence Day [ǐn/də pĕn/dəns dā/] **168**–7
INDIVIDUAL SPORTS [ǐn/də vǐj/oo əl spörts/] **159**
industrial arts [ǐn dŭs/trē əl ärts/] **121**–10
infectious disease [ǐn fĕk/shəs dǐ zēz/] **79** ✦
influenza [ǐn/floo ĕn/zə] **79** ✦
information booth [ǐn/fər mā/shən booth/] **93**–22
ingredients [ǐn grē/dē ənts] **58**–K
INJURIES [ǐn/jə rēz] **78**
ink pad [ǐngk/ păd/] **143**–41
inline [ǐn/līn/]
   ...skates [–skāts/] **161**–10
   ...skating [–skā/tǐng] **159**–9
inquire about the salary [ǐn kwīr/ ə bowt/ dhə săl/ə rē] **141**–K
insect [ǐn/sĕkt]

Index

...bite [–bīt/] **78**–11
...repellent [–rĭ pĕl/ənt] **154**–23
INSECTS [ĭn/sĕkts] **132**
insert [ĭn sürt/] **97**–A
Inside the body [ĭn/sīd/ dhə băd/ē] **75**
instant coffee [ĭn/stənt kö/fē] **55**–51
instructor [ĭn strŭk/tər] **5** ✦, **139**–58
instrument [ĭn/strə mənt] **120**–A
insulation [ĭn/sə lā/shən] **149**–13
insurance [ĭn shoor/əns]
...card [–kärd/] **84**–4
...form [–förm/] **84**–5
intercom [ĭn/tər käm/] **36**–8
interesting [ĭn/trə stĭng, ĭn/tə rĕs/tĭng] **167**–30
international call [ĭn/tər nӑsh/ə nəl köl/] **9**–6
internist [ĭn/tür/nĭst] **86**–2
interpreter [ĭn tür/prə tər] **138**–34
INTERSECTION [ĭn/tər sĕk/shən] **90**–91
interview [ĭn/tər vyoo/] **141**–H
intestinal parasites [ĭn tĕs/tə nəl păr/ə sīts/] **79**–16
intestines [ĭn tĕs/tənz] **75**–42
into [ĭn/too, –tə] **105**–4
introduce [ĭn/trə doos/] **8**–D, F
Invention [ĭn vĕn/shən] **115**
invite [ĭn vīt/] **169**–B
iris [ī/rəs] **129**–20
iron [ī/ərn] **72**–G
iron [ī/ərn] **72**–13
ironed shirt [ī/ərnd shürt/] **72**–20
ironing board [ī/ər nĭng börd/] **72**–14
island [ī/lənd] **117**–8
IV (intravenous drip) [ī/vē/] / [ĭn/trə vē/nəs drĭp/] **87**–27
jack [jăk] **109**–51
jack cheese [jăk/ chēz/] **53**–12
jacket [jăk/ət] **66**–7
jack hammer [jăk/ hăm/ər] **149**–9
jack-o'-lantern [jăk/ə lăn/tərn] **168**–11
jam [jăm] **56**–14
janitor [jăn/ə tər] **138**–35
January [jăn/yoo ĕr/ē] **19**–25
jar [jär(/–)] **56**–2
...of jam [–əv jăm/] **56**–14
jasmine [jăz/mən] **129**–21
jaw [jö] **74**–23
jeans [jēnz] **64**–5
jellyfish [jĕl/ē fĭsh/] **130**–14
jewelry [joo/əl rē] **69**–8
...store [–stör/] **92**–2
job [jäb(/–)] / [–jäb/]
...board [–börd/] **141**–B
get a... [gĕt/ ə–] **28**–G
JOB SAFETY [jäb/ sāf/tē] **147**
JOB SEARCH [jäb/ sürch/] **141**
JOB SKILLS [jäb/ skĭlz/] **140**
JOBS AND OCCUPATIONS A-H [jäbz/ ən äk/yə pā/shənz] **136**–137
JOBS AND OCCUPATIONS H-W [jäbz/ ən äk/yə pā/shənz] **138**–139
jockstrap [jäk/străp/] **67**–14
jog [jäg] **156**–B
join the army [joyn/ dhē är/mē] **28**–F
joystick [joy/stĭk/] **144**–9
judge [jŭj] **99**–6
Judicial [joo dĭsh/əl] **116**
July [joo lī/] **19**–31, **168**–7
jump [jŭmp] **156**–J

jumper [jŭm/pər] **65**–18
jumper cables [jŭm/pər kā/bəlz] **109**–52
jump rope [jŭmp/ rōp/] **153**–5
jumpsuit [jŭmp/soot/] **65**–16
June [joon] **19**–30
junior high school [joon/yər hī/ skool/] **112**–6
Jupiter [joo/pə tər] **127**–5
jury [joor/ē] **99**–8, **116**
Justices [jŭs/tə səz] **116**–10
kangaroo [kăng/gə roo/] **135**–44
keep [kēp] **21**–E
ketchup [kĕch/əp, kăch/–] **60**–23
key [kē(/–)] **37**–31
...chain [–chān/] **69**–43
keyboard [kē/börd/] **120**–20, **144**–7
kick [kĭk] **156**–L
kidney [kĭd/nē] **75**–45
kilometers [kĭ läm/ə tərz, kĭl/ə mē/tərz] **15** ✦
kiss [kĭs] **33**–F
KITCHEN [kĭch/ən] **40**
kitchen [kĭch/ən] **63**–10
...timer [–tī/mər] **59**–18
KITCHEN UTENSILS [kĭch/ən yoo tĕn/səlz] **59**
kitten [kĭt/n] **133**–10
knee [nē(/–)] **74**–17
...socks [–säks/] **67**–25
knee-highs [nē/hīz/] **67**–24
knife [(–)nīf(/)] **41**–22, **63**–27
carving... [kär/vĭng–] **59**–12
multi-use... [mŭl/tē yoos/–, mŭl/tī–] **154**–20
paring... [për/ĭng–] **59**–16
knit [nĭt] **163**–F
knit shirt [nĭt/ shürt/] **65**–20
knitting needles [nĭt/ĭng nēd/lz] **163**–18
koala [kō ä/lə] **135**–45
label [lā/bəl] / [–lā/bəl] **143**–35
prescription... [prĭ skrĭp/shən–] **80**–14
lab technician [lăb/ tĕk nĭsh/ən] **86**–16
ladder [lăd/ər] **149**–2
ladle [lād/l] **59**–7
ladybug [lā/dē bŭg/] **132**–27
lake [lāk] **117**–13
lamb [lăm(/–)] **52**–13, 14, 15
...chops [–chäps/] **52**–15
...shanks [–shăngks/] **52**–13
lamp [lămp] **42**–15, **44**–17
lampshade [lămp/shād/] **44**–18
land [lănd] **111**–O
landlord [lănd/lörd/] **37**–32
language [lăng/gwĭj]
English as a second... [ĭng/glĭsh əz ə sĕk/ənd–] **141**–7
foreign... [för/ən–, fär/–] **141**–8
speak another... [spēk/ ə nä/thər] **140**–J
use the new... [yooz/ thə noo/–] **143** ✦
lantern [lăn/tərn] **154**–22
laptop [lăp/täp/] **144**–14
large [lärj] **70**–4
last [lăst(/–)]
...name [–nām/] **4**–4
...week [–wēk/] **18**–18
late [lāt] **17**–23
latex gloves [lā/tĕks glŭvz/] **87**–33, **147**–17
laugh [lăf] **33**–H
Laundromat [lön/drə măt/] **90**–1
laundry [lön/drē] **72**–1

...basket [–băs/kət] **72**–2
...detergent [–dĭ tür/jənt] **72**–7
...room [–rōōm/] **36**
lawn [lön(/–)] **39**–21
...mower [–mō/ər] **39**–22
lawyer [lö/yər] **99**–B, **138**–36
lay bricks [lā/ brĭks/] **149**–B
leaf [lēf(/–)] **128**–6, **129**–5
...blower [–blō/ər] **39**–4
leaking [lē/kĭng] **48**–3
learn to drive [lürn/ tə drīv/] **28**–E
lease [lēs] **35** ✦
leather [lĕdh/ər]
...boots [–bōōts/] **70**–18
...jacket [–jăk/ət] **66**–3
leave [lēv(/–)] **111**–L
...a message [–ə mĕs/ĭj] **9**–E
...a tip [–ə tĭp/] **62**–J
...work [–würk/] **26**–M
left [lĕft] **13**–1
leg [lĕg(/–)] **74**–6
...of lamb [–əv lăm/] **52**–14
legal [lē/gəl]
...holiday [–häl/ə dā/] **19**–43
...pad [–păd/] **143**–18
LEGAL SYSTEM [lē/gəl sĭs/təm] **99**
leggings [lĕg/ĭngz] **65**–23
Legislative [lĕj/əs lā/tĭv] **116**
lemons [lĕm/ənz] **50**–11
lend [lĕnd] **20** ✦
length [lĕngkth] **15**–16
lengthen [lĕngk/thən] **73**–C
leopard [lĕp/ərd] **135**–25
leotard [lē/ə tärd/] **67**–1
let out [lĕt/ owt/] **73**–F
letter [lĕt/ər] / [–lĕt/ər] **96**–2, **142**–B, D
...carrier [–kăr/ē ər] **96**–6
air... [ër/–] **96**–13
letterhead paper [lĕt/ər hĕd pā/pər] **143**–19
lettuce [lĕt/əs] **51**–1, **60**–17
level [lĕv/əl] **150**–24
librarian [lī brër/ē ən] **98**–1
LIBRARY [lī/brër ē] **98**
library [lī/brër ē] **5**–6, **89**–28, **98**–17, 19, 20
...book [–bōōk/] **98**–20
...card [–kärd/] **98**–19
...clerk [–klürk/] **98**–17
license plate [lī/səns plāt/] **108**–15
lid [lĭd] **59**–24
LIFE EVENTS [līf/ ĭ vĕnts/] **28–29**
lifeguard [līf/gärd/] **155**–18
...station [–stā/shən] **155**–20
lifesaving device [līf/sā/vĭng dĭ vīs/] **155**–19
life vest [līf/ vĕst/] **154**–14
light [līt] **169**–H
light [līt] (weight) **11**–14, **71**–40, (color) **12**–3
light (appliance) [līt(/–)] / [–līt/]
...fixture [–fĭks/chər] **41**–5
...switch [–swĭch/] **44**–19
porch... [pörch/–] **38**–9
lightbulb [līt/bŭlb/] **42**–4
lightning [līt/nĭng] **10**–17
lily [lĭl/ē] **129**–24
limb [lĭm] **128**–3
limes [līmz] **50**–12

line [līn(/–)] / [–līn/] **55**–20
...supervisor [–sōō/pər vī zər] **146**–5
assembly... [ə sĕm/blē–] **146**–8
line dry [līn/ drī/] **72** ✦
linen [lĭn/ən] **70**–17
linen closet [lĭn/ən kläz/ət] **43** ✦
Lines [līnz] **118**
lingerie [län/zhə rā/, –jə–] **67** ✦
lion [lī/ən] **135**–36
lip [lĭp] **74**–30
lipstick [lĭp/stĭk/] **77**–37
Liquid measures [lĭk/wəd mĕzh/ərz] **57**
list [lĭst] **6**–L
listen [lĭs/ən] **2**–C, **85**–D
listen for the dial tone [lĭs/ən fər dhə dī/əl tōn/] **9**–B
liters [lē/tərz] **57** ✦
little [lĭt/l] **11**–1
Little League [lĭt/l lēg/] **158** ✦
live [lĭv] **116**–B
liver [lĭv/ər] (food) **52**–7, (body) **75**–39
livestock [līv/stäk/] **148**–13
LIVING ROOM [lĭv/ĭng rōōm/] **42**
lizard [lĭz/ərd] **131**–41
llama [lä/mə] **135**–26
loading dock [lō/dĭng däk/] **146**–16
load the washer [lōd/ dhə wä/shər, –wö/–] **72**–C
loaf [lōf(/–)] **56**–10
...of bread [–əv brĕd/] **56**–22
loafers [lō/fərz] **68**–19
loan [lōn] **35**–I
Lobby [läb/ē] **37**
lobby [läb/ē] **145**–3
lobster [läb/stər] **53**–23
local call [lō/kəl köl/] **9**–4
lock [läk] **101**–E
lock [läk] (house) **37**–29, **48**–6, (car) **109**–34
lockers [läk/ərz] **5**–7
locket [läk/ət] **69**–33
locksmith [läk/smĭth/] **48**–11
logs [lögz, lägz] **42**–12
lonely [lōn/lē] **30**–18
long [löng(/–)] **23**–3, **71**–34
...underwear [–ŭn/dər wër/] **67**–11
long-distance call [löng/dĭs/təns köl/] **9**–5
long-sleeved shirt [löng/slēvd/ shürt/] **71**–31
look at [lōōk/ ăt/, –ət] **111**–K, **141**–B
look for [lōōk/ för/] / [lōōk/ fər]
...a help wanted sign [–ə hĕlp/ wän/təd sīn/, –wön/–] **141**–C
...a new apartment [–ə nōō/ ə pärt/mənt] **35**–A
...the emergency exit
[–dhē ĭ mür/jən sē ĕg/zət, –ĕk/sət] **111**–J
look in [lōōk/ ĭn]
...the classifieds [–dhə klăs/ə fīdz/] **141**–D
...throat [–thrōt/] **85**–E
look up a word [lōōk/ ŭp ə würd/] **6**–A
loose [lōōs] **71**–42
lose [lōōz] **158** ✦
lost child [löst/ chīld/] **102**–1
loud [lowd] **11**–11
loungewear [lownj/wër/] **67** ✦
love [lŭv(/–)] **30**–19
...seat [–sēt/] **42**–25
low [lō] **71**–46
LPN (licensed practical nurse)
[ĕl/pē/ĕn/] / [lī/sənst prăk/tĭ kəl nürs/] **87**–24

Index

luggage [lŭg/ĭj]
...carrier [–kăr/ē ər] **110**–19
...cart [–kärt/] **145**–6
lug wrench [lŭg/ rĕnch/] **109**–50
lumber [lŭm/bər] **149**–17, **151**
lunar eclipse [lōō/nər ĭ klĭps/] **127** ✦
lunch [lŭnch(/–)] **61**
...benches [–bĕn/chəz] **5**–5
lung [lŭng] **75**–37
LVN (licensed vocational nurse)
[ĕl/vē/ĕn] / [lī/sənst vō kā/shə nəl nürs/] **87**–24
machine [mə shēn/]
...operator [–äp/ə rā tər] **138**–37
...screw [–skrōō/] **150**–27
magazine [măg/ə zēn/, măg/ə zēn/] **98**–7
...holder [–hōl/dər] **42**–22
magnet [măg/nət] **119**–21
magnolia [măg nōl/yə] **128**–9
mailbox [māl/bäks/] **38**–4, **90**–12
mailboxes [māl/bäk/səz] **37**–36
mailer [mā/lər] **143**–32
mailing address [mā/lĭng ə drĕs/, –ă/drĕs] **96**–8
mail [māl/ ĭt] **96**–B
main office [mān/ ö/fəs] **5**–17
make [māk] **106** ✦
make [māk(/–)]
...a deposit [–ə dĭ päz/ət] **97**–C
...an appointment [–ən ə poynt/mənt] **85**–A
...an offer [–ən ö/fər] **35**–H
...a toast [–ə tōst/] **33**–I
...a wish [–ə wĭsh/] **169**–J
...copies [–käp/ēz] **142**–E
...lunch [–lŭnch/] **26**–F
...the bed [–dhə bĕd/] **46**–G
make sure you **understand**
[māk/ shōōr/ yōō ŭn/dər stănd/] **8**–E
male [māl] **4**–13
MALL [möl] **92**–93
mallet [măl/ət] **150**–2
MAMMALS [măm/əlz] **134**–135
Mammals, Sea [sē/ măm/əlz] **131**
man [măn] **22**–11
manager [măn/ĭ jər] **35**–B, **36**–12, **54**–8, **143**–25
mane [mān] **135**–49
mangoes [măng/gōz] **50**–21
mantel [măn/təl] **42**–8
manual [măn/yōō əl] **144**–22
manual labor [măn/yōō əl lā/bər] **140**–D
manufacture [măn/yə făk/chər] **146**–B
map [măp] **3**–12
maple [mā/pəl] **128**–13
March [märch] **19**–27
margarine [mär/jər ən] **54**–39
marigold [măr/ə gōld/] **129**–13
MARINE LIFE, AMPHIBIANS, AND REPTILES
[mə rēn/ līf/ ăm fĭb/ē ənz ən rĕp/tīlz] **130**–**131**
mark [märk] **7**–T
marker [mär/kər] **3**–19
MARKET [mär/kət] **54**–**55**
market [mär/kət] **89**–20
marriage license [măr/ĭj lī/səns] **29**–8
married [măr/ēd] **25**–23, **28**–L
Mars [märz] **127**–6
martial arts [mär/shəl ärts/] **159**–10
mascara [mă skăr/ə] **77**–38

mashed potatoes [măsht/ pə tā/tōz] **61**–11
mask [măsk] **168**–12
masking tape [măs/kĭng tāp/] **151**–49
Master's degree [măs/tərz də grē/] **112** ✦
match [măch] **7**–X
matches [măch/əz] **154**–21
maternity dress [mə tür/nə tē drĕs/] **65**–19
maternity shop [mə tür/nə tē shäp/] **93**–17
MATHEMATICS [măth/ə măt/ĭks] **118**
mattress [mă/trəs] **44**–25
May [mā] **19**–29
mayonnaise [mā/ə nāz/, mā/ə nāz/] **60**–25
meadow [mĕd/ō] **117**–20
measles [mē/zəlz] **79**–5
measure [mĕzh/ər] **15** ✦, **149**–C
Measurement [mĕzh/ər mənt] **15**
MEASUREMENTS [mĕzh/ər mənts] **14**–**15**
MEASURES [mĕzh/ərz] **57**
measure the ingredients [mĕzh/ər dhē ĭn grē/dē ənts] **57**–A
MEAT AND POULTRY [mēt/ n pōl/trē] **52**
meat and poultry section [mēt/ n pōl/trē sĕk/shən] **54**–2
media section [mē/dē ə sĕk/shən] **98**–11
medical [mĕd/ĭ kəl]
...charts [–chärts/] **87**–20
...emergency bracelet [–ĭ mür/jən sē brās/lət] **83**–14
...waste disposal [–wāst/ dĭ spō/zəl] **86**–14
MEDICAL AND DENTAL EXAMS
[mĕd/ĭ kəl ən dĕn/təl ĭg zămz/] **85**
Medical clinic [mĕd/ĭ kəl klĭn/ĭk] **84**
MEDICAL CONDITIONS [mĕd/ĭ kəl kən dĭsh/ənz] **79**
Medical conditions and serious diseases
[mĕd/ĭ kəl kən dĭsh/ənz ən sïr/ē əs dĭ zē/zəz] **79**
MEDICAL EMERGENCIES [mĕd/ĭ kəl ĭ mür/jən sēz] **82**
medication [mĕd/ə kā/shən] **80**–11, 12
...tray [–trā/] **87**–23
medicine cabinet [mĕd/ə sən kăb/ə nət] **43**–19
medium [mē/dē əm] **70**–3
meeting room [mē/tĭng rōōm/] **145**–19
memory [mĕm/ə rē] **144** ✦
men's store [mĕnz/ stör/] **90** ✦
menu [mĕn/yōō] **62**–3
MENU, COFFEE SHOP [kö/fē shäp/ mĕn/yōō] **61**
merchandise [mür/chən dīz/, –dīs/] **152**–24
Mercury [mür/kyə rē] **127**–9
messenger [mĕs/ən jər] **138**–38
messy [mĕs/ē] **11**–16
meter [mē/tər] (measurement) **15**, (taxi) **104**–21
meter [mē/tər] / [–mē/tər]
gas... [găs/–] **48**–14
parking... [pär/kĭng–] **91**–18
mice [mīs] **49**–26
microcassette transcriber [mī/krō kə sĕt/ trăn skrī/bər] **142**–4
microfilm [mī/krə fĭlm/] **98**–5
microfilm reader [mī/krə fĭlm rē/dər] **98**–4
microphone [mī/krə fōn/] **164**–4
microscope [mī/krə skōp/] **119**–4
microwave oven [mī/krə wāv/ ŭv/ən] **40**–13
middle-aged [mĭd/l ājd/] **22**–14
middle initial [mĭd/l ĭ nĭsh/əl] **4**–3
middle school [mĭd/l skōōl/] **112**–6
midnight [mĭd/nīt/] **17**–21
midsize car [mĭd/sīz/ kär/] **106**–3
mile [mīl] **15** ✦
milk [mĭlk] **148**–C
milk [mĭlk(/–)] **54**–35

...shake [–shāk/] **60**–12
milliliters [mĭl/ə lē/tərz] **57** ✦
million [mĭl/yən] **14**
miniblinds [mĭn/ē blīndz/] **43**–11
minivan [mĭn/ē văn/] **106**–10
minute [mĭn/ət] **16**–2
mirror [mĭr/ər] **43**–18, **44**–1
   rearview... [rĭr/vyōō/–] **108**–1
   sideview... [sīd/vyōō/–] **108**–8
missing [mĭs/ĭng] **70**–25
miss the bus [mĭs/ dhə bŭs/] **104** ✦
mistake [mĭ stāk/] **7**–2
mittens [mĭt/nz] **66**–9
mix [mĭks] **58**–K
mixing bowl [mĭk/sĭng bōl/] **59**–31
mobile [mō/bēl] **45**–4
mobile home [mō/bəl hōm/] **34**–8
model (occupation) [mäd/l] **138**–39
model (hobby) [mäd/l] **106** ✦
   ...kit [–kĭt/] **162**–7
   ...trains [–trānz/] **163**–32
models [mäd/lz] **162**–C
modem [mō/dəm, –dĕm] **144**–11
moisturizer [moys/chə rī/zər] **76**–8
molecule [mäl/ĭ kyōōl/] **119**–18
Monday [mŭn/dā, –dē] **18**–2
MONEY [mŭn/ē] **20**
money order [mŭn/ē ör/dər] **20**–16
monitor [män/ə tər] **144**–6
monitors [män/ə tərs] **110**–4
monkey [mŭng/kē] **135**–27
month [mŭnth] **4**–16, **18**–9
monthly statement [mŭnth/lē stāt/mənt] **97**–10
Months of the year [mŭnths/ əv dhə yïr/] **19**
moon [mōōn] **127**–13, 14, 15, 16
moose [mōōs] **134**–1
mop [mäp] **46**–J
mop [(–)mäp(/)]
   dust... [dŭst/–] **47**–17
   wet... [wĕt/–] **47**–16
MORE SCHOOL SUBJECTS [mör/ skōōl/ sŭb/jĭkts] **121**
morning [mör/nĭng] **17**–16
mosque [mäsk] **89**–23
mosquito [mə skē/tō] **132**–23
motel [mō tĕl/] **89**–22
moth [möth] **132**–22
mother [mŭdh/ər] **24**–5, **25**–25
motherboard [mŭdh/ər börd/] **144**–18
mother-in-law [mŭdh/ər ĭn lö/] **24**–13
motorcycle [mō/tər sī/kəl] **91**–19
mountain [mown/tn]
   ...biking [–bī/kĭng] **154**–8
   ...lion [lī/ən] **134**–2
   ...peak [–pēk/] **117**–14
   ...range [–rānj/] **117**–15
   ...time [–tīm/] **17**–27
mouse [mows] (animal) **133**–17, (computer) **144**–8
mouth [mowth] **74**–22
mouthwash [mowth/wäsh/, –wösh/] **77**–23
move [mōōv] **29**–P
move in [mōōv/ ĭn/] **35**–D
Movement [mōōv/mənt] **115**
mover [mōō/vər] **138**–40
movie [mōō/vē] **166**–1
movies [mōō/vēz] **152**–10

movie theater [mōō/vē thē/ə tər] **88**–11
moving van [mōō/vĭng văn/] **106**–14
mow [mō] **39**–C
mudslide [mŭd/slīd/] **102**–6
muffin [mŭf/ən] **60**–14
muffler [mŭf/lər] (clothing) **66**–4, (car part) **108**–11
mug [mŭg] **41**–28
mugging [mŭg/ĭng] **100**–5
multiplication [mŭl/tə plə kā/shən] **118**–3
multi-use knife [mŭl/tē yōōs/ nīf/, mŭl/tī–] **154**–20
mumps [mŭmps] **79**–7
murder [mür/dər] **100**–8
muscle [mŭs/əl] **75**–48
mushrooms [mŭsh/rōōmz/] **51**–26
MUSIC [myōō/zĭk] **120**
musician [myōō zĭsh/ən] **138**–41
music store [myōō/zĭk stör/] **92**–1
mussel [mŭs/əl] **130**–17
mussels [mŭs/əlz] **53**–26
mustache [mŭs/tăsh] **23**–5
mustard [mŭs/tərd] **60**–24
mystery [mĭs/tə rē] **166**–15
nachos [nä/chōz] **60**–10
nail (hardware) [nāl] **150**–29
nail (body) [nāl(/–)]
   ...clipper [–klĭp/ər] **77**–29
   ...polish [–päl/ĭsh] **77**–31
   ...polish remover [–päl/ĭsh rĭ mōō/vər] **77**–32
   ...salon [–sə län/] **91**–25
name [nām] **4**–1, 2, 3, 4, A, C, D
napkin [năp/kĭn] **41**–19, **63**–23
narrow [năr/ō] **71**–45
nasal congestion [nā/zəl kən jĕs/chən] **78**–7
nasal spray [nā/zəl sprā/] **81**–23
NATURAL DISASTERS
   [năch/rəl dĭ zăs/tərz, năch/ər əl–] **102–103**
natural gas [năch/rəl găs/, năch/ər əl–] **126**–3
nature program [nā/chər prō/grăm] **167**–22
near [nïr] **13** ✦
neat [nēt] **11**–15
neck [nĕk] **74**–2
necklaces [nĕk/lə səz] **69**–9
need [nēd] **109**–(54–59)
needle [nēd/l] (sewing) **73**–22, (pine) **128**–12
neighbor [nā/bər] **37**–22
neighborhood [nā/bər hōōd/] **90** ✦
Neighborhood Watch
   [nā/bər hōōd/ wäch/, –wöch/] **101** ✦
nephew [nĕf/yōō] **24**–18
Neptune [nĕp/tōōn] **127**–2
nerve [nürv] **75**–50
nervous [nür/vəs] **30**–11
nest [nĕst] **132**–5
new [nōō(/–)] **71**–32
   ...moon [–mōōn/] **127**–13
Newfoundland time [nōō/fən lənd tīm/, –fənd–] **17**–31
news [nōōz] **167**–17
newspaper [nōōz/pā/pər] **98**–8
newsstand [nōōz/stănd/] **90**–11
newt [nōōt] **130**–26
New Year's Day [nōō/ yïrz/ dā/] **168**–1
next to [nĕkst/ tōō, –tə] **13**–1, 2
next week [nĕkst/ wēk/] **18**–20
nickel [nĭk/əl] **20**–2
niece [nēs] **24**–17

night [nīt] 17–20
nightgown [nīt/gown/] 67–5
night-light [nīt/līt/] 45–3
nightshirt [nīt/shürt/] 67–9
night table [nīt/ tā/bəl] 44–21
nine [nīn] 14
nineteen [nīn/tēn/] 14
nineteenth [nīn/tēnth/] 14
nineteen-year-old [nīn/tēn/yïr ōld/] 22–8
ninety [nīn/tē] 14
ninth [nīnth] 14
nipple [nĭp/əl] 95–27
noisy children [noy/zē chĭl/drən] 11–11
nonfiction [nän/fĭk/shən] 98 ✦
noon [nōōn] 17–17
no outlet [nō/ owt/lĕt, –lət] 107–8
no parking [nō/ pär/kĭng] 107–12
north [nörth] 107, 123, 124
NORTH AMERICA AND CENTRAL AMERICA
    [nörth/ ə mĕr/ə kə ən sĕn/trəl ə mĕr/ə kə] 122–123
nose [nōz] 74–21
not [nät(/–)]
    ...guilty [–gĭi/tē] 99
    ...ripe [–rīp] 50–28
notebook [nōt/bŏŏk/] 3–24
    ...paper [–pā/pər] 3–25
note pad [nōt/ păd/] 143–36
November [nō vĕm/bər] 19–35
nuclear energy [nōō/klē ər ĕn/ər jē] 126–8
numbers [nŭm/bərz] 3–31
NUMBERS AND MEASUREMENTS
    [nŭm/bərz ən mĕzh/ər mənts] 14–15
nurse [nürs] 94–C
nurse [nürs(/–)] 84–10, 87–22, 24, 29, ✦, 138–42, ✦
    ...midwife [–mĭd/wīf/] 86 ✦
    ...practitioner [–prăk tĭsh/ə nər] 86 ✦
Nurse's station [nür/səz stā/shən] 87
nursing home [nür/sĭng hōm/] 34–11
nut (hardware) [nŭt] 150–31
nuts (food) [nŭts] 50–23
nylon [nī/län] 70–19
oak [ōk] 128–18
obey the law [ō bā/ dhə lö/] 116–H
oboe [ō/bō] 120–5
observatory [əb zür/və tör/ē] 127–19
observe [əb zürv/] 119–B
obstetrician [äb/stə trĭsh/ən] 86–1
OCCUPATIONS (A-H) [äk/yə pā/shənz] 136–137
OCCUPATIONS (H-W) [äk/yə pā/shənz] 138–139
ocean [ō/shən] 117–6, 155–1
o'clock [ə kläk/] 16–4
October [äk tō/bər] 19–34
octopus [äk/tə pəs] 130–4
odometer [ō däm/ə tər] 108–21
off [öf] 105–7
OFFICE [ö/fəs] 142–143
Office [ö/fəs] 37
office [ö/fəs] 5–13, 15, 17, 146–1
    ...building [–bĭl/dĭng] 89–24
    ...manager [–măn/ĭ jər] 143–25
official [ə fĭsh/əl] 158–6
oil (cooking) [oyl] 55–49, 57–2
oil (petroleum) [oyl(/–)] 109–55, 126–6
    ...gauge [–gāj/] 108–19
    ...paint [–pānt/] 163–24

...spill [–spĭl/] 126–15
ointment [oynt/mənt] 81–24, 83–9
old [ōld] 71–33
on [än, ön] 13–8
    ...the left [–dhə lĕft/] 13–1
    ...the right [–dhə rīt/] 13–2
once a week [wŭns/ə wēk/] 18–22
one [wŭn(/–)] 14, 15–1, 2, 3, 4, 5, 11, 16–4, 15, 20–1, 12
    ...o'clock [–ə kläk/] 16–4
    ...way [–wā/] 107–6
one billion [wŭn/ bĭl/yən] 14
one-eighth [wŭn/ ātth/, –āth/] 15–1
one-fifteen [wŭn/ fĭf/tēn/] 16–7
one-fifty [wŭn/ fĭf/tē] 16–14
one-forty [wŭn/ för/tē] 16–12
one-fourth [wŭn/ förth/] 15–2
one-half [wŭn/ hăf/] 15–4
one-hundred percent [wŭn/ hŭn/drəd pər sĕnt/] 15–11
one-oh-five [wŭn/ ō fīv/] 16–5
one-ten [wŭn/tĕn/] 16–6
one-third [wŭn/ thürd/] 15–3
one-thirty [wŭn/ thür/tē] 16–10
one-twenty [wŭn/ twĕn/tē] 16–8
onions [ŭn/yənz] 51–28, 58–G, H
online catalog [än/līn/ kăt/l ög/, –äg/, ön/–] 98–9
on time [än/ tīm/, ön/–] 17 ✦
onto [än/tōō, –tə, ön/–] 105–6
open [ō/pən] 2–I
    ...the presents [–dhə prĕz/ənts] 169–L
    don't... [dōnt/–] 101–F
opera [äp/rə] 166–8
operate heavy machinery
    [äp/ə rāt/ hĕv/ē mə shē/nə rē] 140–F
Operating room [äp/ə rā/tĭng rōōm/] 87
operating table [äp/ə rā/tĭng tā/bəl] 87–34
Operations (math) [äp/ə rā/shənz] 118
operator [äp/ə rā/tər] 9–7
ophthalmologist [äf/thəl mäl/ə jĭst, –thə mäl/–, äp/–] 86–7
opossum [ə päs/əm, päs/əm] 134–4
optician [äp tĭsh/ən] 92–8
optometrist [äp täm/ə trĭst] 81–34
orange [ör/ənj, är/–] 12–6
oranges [ör/ən jəz, är/–] 50–10
orangutan [ə răng/ə tăng/, –tăn/] 135–40
orbit [ör/bət] 127–11
orchard [ör/chərd] 148–16
orchestra [ör/kə strə] 120–1
orchid [ör/kĭd] 129–17
order [ör/dər] 62–D
orderly [ör/dər lē] 87–18
order puller [ör/dər pŏŏl/ər] 146–10
Ordinals [ör/dn əlz, örd/nəlz] 14
organ [ör/gən] 120–22
organizer [ör/gə nī/zər] 143–30
ornament [ör/nə mənt] 168–19
orthodontist [ör/thə dän/tĭst] 84–23
orthopedist [ör/thə pē/dĭst] 81–28
Other instruments [ŭdh/ər ĭn/strə mənts] 120
otter [ät/ər] 131–35
ounce [owns] 57–11
out [owt(/–)] 48–2
    ...of focus [–əv fō/kəs] 165–33
    ...of the taxi [–əv dhə tăk/sē] 105–5
OUTDOOR RECREATION [owt/dör rĕk/rē ā/shən] 154
outfit [owt/fĭt] 64 ✦

outlet [owt/lĕt, –lət] **44**–20, **107**–8, **151**–41
oval [ō/vəl] **118**–9
oven [ŭv/ən] **40**–20, **46**–C, **47**–3
...cleaner [–klē/nər] **47**–3
microwave...[mī/krə wāv/–] **40**–13
over [ō/vər] **105**–2
overalls [ō/vər ölz/] **65**–21
overcoat [ō/vər kōt/] **66**–2
overdose [ō/vər dōs/, ō/vər dōs/] **82**–K
overdrawn account [ō/vər drön/ ə kownt/] **97** ✦
overexposed [ō/vər ĭk spōzd/] **165**–34
overflowing [ō/vər flō/ĭng] **49**–17
overhead [ō/vər hĕd/]
...compartment [–kəm pärt/mənt] **110**–10
...projector [–prə jĕk/tər] **2**–4
overjoyed [ō/vər joyd/] **30** ✦
overnight mail [ō/vər nīt/ māl/] **96**–15
over-the-counter medication
[ō/vər dhə kown/tər mĕd/ə kā/shən] **80**–12
owl [owl] **132**–6
owner [ō/nər] **139**–56
oxfords [äks/fərdz] **68**–20
oxygen mask [äk/sĭ jən măsk/] **110**–14
oysters [oy/stərz] **53**–27
Pacific time [pə sĭf/ĭk tīm/] **17**–26
pacifier [păs/ə fī/ər] **95**–29
package [păk/ĭj] **56**–8, **96**–5
...of cookies [–əv kŏŏk/ēz] **56**–20
PACKAGED FOODS [păk/ĭjd fōŏdz/] **56**
packer [păk/ər] **146**–13
packing tape [păk/ĭng tāp/] **143**–42
pager [pā/jər] **9**–16
pail [pāl] **45**–13, **47**–20, **155**–22
pain [pān(/–)]
...reliever [–rĭ lē/vər] **81**–16
paint [pānt] **149**–A, **163**–E
paint [pānt(/–)] / [–pānt/] **151**–20
...pan [–păn/] **151**–45
...roller [–rō/lər] **151**–46
acrylic... [ə krĭl/ĭk–] **162**–47
paintbrush [pānt/brŭsh/] **151**–9, **163**–23
painter [pān/tər] **138**–43
painting [pān/tĭng] **42**–7, **152**–8
pair of scissors [për/ əv sĭz/ərz] **73**–18
paisley [pāz/lē] **70**–13
pajamas [pə jä/məz, –jä/–] **67**–4
palm [päm] (hand) **75**–59, (tree) **128**–15
pan [păn] **40**–24, **59**–5, 13, 26, 28
pancakes [păn/kāks/] **61**–6
pancreas [păng/krē əs] **75**–46
panda [păn/də] **135**–41
panther [păn/thər] **135**–39
panties [păn/tēz] **67**–16
pants [pănts] **64**–8
pantyhose [păn/tē hōz/] **67**–27
papayas [pə pī/əz] **50**–20
paper [pā/pər] (composition) **113**–2
paper [pā/pər] / [–pā/pər]
...bag [–băg/] **55**–22
...clip [–klĭp/] **143**–44
...cutter [–kŭt/ər] **143**–15
...doll [–däl/] **163**–30
...products [–präd/ŭkts] **55**–14
...shredder [–shrĕd/ər] **143**–24
...towels [–tow/əlz] **40**–2, **56**–23

notebook... [nōt/bŏŏk/–] **3**–24, 25, 26
parade [pə rād/] **168**–2
paragraph [păr/ə grăf/] **113**–5
parakeet [păr/ə kēt/] **133**–15
parallel [păr/ə lĕl/] **118**–21
parcel post [pär/səl pōst/] **96**–14
parent [për/ənt] **94**–1
parents [për/ənts] **24**–4
paring knife [për/ĭng nīf/] **59**–16
park [pärk] **91**–D
park [pärk] **88**–8
parka [pär/kə] **66** 8
PARK AND PLAYGROUND [pärk/ ən plā/grownd/] **153**
parking [pär/kĭng]
...garage [–gə räzh/, –räj/] **89**–26
...meter [–mē/tər] **91**–18
...space [–spās/] **36**–15, **90**–5
parochial school [pə rō/kē əl skōŏl/] **112**–3
parsley [pär/slē] **51**–10
part [pärt] **23**–4
partner [pärt/nər] **6**–J
parts [pärts] **146**–7
Parts of a bird [pärts/ əv ə bürd/] **132**
PARTS OF A CAR AND CAR MAINTENANCE
[pärts/ əv ə kär/ ən kär/ mān/tn əns] **108–109**
Parts of a circle [pärts/ əv ə sür/kəl] **118**
Parts of a fish [pärts/ əv ə fĭsh/] **130**
Parts of a flower [pärts/ əv ə flow/ər] **129**
Parts of a square [pärts/ əv ə skwër/] **118**
Parts of a tree [pärts/ əv ə trē/] **128**
PARTY [pär/tē] **169**
Party [pär/tē] **33**
pass [păs] **156**–H
passbook [păs/bŏŏk/] **97**–5
passenger [păs/ən jər] **104**–7, **110**–23
pass out [păs/ owt/] **7**–O
passport [păs/pört/] **29**–9
pasta [päs/tə] **61**–15
...salad [–săl/əd] **53**–15
pastrami [pə strä/mē] **53**–6
patient [pā/shənt] **84**–3
Patient's room [pā/shənts rŏŏm/] **86**
patio [păt/ē ō] **39**–6
...furniture [–für/nĭ chər] **39**–5
patron [pā/trən] **62**–5
pattern (clothes) [păt/ərn] **73**–8
pattern maker [păt/ərn mā/kər] **73** ✦
Patterns (fabric) [păt/ərnz] **70**
pause [pöz] **165**–E
paw [pö] **134**–42
pay [pā(/–)]
...taxes [–tăk/səz] **116**–E
...the check [–dhə chĕk/] **62**–I
...the mortgage [–dhə mör/gĭj] **35**–L
...the rent [–dhə rĕnt/] **35**–F
pay phone [pā/ fōn] **9**–11
pay back [pā/ băk/] **20** ✦
pay for [pā/ för/, –fər] **21**–C
PE (physical education) [pē/ē/] / [fĭz/ĭ kəl ĕj/ə kā/shən]
121–11
peaches [pē/chəz] **50**–5
peacock [pē/käk/] **132**–15
peak [pēk] **117**–14
pearls [pürlz] **69**–30
pears [përz] **50**–6

Index

peas [pēz] **51**–19
pedestrian [pə dĕs/trē ən] **90**–7
...crossing [–krö/sĭng] **107**–10
pediatrician [pē/dē ə trĭsh/ən] **86**–4
peel [pēl] **58**–N
peephole [pēp/hōl/] **37**–27
pelvis [pĕl/vəs] **75**–55
pen [pĕn] **3**–18
pencil [pĕn/səl] **3**–20
...eraser [–ĭ rā/sər] **3**–21
...sharpener [–shär/pə nər] **3**–13, **142**–9
penguin [pĕng/wĭn] **132**–12
peninsula [pə nĭn/sə lə] **117**–7
penny [pĕn/ē] **20**–1
peppers [pĕp/ərz] **51**–7
pepper shaker [pĕp/ər shā/kər] **41**–15
Percents [pər sĕnts/] **15**
Percussion [pər kŭsh/ən] **120**
perfume [pür/fyoōm/, pər fyoōm/] **76**–5
period [pïr/ē əd] **113**–6
periodical section [pïr/ē äd/ĭ kəl sĕk/shən] **98**–6
perm hair [pürm/ hër/] **23**–B
perpendicular [pür/pən dĭk/yə lər] **118**–20
personal check [pür/sə nəl chĕk/] **20**–14
PERSONAL HYGIENE [pür/sə nəl hī/jēn] **76**–**77**
personal identification number (PIN)
[pür/sə nəl ī dĕn/tə fə kā/shən nŭm/bər] **97**–B
PERSONAL INFORMATION [pür/sə nəl ĭn/fər mā/shən] **4**
personal radio-cassette player
[pür/sə nəl rā/dē ō kə sĕt/ plā/ər] **164**–15
pesticide [pĕs/tə sīd/] **49** ✦
...poisoning [–poy/zə nĭng] **126**–14
pet [pĕt(/–)]
...food [–foōd/] **54**–10
...store [–stör/] **92**–6
petal [pĕt/l] **129**–8
petri dish [pē/trē dĭsh/] **119**–6
petroleum [pə trō/lē əm] **126**–6
Pets [pĕts] **133**
pharmacist [fär/mə sĭst] **80**–10
pharmacy [fär/mə sē] **80**–9, **90**–2
Phillips screwdriver [fĭl/ĭps skroō/drī/vər] **150**–26
phone [fōn(/–)] **9**–1
...card [–kärd/] **9**–10
photo [fō/tō]
...album [–ăl/bəm] **165**–32
...shop [–shäp/] **90**–4
photocopier [fō/tə käp/ē ər] **142**–14
photograph [fō/tə grăf/] **44**–7
photographer [fə täg/rə fər] **32**–11
PHOTOGRAPHY [fə täg/rə fē] **164**-**165**
PHYSICAL DESCRIPTION [fĭz/ĭ kəl dĭ skrĭp/shən] **22**
physically challenged [fĭz/ĭ klē chăl/ənjd] **22**–25
physical therapist [fĭz/ĭ kəl thër/ə pĭst] **81**–30
physics [fĭz/ĭks] **119**–3
pi (π) [pī] **118** ✦
piano [pē ăn/ō] **120**–16
pickax [pĭk/ăks/] **149**–20
pick up [pĭk/ ŭp/] / [pĭk/ ŭp/–] **94**–G
...the children [–dhə chĭl/drən] **27**–O
...the receiver [–dhə rĭ sē/vər] **9**–A
pickup truck [pĭk/ŭp trŭk/] **106**–7
picnic [pĭk/nĭk] **153**–D
picnic table [pĭk/nĭk tā/bəl] **153**–8
picture [pĭk/chər]

...book [–boōk/] **45**–17
...dictionary [–dĭk/shə nër ē] **3**–29
pie [pī(/–)] **61**–21
...pan [–păn/] **59**–28
pier [pïr] **155**–16
pierced earrings [pïrst/ ïr/ĭng] **69**–37
pig [pĭg] **133**–8
pigeon [pĭj/ən] **132**–16
pill [pĭl] **81**–26
pillow [pĭl/ō] **42**–20, **44**–9
pillowcase [pĭl/ō kās/] **44**–10
pilot [pī/lət] **110**–12
PIN (personal identification number) [pĭn] **97**–B
pin [pĭn] (jewelry) **69**–36, (sewing) **73**–14
pin [pĭn(/–)] / [–pĭn/]
...cushion [–koōsh/ən] **73**–15
push... [poōsh/–] **143**–43
pine [pīn] **128**–10
pinecone [pīn/kōn/] **128**–11
pineapples [pī/năp/əlz] **50**–2
Ping-Pong [pĭng/päng/, –pöng/] **159**–13
pink [pĭngk] **12**–10
pint [pīnt] **57**–3
pipe [pīp(/–)] **151**–16
...wrench [–rĕnch/] **151**–43
pipes [pīps] **49**–19
pitch [pĭch] **156**–F
pizza [pēt/sə] **60**–7
place [plās(/–)]
...mat [–măt/] **41**–20
...setting [–sĕt/ĭng] **63**–14
place of birth [plās/ əv bürth/] **4**–17
PLACES TO GO [plā/səz tə gō/] **152**
PLACES TO LIVE [plā/səz tə lĭv/] **34**
plaid [plăd] **70**–9
plain [plān] **71**–38
plains [plānz] **117**–19
plan [plăn] **169**–A
plane (tool) [plān] **151**–52
PLANE TRIP [plān/ trĭp/] **111**
Planets [plăn/əts] **127**
plant [plănt] **39**–D, **148**–A
plant [plănt] **39**–B, **42**–18
PLANTS [plănts] **128**
plastic [plăs/tĭk] **70**
...bag [–băg/] **55**–23
...storage container [–stör/ĭj kən tā/nər] **59**–3
...wrap [–răp/] **55**–54
plate [plāt] **41**–24, **63**–15, 16, 17
platform [plăt/förm/] **104**–15
platter [plăt/ər] **41**–3
platypus [plăt/ĭ pəs, –poōs/] **135**–46
play [plā(/–)] **94**–K, **165**–B
...an instrument [–ən ĭn/strə mənt] **120**–A
...cards [–kärdz/] **163**–H
...games [–gāmz/] **162**–C
play [plā] **166**–2
player [plā/ər] **158**–5, **164**–2, 14, 15
PLAYGROUND [plā/grownd/] **153**
playground [plā/grownd/] **36**–6
playpen [plā/pĕn/] **95**–11
pliers [plī/ərz] **150**–7
plug [plŭg] **164**–18
plumber [plŭm/ər] **49**–20
plums [plŭmz] **50**–8

plunger [plŭn/jər] **151**–44
Pluto [plo͞o/tō] **127**–1
plywood [plī/wŏŏd/] **149**–16
p.m. [pē/ĕm/] **16**
pneumatic drill [no͞o măt/ĭk drĭl/] **149**–9
pocket [päk/ət] **73**–4
podium [pō/dē əm] **32**–5
poinsettia [poyn sĕt/ē ə, –sĕt/ə] **129**–23
point [poynt] **2**–F
poison [poy/zən] **82**–J, **147**–3
...ivy [–ī/vē] **128**–25
...oak [–ōk/] **128**–23
...sumac [–so͞o/măk, –sho͞o/–] **128**–24
police [pə lēs/]
...officer [–ö/fə sər] **99**–1, **138**–44
...station [–stā/shən] **89**–19
polish [päl/ĭsh]
...nails [–nālz/] **77**–O
...the furniture [–dhə für/nĭ chər] **46**–K
polka-dotted [pō/kə dät/əd] **70**–8
Pollution [pə lo͞o/shən] **126**
polyester [päl/ē ĕs/tər, päl/ē ĕs/tər] **70**
poncho [pän/chō] **66**–18
pond [pänd] **117**–21, **153**–6
pool (game) [po͞ol] **159**–2
pool (swimming) [po͞ol/–] **37**–16, **145**–16
...service [–sür/vəs] **145**–17
porch light [pörch/ līt/] **38**–9
porcupine [pör/kyə pīn/] **134**–10
Pork [pörk] **52**
pork chops [pörk/ chäps/] **52**–10
porpoise [pör/pəs] **131**–31
port [pört] **144**–17
portable [pör/tə bəl]
...radio-cassette player [–rā/dē ō kə sĕt/ plā/ər] **164**–2
...TV [–tē/vē/] **164**–7
postage [pō/stĭj] **96**–10
postal [pō/stəl]
...scale [–skāl/] **143**–16
...worker [–wür/kər] **138**–45
postcard [pōst/kärd/] **96**–3
Post-it notes [pōst/ĭt nōts/] **143**–34
postmark [pōst/märk/] **96**–9
post office [pōst/ ö/fəs] **89**–29
pot [pät/–] **40**–16, **59**–6
...holders [–hōl/dərz] **59**–29
potato [pə tā/tō]
...chips [–chĭps/] **55**–40
...salad [–săl/əd] **53**–13
potatoes [pə tā/tōz] **51**–21, **61**–11
potty seat [pät/ē sēt/] **95**–10
pouch [powch] **135**–50
POULTRY [pōl/trē] **52**
poultry section [pōl/trē sĕk/shən] **54**–2
pound [pownd] **57**–12
pour [pör/–]
...the eggs into the pan [–dhē ĕgz/ ĭn/tə dhə păn/] **58**–D
...the water [–dhə wö/tər] **62**–C
power [pow/ər] **48**–2
...sander [–săn/dər] **150**–9
...switch [–swĭch/] **144**–4
prairie dog [prër/ē dög/] **133**–22
pregnant [prĕg/nənt] **22**–19
PREPOSITIONS [prĕp/ə zĭsh/ənz] **13**
PREPOSITIONS OF MOTION [prĕp/ə zĭsh/ənz əv mō/shən] **105**

preschool [prē/sko͞ol/] **112**–4
prescription [prĭ skrĭp/shən] **80**–13
...label [–lā/bəl] **80**–14
...medication [–mĕd/ə kā/shən] **80**–11
President [prĕz/ə dənt] **116**–6
pretend [prĭ tĕnd/] **163**–G
price [prīs(/–)] **21**–6
...tag [–tăg/] **21**–1
principal [prĭn/sə pəl] **5**–14
principal's office [prĭn/sə pəlz ö/fəs] **5**–13
print [prĭnt] **4**–C
print [prĭnt] **70**–10
printer [prĭn/tər] (occupation) **138**–46, (computer) **144**–12
print shop [prĭnt/ shäp/] **91**–22
priority mail [prī ör/ə tē māl/, –är/–] **96**–12
prism [prĭz/əm] **119**–20
prison [prĭz/ən] **99**–G
private school [prī/vət sko͞ol/] **112**–2
Problems (clothing) [präb/ləmz] **70**
PROBLEMS, HOUSEHOLD [hows/hōld/ präb/ləmz] **48**–49
produce section [prō/do͞os sĕk/shən] **54**–11
product [präd/ŭkt] **118** ✦
program (computer) [prō/grăm] **144**–21
Programs (TV) [prō/grămz] **167**
projector [prə jĕk/tər] / [–prə jĕk/tər]
carousel slide... [kăr/ə sĕl/ slīd/–] **165**–29
overhead... [ō/vər hĕd/–] **2**–4
prosecuting attorney [präs/ĭ kyo͞o/tĭng ə tür/nē] **99**–10
protect your wallet [prə tĕkt/ yər wä/lət, –wö/–] **101**–D
proud [prowd] **31**–22
prunes [pro͞onz] **50**–26
pruning shears [pro͞o/nĭng shïrz/] **39**–15
psychiatrist [sī kī/ə trĭst, sə–] **86**–6
PUBLIC SAFETY [pŭb/lĭk sāf/tē] **101**
public school [pŭb/lĭk sko͞ol/] **112**–1
public telephone [pŭb/lĭk tĕl/ə fōn/] **91**–21
PUBLIC TRANSPORTATION
[pŭb/lĭk trăns/pər tā/shən] **104**
pudding [pŏŏd/ĭng] **61**–20
pull [pŏŏl(/–)]
...a tooth [–ə to͞oth/] **85**–M
...the wagon [–dhə wăg/ən] **153**–A
pullover sweater [pŏŏl/ō/vər swĕt/ər] **64**–11
pumps [pŭmps] **68**–16
Punctuation [pŭngk/cho͞o ā/shən] **113**
puppet show [pŭp/ət shō/] **152**–14
puppy [pŭp/ē] **133**–12
purple [pür/pəl] **12**–7
purses [pür/səz] **69**–6
push [pŏŏsh] **153**–B
pushpin [pŏŏsh/pĭn/] **143**–43
put away [pŏŏt/ə wā/] / [pŏŏt/ə wā/–]
...the toys [–dhə toyz/] **46**–H
...your pencil [–yər pĕn/səl] **2**–L
put in order [pŏŏt/ ĭn ör/dər] **7**–W
put on [pŏŏt/ än/, –ön/] / [pŏŏt/ än–, –ön–]
...makeup [–māk/ŭp/] **77**–P
...sunscreen [–sŭn/skrēn/] **76**–D
puzzle [pŭz/əl] **45**–22
pyramid [pïr/ə mĭd] **118**–13
quart [kwört] **57**–4
quarter [kwör/tər] (time) **16**, (money) **20**–4
quarter cup [kwör/tər kŭp/] **57**–8
quarter moon [kwör/tər mo͞on/] **127**–15
question mark [kwĕs/chən märk/] **113**–7

Index

quiet [kwī/ət] **11**–12
quill [kwĭl] **134**–23
quiz show [kwĭz/ shō/] **167**–23
quotation marks [kwō tā/shən märks/] **113**–9
quotient [kwō/shənt] **118** ✦
rabbit [răb/ət] **133**–13
raccoon [ră kōōn/] **134**–13
race [rās] **157**–Y
racquetball [răk/ət böl/] **159**–11
radiation [rā/dē ā/shən] **126**–13
radiator [rā/dē ā/tər] **109**–42, 56
radio [rā/dē ō] **44**–16, **108**–31
    …program [-prō/grăm] **166**–4
radioactive [rā/dē ō ăk/tĭv] **147**–6
radiologist [rā/dē ä l/ə jĭst] **86**–5
radishes [răd/ĭ shəz] **51**–5
radius [rā/dē əs] **118**–16
rafting [răf/tĭng] **154**–4
rags [răgz] **47**–6
railroad crossing [rāl/rōd krö/sĭng] **107**–11
rain boots [rān/ bōōts/] **66**–19
raincoat [rān/kōt/] **66**–17
rain forest [rān/ för/əst, fär/–] **117**–1
raining [rā/nĭng] **10**–8
raise [rāz] **2**–A
raisins [rā/zənz] **50**–27
rake [rāk] **39**–F
rake [rāk] **39**–11
ranch [rănch] **34**–12
rancher [răn/chər] **148**–22
RANCHING [răn/chĭng] **148**
rash [răsh] **78**–10
raspberries [răz/bĕr/ēz] **50**–18
rat [răt] **133**–18
rats [răts] **49**–27
rattle [răt/l] **95**–31
rattlesnake [răt/l snāk/] **131**–38
raw [rö] **52**–24
ray [rā] **130**–6
rayon [rā/än] **70**
razor [rā/zər] **77**–25
    …blade [–blād/] **77**–26
read [rēd] **6**–B, **27**–V, **94**–F
Realtor [rē/əl tər] **35**
rearview mirror [rïr/vyōō/ mïr/ər] **108**–1
receipt [rĭ sēt/] **21**–5
receive [rĭ sēv/] **96**–D
receiver [rĭ sē/vər] **9**–2
receptionist [rĭ sĕp/shə nĭst] **84**–2, **138**–47
recharging [rē chär/jĭng] **109**–58
record [rĕk/ərd] **98**–15
record [rĭ körd/] (science) **119**–C, (cassette player) **165**–A
Recreation room [rĕk/rē ā/shən rōōm/] **36**
rec room [rĕk/ rōōm/] **36** ✦
rectangle [rĕk/tăng/gəl] **118**–8
recycle [rē sī/kəl] **46**–B, **126**–A
recycling bin [rē sī/klĭng bĭn/] **47**–2
red [rĕd(/–)] **12**–13
    …hair [–hër/] **23**–14
redwood [rĕd/wōōd/] **128**–1
referee [rĕf/ə rē/] **158**–6
reference [rĕf/rəns]
    …desk [–dĕsk/] **98**–2
    …librarian [lī brër/ē ən] **98**–1
refrigerator [rĭ frĭj/ə rā/tər] **40**–9

register [rĕj/ə stər] **116**–F
registered [rĕj/ə stərd]
    …nurse (RN) [–nürs/] **87**–22
regular price [rĕg/yə lər prīs/] **21**–2
relax [rĭ lăks/] **27**–U
relieved [rĭ lēvd/] **30**–16
religious holiday [rĭ lĭj/əs häl/ə dā/] **19**–44
relish [rĕl/ĭsh] **60**–26
remarried [rē măr/ēd] **25**–27
remote control [rĭ mōt/ kən trōl/] **164**–9
remove [rĭ mōōv/] **97**–F
rent [rĕnt] **28**–I
Renting an apartment [rĕn/tĭng ən ə pärt/mənt] **35**
repair [rĭ për/] **140**–G
repair person [rĭ për/ pür/sən] **48**–10, **138**–48
REPAIRS [rĭ përz/] **48**–49
repeat [rĭ pēt/] **6**–D
report crimes [rĭ pört/ krīmz/] **101**–H
reporter [rĭ pör/tər] **99**–12, **139**–49
Reptiles [rĕp/tīlz] **131**
request [rĭ kwĕst/] **111**–M
rescue breathing [rĕs/kyōō brē/dhĭng] **83**–16
Resident Alien card [rĕz/ə dənt ā/lē ən kärd/] **29**–3
respirator [rĕs/pə rā/tər] **147**–12
Responsibilities (of citizenship)
    [rĭ spän/sə bĭl/ə tēz əv sĭt/ə zən shĭp/] **116**
RESTAURANT [rĕs/tə rənt, –ränt/] **62**–63
restaurant [rĕs/tə rənt, –ränt/] **90**–14
rest rooms [rĕst/ rōōmz/] **5**–8
retire [rĭ tīr/] **29** ✦
return [rĭ türn/] **21**–F
return address [rĭ türn/ ə drĕs/, –ă/drĕs] **96**–7
rewind [rē wīnd/] **165**–D
rewrite [rē rīt/] **113**–D
rhinoceros [rī näs/ər əs] **135**–29
rib cage [rĭb/ kāj/] **75**–53
rice [rīs(/–)] **54**–28, **148**–1
    …pilaf [–pē/läf, –pĭ läf/] **61**–18
ride [rīd] **91**–E, **157**–W
rides [rīdz] **152**–17
right [rīt(/–)] / [–rīt/]
    …turn only [–türn/ ōn/lē] **107**–9
    on the… [än dhə–, ön–] **13**–2
right-of-way [rīt/əv wā/] **107** ✦
Rights and responsibilities [rīts/ ən rĭ spän/sə bĭl/ə tēz] **116**
ring [rĭng] **69**–39
rinse [rĭns] **76**–F
rip [rĭp] **70**–23
ripe [rīp] **50**–29
river [rĭv/ər] **117**–3
RN (registered nurse) [är/ĕn/] **87**–22
roast [rōst] **58**–U
roast [rōst(/–)]
    …beef [–bēf/] **52**–1, **53**–7, **57**–12
    …chicken [–chĭk/ən] **61**–12
roasting [rō/stĭng]
    …pan [–păn/] **59**–13
    …rack [–răk/] **59**–14
robin [räb/ən] **132**–17
rock [räk] **94**–H
rock [räk(/–)] **155**–24
rock band [räk/ bănd/] **120**–2
rocking chair [räk/ĭng chër/] **94**–6
RODENTS [rōd/nts] **133**
roll [rōl(/–)] **56**–11

...of paper towels [–əv pā/pər tow/əlz] **56**–23
roller coaster [rō/lər kō/stər] **152**–15
rollers [rō/lərz] **23**–21
rolling pin [rō/lĭng pĭn/] **59**–30
rolls [rōlz] **54**–30
romance [rō mǎns/, rō/mǎns] **166**–16
Roman numerals [rō/mən nōō/mər əlz] **14**
roof [rōōf] **38**–20, **48**–3
roofer [rōō/fər] **48**–8
roof garden [rōōf/ gär/dn] **36**–5
room service [rōōm/ sür/vəs] **145**–12
rooster [rōō/stər] **133**–6
root [rōōt] **128**–5, **129**–3
rope [rōp] **154**–19
rose [rōz] **129**–15
rotary card file [rō/tə rē kärd/ fīl/] **143**–17
rotten [rät/n] **50**–30
rouge [rōōzh] **77**–36
route [rōōt, rowt] **104**–2
router [row/tər] **150**–12
rubber [rŭb/ər]
  ...band [–bǎnd/] **143**–45
  ...cement [–sə mĕnt/] **143**–38
  ...gloves [–glŭvz/] **47**–4
  ...mat [–mǎt/] **43**–3
  ...stamp [–stǎmp/] **143**–40
rug [rŭg] **44**–23
ruler [rōō/lər] **3**–27
run [rŭn] **156**–C
rural area [rōōr/əl ër/ē ə] **34**–4
rye bread [rī/ brĕd/] **53**–3
sad [sǎd] **31**–20, **167**–28
safe-deposit box [sāf/dĭ päz/ət bäks/] **97**–13
safety [sāf/tē]
  ...boot [–bōōt/] **147**–20
  ...earmuffs [–ïr/mŭfs] **147**–14
  ...glasses [–glǎs/əz] **147**–10
  ...goggles [–gäg/əlz] **147**–9
  ...pin [–pĭn/] **73**–24
  ...seat [–sēt/] **109**–39
  ...vest [–vĕst/] **147**–15
  ...visor [–vī/zər] **147**–11
SAFETY, PUBLIC [pŭb/lĭk sāf/tē] **101**
sailboarding [sāl/bör/dĭng] **160**–10
sailboat [sāl/bōt/] **155**–4
sailing [sā/lĭng] **160**–8
salad [sǎl/əd]
  ...bar [–bär/] **60**–16
  ...dressing [–drĕs/ĭng] **60**–18
  ...fork [–förk/] **63**–24
  ...plate [–plāt/] **63**–17
salamander [sǎl/ə mǎn/dər] **130**–27
salami [sə lä/mē] **53**–5
sale price [sāl/ prīs/] **21**–3
salesclerk [sālz/klürk/] **68**–1, **139**–50
salesperson [sālz/pür/sən] **139**–50
sales tax [sālz/ tǎks/] **21**–7
salmon steak [sǎm/ən stāk/] **53**–19
saltshaker [sölt/shā/kər] **41**–14
sand [sǎnd(/–)] **155**–23
  ...castle [–kǎs/əl] **155**–10
  ...dune [–dōōn/] **117**–5
sandals [sǎn/dlz] **68**–24
sandbox [sǎnd/bäks/] **153**–15
sandpaper [sǎnd/pā/pər] **151**–50

sanitation worker [sǎn/ə tā/shən wür/kər] **139**–51
Saturday [sǎt/ər dā/, –dē] **18**–7
Saturn [sǎt/ərn] **127**–4
saucepan [sös/pǎn/] **59**–25
saucer [sö/sər] **63**–22
sausage [sö/sĭj] **52**–12, **61**–2
sauté [sö tā/, sō–] **58**–H
save [sāv] **126**–B, C
savings account number [sā/vĭngz ə kownt/ nŭm/bər] **97**–6
saxophone [sǎk/sə fōn/] **120**–7
say [sā] **6**–C
scaffolding [skǎf/əl dĭng] **149**–4
scale (weight) [skāl] **43**–26, **84**–7
scales (fish) [skālz] **130**–3
scallions [skǎl/yənz] **51**–17
scallop [skǎl/əp, skäl/–] **130**–18
scallops [skǎl/əps, skäl/–] **53**–25
scanner [skǎn/ər] **144**–13
scared [skërd] **31**–24
scarf [skärf] **66**–4, **70**–15
schedule [skĕj/ōōl, –ōō əl] **104**–3
SCHOOL [skōōl] **5**
school **89**–27
  ...crossing [–krö/sĭng] **107**–13
  adult... [ə dŭlt/–, ăd/ŭlt–] **112**–8
  elementary... [ĕl/ə mĕn/trē–] **112**–5
  high... [hī/–] **112**–7
  junior high... [jōōn/yər hī/–] **112**–6
  middle... [mĭd/l–] **112**–6
  parochial... [pə rō/kē əl–] **112**–3
  private... [prī/vət–] **112**–2
  trade... [trād/–] **112**–9
  vocational... [vō kā/shə nəl–] **112**–9
School Registration Form [skōōl/ rĕj/ə strā/shən förm/] **4**
SCHOOLS, TYPES OF [tīps/ əv skōōlz/] **112**
SCHOOL SUBJECTS, MORE [mör/ skōōl/ sŭb/jĭkts] **121**
SCIENCE [sī/əns] **119**
science fiction story [sī/əns fĭk/shən stör/ē] **166**–12
scissors [sĭz/ərz] **23**–19, **73**–18
score [skör] **158**–1
scorpion [skör/pē ən] **132**–31
scrambled eggs [skrǎm/bəld ĕgz/] **58**, **61**–1
scraper [skrā/pər] **151**–48
screen [skrēn] **2**–2, **144**–6, **152**–12, **165**–28
screen door [skrēn/ dör/] **38**–8
screwdriver [skrōō/drī/vər] **150**–25
  Phillips... [fĭl/ĭps–] **150**–26
scrub [skrŭb] **46**–L
scrub brush [skrŭb/ brŭsh/] **47**–19
scuba [skōō/bə]
  ...diving [–dī/vĭng] **160**–12
  ...tank [–tǎngk/] **155**–8
sculpture [skŭlp/chər] **152**–9
sea [sē(/–)]
  ...anemone [–ə nĕm/ə nē] **130**–21
  ...horse [–hörs/] **130**–23
  ...lion [–lī/ən] **131**–34
  ...urchin [–ür/chən] **130**–20
Sea animals [sē/ ǎn/ə məlz] **130**
SEAFOOD [sē/fōōd/] **53**
seal [sēl] **131**–33
seam [sēm(/–)] **73**–11
  ...ripper [–rĭp/ər] **73**–19
Sea mammals [sē/ mǎm/əlz] **131**
search and rescue team [sürch/ ən rĕs/kyōō tēm/] **103**–17

seashell [sē/shĕl/] **155**–21
Seasons [sē/zənz] **19**
seat [sēt(/–)] **2**–E, **152**–11
...belt [–bĕlt/] **109**–36
seat [sēt] **62**–B
seaweed [sē/wēd/] **155** ✦
second [sĕk/ənd] **14, 16**–1
...floor [–flör/] **36**–2
secretary [sĕk/rə tër/ē] **139**–52, **142**–3
section [sĕk/shən] / [–sĕk/shən]
    dairy... [dër/ē–] **54**–9
    produce... [prō/dōōs–] **54**–11
security [sĭ kyŏŏr/ə tē] **111**–C
    ...gate [–gāt/] **36**–13
    ...guard [–gärd/] **97**–4
    ...system [–sĭs/təm] **36**–9
see [sē] **75**–A
seed [sēd] **129**–1
seedling [sēd/lĭng] **129**–2
seesaw [sē/sö/] **153**–16
See you [sē/ yə] **8**
Selective Service [sə lĕk/tĭv sür/vəs] **116**–F
sell [sĕl] **21**–B, **140**–H
semi [sĕm/ī] **106**–15
semicolon [sĕm/ē kō/lən] **113**–13
Senate [sĕn/ət] **116**–3
Senator [sĕn/ə tər] **116**–4
send [sĕnd] **96**–B
senior citizen [sēn/yər sĭt/ə zən] **22**–12
Senses [sĕn/səz] **75**
sentence [sĕn/tns] **113**–4
sentence the defendant [sĕn/tns dhə dĭ fĕn/dənt] **99**–F
September [sĕp tĕm/bər] **19**–33
serious [sĭr/ē əs] **167**–26
Serious Diseases [sĭr/ē əs dĭ zē/zəz] **79**
serve (sports) [sürv] **157**–N
serve on a jury [sürv/ än ə jŏŏr/ē, –ön–] **116**–G
server [sür/vər] **62**–4, **63**–6, **139**–53
serve the meal [sürv/ dhə mēl/] **62**–F
service elevator [sür/vəs ĕl/ə vā tər] **145** ✦
serviceman [sür/vəs măn/, –mən] **139**–54
servicewoman [sür/vəs wŏŏm/ən] **139**–54
serving dish [sür/vĭng dĭsh/] **41**–6
set [sĕt(/–)]
    ...hair [–hër/] **23**–C
    ...the table [–dhə tā/bəl] **62**–A
set of dishes [sĕt/ əv dĭsh/əz] **41**–2
seven [sĕv/ən] **14**
seventeen [sĕv/ən tēn/] **14**
seventeenth [sĕv/ən tēnth/] **14**
seventh [sĕv/ənth] **14**
seventy [sĕv/ən tē] **14**
sew [sō(/–)]
    ...by hand [–bī hănd/] **73**–A
    ...by machine [–bī mə shēn/] **73**–B
    ...clothes [–klōz/] **140**–L
SEWING AND ALTERATIONS [sō/ĭng ən öl/tə rā/shənz] **73**
sewing machine [sō/ĭng mə shēn/] **73**–10
sex [sĕks] **4**–12
shade [shād] **155**–11
shampoo [shăm pōō/] **76**–9
Shapes [shāps] **118**
share [shër] **6**–I
shark [shärk] **130**–7
shave [shāv] **77**–M

shaving cream [shā/vĭng krēm/] **77**–27
shears [shĭrz] **39**–15
sheep [shēp] **133**–7
sheet [shēt] **44**–13, 14
shelf [shĕlf] **40**–8
Shellfish [shĕl/fĭsh/] **53**
shelter [shĕl/tər] **34**–10
shingles [shĭng/gəlz] **149**–19
shin guards [shĭn/ gärdz/] **161**–13
ship [shĭp] **146**–C
shipping clerk [shĭp/ĭng klürk/] **146**–15
shirt [shürt] **64**–4, **65**–20
shock [shäk] **82**–C
shoe [shōō(/–)]
    ...department [–dĭ pärt/mənt] **68**–3
    ...store [–stör/] **92**–10
shoelace [shōō/lās/] **68**–14
SHOES AND ACCESSORIES [shōōz/ ən ĭk sĕs/ə rēz] **68**–69
shoot [shōōt] **156**–I
shop [shäp] **21**–A
shop [shäp] **121**–10
SHOPPING [shäp/ĭng] **21**
shopping [shäp/ĭng]
    ...basket [–băs/kət] **54**–7
    ...cart [–kärt/] **54**–3
    ...program [–prō/grăm] **167**–25
shore [shör] **117**–12
short [shört] **22**–18, **23**–1, **71**–35
shorten [shör/tn] **73**–D
short-sleeved [shört/slēvd/] **71**–30
shorts [shörts] **64**–13, **67**–3, 12
shortwave radio [shört/wāv/ rā/dē ō] **164**–5
shoulder [shōl/dər] **74**–10
    ...bag [–băg/] **69**–27
    ...harness [–här/nəs] **109**–37
    ...pads [–pădz/] **161**–21
shoulder-length [shōl/dər lĕngkth/] **23**–2
shout [showt] **169**–G
shovel [shŭv/əl] **39**–13, **149**–21
show (puppet) [shō] **152**–14
shower cap [show/ər kăp/] **76**–1
showerhead [show/ər hĕd/] **43**–10
shrimp [shrĭmp] **53**–24, **130**–19
shutter [shŭt/ər] **38**–18
sick [sĭk] **30**–14
side [sīd] **118**–22
sideburns [sīd/bürnz/] **23**–7
sideview mirror [sīd/vyōō/ mĭr/ər] **108**–8
sidewalk [sīd/wök/] **91**–26
sight impaired [sīt/ ĭm përd/] **22**–26
sign [sīn(/–)]
    ...a rental agreement [–ə rĕn/təl ə grē/mənt] **35**–C
    ...your name [–yər nām/] **4**–D
sign [sīn] **91**–29
signature [sĭg/nə chər] **4**–18
Signs [sīnz] **107**
silk [sĭlk] **70**–15
silk scarves [sĭlk/ skärvz/] **68**–4
silver dollar [sĭl/vər däl/ər] **20**–6
simmer [sĭm/ər] **58**–R
sing [sĭng] **120**–B, **169**–I
single [sĭng/gəl]
    ...father [–fä/dhər] **25**–25
    ...mother [–mŭdh/ər] **25**–26
sink [sĭngk] **40**–6, **43**–22, **49**–17

sister [sĭs/tər] **24**–8, **25**–30, 32
sister-in-law [sĭs/tər ĭn lö/] **24**–15
sitcom [sĭt/käm] **167**–18
sit down [sĭt/ down/] **2**–E
situation comedy [sĭch/ōō ā/shən käm/ə dē] **167**–18
six [sĭks] **14**
six-pack [sĭks/päk/] **56**–9
six-pack of soda [sĭks/päk/ əv sō/də] **56**–21
sixteen [sĭks/tēn/] **14**
sixteenth [sĭks/tēnth/] **14**
sixth [sĭksth] **14**
sixty [sĭks/tē] **14**
six-year-old [sĭks/yïr ōld/] **22**–4
Sizes [sī/zəz] **70**
skate [skāt] **157**–V
skateboarding [skāt/bör/dĭng] **159**–12
skating [skā/tĭng] **160**–4, 5
Skeleton [skĕl/ə tn] **75**
ski [skē] **157**–V
ski [skē(/–)]
   ...boots [–bōōts/] **161**–26
   ...cap [–kăp/] **66**–10
   ...mask [–măsk/] **66**–14
   ...poles [–pōlz/] **161**–25
skiing [skē/ĭng] **160**–1, 3, 7
skin [skĭn] **75**–51
skinless [skĭn/ləs] **52** ✦
skirt [skürt] **64**–10, **65**–25
skis [skēz] **161**–24
skull [skŭl] **75**–52
skunk [skŭngk] **134**–12
skyscraper [skī/skrā/pər] **88** ✦
slacks [slăks] **64**–8
sledding [slĕd/ĭng] **160**–6
sledgehammer [slĕj/hăm/ər] **149**–22
sleeping bag [slē/pĭng băg/] **154**–12
sleepy [slē/pē] **30**–3
sleeve [slēv] **73**–6
sleeveless [slēv/ləs] **71**–29
slice [slīs] **58**–O
slide [slīd] (science) **119**–5, (park) **153**–13
slides [slīdz] **165**–31
slide tray [slīd/ trā/] **165**–30
slim [slĭm] **22**–22
sling [slĭng] **80**–8
slippers [slĭp/ərz] **67**–6
slot [slät] **144**–19
slow [slō] **11**–4
small [smöl(/–)] **70**–2
   ...town [–town/] **34**–3
smell [smĕl] **75**–C
smog [smäg(/–), smög(/–)] **126**–10
   ...check [–chĕk/] **109**–57
smoggy [smä/gē, smö/–] **10**–14
smoke detector [smōk/ dĭ tĕk/tər] **37**–25, **45**–11
smoked turkey [smōkt/ tür/kē] **53**–4
snack foods [snăk/ fōōdz/] **55**–16
snail [snāl] **130**–24
snake [snāk] **131**–38, 39
sneeze [snēz] **78**–B
snorkeling [snör/kə lĭng] **160**–11
snowboard [snō/börd/] **161**–23
snowboarding [snō/bör/dĭng] **160**–2
snowing [snō/ĭng] **10**–9
snowstorm [snō/störm/] **10**–20

soap [sōp(/–)] **43**–23, **76**–2
   ...dish [–dĭsh/] **43**–24
   ...pads [–pădz/] **47**–5
soap opera [sōp/ äp/rə] **167**–21
soccer [säk/ər] **158**–12
   ...ball [–böl/] **161**–12
Social Security card [sō/shəl sĭ kyōōr/ə tē kärd/] **29**–5
Social Security number [sō/shəl sĭ kyōōr/ə tē nŭm/bər] **4**–15
socks [säks] **67**–15
soda [sō/də] **55**–52, **60**–4
sofa [sō/fə] **42**–19
soft [söft] **11**–6
softball [söft/böl/] **158**–10
Software [söft/wër/] **144**
solar [sō/lər]
   ...eclipse [–ĭ klĭps/] **127** ✦
   ...energy [–ĕn/ər jē] **126**–1
   ...system [–sĭs/təm] **127**
sole [sōl] (fish) **53**–21, (shoe) **68**–12
solid [säl/əd] **70**–6
Solids [säl/ədz] **118**
son [sŭn] **24**–22
son-in-law [sŭn/ĭn lö/] **24** ✦
sore throat [sör/ thrōt/] **78**–6
Sorry. [sär/ē, sör/ē] **8**
sort [sört] **72**–A
soup [sōōp(/–)] **54**–24
   ...bowl [–bōl/] **63**–18
   ...of the day [–əv dhə dā/] **61**–10
soupspoon [sōōp/spōōn/] **63**–29
sour cream [sow/ər krēm/] **54**–37
south [sowth] **107**, **123**, **124**
soybeans [soy/bēnz/] **148**–3
space [spās(/–)] **127**–22
   ...station [–stā/shən] **127**–18
spades [spādz] **163**–28
spaghetti [spə gĕt/ē] **54**–27
spare tire [spër/ tīr/] **109**–53
sparrow [spär/ō] **132**–8
spatula [spăch/ə lə] **59**–19
speak [spēk] **140**–J
speaker [spē/kər] **36**–8
speakers [spē/kərz] **164**–11
specialist [spĕsh/ə lĭst] **86** ✦
speed [spēd(/–)] **144** ✦
   ...limit [–lĭm/ət] **107**–5
speedometer [spĭ däm/ə tər] **108**–20
spell [spĕl] **4**–A, **6**–E
sphere [sfïr] **118**–14
spices [spī/səz] **55**–46
spider [spī/dər] **132**–30
spinach [spĭn/ĭch] **51**–11
spinal column [spī/nəl käl/əm] **75**–54
spiral notebook [spī/rəl nōt/bōōk/] **3**–26
splint [splĭnt] **83**–11
split skirt [splĭt/ skürt/] **65**–25
sponge [spŭnj] **47**–24
spool of thread [spōōl/ əv thrĕd/] **73**–17
spoon [spōōn] **41**–23, **59**–9
SPORTS [spörts] **158**–160
sports [spörts(/–)]
   ...car [–kär/] **106**–6
   ...coat [–kōt/] **64**–6
   ...shirt [–shürt/] **65**–26
SPORTS EQUIPMENT [spörts/ ĭ kwĭp/mənt] **161**

Index

SPORTS VERBS [spörts/ vürbz/] **156–157**
sprained ankle [sprānd/ ăng/kəl] **78**–18
spray [sprā(/–)]
...gun [–gŭn/] **151**–19
...starch [–stärch/] **72**–12
spring [sprĭng] **19**–37
sprinkler [sprĭng/klər] **39**–8
square [skwër] **118**–6
squash [skwäsh, skwösh] **51**–13
squeegee [skwē/jē] **47**–9
squid [skwĭd] **130**–10
squirrel [skwür/əl] **133**–21
stacking tray [stăk/ĭng trā/] **142**–5
stadium [stā/dē əm] **152**–26
stage [stāj] **32**–4
stain [stān] **70**–22
stairs [stërz] **37**–35, **105**–8, 9
stairway [stër/wā/] **37**–26
stall shower [stöl/ show/ər] **43** ✦
stamp [stămp(/–)] **96**–10
...collection [–kə lĕk/shən] **162**–12
standard [stăn/dərd]
...time [–tīm/] **17**–32
...transmission [–trănz mĭsh/ən, –trăns–] **109**
stand trial [stănd/ trī/əl, –trīl/] **99**–D
stand up [stănd/ ŭp/] **2**–D
stand-up comedy [stănd/ŭp/ kăm/ə dē] **166**–5
staple [stā/pəl] **142**–G
staple [stā/pəl] **143**–29
stapler [stā/plər] **143**–28
star [stär] **127**–23
starfish [stär/fĭsh/] **130**–15
start [stärt(/–)] **157**–X
...school [–skōol/] **28**–B
starving [stär/vĭng] **30** ✦
state [stāt] **4**–8
station wagon [stā/shən wăg/ən] **106**–8
stay [stā] **101**–B
steak [stāk(/–)] **52**–2, **61**–13
...knife [–nīf/] **63**–26
steam [stēm] **58**–I
steamer [stē/mər] **59**–4
steel-wool soap pads [stēl/wōol/ sōp/ pădz/] **47**–5
steering wheel [stïr/ĭng wēl/] **108**–26
steers [stïrz] **148**–21
stem [stĕm] **129**–4
stepbrother [stĕp/brŭdh/ər] **25**–33
stepdaughter [stĕp/dö/tər] **25** ✦
stepfather [stĕp/fä/dhər] **25**–28
stepladder [stĕp/lăd/ər] **47**–7
stepmother [stĕp/mŭdh/ər] **25**–31
steps [stĕps] **38**–13, **48**–7
stepsister [stĕp/sĭs/tər] **25**–32
stereo system [stĕr/ē ō sĭs/təm] **42**–14
sterile pad [stĕr/əl păd/] **83**–4
stethoscope [stĕth/ə skōp/] **84**–8
stewing beef [stōo/ĭng bēf/] **52**–3
stick shift [stĭk/ shĭft/] **109**–48
stir [stür] **58**–E
stir-fry [stür/frī/] **58**–W
stitches [stĭch/əz] **83**–15
stock clerk [stäk/ klürk/] **139**–55
stockings [stäk/ĭngz] **67**–26
stomach [stŭm/ək] **75**–41
stomachache [stŭm/ək āk/] **78**–4

stop [stäp] **165** F
stop [stäp] **107**–3
stopover [stäp/ō/vər] **111** ✦
stopped up [stäpt/ ŭp/] **49**–18
storage locker [stör/ĭj läk/ər] **36**–14
store [stör(/–)] / [–stör/]
...owner [–ō/nər] **139**–56
candy... [kăn/dē–] **92**–3
card... [kärd/–] **92**–7
convenience... [kən vēn/yəns–] **90**–3
department... [dĭ pärt/mənt–] **93**–13
electronics... [ĭ lĕk trän/ĭks–] **93**–18
jewelry... [jōo/əl rē–] **92**–2
music... [myōo/zĭk–] **92**–1
pet... [pĕt/–] **92**–6
shoe... [shōo/–] **92**–10
toy... [toy/–] **92**–5
video... [vĭd/ē ō–] **93**–15
storm [störm] **10**–16, 18, 20, 21
storm door [störm/ dör/] **38**–12
stove [stōv] **40**–18, **154**–16
stow [stō] **111**–H
straight [strāt(/–)]
...hair [–hër/] **23**–9
...line [–līn/] **118**–18
strainer [strā/nər] **59**–22
stranger [strān/jər] **101**–F
straw [strö] **60**–20
strawberries [strö/bĕr/ēz] **50**–17
straw hat [strö/ hăt/] **66**–23
stream [strēm] **117** ✦
street [strēt(/–)] **90**–9
...vendor [–vĕn/dər] **91**–30
streetlight [strēt/līt/] **91**–23
strep throat [strĕp/ thrōt/] **79**–4
stretch [strĕch] **157**–Q
stretcher [strĕch/ər] **87**–28
string beans [strĭng/ bēnz/] **51**–25
string of pearls [strĭng/ əv pürlz/] **69**–30
Strings [strĭngz] **120**
striped [strīpt] **70**–7
stroller [strō/lər] **94**–2
stucco [stŭk/ō] **149**–14
student [stōod/nt] **2**–3, **139**–57
STUDYING [stŭd/ē ĭng] **6**–7
stuffed animals [stŭft/ ăn/ə məlz] **45**–23
subcompact [sŭb/käm/păkt] **106**–1
subtraction [səb trăk/shən] **118**–2
suburbs [sŭb/ürbz] **34**–2
subway [sŭb/wā/] **104**–9
sugar [shōog/ər] **55**–48, **60**–21
...bowl [–bōl/] **41**–12
...substitute [–sŭb/stə tōot/] **60**–22
suit [sōot] (clothing) **64**–2, (diving) **155**–7
summer [sŭm/ər] **19**–38
sun [sŭn] **127**–10
sunbather [sŭn/bā/dhər] **155**–17
sunblock [sŭn/bläk/] **155**–13
sunburn [sŭn/bürn/] **78**–14
Sunday [sŭn/dā, –dē] **18**–1
sunflower [sŭn/flow/ər] **129**–10
sunglasses [sŭn/glăs/əz] **66**–21
sunny [sŭn/ē] **10**–6
sunscreen [sŭn/skrēn/] **76**–6, **155**–13
superintendent [sōo/prĭn tĕn/dənt, sōo/pər ĭn–] **36**–12

supervise people [sōo/pər vīz pē/pəl] **140**–K
supply cabinet [sə plī/ kăb/ə nət] **142**–13
Supreme Court [sə prēm/ kört/] **116**–8
surfboard [sürf/börd/] **155**–5
surfing [sür/fĭng] **160**–9
surgeon [sür/jən] **87**–30
surge protector [sürj/ prə tĕk/tər] **144**–10
surgical [sür/jĭ kəl]
...cap [–kăp/] **87**–31
...gown [–gown/] **87**–32
...nurse [–nürs/] **87**–29
surprised [sər prīzd/, sə–] **31**–31
suspect [sŭs/pĕkt] **99**–A
suspenders [sə spĕn/dərz] **68**–2
SUV (sports utility vehicle)
[ĕs/yōo/vē/] / [spörts/ yōo tĭl/ə tē vē/ĭ kəl] **106**–9
swallow [swäl/ō] **82**–J
swap meet [swäp/ mēt/] **152**–22
sweater [swĕt/ər]
cardigan... [kär/də gən–] **65**–27
crewneck... [krōo/nĕk/–] **71**–26
pullover... [pool/ō/vər–] **64**–11
turtleneck... [tür/tl nĕk/–] **71**–28
V-neck... [vē/nĕk/–] **71**–27
sweatpants [swĕt/pănts/] **64**–15
sweatshirt [swĕt/shürt/] **64**–14
sweep [swēp] **46**–E
sweet peppers [swēt/ pĕp/ərz] **51**–7
swim [swĭm] **157**–T
swimming [swĭm/ĭng]
...pool [–pool/] **37**–16
...trunks [–trŭngks/] **66**–22
swimsuit [swĭm/sōot/] **66**–26
swing [swĭng] **157**–O
swings [swĭngz] **153**–12
Swiss cheese [swĭs/ chēz/] **53**–11
swivel chair [swĭv/əl chër/] **143**–22
swollen [swō/lən] **78**–16
swordfish [sörd/fĭsh/] **130**–12
SYMPTOMS AND INJURIES [sĭmp/təmz ən ĭn/jə rēz] **78**
synagogue [sĭn/ə gäg/] **88**–9
synthetic materials [sĭn thĕt/ĭk mə tïr/ē əlz] **70**
syringe [sə rĭnj/] **84**–14
syrup [sïr/əp, sür/–] **61**–5
table [tā/bəl] / [–tā/bəl]
dining room... [dī/nĭng rōom/–] **41**–17
night... [nīt/–] **44**–21
picnic... [pĭk/nĭk–] **153**–8
tablecloth [tā/bəl klöth/] **41**–18
tablespoon [tā/bəl spōon/] **57**–7
tablet [tăb/lət] **81**–25
table tennis [tā/bəl tĕn/əs] **159**–13
tackle [tăk/əl] **156**–M
taco [tä/kō] **60**–9
tail [tāl] **134**–22
taillight [tāl/līt/] **108**–14
tailor [tā/lər] **73**–9
take [tāk(/–)]
...a bath [–ə băth/] **76**–B
...a citizenship test [–ə sĭt/ə zən shĭp tĕst/] **116**–C
...a message [–ə mĕs/ĭj] **142**–A
...a nap [–ə năp/] **94**–L
...a picture [–ə pĭk/chər] **32**–D
...a seat [–ə sēt/] **2**–E
...a shower [–ə show/ər] **26**–C, **76**–A

...medicine [–mĕd/ə sən] **80**–F
...ownership [–ō/nər shĭp/] **35**–J
...the bus [–dhə bŭs/] **26**–H, **104** ✦
...the children to school [–dhə chĭl/drən tə skōol/] **26**–G
...the order [–dhē ör/dər] **62**–E
...(your) temperature [–yər tĕm/prə chər] **85**–C
take care of [tāk/ kër/ əv] **140**–L
take in [tāk/ ĭn/] **73**–E
take off [tāk/ öf/] **111**–L
take out [tāk/ owt/] **2**–K, **46**–Q
take out (food) [tāk/ owt/] **62** ✦
talcum powder [tăl/kəm pow/dər] **76**–3
talk [tök] **2**–B, **7**–P, **35**–B, G, **141**–A, I
talk show [tök/ shō/] **167**–20
tall [töl] **22**–16
tambourine [tăm/bə rēn/] **120**–19
tangerines [tăn/jə rēnz/] **50**–13
tank top [tăngk/ tăp/] **67**–2
tape [tāp(/–)] **83**–5, **143**–39, 42
...deck [–dĕk/] **108**–30
...measure [–mĕzh/ər] **73**–13, **150**–22
target [tär/gət] **161**–8
tartar [tär/tər] **84**–17
taste [tāst] **75**–D
taxi [tăk/sē] **104**–18
...driver [–drī/vər] **104**–20
...license [–lī/səns] **104**–22
...stand [–stănd/] **104**–19
TB (tuberculosis) [tē/bē/] / [tōo bür/kyə lō/səs] **79**–13
tea [tē] **60**–5, **61**–24
teach [tēch] **140** ✦
teacher [tē/chər] **2**–5, **5**–2, **139**–58
teakettle [tē/kĕt/l] **40**–17
team [tēm] **103**–17, **158**–3
TEAM SPORTS [tēm/ spörts/] **158**
teapot [tē/pät/] **41**–11
tear [tër] **70**–23
teaspoon [tē/spōon/] **57**–6, **63**–28
technician [tĕk nĭsh/ən] **86**–8, 16
teddy bear [tĕd/ē bër/] **45**–10
teenagers [tē/nā/jərz] **22**–6
teeth [tēth] **74**–25, **77**–J, K, **85**–I
teething ring [tē/dhĭng rĭng/] **95**–30
telemarketer [tĕl/ə mär/kə tər] **139**–59
TELEPHONE [tĕl/ə fōn/] **9**
telephone [tĕl/ə fōn/] **9**–1, 15
...book [–book/] **9**–15
...card [–kärd/] **9**–10
...number [–nŭm/bər] **4**–11
telescope [tĕl/ə skōp/] **127**–21
television (TV) [tĕl/ə vĭzh/ən] **42**–26, **164**–6
...program [–prō/grăm] **166**–3
teller [tĕl/ər] **97**–1
Temperature (weather) [tĕm/prə chər] **10**
temperature (fever) [tĕm/prə chər] **78**–8
temperature gauge [tĕm/prə chər gāj/] **108**–23
ten [tĕn] **14**, **15**–7, **16**–6, **20**–9
tenant [tĕn/ənt] **37**–33
tennis [tĕn/əs] **159**–14
...court [–kört/] **153**–7
...racket [–răk/ət] **161**–2
...shoes [–shōoz/] **68**–22
tent [tĕnt] **154**–10
tenth [tĕnth] **14**
ten-year-old [tĕn/yïr ōld/] **22**–5

termites [tür/mīts] **49**–22
terrified [tĕr/ə fīd/] **30** ✦
test tube [tĕst/ tōōb/] **119**–16
textbook [tĕkst/bŏŏk/, tĕks/–] **3**–22
thank [thăngk] **8**–H
Thanksgiving [thăngks gĭv/ĭng] **168**–15
Thank you [thăngk/ yōō] **8**
theater [thē/ə tər] / [thē/ə tər] **88**–10
   …arts [–ärts/] **121**–12
   movie… [–mōō/vē–] **88**–11
thermometer [thər măm/ə tər] **84**–15
thick book [thĭk/ bŏŏk/] **11**–7
thigh [thī] **74**–16
thighs [thīz] **52**–21
thimble [thĭm/bəl] **73**–20
thin [thĭn] **11**–8, **22**–22
third [thürd(/–)] **14**
   …floor [–flör/] **36**–3
thirsty [thür/stē] **30**–2
thirteen [thür/tēn/] **14**
thirteenth [thür/tēnth/] **14**
thirteen-year-old [thür/tēn/yïr ōld/] **22**–7
thirty [thür/tē] **14**
this week [dhĭs/ wēk/] **18**–19
thorn [thörn] **129**–28
thousand [thow/zənd] **14**
thread [thrĕd] **73**–17
three [thrē(/–)] **14**
   …times a week [–tīmz/ ə wēk/] **18**–24
three-fourths [thrē/förths/] **15**–5
three-piece suit [thrē/pēs/ sōōt/] **64**–1
throat [thrōt(/–)] **75**–36
   …lozenges [–läz/ən jəz] **81**–21
through [thrōō] **105**–11
throw [thrō] **156**–D
throw pillow [thrō/ pĭl/ō] **42**–20
throw up [thrō/ ŭp/] **78**–E
thumb [thŭm] **75**–56
thunderstorm [thŭn/dər störm/] **10**–16
Thursday [thürz/dā, –dē] **18**–5
tick [tĭk] **132**–28
ticket [tĭk/ət] **104**–14
tidal wave [tīd/l wāv/] **103**–15
tide [tīd] **155** ✦
tie [tī] **94**–I
tie [tī] (clothing) **69**–40, (sports) **158** ✦
ties [tīz] (clothing) **69**–10
tiger [tī/gər] **135**–37
tight [tīt] **71**–43
tights [tīts] **66**–11
tile [tīl] **43**–9
TIME [tīm] **16**–17
time clock [tīm/ kläk/] **146**–4
Time zones [tīm/ zōnz/] **17**
tire [tīr] **108**–10, **109**–53
tired [tīrd] **31**–33
tires [tīrz] **109**–59
title [tīt/l] **98**–21, **113**–3
toad [tōd] **130**–28
toast [tōst] **33**, **61**–3
toaster [tō/stər] **40**–7
   …oven [–ŭv/ən] **40**–15
today [tə dā/] **18**–15
toddler [täd/lər] **22**–3
toe [tō(/–)] **68**–15, **75**–63

…guard [–gärd/] **147**–21
toenail [tō/nāl/] **75**–64
toggle bolt [täg/əl bōlt/] **150**–33
toilet [toy/lət] **43**–17, **49**–18
   …brush [–brŭsh/] **43**–16
   …paper [–pā/pər] **43**–15
token [tō/kən] **104**–11
tomatoes [tə mā/tōz] **51**–23
tomorrow [tə mär/ō, –mör/ō] **18**–16
tongs [tängz, töngz] **59**–23, **119**–15
tongue [tŭng] **74**–26
too big [tōō/ bĭg/] **70**–21
TOOLS AND BUILDING SUPPLIES
   [tōōlz/ ən bĭl/dĭng sə plīz/] **150**–**151**
too small [tōō/ smöl/] **70**–20
toothache [tōōth/āk/] **78**–2
toothbrush [tōōth/brŭsh/] **43**–20, **77**–20
   …holder [–hōl/dər] **43**–21
toothpaste [tōōth/pāst/] **77**–21
tornado [tör nā/dō] **103**–13
total [tōt/l] **21**–8, **118** ✦
tote bag [tōt/ băg/] **69**–29
touch [tŭch] **75**–E
towel [tow/əl] **43**–8, 12, 13
   …rack [–răk/] **43**–8
townhouse [town/hows/] **34**–7
tow truck [tō/ trŭk/] **106**–13
toy [toy(/–)]
   …chest [–chĕst/] **45**–24
   …store [–stör/] **92**–5
toys [toyz] **46**–H, **94**–5
track [trăk] (athletic) **5**–11, (train) **104**–10
track and field [trăk/ ən fēld/] **159**–17
trackball [trăk/böl/] **144**–15
track lighting [trăk/ lī/tĭng] **42**–3
tractor [trăk/tər] **148**–9
   …trailer [–trā/lər] **106**–15
trade school [trād/ skōōl/] **112**–9
traffic light [trăf/ĭk līt/] **90**–6
TRAFFIC SIGNS [trăf/ĭk sīnz/] **107**
tragedy [trăj/ə dē] **166**–11
trailer [trā/lər] **106**–17
train [trăn(/–)] **104**–17
   …station [–stā/shən] **104**–13
training pants [trā/nĭng pănts/] **95**–24
transcribe [trăn skrīb/] **142**–C
transcriber (medical) [trăn skrī/bər] **142**–4
transfer [trăns für/, trăns/fər] **97**–E
transfer [trăns/fər] **104**–6
translator [trănz/lā/tər, trăns/–] **138**–34
transmission [trănz mĭsh/ən, trăns–]
   automatic… [ö/tə măt/ĭk–] **109**
   standard… [stăn/dərd–] **109**
TRANSPORTATION, PUBLIC [pŭb/lĭk trăns/pər tā/shən] **104**
trash [trăsh(/–)]
   …bags [–băgz/] **47**–12
   …bin [–bĭn/] **37**–20
   …chute [–shōōt/] **37**–24
travel [trăv/əl] **29**–N
travel [trăv/əl]
   …agency [–ā/jən sē] **92**–9
   …agent [–ā/jənt] **139**–60
traveler's check [trăv/lərz chĕk/] **20**–17
tray [trā(/–)] **41**–10, **62**–H, **63**–7
   …table [–tā/bəl] **110**–16

treatment [trēt/mənt] **80** ✦
TREES AND PLANTS [trēz/ ən plănts/] **128**
trench coat [trĕnch/ kōt/] **66**–20
triangle [trī/ăng/gəl] **118**–7
tricycle [trī/sĭ kəl] **153**–9
trigonometry [trĭg/ə năm/ə trē] **118**–27
trim [trĭm] **39**–E
tripe [trīp] **52**–8
tripod [trī/päd] **165**–20
trombone [träm bōn/] **120**–12
trout [trowt] **53**–16
trowel [trow/əl] **39**–14, **149**–12
truck driver [trŭk/ drī/vər] **139**–61
TRUCKS [trŭks] **106**
trumpet [trŭm/pət] **120**–13
trunk [trŭngk] (car) **109**–49, (tree) **128**–4, (animal) **135**–47
T-shirt [tē/shürt/] **64**–12, **70**–16, **72**–15, 16, 17, 18
tuba [tōō/bə] **120**–14
tube [tōōb(/–)] **56**–12
   …of toothpaste [–əv tōōth/pāst/] **56**–24
Tuesday [tōōz/dā, –dē] **18**–3
tulip [tōō/ləp] **129**–11
tuna [tōō/nə] **54**–25, **130**–9
tuner [tōō/nər] **164**–13
tunic [tōō/nĭk] **65**–22
tunnel [tŭn/əl] **105**–11
turbulence [tür/byə ləns] **111**–N
turkey [tür/kē] **52**–17, **53**–4, **168**–17
turn [türn(/–)]
   …left [–lĕft/] **107**–C
   …right [–rīt/] **107**–B
turn in [türn/ ĭn/] **113**–E
turnips [tür/nəps] **51**–14
turn signal [türn/ sĭg/nəl] **108**–4
turntable [türn/tā/bəl] **164**–12
turquoise [tür/koyz, –kwoyz] **12**–4
turtle [tür/tl] **131**–42
turtleneck [tür/tl nĕk/] **64**–7
   …sweater [–swĕt/ər] **71**–28
tusk [tŭsk] **135**–48
tuxedo [tŭk sē/dō] **65**–28
TV (television) [tē/vē/] **42**–26, **164**–6
   …antenna [–ăn tĕn/ə] **38**–22
tweezers [twē/zərz] **83**–2
twelfth [twĕlfth] **14**
twelve [twĕlv] **14**
twentieth [twĕn/tē əth] **14**
twenty [twĕn/tē] **14**, **16**–8, 9, **20**–10
twenty-five after one [twĕn/tē fīv/ ăf/tər wŭn/] **16**–9
twenty-five to two [twĕn/tē fīv/ tə tōō/] **16**–11
twenty percent [twĕn/tē pər sĕnt/] **15**–8
twenty to two [twĕn/tē tə tōō/] **16**–12
twice a week [twīs/ ə wēk/] **18**–23
twig [twĭg] **128**–1
two [tōō] **14**
two-story house [tōō/stör/ē hows/] **38** ✦
type [tīp] **140**–M, **142**–D
Types of entertainment [tīps/ əv ĕn/tər tān/mənt] **166**
Types of material [tīps/ əv mə tïr/ē əl] **70**
Types of math [tīps/ əv măth/] **118**
TYPES OF SCHOOLS [tīps/ əv skōōlz/] **112**
Types of stories [tīps/ əv stör/ēz] **166**
Types of TV programs [tīps/ əv tē/vē/ prō/grămz] **167**
typewriter [tīp/rī/tər] **142**–2
   …cartridge [–kär/trĭj] **143**–31

ugly [ŭg/lē] **11**–22
umbrella [ŭm brĕl/ə] **66**–16, **155**–9
umpire [ŭm/pīr] **158** ✦
uncle [ŭng/kəl] **24**–11
uncomfortable [ŭn kŭmf/tə bəl, –tər–] **30**–8
under [ŭn/dər] **13**–9, **105**–1
underexposed [ŭn/dər ĭk spōzd/] **165**–35
underline [ŭn/dər līn/] **7**–V
underpants [ŭn/dər pănts/] **67**–17
undershirt [ŭn/dər shürt/] **67**–10
uniform [yōō/nə förm/] **65**–17, **161**–16
UNIVERSE [yōō/nə vürs/] **127**
university [yōō/nə vür/sə tē] **112**–10
unload [ŭn lōd/] **72**–E
unpack [ŭn păk/] **35**–E
unscented [ŭn sĕn/təd] **77** ✦
up [ŭp] **105**–9
upset [ŭp sĕt/] **31**–30
upstairs [ŭp/stërz/] **38** ✦
Uranus [yōōr/ə nəs, yōō rā/nəs] **127**–3
urban area [ür/bən ër/ē ə] **34**–1
use [yōōz(/–)] **140**–N
   …deodorant [–dē ō/dər ənt] **76**–C
user's manual [yōō/zərz măn/yōō əl] **144**–22
U.S. GOVERNMENT AND CITIZENSHIP
   [yōō/ĕs/ gŭv/ər mənt ən sĭt/ə zən shĭp/] **116**
U.S. HISTORY [yōō/ĕs/ hĭs/tə rē] **114**–**115**
Using a pay phone [yōō/zĭng ə pā/ fōn/] **9**
Using the ATM machine [yōō/zĭng dhē ā/tē/ĕm/ mə shēn/] **97**
U.S. MAIL [yōō/ĕs/ māl/] **96**
utilities [yōō tĭl/ə tēz] **35** ✦
U-turn OK (sign) [yōō/türn/ ō kā/] **107**–7
vacancy sign [vā/kən sē sīn/] **36**–11
vacation [vā kā/shən] **19**–46
vaccination [văk/sə nā/shən] **80** ✦
vacuum [văk/yōōm] **46**–I
vacuum cleaner [văk/yōōm klē/nər] **47**–13
   …attachments [–ə tăch/mənts] **47**–14
   …bag [–băg/] **47**–15
valedictorian [văl/ə dĭk tör/ē ən] **32**–8
Valentine's Day [văl/ən tīnz dā/] **168**–4
valet parking [văl/ā pär/kĭng] **145**–1
valley [văl/ē] **117**–18
van [văn] **106**–10, 14
vandalism [văn/də lĭz/əm] **100**–1
vase [vās, vāz, väz] **41**–9
vault [völt] **97**–2
VCR (videocassette recorder)
   [vē/sē/är/] / [vĭd/ē ō kə sĕt/ rĭ kör/dər] **164**–8
veal cutlets [vēl/ kŭt/ləts] **52**–6
vegetable [vĕj/tə bəl]
   …casserole [–kăs/ə rōl/] **58**
   …garden [–gär/dn] **148**–12
   …peeler [–pē/lər] **59**–15
VEGETABLES [vĕj/tə bəlz] **51**
vegetables [vĕj/tə bəlz] **55**–43
vegetarian [vĕj/ə tër/ē ən] **52** ✦
vein [vān] **75**–44
vendor [vĕn/dər] **91**–30
Venus [vē/nəs] **127**–8
vest [vĕst] **65**–24, **66**–13
veterinarian [vĕt/ər ə nër/ē ən] **139**–62
Vice President [vīs/ prĕz/ə dənt] **116**–7
victim [vĭk/təm] **100** ✦
video [vĭd/ē ō]

Index

...camera [kăm/rə] **165**–19
...game system [–gām/ sĭs/təm] **162**–1
...store [–stör/] **93**–15
videocassette [vĭd/ē ō kə sĕt/] **98**–13, **164**–8, 10
view [vyōō] **11**–21, 22
vine [vīn] **128**–22
vineyard [vĭn/yərd] **148**–14
violet [vī/ə lət, vī/lət] **129**–22
violin [vī/ə lĭn/] **120**–8
vise [vīs] **150**–21
visor [vī/zər] **147**–11
vital signs monitor [vīt/l sīnz/ män/ə tər] **87**–21
vitamins [vī/tə mənz] **81**–19
V-neck sweater [vē/nĕk/ swĕt/ər] **71**–27
vocational school [vō kā/shə nəl skōōl/] **112**–9
volcanic eruption [väl kän/ĭk ĭ rŭp/shən] **103**–14
volleyball [väl/ē böl/] (sport) **158**–14, (equipment) **161**–3
Volume [väl/yəm, –yōōm] **57**
volunteer [väl/ən tïr/] **87**–19
vomit [väm/ət] **78**–E
vote [vōt] **116**–D
waffles [wä/fəlz, wö/–] **61**–4
waist [wāst] **74**–4
waistband [wāst/bănd/] **73**–3
wait [wāt] **90**–B
waiter [wā/tər] **62**–4
waiting room [wā/tĭng rōōm/] **84**–1
wait on customers [wāt/ än kŭs/tə mərz, –ön–] **140**–O
waitress [wā/trəs] **63**–6
wake up [wāk/ ŭp/] **26**–A
walk [wök] **101**–A, **156**–A
walker [wö/kər] **80**–5, **95**–12
wall [wöl(/–)] **42**–6, **48**–4
...unit [–yōō/nət] **42**–13
wallet [wä/lət, wö/–] **69**–26
wallpaper [wöl/pā/pər] **45**–5
walrus [wöl/rəs] **131**–32
War [wör] **114**
warehouse [wër/hows/] **146**–9
warm [wörm] **10**–2
warning label [wör/nĭng lā/bəl] **80**–15
wash [wäsh(/–), wösh(/–)]
...hair [–hër/] **76**–E
...the dishes [–dhə dĭsh/əz] **46**–M
...the windows [–dhə wĭn/dōz] **46**–D
washcloth [wäsh/klöth/, wösh/–] **43**–14
washer [wä/shər, wö/–] **72**–3, **150**–32
wasp [wäsp, wösp] **132**–18
wastebasket [wāst/băs/kət] **43**–25, **46**–F
watch [wäch, wöch] **69**–34
watch TV [wäch/ tē/vē/, wöch/–] **27**–5
water [wö/tər] **39**–B
water [wö/tər] **117**, **155**–1
...fountain [–fown/tn] **153**–11
...glass [–glăs/] **63**–19
...pollution [–pə lōō/shən] **126**–12
...polo [–pō/lō] **158**–15
watercolor [wö/tər kŭl/ər] **163**–25
waterfall [wä/tər föl/] **117**–2
watering can [wö/tər ĭng kăn/] **39**–17
watermelons [wö/tər mĕl/ənz] **50**–24
waterskiing [wö/tər skē/ĭng] **160**–7
WATER SPORTS [wö/tər spörts/] **160**
wave [wāv] **155**–6
wavy [wā/vē] **23**–10

Ways to pay [wāz/ tə pā/] **20**
WEATHER [wĕdh/ər] **10**
Wednesday [wĕnz/dā, –dē] **18**–4
weed [wēd] **39**–A
week [wēk] **18**–11
weekdays [wēk/dāz/] **18**–12
weekend [wēk/ĕnd/] **18**–13
weigh [wā] **57**–B
weight [wāt] **22**–21, **57**
weightlifting [wāt/lĭf/tĭng] **159**–15
weights [wāts] **161**–19
WEIGHTS AND MEASURES [wāts/ ən mĕzh/ərz] **57**
welder [wĕl/dər] **139**–63
well [wĕl] **30**–15
west [wĕst] **107**, **123**, **124**
western [wĕs/tərn] **166**–9
wet [wĕt(/–)] **72**–17
...mop [–mäp/] **47**–16
...suit [–sōōt/] **155**–7
whale [wāl] **131**–29
wheat [wēt(/–)] **148**–2
...bread [–brĕd/] **53**–2
wheelbarrow [wēl/băr/ō] **39**–16
wheelchair [wēl/chër/] **80**–6
whisk [wĭsk] **59**–21
whiskers [wĭs/kərz] **134**–18
white [wīt(/–)] **12**–14
...bread [–brĕd/] **53**–1
White House [wīt/ hows/] **116**–5
whole [hōl(/–)] **15**–6
...salmon [–săm/ən] **53**–18
wide [wīd] **71**–44
widow [wĭd/ō] **29** ✦
widower [wĭd/ō ər] **29** ✦
width [wĭdth, wĭtth] **15**–17
wife [wīf] **24**–20, **25** ✦
wild animals [wīld/ ăn/ə məlz] **133** ✦
willow [wĭl/ō] **128**–14
win [wĭn] **158** ✦
wind [wĭnd] **126**–2
windbreaker [wĭnd/brā/kər] **66**–24
window [wĭn/dō] **38**–17, **42**–17
...pane [–pān/] **149**–15
...shade [–shād/] **44**–6
windshield [wĭnd/shēld/] **108**–2
...wipers [–wī/pərz] **108**–3
windy [wĭn/dē] **10**–10
wine glass [wīn/ glăs/] **63**–20
wing [wĭng] **132**–2
wings [wĭngz] **52**–20
winter [wĭn/tər] **19**–40
WINTER SPORTS AND WATER SPORTS [wĭn/tər spörts/ ən wö/tər spörts/] **160**
wipes [wīps] **95**–17
wipe the counter [wīp/ dhə kown/tər] **46**–O
wire [wīr(/–)] **151**–13
...stripper [–strĭp/ər] **151**–37
wish [wĭsh] **169**–J
withdraw cash [wĭdh drö/ kăsh/, wĭth–] **97**–D
witness [wĭt/nəs] **99**–11
wolf [wŏŏlf] **134**–5
woman [wŏŏm/ən] **22**–10
wood [wŏŏd(/–)] **149**–17, **151**–18
...screw [–skrōō/] **150**–28
wooden spoon [wŏŏd/n spōōn/] **59**–9

woodpecker [wŏŏd/pĕk/ər] **132**–9
Woodwinds [wŏŏd/wĭndz/] **120**
woodworking kit [wŏŏd/wûr/kĭng kĭt/] **162**–16
wool [wŏŏl(/–)] **70**–14
...scarf [–skärf/] **66**–4
work [wûrk/] **26**–K, **140**–P
workbook [wûrk/bŏŏk/] **3**–23
Work in a group [wûrk/ ĭn ə grŏŏp/] **6**
working [wûr/kĭng] **48**–1
work out [wûrk/ owt/] **157**–P
Work with a partner [wûrk/wĭdh/ ə pärt/nər, –wĭth/–] **6**
WORLD [wûrld] **124**–**125**
worm [wûrm] **130**–22
worried [wûr/ēd] **30**–13
wrap [răp] **169**–D
wrench [rĕnch] **109**–50, **151**–42, 43
wrestling [rĕs/lĭng] **159**–16
wrinkled [rĭng/kəld] **72**–19
wrist [rĭst] **69**–34, **75**–60
wristwatch [rĭst/wäch/, –wöch/] **69**–34
write [rīt] **2**–G, **113**–A
writer [rī/tər] **139**–64
writing assignment [rī/tĭng ə sīn/mənt] **113**–1
wrong [röng(/–)]
...number [–nŭm/bər] **9** ✦
...way [–wā/] **107**–4
X-ray [ĕks/rā/]
...technician [–tĕk nĭsh/ən] **86**–8
xylophone [zī/lə fōn/] **120**–17
yams [yămz] **51**–22
YARD [yärd] **39**
yard [(–)yärd(/)]
front... [frŭnt/–] **38**–15
yard (measurement) [yärd] **15** ✦
yardstick [yärd/stĭk/] **151**–15
yarn [yärn] **163**–17
year [yïr] **4**–16, **18**–8
yellow [yĕl/ō] **12**–12
yesterday [yĕs/tər dā/, –dē] **18**–17
yield [yēld] **107** ✦
yogurt [yō/gərt] **54**–33, **60**–11
young [yŭng] **22**–13
zebra [zē/brə] **135**–34
zero [zïr/ō] **14**
ZIP code [zĭp/ kōd/] **4**–9
zipper [zĭp/ər] **73**–16
zoo [zŏŏ] **152**–1
zookeeper [zŏŏ/kē/pər] **152**–3
zoom lens [zŏŏm/ lĕnz/] **165**–25
zucchini [zŏŏ kē/nē] **51**–4

Geographical Index

Continents

Africa [ăf/rĭ kə] **125–5**
Antarctica [ănt ärk/tĭ kə, –är/tĭ–] **125–7**
Asia [ā/zhə] **125–4**
Australia [ö strāl/yə] **125–6**
Europe [yŏŏr/əp] **125–3**
North America [nörth/ ə měr/ə kə] **124–1**
South America [sowth/ ə měr/ə kə] **124–2**

Countries and other locations

Afghanistan [ăf găn/ə stăn/] **124–125**
Albania [ăl bā/nē ə] **124–125**
Algeria [ăl jïr/ē ə] **124–125125**
American Samoa [ə měr/ə kən sə mō/ə] **124–125**
Andorra [ăn dör/ə] **124–125**
Angola [ăng gō/lə] **124–125**
Argentina [är/jən tē/nə] **124–125**
Armenia [är mē/nē ə] **124–125**
Australia [ö strāl/yə] **124–125**
Austria [ö/strē ə] **124–125**
Azerbaijan [ăz/ər bī jän/] **124–125**
Bahamas [bə hä/məz] **122–125**
Bahrain [bä rān/] **124–125**
Bangladesh [băng/glə děsh/, băng/–] **124–125**
Barbados [bär bā/dōs] **124–125**
Belarus [bē/lə rōōs/, byěl/ə–] **124–125**
Belgium [běl/jəm] **124–125**
Belize [bə lēz/] **124–125**
Benin [bə nĭn/, –nēn/] **124–125**
Bermuda [bər myōō/də] **122–125**
Bhutan [bōō tän/] **124–125**
Bolivia [bə lĭv/ē ə] **124–125**
Borneo [bör/nē ō] **124–125**
Bosnia-Herzegovina [bäz/nē ə hër/tsə gō vē/nə] **124–125**
Botswana [bät swä/nə] **124–125**
Brazil [brə zĭl/] **124–125**
Brunei [brōō nī/] **124–125**
Bulgaria [bŭl gër/ē ə] **124–125**
Burkina Faso [bər kē/nə fä/sō] **124–125**
Burundi [bōō rŏŏn/dē] **124–125**
Cambodia [kăm bō/dē ə] **124–125**
Cameroon [kăm/ə rōōn/] **124–125**
Canada [kăn/ə də] **122–125**
Cape Verde [kāp/ vürd/] **124–125**
Central African Republic [sěn/trəl ăf/rĭ kən rĭ pŭb/lĭk]
  124–125
Chad [chăd] **124–125**
Chile [chĭl/ē] **124–125**
China [chī/nə] **124–125**
Colombia [kə lŭm/bē ə] **124–125**
Comoros [kăm/ə rōz] **124–125**
Congo [käng/gō] **124–125**
Costa Rica [kōs/tə rē/kə, käs/–] **122–125**
Croatia [krō ā/shə] **124–125**
Cuba [kyōō/bə] **122–125**
Cyprus [sī/prəs] **124–125**
Czech Republic [chěk/ rĭ pŭb/lĭk] **124–125**
Democratic Republic of the Congo [děm/ə krăt/ĭk rĭ pŭb/lĭk
  əv dhə käng/gō] **124–125**
Denmark [děn/märk] **124–125**
Djibouti [jĭ bōō/tē] **124–125**
Dominica [däm/ə nē/kə] **124–125**
Dominican Republic [də mĭn/ĭ kən rĭ pŭb/lĭk] **122–125**
Ecuador [ěk/wə dör/] **124–125**
Egypt [ē/jĭpt] **124–125**
El Salvador [ěl săl/və dör/] **122–125**

Equatorial Guinea [ē/kwə tör/ē əl gĭn/ē, ěk/wə–] **124–125**
Eritrea [ěr/ə trē/ə] **124–125**
Estonia [ě stō/nē ə] **124–125**
Ethiopia [ē/thē ō/pē ə] **124–125**
Fiji [fē/jē] **124–125**
Finland [fĭn/lənd] **124–125**
France [frăns] **124–125**
French Guiana [frěnch/ gē ăn/ə, –ä/nə] **124–125**
French Polynesia [frěnch/ päl/ə nē/zhə] **124–125**
Gabon [gă bōn/] **124–125**
Georgia [jör/jə] **124–125**
Germany [jür/mə nē] **124–125**
Ghana [gä/nə] **124–125**
Greece [grēs] **124–125**
Greenland [grēn/lənd, –lănd/] **122–125**
Grenada [grə nā/də] **124–125**
Guatemala [gwä/tə mä/lə] **122–125**
Guinea [gĭn/ē] **124–125**
Guinea-Bissau [gĭn/ē bĭ sow/] **124–125**
Guyana [gī ăn/ə] **124–125**
Haiti [hā/tē] **122–125**
Honduras [hän dŏŏr/əs] **122–125**
Hong Kong [häng/ käng/] **124–125**
Hungary [hŭng/gə rē] **124–125**
Iceland [īs/lənd] **124–125**
India [ĭn/dē ə] **124–125**
Indonesia [ĭn/də nē/zhə] **124–125**
Iran [ĭ rän/, ĭ răn/] **124–125**
Iraq [ĭ räk/, ĭ răk/] **124–125**
Ireland [īr/lənd] **124–125**
Israel [ĭz/rē əl, –rā–] **124–125**
Italy [ĭt/l ē] **124–125**
Ivory Coast [īv/rē kōst/] **124–125**
Jamaica [jə mā/kə] **122–125**
Japan [jə păn/] **124–125**
Java [jä/və] **124–125**
Jordan [jör/dn] **124–125**
Kazakhstan [kä/zäk stän/] **124–125**
Kenya [kěn/yə, kēn/–] **124–125**
Kiribati [kïr/ə băs/] **124–125**
Kuwait [kōō wāt/] **124–125**
Kyrgyzstan [kïr/gĭ stän/, –stän/] **124–125**
Laos [lows, lä/ōs] **124–125**
Latvia [lăt/vē ə] **124–125**
Lebanon [lěb/ə nən, –nän/] **124–125**
Lesotho [lə sō/tō, –sōō/tōō] **124–125**
Liberia [lī bïr/ē ə] **124–125**
Libya [lĭb/ē ə] **124–125**
Liechtenstein [lĭk/tən stīn/] **124–125**
Lithuania [lĭth/ōō ā/nē ə] **124–125**
Luxembourg [lŭk/səm bürg/] **124–125**
Macedonia [măs/ə dō/nē ə] **124–125**
Madagascar [măd/ə găs/kər] **124–125**
Malawi [mə lä/wē] **124–125**
Malaysia [mə lā/zhə] **124–125**
Maldives [möl/dēvz, –dīvz] **124–125**
Mali [mä/lē] **124–125**
Malta [möl/tə] **124–125**
Marshall Islands [mär/shəl ī/ləndz] **124–125**
Mauritania [mör/ə tā/nē ə] **124–125**
Mauritius [mö rĭsh/əs] **124–125**
Mexico [měk/sĭ kō/] **122–125**
Micronesia [mī/krə nē/zhə] **124–125**
Moldova [mäl dō/və, möl–] **124–125**
Monaco [män/ə kō/] **124–125**

Mongolia [mäng gō/lē ə] **124–125**
Montenegro [män/tə nē/grō, –nē/–] **124–125**
Morocco [mə räk/ō] **124–125**
Mozambique [mō/zəm bēk/] **124–125**
Myanmar [myän/mär] **124–125**
Namibia [nə mĭb/ē ə] **124–125**
Nauru [nä ōō/rōō] **124–125**
Nepal [nə pöl/, –päl/] **124–125**
Netherlands [nĕdh/ər ləndz] **124–125**
New Guinea [nōō/ gĭn/ē] **124–125**
New Zealand [nōō/ zē/lənd] **124–125**
Nicaragua [nĭk/ə rä/gwə] **122–125**
Niger [nī/jər, nē zhër/] **124–125**
Nigeria [nī jïr/ē ə] **124–125**
North Korea [nörth/ kə rē/ə] **124–125**
Norway [nör/wā] **124–125**
Oman [ō män/] **124–125**
Pakistan [păk/ə stän/] **124–125**
Palau [pə low/] **124–125**
Panama [păn/ə mä/] **122–125**
Papua New Guinea [păp/yōō ə nōō/ gĭn/ē] **124–125**
Paraguay [păr/ə gwī/, –gwä/] **124–125**
Peru [pə rōō/] **124–125**
Philippines [fĭl/ə pēnz/, fĭl/ə pēnz/] **124–125**
Poland [pō/lənd] **124–125**
Portugal [pör/chə gəl] **124–125**
Puerto Rico [pwër/tə rē/kō, pör/tə–] **122–125**
Qatar [kä/tär, kə tär/] **124–125**
Romania [rō mä/nē ə, rōō–] **124–125**
Russia [rŭsh/ə] **124–125**
Rwanda [rōō än/də] **124–125**
Saudi Arabia [sow/dē ə rä/bē ə, sö/dē–] **124–125**
Senegal [sĕn/ə göl/, –gäl/] **124–125**
Serbia [sür/bē ə] **124–125**
Seychelles [sā shĕlz/, –shĕl/] **124–125**
Sierra Leone [sē ĕr/ə lē ōn/, –lē ō/nē] **124–125**
Singapore [sĭng/ə pör/] **124–125**
Slovakia [slō vä/kē ə] **124–125**
Slovenia [slō vē/nē ə] **124–125**
Solomon Islands [säl/ə mən ī/ləndz] **124–125**
Somalia [sə mä/lē ə] **124–125**
South Africa [sowth/ ăf/rĭ kə] **124–125**
South Korea [sowth/ kə rē/ə] **124–125**
Spain [spān] **124–125**
Sri Lanka [srē/ läng/kə, shrē/–] **124–125**
Sudan [sōō dän/] **124–125**
Sumatra [sōō mä/trə] **124–125**
Suriname [sōōr/ə nä/mə] **124–125**
Swaziland [swä/zē länd/] **124–125**
Sweden [swēd/n] **124–125**
Switzerland [swĭt/sər lənd] **124–125**
Syria [sïr/ē ə] **124–125**
Tahiti [tə hē/tē] **124–125**
Taiwan [tī/wän/] **124–125**
Tajikistan [tä jĭk/ə stän/, –stän/] **124–125**
Tanzania [tăn/zə nē/ə] **124–125**
Tasmania [tăz mā/nē ə] **124–125**
Thailand [tī/länd/, –lənd] **124–125**
The Gambia [dhə găm/bē ə] **124–125**
Togo [tō/gō] **124–125**
Tonga [täng/gə] **124–125**
Tunisia [tōō nē/zhə] **124–125**
Turkey [tür/kē] **124–125**
Turkmenistan [türk mĕn/ə stän/, –stän/] **124–125**
Uganda [yōō găn/də] **124–125**

Ukraine [yōō/krān, yōō krān/] **124–125**
United Arab Emirates [yōō nī/təd ăr/əb ĕm/ər əts] **124–125**
United Kingdom [yōō nī/təd kĭng/dəm] **124–125**
United States of America [yōō nī/təd stāts/ əv ə mĕr/ə kə] **122–125**
Uruguay [yōōr/ə gwī/, –gwä/] **124–125**
Uzbekistan [ōōz bĕk/ə stän/, –stän/] **124–125**
Venezuela [vĕn/ə zwä/lə] **124–125**
Vietnam [vē/ĕt näm/, –năm/] **124–125**
Western Sahara [wĕs/tərn sə här/ə] **124–125**
Western Samoa [wĕs/tərn sə mō/ə] **124–125**
Yemen [yĕm/ən] **124–125**
Zambia [zăm/bē ə] **124–125**
Zimbabwe [zĭm bäb/wä] **124–125**

Bodies of water

Arabian Sea [ə rā/bē ən sē/] **124–125**
Arctic Ocean [ärk/tĭk ō/shən] **122–125**
Baffin Bay [băf/ən bā/] **122–125**
Baltic Sea [böl/tĭk sē/] **124–125**
Barents Sea [băr/ənts sē/] **124–125**
Beaufort Sea [bō/fərt sē/] **122–125**
Bering Sea [bër/ĭng sē/, bïr/–] **122–125**
Black Sea [blăk/ sē/] **124–125**
Caribbean Sea [kăr/ə bē/ən sē/, kə rĭb/ē ən–] **122–125**
Caspian Sea [kăs/pē ən sē/] **124–125**
Coral Sea [kör/əl sē/] **124–125**
East China Sea [ēst/ chī/nə sē/] **124–125**
Greenland Sea [grēn/lənd sē/, –lănd/–] **124–125**
Gulf of Alaska [gŭlf/ əv ə lăs/kə] **122–125**
Gulf of California [gŭlf/ əv kăl/ə förn/yə] **122–125**
Gulf of Honduras [gŭlf/ əv hän dōōr/əs] **122–125**
Gulf of Mexico [gŭlf/ əv mĕk/sĭ kō/] **122–125**
Gulf of St. Lawrence [gŭlf/ əv sānt/ lör/əns, –lär/–] **122–125**
Hudson Bay [hŭd/sən bā/] **122–125**
Indian Ocean [ĭn/dē ən ō/shən] **124–125**
Labrador Sea [lăb/rə dör/ sē/] **122–125**
Mediterranean Sea [mĕd/ə tə rā/nē ən sē/] **124–125**
North Atlantic Ocean [nörth/ ət lăn/tĭk ō/shən] **122–125**
North Pacific Ocean [nörth/ pə sĭf/ĭk ō/shən] **122–125**
North Sea [nörth/ sē/] **124–125**
Norwegian Sea [nör wē/jən sē/] **124–125**
Persian Gulf [pür/zhən gŭlf/] **124–125**
Philippine Sea [fĭl/ə pēn/ sē/] **124–125**
Red Sea [rĕd/ sē/] **124–125**
Sea of Japan [sē/ əv jə păn/] **124–125**
Sea of Okhotsk [sē/ əv ō kätsk/] **124–125**
South Atlantic Ocean [sowth/ ət lăn/tĭk ō/shən] **124–125**
South China Sea [sowth/ chī/nə sē/] **124–125**
Southern Ocean [sŭdh/ərn ō/shən] **124–125**
South Pacific Ocean [sowth/ pə sĭf/ĭk ō/shən] **124–125**

The United States of America
Capital: Washington, D.C. (District Of Columbia)
   [wä/shĭng tən dē/sē/, wö/–]

Regions of the United States

Mid-Atlantic States [mĭd/ət lăn/tĭk stāts/] **123–10**
Midwest [mĭd/wĕst/] **123–9**
New England [nōō/ ĭng/glənd] **123–11**
Pacific States [pə sĭf/ĭk stāts/] **123–7**
Rocky Mountain States [räk/ē mown/tn stāts/] **123–8**
South [sowth] **123–13**
Southeast [sowth/ēst/] **123–13**
Southwest [sowth/wĕst/] **123–12**
West Coast [wĕst/ kōst/] **123–7**

Geographical Index

States of the United States

Alabama [ăl/ə băm/ə] **122–123**
Alaska [ə lăs/kə] **122–125**
Arizona [ăr/ə zō/nə] **122–123**
Arkansas [är/kən sö/] **122–123**
California [kăl/ə förn/yə] **122–123**
Colorado [kăl/ə răd/ō, –ra/dō] **122–123**
Connecticut [kə nĕt/ĭ kət] **122–123**
Delaware [dĕl/ə wër/] **122–123**
Florida [flör/ə də, flär/–] **122–123**
Georgia [jör/jə] **122–123**
Hawaii [hə wī/ē] **122–123**
Idaho [ī/də hō/] **122–123**
Illinois [ĭl/ə noy/] **122–123**
Indiana [ĭn/dē ăn/ə] **122–123**
Iowa [ī/ə wə] **122–123**
Kansas [kăn/zəs] **122–123**
Kentucky [kən tŭk/ē] **122–123**
Louisiana [loo ē/zē ăn/ə] **122–123**
Maine [mān] **122–123**
Maryland [mër/ə lənd] **122–123**
Massachusetts [măs/ə choo/səts] **122–123**
Michigan [mĭsh/ĭ gən] **122–123**
Minnesota [mĭn/ə sō/tə] **122–123**
Mississippi [mĭs/ə sĭp/ē] **122–123**
Missouri [mə zoor/ē, –zoor/ə] **122–123**
Montana [măn tăn/ə] **122–123**
Nebraska [nə brăs/kə] **122–123**
Nevada [nə văd/ə, –vä/də] **122–123**
New Hampshire [noo/ hămp/shər] **122–123**
New Jersey [noo/ jür/zē] **122–123**
New Mexico [noo/ mĕk/sĭ kō/] **122–123**
New York [noo/ yörk/] **122–123**
North Carolina [nörth/ kăr/ə lī/nə] **122–123**
North Dakota [nörth/ də kō/tə] **122–123**
Ohio [ō hī/ō] **122–123**
Oklahoma [ō/klə hō/mə] **122–123**
Oregon [ör/ĭ gən, –gän/, är/–] **122–123**
Pennsylvania [pĕn/səl văn/yə] **122–123**
Rhode Island [rōd/ ī/lənd] **122–123**
South Carolina [sowth/ kăr/ə lī/nə] **122–123**
South Dakota [sowth/ də kō/tə] **122–123**
Tennessee [tĕn/ə sē/] **122–123**
Texas [tĕk/səs] **122–123**
Utah [yoo/tö, –tä] **122–123**
Vermont [vər mänt/] **122–123**
Virginia [vər jĭn/yə] **122–123**
Washington [wä/shĭng tən, wö/–] **122–123**
West Virginia [wĕst/ vər jĭn/yə] **122–123**
Wisconsin [wĭs kän/sən] **122–123**
Wyoming [wī ō/mĭng] **122–123**

Canada
Capital: Ottawa [ät/ə wə]

Regions of Canada
Atlantic Provinces [ət lăn/tĭk prăv/ən səz] **123–6**
British Columbia [brĭt/ĭsh kə lŭm/bē ə] **123–2**
Northern Canada [nör/dhərn kăn/ə də] **123–1**
Ontario [än tër/ē ō/] **123–4**
Prairie Provinces [prĕ/ē prăv/ən səz] **123–3**
Quebec [kwĭ bĕk/] **123–5**

Provinces of Canada
Alberta [ăl bür/tə] **122–123**
British Columbia [brĭt/ĭsh kə lŭm/bē ə] **122–123**
Manitoba [măn/ə tō/bə] **122–123**

New Brunswick [noo/ brŭnz/wĭk] **122–123**
Newfoundland [noo/fən lənd] **122–123**
Northwest Territories [nörth/wĕst/ tĕr/ə tör/ēz] **122–123**
Nova Scotia [nō/və skō/shə] **122–123**
Ontario [än tër/ē ō/] **122–123**
Prince Edward Island [prĭns/ ĕd/wərd ī/lənd] **122–123**
Quebec [kwĭ bĕk/] **122–123**
Saskatchewan [să skăch/ə wən, –wän/] **122–123**
Yukon Territory [yoo/kän tĕr/ə tör/ē] **122–123**

Mexico
Capital: Mexico (City) [mĕk/sĭ kō/ (sĭt/ē)]

Regions of Mexico
Chiapas Highlands [chē ä/pəs hī/ləndz] **123–18**
Gulf Coastal Plain [gŭlf/ kō/stəl plăn/] **123–16**
Pacific Northwest [pə sĭf/ĭk nörth/wĕst] **123–14**
Plateau of Mexico [plă tō/ əv mĕk/sĭ kō/] **123–15**
Southern Uplands [sŭdh/ərn ŭp/ləndz] **123–17**
Yucatan Peninsula [yoo/kə tăn/ pə nĭn/sə lə, yoo/kə tän/–] **123–19**

States of Mexico
Aguascalientes [ä/gwəs kăl yĕn/täs] **122–123**
Baja California Norte [bä/hä kăl/ə förn/yə nör/tā] **122–123**
Baja California Sur [bä/hä kăl/ə förn/yə soor/] **122–123**
Campeche [kăm pā/chā, kăm pē/chē] **122–123**
Chiapas [chē ä/pəs] **122–123**
Chihuahua [chĭ wä/wä, –wə] **122–123**
Coahuila [kō/ə wē/lə] **122–123**
Colima [kə lē/mə] **122–123**
Distrito Federal [dĭ strē/tō fĕd/ə räl/] **122–123**
Durango [doo răng/gō, –răng/–] **122–123**
Guanajuato [gwä/nə hwä/tō] **122–123**
Guerrero [gə rër/ō] **122–123**
Hidalgo [hĭ dăl/gō, ē dhäl/gō] **122–123**
Jalisco [hə lĭs/kō, –lēs/–] **122–123**
México [mĕk/sĭ kō/, mĕ/hē kō] **122–123**
Michoacán [mē/chō ä kän/] **122–123**
Morelos [mö rĕl/ōs] **122–123**
Nayarit [nä/yə rēt/] **122–123**
Nuevo León [nwä/vō lā ōn/] **122–123**
Oaxaca [wə hä/kə, wä–] **122–123**
Puebla [pwĕb/lä] **122–123**
Querétaro [kə rĕt/ə rō/] **122–123**
Quintana Roo [kēn tä/nə rō/] **122–123**
San Luis Potosí [sän/ loo ēs/ pō/tə sē/] **122–123**
Sinaloa [sē/nə lō/ə] **122–123**
Sonora [sə nör/ə] **122–123**
Tabasco [tə băs/kō] **122–123**
Tamaulipas [tä/mow lē/pəs] **122–123**
Tlaxcala [tlä skä/lə] **122–123**
Veracruz [vĕr/ə krooz/, –kroos/] **122–123**
Yucatán [yoo/kə tăn/, –tän/] **122–123**
Zacatecas [zä/kə tā/kəs, sä/–] **122–123**

1 달러 **20**–7
1 달러 은화 **20**–6
1 센트 **20**–1
10 달러 **20**–9
10 센트 **20**–3
10 퍼센트 **15**–7
100 달러 **20**–12
100 퍼센트 **15**–11
10대 청소년 **22**–6
10세 소녀 **22**–5
10월 **19**–34
11월 **19**–35
12월 **19**–36
13세 소년 **22**–7
1812년 전쟁 **114**
18세가 되다 **116**–A
19세 소녀 **22**–8
1시간동안 약한 불에 끓인다 **58**–R
1월 **19**–25
1층 **36**–1
20 달러 **20**–10
20 퍼센트 **15**–8
25 센트 **20**–4
2단 침대 **45**–1
2분의 1 **15**–4
2월 **19**–26
2인용 소파 **42**–25
2층 **36**–2
350°에서 45분간 굽는다 **58**–L
35mm 카메라 **165**–24
3분의 1 **15**–3
3월 **19**–27
3층 **36**–3
4분의 1 **15**–2
4분의 3 **15**–5
4월 **19**–28
4층 **36**–4
5 달러 **20**–8
5 센트 **20**–2
50 달러 **20**–11
50 센트 은화 **20**–5
50 퍼센트 **15**–9
5월 **19**–29
6 개들이 팩 **56**–9
6세 소년 **22**–4
6월 **19**–30
7월 **19**–31
7월 4일 **168**–7
80 퍼센트 **15**–10
8분의 1 **15**–1
8월 **19**–32
9월 **19**–33
ATM (자동 현금 인출기) 사용방법 **97**
ATM (자동현금인출기) **97**–3
ATM 카드 **97**–9
ATM 카드를 넣으십시오 **97**–A
ATM 카드를 빼십시오 **97**–F
C-클램프 **150**–6
CD ROM 디스크 **144**–2
CD 컴팩트 디스크 **98**–14
CD 플레이어 **164**–14
CPR (심폐기능 소생법) **83**–17
CPU (중앙 처리 장치) **144**–1
HIV (인체 면역 결핍 바이러스) **79**–10
PIN 번호를 입력하십시오 **97**–B
SUV (스포츠 유틸리티 카) **106**–9

TV 보급 **115**
TV 프로그램 종류 **167**
U 회전 허용 **107**–7
VCR/ 비디오 카세트 레코더 **164**–8
가격 **21**–6
가격표 **21**–1
가구 광택제 **47**–18
가구를 배치하다 **35**–K
가구에 광을 내다 **46**–K
가구의 먼지를 털다 **46**–A
가구점 **88**–13
가득찬 잔 **11**–9
가르마타다 **23**–4
가리비 **53**–25, **130**–18
가면 **168**–12
가면 복장 **168**–13
가뭄 **103**–10
가방 카트 **145**–6
가벼운 상자 **11**–14
가사 **46**
가사 보조원 **137**–31
가스계량기 **48**–14
가스미터 **48**–14
가슴 **52**–19, **74**–13
가습기 **80**–2
가시 **129**–28
가오리 **130**–6
가옥 **34**–6
가위 **23**–19, **73**–18
가을 **19**–39
가자미 **130**–13
가재 **53**–23
가전제품을 수리하다 **140**–G
가정 해충 **49**
가정부 **138**–33
가정학 **121**–9
가제 **83**–6
가족 **24**–25, **134**–19
가죽 부츠 **70**–18
가죽 자켓 **66**–3
가지 **51**–18, **128**–2
가지고 있다 **21**–E
가축과 설치류 동물 **133**
가축 **148**–13
가축 우리 **148**–17
각도 **118**–24
간 **75**–39
간식 **55**–16
간편화 **68**–19
간호사 **84**–10, **138**–42
간호원실 **87**
갈기 **135**–49
갈라진 스커트 **65**–25
갈색 **12**–11
갈색 머리 **23**–17
갈퀴 **39**–11
감기 **79**–1
감기용 정제약 **81**–17
감옥으로 가다 **99**–G
감자 **51**–21
감자 샐러드 **53**–13
감자 칩 **55**–40
감자 튀김 **60**–2
감춰놓다 **169**–E
갑각류 **53**
값을 제의하다 **35**–H

강 **117**–3
강당 **5**–3
강도 **100**–6
강모 비누실 다발 **47**–5
강아지 **133**–12
강판 **59**–2
강풍 낙엽 청소기 **39**–4
개 **133**–11
개구리 **130**–25
개마 핥기 **135**–24
개미 **49**–24
개인 수표 **20**–14
개인 스포츠 **159**
개인 위생 **76**–77
개코원숭이 **135**–32
객실 **145**–10
갱 폭력 **100**–2
거들 **67**–18
거리 **90**–9
거미 **132**–30
거스름돈 **21**–9
거실 **42**
거울 **43**–18, **44**–1
거위 **132**–14
거품기 **59**–21
건강 관리 **80**–81
건강상태 및 중병 **79**
건강 위급 상황 **82**
건강진단과 치아검사 **85**
건강한 **30**–15
건량 **57**
건물 관리인 **138**–35
건설 작업자 **149**–1
건조기 **72**–4
건조기에 넣는 종이 소프너 **72**–5
건조기에서 옷을 꺼내다 **72**–E
건초 **148**–18
건축 **149**
건축가 **136**–4
건포도 2분의 1 컵 **57**–9
건포도 **50**–27
걷다 **156**–A
걸프 해안 평원 **123**–16
걸프전 **115**
검사 **99**–10
검안사 **81**–34
검은 머리 **23**–15
검정색 **12**–15
겁이 난 **31**–24
겉문 **38**–18
게 **53**–22, **130**–16
게시판 **3**–14
게이트 **110**–5
게이트에서 체크인 하십시오 **111**–D
게임 **152**–18
게임 쇼 **167**–23
게임을 하다 **162**–B
겨울 **19**–40
겨자 소스 **60**–24
격자 무늬 **70**–9
견과류 **50**–23
견인차 **106**–13
결과를 기록하다 **119**–C
결승점에 닿다 **157**–Z
결핵 **79**–13
결혼 증서 **29**–8

결혼하고 있다 **25**–23
결혼하다 **28**–L
경고문 **80**–15
경기장 **5**–12, **152**–26
경마 **159**–18
경비원 **97**–4, **99**–3
경적 **108**–24
경제학 **121**–6
경주로 **5**–11
경주하다 **157**–Y
경찰 **138**–44
경찰관 **99**–1
경찰서 **89**–19
경험을 말하다 **141**–I
계곡 **117**–18
계기판 **108**–17
계단 **37**–26, **37**–35
계단이 부서졌다 **48**–7
계모 **25**–31
계부 **25**–28
계산기 **142**–8
계산대 **55**–17, **60**–13
계산서를 물다 **62**–I
계산원 **136**–14
계절 **19**
고구마 **51**–22
고기류 **52**, **54**–2
고기잡이 그물 **154**–17
고대기 **76**–15
고등학교 **112**–7
고래 **131**–39
고리 나사 **150**–35
고리 모양의 물리개 **95**–30
고릴라 **135**–30
고모 **24**–10
고무 도장 **143**–40
고무 매트 **43**–3
고무 밴드 **143**–45
고무 장갑 **47**–4, **147**–17
고무풀 **143**–38
고속 앞으로 **165**–C
고속도로 위로 **105**–6
고습도치 **134**–10
고양이 **133**–9
고용이 되다 **141**–L
고장과 수리 **48**–49
고장난 지퍼 **70**–24
고층 건물 **89**–25
고혈압 **79**–15
곡괭이 **149**–20
곡선 **118**–19
곧은 머리 **23**–9
골격 **75**
골목 **37**–21
골무 **73**–20
골반 **75**–55
골프 **159**–7
골프 채 **161**–1
곰 **134**–11
곰인형 **45**–10
곱슬 머리 **23**–11
곱하기 **118**–3
공 **45**–16
공구와 건물보수 용품 **150**–**151**
공기 정화기 **80**–4
공놀이터 **153**–1
공립학교 **112**–1

공부하기 **6**–7
공상과학 **166**–12
공식 **119**–19
공예를 하다 **162**–D
공원 **88**–8
공원과 놀이터 **153**
공인 간호사 **87**–22
공작 **132**–15
공장 **146**
공장 근로자 **146**–6
공장 주인 **146**–2
공중 안전 **101**
공중 전화 **9**–11
공중전화 **91**–21
공중전화 사용 **9**
공책 **3**–24, **3**–26
공책 종이 **3**–25
공포 **166**–14
공항 **110**
공항 직원 **110**–2
공항 터미널 **110**–1
공해 **126**, **126**–10
과녁 **161**–8
과도 **59**–16
과산화수소 **83**–8
과수원 **148**–16
과일 **50**
과제를 나누어 주세요 **7**–O
과제를 모으세요 **7**–Q
과학 **119**
관객 **32**–10
관리인 **36**–12
관리인이 있는 주차장 **145**–1
관목 **39**–20
관제탑 **110**–7
관찰하다 **119**–B
관측소 **127**–19
광고란을 보다 **141**–D
교과서 **3**–22
교사 **5**–2, **139**–58
교실 **2**–3, **5**–1
교외 **34**–2
교장 **5**–14
교장실 **5**–13
교정치과의 **84**–23
교차로 **90**–**91**
교환수 **9**–7
교환하다 **21**–G
교회 **88**–6
구 **14**
구강 위생사 **84**–16
구겨진 셔츠 **72**–19
구근 **129**–9
구급 서비스 (911) **9**–9
구두 앞 편자 **68**–15
구두굽 **68**–13
구두끈 **68**–14
구름낀 **10**–7
구명 조끼 **154**–14
구부리다 **157**–R
구불거리는 머리 **23**–10
구슬 목걸이 **69**–32
구십 **14**
구운 감자 **61**–14
구운 닭고기 **61**–12
구인 광고 사인을 찾아보다 **141**–C
구조대원 **155**–18

구조대원실 **155**–20
구체 **118**–14
구토하다 **78**–E
구형 **118**–8
국기 **168**–9
국자 **59**–7
국제 전화 **9**–6
국제연합 **114**
국화 **129**–19
군에 입대하다 **28**–F
굴 **53**–27
굴뚝 **38**–21
굽기용 쇠선반 **59**–14
굽기용 팬 **59**–13
굽는다 **58**–V
궁형 톱 (금속판 절단용) **150**–5
권리와 의무 **116**
권리장전 **115**
궤도 **127**–11
귀 **74**–28
귀뚜라미 **132**–24
귀마개 **66**–12, **147**–13
귀먼 **22**–27
귀앓이 **78**–3
귀여운 **22**–24
귀중품 보관함 **97**–13
귀화 증명서 **29**–6
귤 **50**–13
그네 **153**–12
그네를 밀다 **153**–B
그늘 **155**–12
그래픽 아티스트 **137**–29
그룹으로 공부하기 **6**
그릇 말리는 수건 **47**–22
그릇 배수기 **40**–3
그릇 세척 용제 **47**–21
그릇을 말리다 **46**–N
그릇을 썼다 **46**–M
그릴 치즈 샌드위치 **61**–8
그림 **42**–7, **152**–8
그림 그리다 **163**–E
그림 붓 **163**–23
그림 사전 **3**–29
그림을 가리키세요 **2**–F
그림을 그리세요 **6**–M
그림책 **45**–17
극장 **88**–10, **88**–11
근대 **51**–6
근무시간을 물어보다 **141**–F
근육 **75**–48
글러브 **161**–17
금고 **97**–2
금발 머리 **23**–16
금붕어 **133**–16
금성 **127**–8
금요일 **18**–6
금잔화 **129**–13
금전 등록기 **55**–18
금전 등록기를 사용하다 **140**–N
급료를 물어보다 **141**–K
기 **33**–15
기계 나사 **150**–27
기계 작동자 **138**–37
기내휴대물을 보관함에
　넣으십시오 **111**–H
기념일 **19**–42
기니피그 (쥐의 일종) **133**–14

기름 한 컵 **57**–2
기린 **135**–33
기분이 나쁜 **31**–30
기수 **14**
기어 전환장치 **108**–27
기어오르는 놀이 기구 **153**–14
기온 **10**
기장을 늘이다 **73**–C, **73**–D
기저귀 갈이용 탁자 **45**–12
기저귀 바지 **95**–24
기저귀 통 **95**–23
기저귀 핀 **95**–22
기저귀를 갈아주다 **94**–E
기저귀통 **45**–13
기침시럽 **81**–20
기침하다 **78**–A
기타 **120**–11
기타 학교 과목 **121**
기하 **118**–26
긴 내의 **67**–11
긴 머리 **23**–3
긴 상의 **65**–22
긴 치마 **71**–34
긴소매 셔츠 **71**–31
길을 건너시오 **90**–A
길이 **15**–16
깃대 **134**–23
깃털 **132**–5
깃털 총체 **47**–1
깊이 **15**–15
깍지 강낭콩 **51**–25
깔때기 **119**–12
깡통 따개 **59**–1
깨끗한 티셔츠 **72**–16
껌 **55**–42
꼬리 **134**–22
꼭끼는 바지 **71**–43
꽃 **129**, **129**–7
꽃가게 **92**–12
꽃다발 **129**–27
꽃무늬 **70**–12
꽃병 **41**–9
꽃양배추 **51**–16
꽃잎 **129**–8
꾸러미 **56**–8
꿀벌 **132**–26
끈없는 가벼운 구두 **68**–16
끌 **151**–51
나누기 **118**–4
나무 나사 **150**–28
나무 숫가락 **59**–9
나무와 화초 **128**
나무 울타리를 다듬으세요 **39**–E
나무딸기 **50**–18
나무를 심으세요 **39**–D
나무메 **150**–2
나무의 구조 **128**
나방 **132**–22
나비 **132**–20
나비 넥타이 **69**–40
나쁜 개 **11**–18
나이와 신체 묘사 **22**
나이 지긋한 **22**–15
나이프 **63**–27
나일론 스타킹 **70**–19
나초 **60**–10

낙심한 **31**–28
낙옆을 긁어 모으세요 **39**–F
낙타 **135**–38
낚시 **154**–5
낚싯대 **154**–18
난초 **129**–17
날 닭고기 **52**–24
날개 **52**–20, **132**–2
날씨 **10**
날씬한 **22**–22
날짜 **18**–14
남 **4**–13
남극대륙 **125**–7
남동부 **123**–13
남동생 **24**–9
남미 **124**–2
남부 **123**–13
남부 고원 **123**–17
남북전쟁 **115**
남서부 **123**–12
남자 **22**–11
남자 지갑 **69**–26
남자 팬티 **67**–13
남자용 긴 잠옷 **67**–9
남자형제 **24**–9
남편 **24**–19
낮은 굽 **71**–46
낮잠을 자다 **94**–L
내과 의사 **86**–2
내려주다 **94**–A
내일 **18**–16
냄비 **40**–16, **59**–6
냄비 집게 **59**–29
냄새 맡다 **75**–C
냅킨 **41**–19, **63**–23
냉난방 장치 **37**–19
냉동 생선 **53**–30
냉동 식품 **55**–12
냉동 요구르트 **60**–11
냉동고 **40**–10
냉동야채 **55**–43
냉수 **43**–7
냉장고 **40**–9
냉전 **114**
냉차 **60**–5
너구리 **134**–13
너무 작은 **70**–20
너무 큰 **70**–21
너비 **15**–17
너트 **150**–31
널찍한 주택 갑판 **38**–16
넓은 넥타이 **71**–44
넓적다리 **52**–21
네일 살롱 **91**–25
넥타이 **69**–10
넷째 **14**
년 **4**
노란색 **12**–12
노래를 부르다 **120**–B
노선 **104**–2
노예 **114**, **115**
노예제도 폐지 **115**
노인 **22**–12
노출 부족 **165**–35
노출 초과 **165**–34
노트북 **143**–36

녹음하다 **165**–A
놀다 **94**–K
놀란 **31**–31
놀러가는 곳 **152**
놀이 틀 위를 기어오르다 **153**–C
농구 **158**–8
농구 코트 **158**–7
농구공 **161**–4
농기구 **148**–10
농부 **148**–15
농사꾼 **148**–8
농사일과 목장일 **148**
농산물 재배자 **148**–15
농작물 **148**
농장 **34**–13
농장 동물 **133**
높은 굽 구두 **71**–47
높은 의자 **95**–7
높이 **15**–14
뇌 **75**–35
뇌암 **79**–12
뇌우 **10**–16
누군가에게 인사하세요 **8**–A
누나 **24**–8
누룩뱀 **131**–39
눈 **74**–27
눈금새긴 원통 **119**–10
눈꺼풀 **74**–33
눈먼 **22**–26
눈보라 **10**–20, **103**–11
눈썹 **74**–32
눈썹그리는 연필 **77**–33
눈약 **81**–22
눈오는 **10**–9
눈을 검사하다 **85**–F
뉴스 **167**–17
뉴잉글랜드 **123**–11
뉴펀들랜드 표준시 **17**–31
느낌 **30**–31
느낌표 **113**–8
느릅나무 **128**–17
느린 운전사 **11**–4
늑대 **134**–5
늦은 **17**–23
니켈 **20**–2
니트 셔츠 **65**–20
다 될 때까지 익힌다 **58**–F
다람쥐 **133**–21
다른 사람의 평을 받다 **113**–C
다리 **74**–6
다리 아래 **105**–1
다리 위 **105**–2
다리미 **72**–13
다리미판 **72**–14
다린 셔츠 **72**–20
다섯 가지 닭고기 요리법 **58**
다섯째 **14**
다용도 칼 **154**–20
다우림 **117**–1
다음 주 **18**–20
다이닝룸 **62**–2
다이빙 마스크 **155**–3
다이빙하다 **157**–S
다이아몬드 **163**–27
다임 **20**–3
다진 쇠고기 **52**–4

다치다 **82**–A
다친 **30**–17
단어들을 순서대로 놓으세요 **7**–W
단어를 말하세요 **6**–C
단어를 반복해 말하세요 **6**–D
단어를 베껴 쓰세요 **6**–F
단어를 읽으세요 **6**–B
단어를 찾아보세요 **6**–A
단어에 밑줄을 치세요 **7**–V
단어에 선을 그어 지우세요 **7**–U
단어의 철자를 쓰세요 **6**–E
단열재 **149**–13
단추 **73**–21
단추구멍 **73**–12
단파 라디오 **164**–5
단풍나무 **128**–13
달(월) **18**–9
달걀 **54**–34
달걀 3개를 깨뜨린다 **58**–A
달걀 교반기 **59**–20
달걀 한 카톤 **56**–16
달걀을 팬에 붓는다 **58**–D
달력 **18**–19
달팽이 **130**–24
닭고기 **52**–16
닭고기 수프 **58**
닭고기를 삶는다 **58**–P
닭고기를 자른다 **58**–M
닭다리 **52**–22
담배 라이터 **108**–32
담요 **44**–12
담요 잠옷 **67**–7
담요를 달라고 하십시오 **111**–M
답안지에 표시하세요 **7**–T
당구 **159**–2
당근 **51**–3
당근 껍질을 벗긴다 **58**–N
당근을 얇게 썬다 **58**–O
당나귀 **133**–2
당뇨병 **79**–9
당좌예금구좌번호 **97**–8
당황한 **31**–25
대 **70**–14
대각선 **118**–23
대공황 **114**
대구 **130**–8
대기실 **84**–1
대들보 **149**–3
대륙 **124**
대륙횡단 기차 **115**
대머리 **23**–12
대법관 **116**–10
대법원 **116**–8
대법원장 **116**–9
대서양 표준시 **17**–30
대수 **118**–25
대양 **155**–1
대중교통 **104**
대추 **50**–25
대통령 **116**–6
대패 **151**–52
대학 기숙사 **34**–9
대학 학위 **29**–7
대학교 **112**–10
대학에 들어가다 **28**–J
대합 조개 **53**–28

대형 치 **106**–4
대형 핸드백 **69**–29
대화를 끝내세요 **8**–C
대화를 시작하세요 **8**–B
더러운 티셔츠 **72**–15
더운 **10**–1, **30**–1
더하기 **118**–1
던지다 **156**–D, **156**–F
덤프 트럭 **106**–12
덩굴옻나무 **128**–25
덩어리 **56**–10
데스크 직원 **145**–9
데이지 **129**–14
도가니 집게 **119**–15
도끼 **150**–3
도너츠 **60**–15
도너츠 가게 **91**–20
도롱뇽 **130**–27
도마 **40**–27
도마뱀 **131**–41
도서관 **5**–6
도서관 **89**–28, **98**
도서관 서기 **98**–17
도서관 책 **98**–20
도서관 카드 **98**–19
도시 **34**–1
도어맨 **145**–2
도착 **111**–O
도회 지역 **34**–1
독립기념일 **168**–7
독립선언문 **115**
독립전쟁 **115**
독성 **147**–3
독수리 **132**–10
독신모 **25**–25
독신부 **25**–26
독약을 삼키다 **82**–J
독있는 오크 **128**–23
독있는 옻나무 **128**–24
돌고래 **131**–30
돌고래 무리 **131**–31
동계 스포츠와 수중 스포츠 **160**
동그라미 **118**–5
동남 아시아 인 **115**
동맥 **75**–43
동물 **152**–2
동물 사육자 **152**–3
동물원 **152**–1
동부 표준시 **17**–29
동상을 입다 **82**–G
동작 관련 전치사 **105**
동전 **20**
동전 수집 **162**–13
동전 지갑 **69**–25
동전을 넣으세요 **9**–C
돼지 **133**–8
돼지고기 **52**
돼지고기찹 **52**–10
돼지부분육 **52**–10
되감기 **165**–D
두개골 **75**–52
두꺼비 **130**–28
두꺼비집-퓨즈 상자 **48**–13
두꺼운 자켓 **71**–41
두꺼운 책 **11**–7
두루말이 **56**–11

두통 **78**–1
둘째 **14**
둥우리 **132**–3
뒤에 **13**–3
뒷마당 **38**–2
뒷좌석 **109**–38
드라이버 **150**–25
드라이브 스루 윈도우 **90**–13
드라이브웨이 **38**–5
드라이어 **23**–20
드라이월 **149**–18
드럼 **120**–18
드레스 **64**–3
드리블하다 **156**–K
드릴 **84**–21
드릴 비트 **150**–23
득점 **158**–1
들다 **75**–B
들보 **149**–3
들소 **134**–6
들여다 보는 구멍 **37**–27
들쥐 **133**–19
들통 **47**–20
등 **74**–11
등기 우편 **96**–11
등불 **154**–22
등산화 **68**–21
디너 접시 **63**–15
디너 포크 **63**–25
디스크 드라이브 **144**–3
디스크 자키/DJ **33**–17
디자이너 **146**–3
디자인하다 **146**–A
디저트 쟁반 **63**–7
따뜻한 **10**–2
따옴표 **113**–9
딱따구리 **132**–9
딱딱한 의자 **11**–5
딱정벌레 **132**–19
딸 **24**–21
딸기 **50**–17
딸랑이 **95**–31
떨어지다 **82**–O
떨어진 단추 **70**–25
떼어낼 수 있는 테이블 **95**–9
뚜껑 **59**–24
뚜껑있는 찜냄비 **59**–11
뛰다 **156**–C
뜨개 바늘 **163**–18
뜨개실 **163**–17
뜰 **39**
라디에이터 **109**–42
라디오 **108**–31
라디오 프로그램 **166**–4
라마 **135**–26
라인 조장 **146**–5
라임 **50**–12
라켓볼 **159**–11
래프팅 **154**–4
램프 **44**–17
램프갓 **44**–18
랩톱 **144**–14
러그렌치 **109**–50
러시아 인 **115**
레깅 **65**–23
레몬 **50**–11

레슬링 **159**–16
레이블 **143**–35
레코드 **98**–15
레터헤드 편지지
　(회사명이 들어 있는) **143**–19
레프리 **158**–6
렌치 **151**–43
로마 숫자 **14**
로맨스 **166**–16
로비 **145**–3
로빈 **132**–17
로스트 비프 1 파운드 **57**–12
로스트 비프 **53**–7
로스트비프 **52**–1
로스트하다 **58**–U
로켓 **69**–33
로프 **154**–19
록 밴드 **120**–2
록키 산 주 **123**–8
록킹 의자 **94**–6
롤러 **23**–21
롤러 스케이트 **161**–10
롤러 스케이팅 **159**–9
롤러코스터 **152**–15
롤빵 **54**–30
루이지애나 구입지 **114**
루즈 **77**–36
루터 **150**–12
룸 서비스 **145**–12
를 사려고 다니다 **21**–A
리걸 패드 **143**–18
리넨 자켓 **70**–17
리모콘 **164**–9
립스틱 **77**–37
링컨 암살 **115**
마가린 **54**–39
마늘 **51**–29
마늘 압착기 **59**–10
마늘빵 **61**–16
마루를 걸레질하다 **46**–J
마루바닥을 문질러 닦다 **46**–L
마루바닥을 쓸다 **46**–E
마른 티셔츠 **72**–18
마스카라 **77**–38
마스킹 테이프 **151**–49
마시다 **60**–B
마요네즈 **60**–25
마우스 **144**–8
마이크 **164**–4
마이크로카셋 녹음기 **142**–4
마이크로필름 **98**–5
마이크로필름 판독기 **98**–4
마취사 **87**–35
마취제 주사를 놓다 **85**–J
마침표 **113**–6
마커 **3**–19
막다른 길 **107**–8
만 **14, 117**–9
만월 **127**–16
만지다 **75**–E
만화 **167**–19
말 **133**–4
말미잘 **130**–21
말벌 **132**–18
말타기 **154**–9
맑게 갠 **10**–6

맛보다 **75**–D
망고 **50**–21
망원경 **127**–21
망치 **150**–1
망치질하다 **149**–D
맞는 항목끼리 짝지우세요 **7**–X
맡긴 사람 **94**–G
매니저와 이야기하다 **35**–B
매니큐어 제거제 **77**–32
매부 **24**–16
매시포테이토 **61**–11
매일 **18**–21
매트리스 **44**–25
머그 **41**–28
머리 **74**–1
머리를 감다 **76**–E
머리를 말리다 **76**–H
머리를 빗다 **76**–G, **76**–I
머리를 세트하다 **23**–C
머리를 염색하다 **23**–D
머리를 자르다 **23**–A
머리를 파마하다 **23**–B
머리를 헹구다 **76**–F
머리위 짐칸 **110**–10
머리카락 **74**–19
머리핀 **76**–18
머플러 **108**–11
머핀 **60**–14
먹다 **60**–A
먼지 방지용 프릴 **44**–22
멀미 봉투 **110**–15
멍 **78**–12
메기 **53**–17
메뉴 **62**–3
메뉴보고 주문하다 **62**–D
메뚜기 **132**–25
메세지를 남기세요 **9**–E
메스껍다 **78**–D
메시지를 받다 **142**–A
메시지를 적다 **142**–C
메일리 **143**–32
멕시코 고원 **123**–15
멕시코 지역 **123**
멕시코와 미국과의전쟁 **114**
멜로 드라마 **167**–21
멜론 **50**–15
멜빵 **68**–2
면 **118**–22
면 티셔츠 **70**–16
면담을 하다 **141**–H
면도날 **77**–26
면도용 크림 **77**–27
면도칼 **77**–25
면도하다 **77**–M
명왕성 **127**–1
모기 **132**–23
모니터 **144**–6
모델 **138**–39
모델 기차 **163**–32
모뎀 **144**–11
모래 **155**–23
모래 놀이통 **153**–15
모래 바람 **10**–21
모래 언덕 **117**–5
모래성 **155**–10
모래주머니 **52**–23

모르는 사람에게 문을 열어주지
　마십시오 **101**–F
모빌 **45**–4
모양 **118**
모자 **66**–1, **66**–6, **68**–5
모충 **132**–21
모텔 **89**–22
모퉁이 **91**–17, **107**–1
모퉁이 주위 **105**–10
모험 **166**–13
모형 키트 **162**–7
모형을 만들다 **162**–C
목 **74**–2
목걸이 **69**–9
목걸이 줄 **69**–31
목공 키트 **162**–16
목구멍(인후) **75**–36
목록에 대해서 논의하세요 **6**–L
목록을 같이 생각해 보세요 **6**–K
목마른 **30**–2
목발 **80**–1
목성 **127**–5
목수 **48**–12, **136**–13
목아픔 **78**–6
목안을 검사하다 **85**–E
목알약 **81**–21
목요일 **18**–5
목욕 파우더 **76**–3
목욕가운 **67**–8
목욕용 큰 수건 **43**–12
목욕하다 **76**–B
목장 **34**–12
목장주 **148**–22
목재 **149**–17, **151**–18
목화 **148**–6
몹시 추운 **10**–5
못 **150**–29
무 **51**–5
무거운 상자 **11**–13
무게와 단위 **57**
무균 패드 **83**–4
무늬 **70**
무당벌레 **132**–27
무대 **32**–4
무도장 **33**–16
무릎 **74**–17
무릎 가드 **161**–13
무릎 양말 **67**–25
무선 전화기 **9**–12
무술 **159**–10
무스 **134**–1
무용 타이츠 **67**–1
무지 초록색 **70**–6
무카페인 커피 **61**–23
문 사슬 **37**–28
문 손잡이 **37**–30
문단 **113**–5
문어 **130**–4
문을 열다 **169**–F
문을 잠그십시오 **101**–E
문장 **113**–4
문장을 받아 쓰세요 **6**–N
문제점들 **70**
물 **155**–1
물 1 온스 **57**–1
물 건너 **105**–3

문 절약 **126**–B
물개 **131**–33
물건 담아주는 사람 **55**–21
물건을 받아 오다 **94**–G
물건을 수집하다 **162**–A
물걸레 **47**–16
물고기의 부분 **130**
물리 **119**–3
물리치료사 **81**–30
물방울 **70**–8
물뿌리개 **39**–17
물에 빠지다 **82**–I
물을 따르다 **62**–C
물음표 **113**–7
물잔 **63**–19
물집 **78**–15
뮤직 스토어 **92**–1
미국 역사 **114**–**115**
미국 우편 **96**
미국 인디언 **114**, **115**
미국 정부와 시민권 **116**
미국 지역 **123**
미국시민과 해방된 노예들 **114**
미국에서 5 년동안 살다 **116**–B
미국에서 알래스카 구입 **115**
미국헌법 제정 **115**
미끄럼틀 **153**–13
미니밴 **106**–10
미드 애틀란틱 주 **123**–10
미등 **108**–14
미디어 섹션 **98**–11
미술 **121**–1
미술관 **152**–7
미식 축구 **158**–11
미식축구 공 **161**–22
미아 **102**–1
미용사 **137**–30
미장원 **93**–16
미적분 **118**–28
미주리 타협 **114**
미터 **104**–21
믹스용 그릇 **59**–31
민권운동 **115**
밀 **148**–2
밀가루 **55**–45
밀가루 한 봉지 **56**–19
밀가루 한 컵 **57**–10
밀방망이 **59**–30
밀빵 **53**–2
밀집모자 **66**–23
밀크 쉐이크 **60**–12
바구니 **42**–2
바나나 **50**–3
바늘 **73**–22
바늘겨레 **73**–15
바다 **117**–6
바다 동물 **130**
바다 사자 **131**–34
바다생물, 양서류 그리고 파충류 **130**–**131**
바다 포유동물 **131**
바디 로숀 **76**–7
바람 **126**–2
바람부는 **10**–10
바베큐 석쇠 **39**–7
바베큐하다 **58**–T

바순 **120** 6
바스 **120**–10, **130**–11
바운드 시키다 **156**–K
바위 **155**–24
바이스 **150**–21
바이올린 **120**–8
바인더 **3**–24
바켓 **47**–20
바퀴 달린 들것 **87**–28
바퀴벌레 **49**–25
박수치다 **32**–B
박쥐 **134**–7
반 양말 **67**–24
반도 **117**–7
반바지 **64**–13
반소매 셔츠 **71**–30
반송 주소 **96**–7
반지 **69**–39
반지름 **118**–16
반창고 **83**–3
반환하다 **21**–F
받다 **156**–E
받으십시오 **96**–D
받침 접시 **63**–22
발 **74**–7, **134**–20
발가락 **75**–63
발가락 보호 **147**–21
발굽 **134**–17
발깔개 **47**–6
발꿈치 **75**–62
발레 **166**–7
발목 **75**–61
발목을 삐다 **78**–18
발신음을 들으세요 **9**–B
발음 **113**
발진 **78**–10
발코니 **37**–17
발톱 **75**–64, **132**–4
발판 **149**–4
발판 사닥다리 **47**–7
밤 **17**–20
밥 필레프 **61**–18
방광 **75**–47
방바닥 **44**–24
방사능 **126**–13, **147**–6
방사선과 의사 **86**–5
방울뱀 **131**–38
방충제 **154**–23
방학 **19**–46
방향 **107**
방향과 교통 표지판 **107**
방향 지시등 **108**–4, **108**–18
밭 **148**–7
배 **50**–6, **74**–3
배고픈 **30**–5
배관공 **49**–20
배구 **158**–14
배구공 **161**–3
배낭 **154**–15
배낭메고 걷기 **154**–7
배달원 **137**–18
배달하십시오 **96**–C
배부른 **30**–6
배수구 **43**–4
배심원 **99**–8

배심원 임무를 수행히다 **116**–G
배우 **136**–2
배터리 **109**–43, **151**–40
배터리 충전기 **165**–23
배터리 팩 **165**–22
백 **14**
백 팩 **69**–28
백과사전 **98**–18
백만 **14**
백미러 **108**–1
백악관 **116**–5
백일 **14**
백합 **129**–24
백호 **149**–8
백화점 **93**–13
밸런타인스 데이 **168**–4
뱀장어 **130**–5
뱃놀이 **154**–2
버너 **40**–19
버드나무 **128**–14
버섯 **51**–26
버스 **90**–15, **104**–4
버스 운전사 **104**–8
버스 정류장 **104**–1
버스 정류장 **91**–16
버스로 학교에 가다 **26**–H
버지니아에 최초 영국인 **114**
버지니아에서 최초로 아프리카 노예 **114**
버지지나에 최초로 세운 인디언
　　보호구역 **114**
버킷 **155**–22
버터 **54**–36
번개 **10**–17
번역사 **138**–34
번호를 돌리세요 **9**–D
번호판 **108**–15
벌레 **130**–22
벌레에게 물린 상처 **78**–11
벌새 **132**–11
범죄 **100**
범죄를 보면 경찰에 보고하십시오 **101**–H
범퍼 **108**–7
법원 **89**–18
법원 속기사 **99**–12
법을 지키다 **116**–H
법정 **99**–7
법정 간수 **99**–13
법정 휴일 **19**–43
법정에 출두하다 **99**–C
법제도 **99**
벙어리 장갑 **66**–9
베게 **44**–9
베갯잇 **44**–10
베니어판 **149**–16
베이비 파우더 **95**–18
베이지색 **12**–9
베이컨 **52**–11, **61**–7
베인 상처 **78**–13
벤치 **153**–10
벨 캡틴 **145**–4
벨트 **69**–11
벨트 버클 **69**–41
벼룩 **49**–23
벼룩시장 **152**–22
벽 **42**–6

벽난로 **42**–9
벽난로 불 **42**–10
벽돌 **149**–11
벽돌공 **136**–9
벽돌을 쌓다 **149**–B
벽로선반 **42**–8
벽에 금이갔다 **48**–4
벽장 **42**–13
벽지 **45**–5
변기 **43**–17
변기 세척솔 **43**–16
변기가 막혔다 **49**–18
변호사 **138**–36
변호사를 고용하다 **99**–B
별 **127**–23
별자리 **127**–24
병 **56**–1, **56**–2
병 회수 **54**–1
병든 **30**–14
병원 **86**–87
병원 **88**–7
병원 건강 기록부 **87**–20
병원 의료진 **86**
병원 침대 **86**–11
병원가운 **86**–15
보관함 **36**–14
보기 흉한 광경 **11**–22
보넷 **108**–6
보다 **75**–A
보도 **91**–26
보드게임 **162**–3
보라색 **12**–7
보름달 **127**–16
보석류 **69**–8
보석상 **92**–2
보습제 **76**–8
보안검사를 통과하십시오 **111**–C
보안용 문 **36**–13
보온 패드 **80**–3
보일러가 고장났다 **49**–15
보조원 **87**–18
보존 **126**, **126**–B, **126**–C
보청기 **81**–33
보풀 트랩을 제거하다 **72**–D
보행기 **95**–12
보행보조기 **80**–5
보행자 **90**–7
보험 카드 **84**–4
보험양식 **84**–5
보호 안경 **147**–9, **147**–10
보호소 **34**–10
보호펜 **95**–11
복도 **54**–5
복사기 **142**–14
복사를 하다 **142**–E
복사센터 **91**–22
복숭아 **50**–5
복지후생에 대하여 물어보다 **141**–J
복통 **78**–4
본체 기판 **144**–18
볼 **74**–29
볼륨 **145**–20
볼링 **159**–3
볼링 볼 **161**–5
볼연지 **77**–36
볼트 **150**–30

봄 **19**–37
봉제 동물 완구 **45**–23
봉지 **56**–7
봉투 **96**–1, **143**–20
봉합 바늘 **83**–15
부동산업자와 이야기하다 **35**–G
부두 **155**–16
부두 근로자 **137**–21
부드러운 의자 **11**–6
부리 **132**–1
부모 **24**–4, **94**–1
부목 **83**–11
부식성 **147**–4
부어오른 손가락 **78**–16
부엌용 타이머 **59**–18
부인 **24**–20
부주의한 **147**–23
부추 **51**–17
부츠 **68**–18
부통령 **116**–7
부페 **33**–13
부품 **146**–7
부품을 조립하다 **140**–A
북 캐나다 **123**–1
북미 **124**–1
북미주와 중미 **122**–123
북유럽인들이 대서양 연안에 설립한
　식민지들 **114**
분 **16**–2
분수 **15**, **92**–11
분자 **119**–18
분젠 가스 버너 **119**–9
분필 **3**–16
분홍색 **12**–10
불가사리 **130**–15
불꽃 가리개 **42**–11
불꽃 놀이 **168**–8
불도저 **149**–6
불법 마약 **100**–4
불이 환한 거리로만 가십시오 **101**–B
불편한 **30**–8
브라자 **67**–20
브레이스 **81**–31
브레이크 페달 **109**–46
브로일러 **40**–21
브로콜리 **51**–15
브로콜리를 찐다 **58**–I
브리티시 콜럼비아 **123**–2
브이넥 스웨터 **71**–27
블라우스 **64**–9
블라인드 **43**–11
블록 **107**–2
블루베리 **50**–19
비극 **166**–11
비누 **43**–23, **76**–2
비누 접시 **43**–24
비늘 **130**–3
비닐 봉투 **55**–23
비닐랩 **55**–54
비둘기 **132**–16
비디오 가게 **93**–15
비디오 게임 **162**–1
비디오 카메라 **165**–19
비디오 카세트 **164**–10
비디오 테이프 **98**–13
비버 **134**–9

비상 브레이크 **109**–44
비상 카드를 보십시오 **111**–K
비상구 **37**–23
비상구 계단 **36**–7
비상구를 찾으십시오 **111**–J
비상시와 천재지변 **102**–103
비서 **139**–52, **142**–3
비싼 반지 **11**–19
비오는 **10**–8
비옷 **66**–17
비용 **21**–6
비처빙약 **80**–12
비치 가운(걸쳐 입는 옷) **66**–25
비치 타월 **155**–15
비치 파라솔 **155**–9
비커 **119**–13
비키니 **67**–16
비타민 **81**–19
비품 보관함 **142**–13
비행기 **110**–9
비행기 추락 **102**–3
비행기에 탑승하십시오 **111**–F
빈 방 광고문 **36**–11
빈 잔 **11**–10
빈 칸을 채우세요 **7**–R
빈그릇 운반인 **63**–9
빗 **23**–22, **76**–13
빗자루 **47**–10
빠른 운전사 **11**–3
빨간색 **12**–13
빨강 머리 **23**–14
빨대 **60**–20
빨래 **72**–1
빨래 바구니 **43**–1
빨래 집게 **72**–10
빨래를 개다 **72**–F
빨래를 분류하다 **72**–A
빨래방 **90**–1
빨래통 **72**–2
빨랫줄 **72**–9
빵 **54**–29
빵 한 덩어리 **56**–22
빵과 버터 접시 **63**–16
빵바구니 **63**–8
삐기 **118**–2
뼈 **75**–49
뼈가 부러지다 **82**–P
뿌리 **128**–5
뿌리 **129**–3
뿔 **134**–21
사 **14**
사각 팬티 **67**–12
사과 **50**–4
사과 쥬스 **55**–50
사과 쥬스 1 갤런 **57**–5
사과하세요 **8**–I
사다 **21**–C
사닥다리 **149**–2
사람을 관리하다 **140**–K
사랑에 빠지다 **28**–K
사랑에 빠진 **30**–19
사료 **148**–D
사립학교 **112**–2
사막 **117**–4
사무 보조원 **142**–12
사무실 **142**–143

사무실 매니저 **143** 25
사무실 빌딩 **89**–24
사무원 **5**–18, **136**–3
사물 묘사하기 **11**
사물함 **108**–33
사물함 **5**–7
사발 **41**–25
사슴 **134**–14
사슴뿔 **134**–16
사십 **14**
사업가 **136**–10
사용 설명서 **144**–22
사워크림 **54**–37
사이드 미러 **108**–8
사이에 **13**–10
사이즈 **70**
사이클링 **159**–4
사자 **135**–36
사전 **3**–28
사전 공부 **6**
사진 **44**–7
사진 앨범 **165**–32
사진 현상소 **90**–4
사진사 **32**–11
사진을 찍다 **32**–D
사촌 **24**–12
사회 보장 카드 **29**–5
산과의사 **86**–1
산맥 **117**–15
산봉우리 **117**–14
산성 비 **126**–11
산소 마스크 **110**–14
산악 자전거 타기 **154**–8
산업미술 **121**–10
산지 표준시 **17**–27
산타페의 스페인 사람들 **114**
살구 **50**–7
살균제 **95**–19
살라미 **53**–5
살수장치 **39**–8
살인 **100**–8
살충제 중독 **126**–14
삼 **14**
삼각 붕대 **80**–8
삼각법 **118**–27
삼각형 **118**–7
삼발이 **165**–20
삼십 **14**
삼촌 **24**–11
삽 **149**–21
삽 **39**–13
삽입형 귀고리 **69**–37
상담 교사 **5**–16
상담 교사실 **5**–15
상어 **130**–7
상업교육 **121**–2
상원 **116**–3
상원의원 **116**–4
상자 **56**–6
상점 주인 **139**–56
상추 **51**–1
상추 **60**–17
상태가 좋은 **30**–15
상품 **152**–24
새, 곤충 그리고 거미류 **132**
새 신발 **71**–32

새 아파트를 찾아 보다 **35**–A
새끼 고양이 **133**–10
새우 **130**–19
새우 **53**–24
새의 부분 명칭 **132**–1
색깔 **12**
색소폰 **120**–7
색종이 조각 **168**–3
색칠책 **45**–20
샌드페이퍼 **151**–50
샌들 **68**–24
샐러드 드레싱 **60**–18
샐러드 바 **60**–16
샐러드 접시 **63**–17
샐러드 포크 **63**–24
생년월일 **4**–16
생명 징후 검사기 **87**–21
생물 **119**–1
생물학적 위험 **147**–5
생선 **53**
생선 튀김 **61**–17
생수 **55**–53
생일 **19**–41
"생일 축하합니다" 노래를 부르다 **169**–I
생쥐 **133**–17
생쥐 **49**–26
샤워기 앞부분 **43**–10
샤워를 하다 **26**–C
샤워캡 **76**–1
샤워하다 **76**–A
샴푸 **76**–9
서랍 **40**–23, **44**–3
서랍장 **45**–8
서로 이야기하세요 **7**–P
서류를 파일에 넣다 **142**–H
서류함 **142**–10
서명 **4**–18
서명하세요 **4**–D
서버 **63**–6
서부영화 **166**–9
서브하다 **157**–N
서비스 요원 **139**–54
서빙 접시 **41**–6
서수 **14**
서식에 기입하세요 **4**–B
서양 자두 **50**–26
서양 장기 **162**–6
서양호랑가시나무 **128**–19
서양호박 **51**–4
서점 **92**–4
서지 보호기 **144**–10
"서프라이즈" 하고 고함치다 **169**–G
서프보드 **155**–5
서핑 **160**–9
서해안 **123**–7
석고붕대 **81**–29
석방되다 **99**–H
석유 **126**–6
석유 유출 **126**–15
석탄 **126**–4
선 **118**
선글라스 **66**–21
선물 **33**–18
선물가게 **145**–7
선물을 뜯어보다 **169**–L
선물을 싸다 **169**–D

선반 **40**–8
선발 징병제에 등록하다 **116**–F
선블록 **155**–13
선생 **2**–5
선생님께 이야기하세요 **2**–B
선수 **158**–5
선스크린 **76**–6, **155**–13
선스크린을 바르다 **76**–D
선인장 **128**–21
설치류 **133**
설탕 **55**–48, **60**–21
설탕 그릇 **41**–12
설탕 대체품 **60**–22
설탕 테이블스푼 하나 **57**–7
섬 **117**–8
섬게 **130**–20
성 **4**–4
성냥 **154**–21
성별 **4**–12
성인 **22**–9
성인학교 **112**–8
세계 **124**–125
세관 **110**–20
세관직원 **110**–21
세금을 내다 **116**–E
세룰라폰 **9**–13
세면대 **43**–22
세미 트랙터 트레일러 **106**–15
세미콜론 **113**–13
세발 자전거 **153**–9
세일가격 **21**–3
세일보딩 **160**–10
세제 **47**–23, **72**–7
세제를 넣다 **72**–B
세탁기 **72**–3
세탁기에 빨래를 넣다 **72**–C
세탁소 **91**–24
세탁하기 **72**
센불에 볶는다 **58**–W
센티미터(cm) **15**–12
셀러리 **51**–9
셋째 **14**
셔츠 **64**–4
소 **70**–2
소금 티스푼 하나 **57**–6
소금통(식탁용) **41**–14
소나무 **128**–10
소다 **55**–52
소매 **73**–6
소매없는 셔츠 **71**–29
소매없는 원피스 **65**–18
소매없는 짧은 상의 **67**–2
소맷부리 **73**–5
소방서 **88**–1
소방수 **102**–8
소방원 **137**–24
소방차 **102**–9
소세지 **52**–12, **61**–2
소셜시큐리티번호 **4**–15
소스 냄비 **59**–25
소아과 의사 **86**–4
소아용 침대 **45**–6
소원을 말하다 (속으로) **169**–J
소의 위 **52**–8
소파 **42**–19
소파 옆 소탁자 **42**–21

소포 우편 **96**–14
소프트볼 **158**–10
소프트웨어 **144**
소형 라디오 **164**–15
소형 차 **106**–2
소화기 **147**–22
소화전 **91**–28
속눈썹 **74**–34
속달 우편 **96**–12
속도 계기 **108**–20
속셔츠 **67**–10
손 **74**–8
손가락 **75**–57
손님 **62**–5, **145**–11
손님 접대하다 **140**–O
손님들 **33**–14
손님들을 초대하다 **169**–B
손님을 앉히다 **62**–B
손목 **75**–60
(손목)시계 **69**–34
손바닥 **75**–59
손뼉치다 **32**–C
손수건 **69**–42
손으로 바느질하다 **73**–A
손을 올리세요 **2**–A
손자 **24**–7
손자를 보다 **29**–Q
손톱 **75**–58
손톱 광택제(매니큐어) **77**–31
손톱 깎기 **77**–29
손톱에 매니큐어 칠하다 **77**–O
손톱을 깎다 **77**–N
손톱줄 **77**–30
솔 **23**–18
솔기 **73**–11
솔기 터는 기구 **73**–19
솔방울 **128**–11
솔빗 **76**–14
송금환 **20**–16
송아지 고기 카틀렛 **52**–6
송어 **53**–16
쇠간 **52**–7
쇠갈비 **52**–5
쇠고기 **52**
쇠사슬 **150**–36
쇼크 상태에 있다 **82**–C
쇼핑 **21**
쇼핑 바구니 **54**–7
쇼핑 카트 **54**–3
쇼핑 프로그램 **167**–25
쇼핑센터 **92**–93
숄더 백 **69**–27
수갑 **99**–2
수건걸이 **43**–8
수구 **158**–15
수달 **131**–35
수도꼭지 **43**–6
수도꼭지가 새다 **49**–16
수동 변속 레버 **109**–48
수두 **79**–6
수력발전 **126**–5
수리공 **48**–10, **138**–48
수박 **50**–24
수상스키 **160**–7
수색구조팀 **103**–17
수선화 **129**–26

수성 **127**–9
수세미 **47**–19
수송아지 **148**–21
수송하다 **146**–C
수술대 **87**–34
수술실 **87**
수술실 간호원 **87**–29
수술용 가운 **87**–32
수술용 고무 장갑 **87**–33
수술용 캡 **87**–31
수업 공부 **7**
수염 **134**–18
수영 팬츠 **66**–22
수영복 **66**–26
수영장 **37**–16, **145**–16
수영장 서비스 **145**–17
수영하다 **157**–T
수요일 **18**–4
수위 **36**–10
수의사 **139**–62
수준기 **150**–24
수직 **118**–20
수질 오염 **126**–12
수채화 물감 **163**–25
수탉 **133**–6
수통 **154**–24
수표책 **97**–7
수프 **54**–24
수프 한 캔 **56**–15
수프스푼 **63**–29
수프용 그릇 **63**–18
수학 **118**
수학의 종류 **118**
수화기 **9**–2
수화기를 드세요 **9**–A
수화기를 제자리에 놓으세요 **9**–F
수화물 **96**–5
수화물 찾는 곳 **110**–17
수화물 캐리어 **110**–19
수화물을 찾으십시오 **111**–P
숙모 **24**–10
숙제를 하다 **27**–T
순무 **51**–14
숨을 못쉬다 **82**–N
숫가락 **41**–23
숫자 **3**–31
숫자와 단위 **14**–15
숲 **117**–11
쉬다 **27**–U
쉬운 문제 **11**–23
쉼표 **113**–10
슈트하다 **156**–I
스노보드 **161**–23
스노보딩 **160**–2
스노클링 **160**–11
스리피스 정장 **64**–1
스모그 **126**–10
스모그가 많은 **10**–14
스무번째 **14**
스왑미트 **152**–22
스위스 치즈 **53**–11
스윙하다 **157**–O
스캐너 **144**–13
스컹크 **134**–12
스케이트 타다 **157**–V
스케이트보딩 **159**–12

스코틀랜드, 아일랜드, 독일 **115**
스쿠버 다이빙 **160**–12
스쿠버 탱크 **155**–8
스퀴지 **47**–9
스크램블드 달걀 **58**
스크램블드 에그 **61**–1
스크레이퍼 **151**–48
스크린 **165**–28
스키 **161**–24
스키 마스크 **66**–14
스키 모자 **66**–10
스키 폴 **161**–25
스키를 타다 **157**–U
스키화 **161**–26
스타킹 **67**–26
스태킹 트레이 **142**–5
스탠드업 코메디 **166**–5
스테레오 전축 **42**–14
스테이션 웨곤 **106**–8
스테이크 **52**–2, **61**–13
스테이크용 나이프 **63**–26
스테이크용 연어 **53**–19
스테이플 **143**–29
스테이플러 **143**–28
스테이플러로 찍다 **142**–G
스토리 종류 **166**
스토브 **40**–18
스튜용 쇠고기 **52**–3
스트레치하다 **157**–Q
스파게티 **54**–27
스페이드 **163**–28
스페인과 미국 전쟁 **115**
스포츠 동사 **156**–157
스포츠 셔츠 **65**–26
스포츠 카 **106**–6
스포츠 코트 **64**–6
스포츠용 잠바 **66**–24
스폰지 **47**–24
스프레이 건 **151**–19
스피커 **36**–8, **164**–11
슬라이드 **119**–5, **165**–31
슬라이드 트레이 **165**–30
슬롯 **144**–19
슬리퍼 **67**–6
슬리핑백 **154**–12
슬픈 **31**–20
슬픈 책 **167**–28
습한 **10**–12
승강기 **37**–34
승객 **104**–7, **110**–23
승무원 **110**–13
승차권 **104**–14
시 **4**–7, **16**–3
시가지 **88**–89
시각 장애인 **22**–26
시간 **16**–17
시계 **3**–10
시계 라디오 **164**–1
시계겸용 라디오 **44**–16
시골 **34**–4
시궁쥐 **49**–27
시금치 **51**–11
시끄러운 아이들 **11**–11
시내 전화 **9**–4
시누이 **24**–15
시럽 **61**–5

시력 검사표 **84**–11
시리얼 한 박스 **56**–18
시민권 시험을 보다 **116**–C
시민권 신청 자격 **116**
시민이 되다 **28**–H
시소 **153**–16
시아버지 **24**–14
시어머니 **24**–13
시원한 **10**–3
시장 **54**–**55**, **89**–20
시장에 가다 **26**–L
시청 **89**–17
시트를 갈다 **46**–Q
시험관 **119**–16
식기 세척기 **63**–13
식기 세척실 **63**–12
식기 세트 **41**–2
식기세척기 **40**–4
식당 **41**, **62**–5, **62**–**63**
식당 구역 **93**–14
식물 **42**–18
식물에 물을 주세요 **39**–B
식물원 **152**–4
식민지 거주자들과 비노예 흑인 **115**
식민지 주민 **114**
식사습관을 바꾸다 **80**–C
식용유 **55**–49
식탁 **41**–17
식탁 의자 **41**–16
식탁보 **41**–18
식탁을 차리다 **62**–A
식탁을 치우다 **62**–G
식품 가공기 **40**–26
신경 **75**–50
신고서 **110**–22
신문 **98**–8
신문기자 **139**–49
신문매점 **90**–11
신문을 읽다 **27**–V
신문을 재활용하다 **46**–B
신발 가게 **92**–10
신발과 액세서리 **68**–**69**
신발끈을 매다 **94**–I
신발류 **68**–3
신발밑창 **68**–12
신상 정보 **4**
신선한 생선 **53**–29
신용 카드 **20**–15
신월 **127**–13
신장 **75**–45
신체 **74**–**75**
신체 내부 **75**
신체 부자유인 **22**–25
신체장애자 주차 **107**–14
신호등 **90**–6, **91**–23
신호등을 기다리시오 **90**–B
실내 화초 **129**–29
실로폰 **120**–17
실습 **121**–10
실크 스카프 **68**–4, **70**–15
실패 **73**–17
실편 **76**–19
실험실 기사 **86**–16
실험하다 **119**–A
심각한 책 **167**–26
심장 **75**–38

심징 빅동을 듣다 **85**–D
심장마비를 일으키다 **82**–D
심장병 **79**–14
심장병 전문의 **86**–3
심판 **158**–6
심폐기능 소생법 **83**–18
십 **14**
십구 **14**
십만 **14**
십사 **14**
십삼 **14**
십억 **14**
십오 **14**
십육 **14**
십이 **14**
십일 **14**
십자 드라이버 **150**–26
십칠 **14**
십팔 **14**
싱크 **40**–6
싱크물이 넘치다 **49**–17
싹 **129**–6
싼 반지 **11**–20
쌀 **54**–28, **148**–1
쌓기 장난감 **45**–15
써는 칼 **59**–12
썩은 **50**–30
썰매타기 **160**–6
쓰레기 낙하장치 **37**–24
쓰레기를 내다놓다 **46**–R
쓰레기봉지 **47**–12
쓰레기차 **91**–27
쓰레기통 **37**–20, **39**–3, **43**–25
쓰레기통을 비우다 **46**–F
쓰레받기 **47**–11
쓰로우 필러 **42**–20
쓸개 **75**–40
씨 **129**–1
씨 뿌리기 **129**–2
아가미 **130**–2
아기 **22**–2
아기 돌보는 사람 **136**–12
아기 모니터 **45**–9
아기 백팩 **95**–15
아기 보호망 **95**–11
아기 캐리어 **95**–14
아기를 낳다 **29**–M
아나운서 **152**–27
아늑한 곳 **94**–4
아들 **24**–22
아래에 **13**–7, **13**–9
아래턱 **74**–23
아르마딜로 **134**–8
아르메니아 인 남유럽 및 동유럽 인 **115**
아름다운 경치 **11**–21
아메리카삼나무 **128**–7
아메리칸 치즈 **53**–9
아버지 **24**–6
아보카도 **50**–14
아스파라거스 **51**–24
아시아 **125**–4
아이라이너 **77**–35
아이새도우 **77**–34
아이스 박스 **155**–11
아이스 스케이트 **161**–9
아이스 스케이팅 **160**–4

아이스 하키 **158**–13
아이스크림 **55**–44
아이스크림 판매대 **93**–20
아이티 인 **115**
아일랜드인 **114**
아침 **17**–16
아침 식사를 하다 **26**–E
아코디언 **120**–21
아크릴 페인트 **162**–9
아티초크 **51**–20
아파트 **36**–**37**
아파트 건물 **34**–5
아파트 번호 # **4**–6
아파트 임대하기 **35**
아파트를 임대하다 **28**–I
아포스트로피 **113**–11
아프리카 **125**–5
아프터쉐이브 **77**–28
아픈 **30**–12
아홉째 **14**
악기를 연주하다 **120**–A
악어 **131**–36
안개긴 **10**–11
안경 **81**–35
안경점 **92**–8
안과 의사 **86**–7
안내소 **93**–22
안내판 **93**–19
안도된 **30**–16
안뜰 **37**–18, **39**–16
안뜰용 가구 **39**–5
안락의자 **42**–24
안보 장치 **36**–9
안에 **13**–5
안전 귀가리개 **147**–14
안전 마스크 **147**–11
안전 벨트 **109**–36
안전 벨트를 매십시오 **111**–I
안전 장화 **147**–20
안전 조끼 **147**–15
안전모 **147**–19
안전핀 **73**–24
앉으세요 **2**–E
알라스카 표준시 **17**–25
알레르기 **79**–8
알레르기 반응을 보이다 **82**–E
알루미늄 포일 **55**–55
알약 **81**–26
알파벳 **3**–30
알파파 **148**–5
암스트롱 달 착륙 **115**
암청색 **12**–2
암탉 **133**–5
압축공기 드릴 **149**–9
압편 **143**–43
앞니 **135**–48
앞마당 **38**–15
앞머리 **23**–8
앞문 **38**–11
앞에 **13**–4
앞유리 **108**–2
앞유리 와이퍼 **108**–3
앞좌석 **109**–35
애완동물 **133**
애완동물 가게 **92**–6
애완동물 식품 **54**–10

애틀란틱 프로빈스 **123**–6
액량 **57**
액셀러레이터 **109**–47
액션 **166**–13
액션 인물 **163**–31
액체류를 마시다 **80**–B
야간등 **45**–3
야구 **158**–9
야구 게임 **152**–25
야구 모자 **66**–27
야구 방망이 **161**–14
야구 카드 **162**–11
야구공 **161**–18
야드 자 **151**–15
야외 활동 **154**
야채 **51**
야채 껍질 제거기 **59**–15
야채 샐러드 **60**–8
야채 찜냄비 요리 **58**
야채를 첨가한다 **58**–Q
약 접시 **87**–23
약국 **80**–9, **90**–2
약속 **19**–45
약을 과량복용하다 **82**–K
약을 먹다 **80**–F
약제사 **80**–10
약품 진열장 **43**–19
얇은 자켓 **71**–40
얇은 책 **11**–8
양 **133**–7
양 다리고기 **52**–14
양 정강이 살 **52**–13
양고기 **52**
양고기춥 **52**–15
양궁 **159**–1
양념 **60**–26
양념류 **55**–46
양로원 **34**–11
양말 **67**–15
양배추 **51**–2
양배추 샐러드 **53**–14
양부분육 **52**–15
양서류 **130**
양재사 **73**–2
양치수 **77**–23
양치질하다 **77**–L
양탄자 **44**–23
양파 **51**–28
양파를 살짝 기름에 익힌다 **58**–H
양파를 잘게 썬다 **58**–G
어깨 **74**–10
어깨 길이의 머리 **23**–2
어깨 벨트 **109**–37
어깨 패드 **161**–21
어댑터 **164**–17
어려운 문제 **11**–24
어린이 **22**–1
어린이 안전 시트 **95**–13
어린이 침실 **45**
어린이 카 시트 **109**–39
어린이 프로그램 **167**–24
어린이를 볼보다 **140**–L
어린이용 변기 **95**–10
어머니 **24**–5
어부 **136**–15
어제 **18**–17

어지럽다 **78**–C
어질러진 옷장 **11**–16
언덕 **117**–16
얼굴 **74**
얼룩 **70**–22
얼룩 다람쥐 **133**–20
얼룩말 **135**–34
얼어붙는 **10**–5
얼음이 덮인 **10**–13
얼음찜질 팩 **83**–13
엄지 손가락 **75**–56
엉덩이 **74**–12
에너지와 환경 **126**
에너지 자원 **126**
에너지 절약 **126**–C
에스컬레이터 **93**–21
에어백 **108**–16
에어컨 **108**–28
에어콘 **37**–19
엑스레이 기사 **86**–8
엑스레이를 찍다 **85**–H
엔지니어 **137**–23
엔진 **109**–41
엔터테인먼트 **166**–167
엔터테인먼트의 종류 **166**
여 **4**–14
여과기 **59**–17
여권 **29**–9
여덟째 **14**
여동생 **24**–8
여름 **19**–38
여섯째 **14**
여성 참정권 **114**
(여성용)양말 대님 **67**–19
여우 **134**–15
여자 **22**–10
여자 팬티 **67**–17
여자조카 **24**–17
여자형제 **24**–8
여행사 **92**–9
여행사 직원 **139**–60
여행자 수표 **20**–17
여행하다 **29**–N
역겨운 **30**–9
역기 **161**–19
역도 **159**–15
역사적 및 정치적 사건 **114**
연결 코드 **151**–14
연고 **81**–24
연극 **166**–2
연극예술 **121**–12
연기 탐지기 **37**–25, **45**–11
연단 **32**–5
연료 계기 **108**–22
연료 탱크 **108**–12
연료분사 장치 **109**–40
연립 주택 **34**–7
연못 **117**–21
연산 **118**
연석 **90**–10
연설하다 **32**–E
연속 코메디 **167**–18
연습장 **3**–23
연어 한 마리 **53**–18
연필 **3**–20
연필 깎이 **3**–13

연필 지우개 **3**–21
연필을 꺼내세요 **2**–K
연필을 치우세요 **2**–L
연회 요리 담당자 **33**–12
열 **78**–8
열넷째 **14**
열다섯째 **14**
열두째 **14**
열번째 **14**
열셋째 **14**
열쇠 **37**–31
열쇠 고리 **69**–43
열아홉째 **14**
열여덟째 **14**
열여섯째 **14**
열일곱째 **14**
열파 **10**–15
열한번째 **14**
염려되는 **30**–13
염소 **133**–1
엽서 **96**–3
엽서에 주소를 쓰십시오 **96**–A
영 **14**
영수증 **21**–5
영양 **135**–35
영양사 **87**–25
영어 제2외국어 **121**–7
영원 **130**–26
영작문 **113**
영주권 **29**–3
영화 **152**–10, **166**–1
옆, 오른쪽에 **13**–2
옆, 왼쪽에 **13**–1
엽서에 주소를 쓰십시오
옆선을 늘여 내다 **73**–F
옆선을 줄여 넣다 **73**–E
예비 타이어 **109**–53
예쁜 **22**–23
예술가 **136**–5
예약을 하다 **85**–A
예약일지 **143**–27
오 **14**
오거나이저 **143**–30
오늘(금일) **18**–15
오늘의 수프 **61**–10
오디오 테이프 **98**–12
오랑우탄 **135**–40
오렌지 **50**–10
오르간 **120**–22
오리 **132**–13
오리 고기 **52**–18
오리 너구리 **135**–46
오리 연못 **153**–6
오리털 자켓 **66**–15
오리털 조끼 **66**–13
오버롤 **65**–21
오버헤드 프로젝터 (OHP) **2**–4
오보에 **120**–5
오븐 **40**–20
오븐 클리너 **47**–3
오븐 토스터 **40**–15
오븐을 청소하다 **46**–C
오십 **14**
오이 **51**–12
오일 **126**–6
오자 교정액 **143**–33

오징어 **130**–10
오케스트라 **120**–1
오크 **128**–18
오토바이 **91**–19
오페라 **166**–8
오한 **78**–9
오후 **17**–18
옥상 정원 **36**–5
옥수수 **51**–27, **148**–4
옥스포드화 **68**–20
온도 **78**–8
온도 계기 **108**–23
온라인 카탈로그 **98**–9
온수 **43**–5
온실 **152**–5
온타리오 **123**–4
올빼미 **132**–6
옷감 소프너 **72**–6
옷걸이 **72**–11
옷단의 안선 **73**–1
옷을 걸다 **72**–H
옷을 다리미질하다 **72**–G
옷을 바느질하다 **140**–I
옷을 입다 **26**–D, **94**–J
옷장 **44**–4
와셔 **150**–32
와시클로스 **43**–14
와이어 스트리퍼 **151**–37
와플 **61**–4
완두콩 **51**–19
완충 패드 **45**–7
외과 의사 **87**–30
외국어 **121**–8
외국어를 말하다 **140**–J
외로운 **30**–18
외바퀴 손수레 **39**–16
외야석 **5**–10
외투 **66**–2
요구르트 **54**–33
요구르트 1 파인트 **57**–3
요금 **104**–5
요금 카드 **104**–12
요람 **45**–19
요리사 **137**–17
요리용 믹서 **40**–12
요리하다 **140**–C
요일 **18**
요통 **78**–5
요트 **155**–4
요트 경기 **160**–8
욕실 **43**
욕실용 매트 **43**–27
욕탕 **43**–2
용기 **56**–5
용기와 포장식품 **56**
용의자를 체포하다 **99**–A
용접공 **139**–63
용지 순서를 맞추다 **142**–F
우박 **10**–19
우박 폭풍 **10**–18
우산 **66**–16
우유 **54**–35, **148**–C
우유 1 쿼트 **57**–4
우주 **127**, **127**–12, **127**–22
우주 비행사 **127**–17
우주 정류장 **127**–18

우체국 **89**–29
우체국 소인 **96**–9
우체부 **96**–6
우편 주소 **96**–8
우편 집배원 **138**–45
우편물 저울 **143**–16
우편번호 **4**–9
우편으로 보내십시오 **96**–B
우편함 **37**–36, **38**–4, **90**–12
우표 **96**–10
우표 수집 **162**–12
우회전 하시오 **107**–B
우회전만 허용 **107**–9
운동경기용 서포터 **67**–14
운동기구 **161**
운동장 **36**–6
운동하다 **27**–W, **80**–D, **157**–P
운동화 **68**–23
운디드 니 전투 **115**
운전 면허증 **29**–4
운전교육 **121**–5
운전을 배우다 **28**–E
울 스웨터 **70**–14
울 스카프 **66**–4
울다 **32**–C
울타리 **38**–3, **148**–19
웃다 **33**–H
워터 히터가 고장났다 **48**–1
원숭이 **135**–27
원의 부분 **118**
원자 **119**–17
원자력 에너지 **126**–8
원주 **118**–15
원추형 **118**–11
원통 **118**–12
원형 컨베이어 **110**–18
원형 톱 **150**–10
월 **4**
월 계산서 **97**–10
월남전쟁 **115**
월명 **19**
월요일 **18**–2
웨곤을 잡아당기다 **153**–A
웨이터 **62**–4, **139**–53
웨이트레스 **63**–6
위 **75**–41
위에 **13**–6, **13**–8
위험 폐기물 **126**–9
위험물질 **147**–7
위험한 상황 **147**–8
유니폼 **65**–17, **161**–16
유대회당 **88**–9
유량계 **108**–19
유럽 **125**–3
유리 끼운 덧문 **38**–12
유리 클리너 **47**–8
유리창이 깨졌다 **48**–5
유리컵 **41**–26
유모차 **94**–2, **95**–16
유방 **74**–14
유아 **22**–3
유아용 유동식 **95**–25
유원지 **152**–13
유제품 **54**–9
유치원 **112**–4
유타칸 반도 **123**–19

유행성 감기 **79**–2
유화 **163**–24
육 **14**
육상 경기 **159**–17
육상 우편 **96**–14
육십 **14**
육체 노동을 하다 **140**–D
융자금을 얻다 **35**–I
은하계 **127**–26
은행 **88**–3, **97**
~을 **21**–A
음료수 **55**–15
음료수 대 **153**–11
음식 무게를 달다 **57**–B
음식 준비 **58**
음식을 먹이다 **94**–D
음식을 서브하다 **62**–F
음식찌거기처리기 **40**–5
음악 **120**
음악가 **138**–41
음주 운전 **100**–3
음주 운전하지 마십시오 **101**–G
응급 의료 테크니션 **87**–26
응급 치료 상자 **83**–1
응급 치료 설명서 **83**–7
응급 호흡법 **83**–16
응급실 **87**
응급치료 **83**
응급환자식별 팔찌 **83**–14
응용 프로그램 **144**–21
의료 폐기물 처리기 **86**–14
의복 I **64–65**
의복 II **66**
의복 III **67**
의복 묘사 **70–71**
의붓 남자형제 **25**–33
의붓 아버지 **25**–28
의붓 어머니 **25**–31
의붓 여자형제 **25**–32
의사 **84**–6, **137**–22
의식을 잃다 **82**–B
의자 **2**–7
이 **14**, **74**–25
이 라디에이터는 냉각수가
　필요하다 **109**–56
이 배터리는 재충전이 필요하다 **109**–58
이 자동차는 스모그 검사가
　필요하다 **109**–57
이 자동차는 오일이 필요하다 **109**–55
이 자동차는 휘발유가 필요하다 **109**–54
이 타이어는 공기가 필요하다 **109**–59
이동식 주택 **34**–8
이류 **111**–L
이른 **17**–22
이를 닦다 **77**–J
이를 드릴하다 **85**–K
이를 뽑다 **85**–M
이를 클린하다 **85**–I
이를 플로스하다 **77**–K
이름 **4**–1, **4**–2
이름을 정자로 쓰세요 **4**–C
이름의 철자를 쓰세요 **4**–A
이마 **74**–20
이모 **24**–10
이민 **114**
이민하다 **28**–C

이발소 **88**–15
이번 주(금주) **18**–19
이복 **25**–29, **25**–30
이부 남자형제 **25**–29
이부 여자형제 **25**–30
이불 **45**–2
이브닝 가운 **65**–29
이사하다 **29**–P
이삿짐 배달원 **138**–40
이삿짐 트럭 **106**–14
이십 **14**
이십이 **14**
이십일 **14**
이야기책을 읽어주다 **94**–F
이염 **79**–3
이웃 **37**–22
이유식 **95**–28
이젤 **163**–21
이중 냄비 **59**–8
이차세계대전 **114**
이차세계대전 피난민 이민 **114**
이착륙 모니터 **110**–4
이하선염 **79**–7
이해하고 있는지 **8**–E
이혼했다 **25**–24
익은 **50**–29
익지 않은 **50**–28
인구 **114**
인디언 제거 법안 **114**
인명구조 기구 **155**–19
인생 경로 **28**–29
인쇄 기술자 **138**–46
인쇄소 **91**–22
인스턴트 커피 **55**–51
인치(in) **15**–13
인터네트 보급 **115**
인터콤 **36**–8
인형 **45**–18
인형 만드는 키트 **162**–1, **162**–15
인형 집 **45**–14
인형극 **152**–14
인화물질 **147**–2
일 **4**, **14**, **18**–10
일 주에 두 번 **18**–23
일 주에 세 번 **18**–24
일 주에 한 번 **18**–22
일곱째 **14**
일과 **26**–27
일광욕하는 사람 **155**–17
일광절약시간 (서머타임) **17**–33
일꾼 **148**–20
일등상 **152**–20
일방통행 **107**–6
일본인 **115**
일상 회화 **8**
일어나다 **26**–B
일어서세요 **2**–D
일요일 **18**–1
일정표 **104**–3
일차세계대전 **114**
일하다 **26**–K
일회용 기저귀 **95**–20
임대 계약서에 서명하다 **35**–C
임대료를 지불하다 **35**–F
임대인 **37**–33
임산부 옷가게 **93**–17

임산부용 드레스 **65**–19
임신한 **22**–19
입 **74**–22
입금용지 **97**–12
입금을 하십시오 **97**–C
입방체 **118**–10
입술 **74**–30
입주하다 **35**–D
입체 **118**
잇몸 **74**–24
잉꼬 **133**–15
잉크 스탬프 패드 **143**–41
잎 **128**–6, **129**–5
자 **3**–27
자금 이체 **97**–E
자기그릇 캐비닛 **41**–1
자녀를 데려오다 **27**–O
자녀를 학교에 데려다 주다 **26**–G
자다 **27**–X, **27**–Y
자동 응답기 **9**–14
자동차 기술자 **136**–7
자동차 딜러 **88**–4
자동차 부속과 자동차 정비 **108**–109
자동차 사고 **102**–2
자동차를 운전하시오 **90**–C
자동차를 주차하십시오 **91**–D
자동차를 팔다 **140**–H
자동차와 트럭 **106**
자두 **50**–8
자라 **131**–42
자랑스러운 **31**–22
자루 걸레 **47**–17
자리에 앉으세요 **2**–E
자몽 **50**–9
자물쇠가 부서졌다 **48**–6
자물쇠 제조공 **48**–11
자석 **119**–21
자수 **163**–19
자신을 소개하세요 **8**–D
자연 프로그램 **167**–22
자원 봉사자 **87**–19
자작나무 **128**–8
자전거 길 **153**–2
자전거 타기용 반바지 **67**–3
자전거 타는 사람 **153**–3
자전거(두바퀴) **153**–4
자전거를 타십시오 **91**–E
자정 **17**–21
자켓 **66**–7
작가 **139**–64
작문 **113**–2
작문 숙제 **113**–1
작문을 다시 쓰다 **113**–D
작문을 수정하다 **113**–B
작문을 제출하다 **113**–E
작업 안전 **147**
작은 가지 **128**–1
작은 마을 **34**–3
작은 손 **11**–1
작은 수건 **43**–13
작은 입상 **162**–10
잔디 깎는 기계 **39**–22
잔디(밭) **39**–21
잔디를 깎으세요 **39**–C
잔액 **97**–11
잔치 **168**–16

잘 정리된 옷장 **11**–15
잘 휘젓는다 **58**–B
잠금장치 **109**–34
잠수복 **155**–7
잠에서 깨다 **26**–A
잠옷 **67**–5
잠이 들다 **27**–Y
잠자리에 들다 **27**–X
잡다 **94**–B
잡지 **98**–7
잡지 꽂이대 **42**–22
장 **75**–42
장갑 **66**–5
장거리 전화 **9**–5
장과 **128**–20
장난감 **94**–5
장난감 가게 **92**–5
장난감 상자 **45**–24
장난감들을 치우다 **46**–H
장내 기생충 **79**–16
장모 **24**–13
장미 **129**–15
장식 **168**–19
장식편 **69**–36
장인 **24**–14
장작 **42**–12
장화 **66**–19
재단사 **73**–9
재료를 섞는다 **58**–K
재료를 측량하다 **57**–A
재미있는 책 **167**–27
재봉 및 수선 **73**
재봉사 **137**–27
재봉틀 **73**–10
재봉틀로 바느질하다 **73**–B
재생하다 **165**–B
재스민 **129**–21
재채기하다 **78**–B
재판관 **99**–6
재판을 받다 **99**–D
재혼했다 **25**–27
재활용 **126**–A
재활용 통 **47**–2
잭 **109**–51
잭 치즈 **53**–12
잭-오-랜턴 **168**–11
잭해머 **149**–9
잼 한 병 **56**–14
쟁반 **41**–10
쟁반을 나르다 **62**–H
쟁반접시 **41**–3
저녁 **17**–19
저녁 식사를 요리하다 **27**–P
저녁 식사를 하다 **27**–R
저울 **43**–26, **84**–7, **119**–11
저자 **98**–22
저축예금 계좌번호 **97**–6
적재 도크 **146**–16
전갈 **132**–31
전구 **42**–4
전기 깡통 따개 **40**–14
전기 면도기 **77**–24
전기 믹서 **40**–25
전기 연필깎개 **142**–9
전기 위험 **147**–1
전기 충격을 받다 **82**–F

전기 테이프 151–38
전기공 48–9
전등 115
전동 드릴 150–8
전동 샌더 150–9
전등 스위치 44–19
전방 통로 38–14
전산학 121–4
전선 151–13
전시회 152–21
전신용 슬립 67–22
전원 스위치 144–4
전원 지역 34–4
전원이 나갔다 48–2
전자 렌지 40–13
전자 키보드 120–20
전자제품 가게 93–18
전자제품과 사진 164–165
전정 가위 39–15
전조등 108–5
전철 104–17
전철역 104–13
전치사 13
전화 9–1, 115
전화 번호 4–11
전화 번호부 9–15
전화 카드 9–10
전화를 걸어 문의하다 141–E
전화번호 안내 서비스 (411) 9–8
젊은 22–13
점수 158–1
점심 벤치 5–5
점심을 만들다 26–F
점원 68–1
점적기 119–14
점토 162–14
점퍼 케이블 109–52
점프수트 65–16
점프하다 156–J
점화장치 108–25
접수원 84–2, 138–47
접시 41–24
접시 놓기 63–14
접시 받침 41–20
젓는다 58–E
정기간행물 섹션 98–6
정답에 동그라미를 치세요 7–S
정맥 75–44
정맥 영양 주사 87–27
정사각형 118–6
정사각형의 부분 118
정상가 21–2
정수 15–6
정신과 의사 86–6
정오 17–17
정원사 137–26, 152–6
정월 초하루 168–1
정장 64–2
정장 드레스 71–36
정제약 81–25
정지 107–3
정지 및 방출 165–F
정형외과 의사 81–28
젖꼭지 95–27
젖먹이다 94–C
젖병 95–26

젖소 133–3
젖은 티셔츠 72–17
젖은 티슈 95–17
제 1대 대통령 워싱턴 115
제과 기술자 136–8
제과류 54–6, 55–13
제과점 89–16
제동등 108–13
제목 98–21, 113–3
제비꽃 129–22
제빙기 145–18
제산제 81–18
제조하다 146–B
제한 속도 107–5
조각품 152–9
조개 155–21
조깅하다 156–B
조끼 65–24
조리대 40–22
조리대를 닦아내다 46–O
조리한 닭고기 52–25
조립 라인 146–8
조립공 136–6
조명 기구 41–5
조모 24–2
조부 24–3
조부모 24–1
조카 24–18
졸리는 30–3
졸업 32–33
졸업 가운 32–2
졸업 증서 29–2, 32–7
졸업모 32–3
졸업반 32–1
졸업생 32–6
졸업생 대표 32–8
졸업하다 28–D, 32–A
좁은 넥타이 71–45
종교적 휴일 19–44
종려 128–15
종아리 74–18
종업원 62–4
종이 봉투 55–22
종이 인형 163–30
종이 재단기 143–15
종이 제품 55–14
종이 타월 40–2
종이타월 두루말이 하나 56–23
좌석 2–7, 152–11
좌석을 찾으십시오 111–G
좌회전 하시오 107–C
죄수 99–14
주 4–8, 18–11
주 사무실 5–17
주거 장소 34
주걱 59–19
주다 21–D
주말 18–13
주머니 135–50
주머니 쥐 134–4

주문 담당자 146–10
주문을 받다 62–E
주방 40, 63–10
주방 용구 59
주방장 63–11
주방장 샐러드 61–9
주부 137–32
주사 84–14
주사 맞다 80–E
주사위 162–4
주소 4–5
주유소 88–12
주유소 종업원 137–28
주차 공간 36–15, 90–5
주차 미터 91–18
주차금지 107–12
주차장 (옥내) 89–26
주택 38
주택 융자금을 지불하다 35–L
주행 기록계 108–21
주황색 12–6
죽다 29–R
줄 55–20
줄기 128–4, 129–4
줄넘기 줄 153–5
줄무늬 70–7
줄자 73–13, 150–22
줌 렌즈 165–25
중 70–3
중간 이름의 첫자 4–3
중고품시장 152–22
중국인, 스칸디나비아 인 115
중년의 22–14
중단 165–E
중동인 115
중량 57
중부 표준시 17–28
중서부 123–9
중앙 아메리카 인 115
중장비를 운전하다 140–F
중학교 112–6
중형 차 106–3
쥐 49–27, 133–18
증거 99–9
증권시장 폭락 114
증상과 상해 78
증인 99–11
지갑을 보호하십시오 101–D
지게차 146–14
지구 3–9, 127–7
지난 주 18–18
지느러미 130–1
지도 3–12
지도책 98–3
지루한 31–26
지루한 책 167–29
지름 118–17
지리 117
지배인 36–12, 54–8
지불 방법 20
지불하다 21–C
지붕 38–20
지붕 수리공 48–8
지붕널 149–19
지붕이 새다 48–3
지시를 따라하기 7

지역 번호 **4**–10
지열 에너지 **126**–7
지진 **102**–5
지팡이 **80**–7
지퍼 **73**–16
지폐 **20**
지하철 **104**–9
직사각형 **118**–8
직선 **118**–18
직업 (A–H, 영어순) **136–137**
직업 (H–W, 영어순) **138–139**
직업 게시판을 보다 **141**–B
직업 찾기 **141**
직업 특기 **140**
직업학교 **112**–9
직장을 구하다 **28**–G
직행하시오 **107**–A
진공 청소기 **47**–13
진공 청소기 부착물 **47**–14
진공 청소기 안주머니 **47**–15
진드기 **132**–28
진료대 **84**–13
진료소 **84**
진열장 **69**–7
진주 목걸이 **69**–30
진찰실 **84**–9
진통제 **81**–16
진흙 사태 **102**–6
질녀 **24**–17
질문에 답하세요 **6**–H
질문을 하세요 **6**–G
질병과 건강상태 **79**
질식되다 **82**–L
짐을 체크하십시오 **111**–B
짐을 풀다 **35**–E
집 **34**–6
집 구하기 **35**
집게 **59**–23
집소유권을 얻다 **35**–J
집안일 **46**
집에 도착하다 **27**–Q
집에 오다 **27**–Q
집을 사기 **35**–1
집을 사다 **29**–O
집을 청소하다 **27**–N
집을 치장하다 **169**–C
집주인 **37**–32
짜다 **163**–F
짝과 함께 공부하기 **6**
짝을 도와 주세요 **6**–J
짧은 구레나룻 **23**–7
짧은 머리 **23**–1
짧은 치마 **71**–35
찜통 **59**–4
찢어진 **70**–23
차 **61**–24
차 주전자 **41**–11
차고 **38**–6
차고문 **38**–7
차다 **156**–L
차로 출근하다 **26**–I
차양 **44**–6
차장 **104**–16
차주전자 **40**–17
착륙 **111**–O
착한 개 **11**–17

찬 **30**–4
찬장 **40**–1, **41**–1
참고도서 사서 **98**–1
참고도서부 **98**–2
참새 **132**–8
참치 **54**–25, **130**–9
창고 **146**–9
창고원 **139**–55
창구 계원 **97**–1
창문 **38**–17, **42**–17
창문을 닦다 **46**–D
창유리 **149**–15
채소류 **54**–11
채소밭 **148**–12
책가방 **69**–28
책상 **2**–6, **142**–1
책상 깔개 **142**–7
책을 같이 보세요 **6**–I
책을 덮으세요 **2**–J
책을 펴세요 **2**–I
책장 **3**–8, **42**–1
처남 **24**–16
처방 **80**–13
처방약 **80**–11
처방표 **80**–14
척추 **75**–54
척추 지압사에게 가다 **81**–H
천 **14**
천 종류 **70**
천문학자 **127**–20
천식 **79**–11
천연가스 **126**–3
천왕성 **127**–3
천일 **14**
천장 **42**–5
천장 팬 **41**–4
철도 건널목 **107**–11
철로 **104**–10
철물점 **88**–14
첫 번째 비행 **114**
첫째 **14**
청각 장애인 **22**–27
청력 전문의 **81**–32
청록색 **12**–4
청바지 **64**–5
청소 용구 **47**
청소 카트 **145**–14
청소부 **145**–15
청진기 **84**–8
체 **59**–22
체격이 큰 **22**–20
체다 치즈 **53**–10
체로키족의 눈물의 산길 **114**
체리 **50**–16
체리 피커 **149**–5
체스 **162**–6
체온계 **84**–15
체온을 재다 **85**–C
체육 **121**–11
체육관 **5**–9
체조 **159**–8
체커스 **162**–5
체크 무늬 **70**–11
체크아웃 데스크 **98**–16
체크인 카운터 **110**–3
첼로 **120**–9

초 **16**–1, **41**–7
초강력 열쇠장치 **37**–29
초등학교 **112**–5
초록색 **12**–8
초빙 연사 **32**–9
초소형 차 **106**–1
초승달 **127**–14
초안을 쓰다 **113**–A
초원 **117**–20
초인종 **38**–10
초점이 안맞다 **165**–33
초조한 **30**–11
초콜릿 **55**–41
촛대 **41**–8
촛불을 불어 끄다 **169**–K
촛불을 켜다 **169**–H
총 **100**–9
총액 **21**–8
최초 사운드 필름 **114**
최초 원자탄 **114**
추리 **166**–15
추수 **148**–B
추수감사절 **168**–15
추운 **10**–4, **30**–4
축구 **158**–12
축구 헬멧 **161**–20
축구공 **161**–12
축배를 들다 **33**–I
축제일 **168**
축하 카드 **96**–4
출구 없음 **107**–8
출발 **111**–L
출발하다 **157**–X
출생 증명서 **29**–1
출생 지 **4**–17
출하담당 계원 **146**–15
출혈하다 **82**–M
춤추다 **33**–J
충전재 **84**–22
충치 **84**–20
충치 구멍을 메꾸다 **85**–L
췌장 **75**–46
취미와 게임 **162–163**
취업원서를 작성하다 **141**–G
측량치를 환산하다 **57**–C
측정법 **15**
측정하다 **149**–C
층계 **38**–13
층계 아래 **105**–8
층계 위 **105**–9
층층나무 **128**–16
치과 병원 **84**
치과 보조원 **84**–19, **137**–19
치과의사 **84**–18, **137**–20
치다 **156**–G
치료소 **84**
치마 **64**–10
치석 **84**–17
치솔 **43**–20, **77**–20
치솔통 **43**–21
치아 교정기 **84**–24
치아파스 고지 **123**–18
치약 **77**–21
치약 튜브 하나 **56**–24
치자나무 **129**–16
치장 벽토 **149**–14

치즈 1 온스 **57**–11
치즈 **54**–38
치즈를 간다 **58**–J
치즈버거 **60**–3
치통 **78**–2
친구들에게 말하다 **141**–A
친구를 소개하세요 **8**–F
친구를 칭찬하세요 **8**–G
친구에게 감사하세요 **8**–H
친구와 같이 걸으십시오 **101**–A
칠 **14**
칠리고추 **51**–8
칠면조 **168**–17
칠면조 고기 **52**–17
칠십 **14**
칠판 **2**–1
칠판 지우개 **3**–17
칠판에 쓰세요 **2**–G
칠판을 지우세요 **2**–H
침대 **44**–8
침대 곁 소탁자 **44**–21
침대 매트레스 시트 **44**–14
(침대)머리판 **44**–15
침대 스프링 **44**–26
침대 옆 작은 탁자 **86**–9
침대 이불 시트 **44**–13
침대 조절기 **86**–12
침대 커버 **44**–11
침대를 정돈하다 **46**–G
침대틀 **44**–27
침상에서 요양하다 **80**–A
침실 **44**
침엽 **128**–12
침을 맞다 **81**–G
침착한 **30**–10
침판지 **135**–28
카네이션 **129**–18
카누 타기 **154**–3
카니발 **152**–16
카드 **168**–5
카드 가게 **92**–7
카드 카탈로그 **98**–10
카드놀이를 하다 **163**–H
카디건 스웨터 **65**–27
카메라 케이스 **165**–27
카세트 녹음기 **164**–3
카세트 플레이어 **3**–11, **164**–2, **164**–15
카세트를 들으세요 **2**–C
카운티 페어 **152**–19
카톤 **56**–4
카톨릭 학교 **112**–3
카트 **91**–31
카트리지 **162**–2
카터지치즈 한 통 **56**–17
카페테리아 **5**–4
카페트 **42**–27
카페트를 진공 청소하다 **46**–I
칸막은 좌석 **60**–19
칸막이 문 **38**–8
칼 **41**–22
칼라 **73**–7
캐나다 지역 **123**
캐로셀 슬라이드 프로젝터 **165**–29
캐미솔 **67**–21
캐비닛 **40**–1
캐주얼 드레스 **71**–37

케처 미스크 **161**–15
캔 **56**–3
캔디 **168**–14
캔디 가게 **92**–3
캔디바 **55**–41
캔버스 **163**–22
캘리포니아에서 금 발견 **115**
캠코더 **165**–21
캠퍼 **106**–11
캠프파이어 **154**–11
캠핑 **154**–1
캠핑 스토브 **154**–16
캡 **106**–16
캡슐약 **81**–27
캥거루 **135**–44
커튼 **42**–16
커튼 **44**–5
커피 **61**–22
커피 메이커 **40**–11
커피 숍 **88**–2
커피 숍 메뉴 **61**
커피 탁자 **42**–23
커피컵 **41**–27
컨디셔너 **76**–10
컨버터블 **106**–5
컨베이어 벨트 **146**–12
컴퓨터 **144**
컴퓨터 **3**–15
컴퓨터 보급 **115**
컴퓨터 웍스테이션 **143**–21
컴퓨터 프로그래머 **136**–16
컴퓨터를 사용하다 **140**–P
컵 **63**–21
케네디 암살 **115**
케이블 **144**–16
케이크 **54**–32, **61**–19
케이크팬 **59**–26
케익재료 **55**–47
케첩 **60**–23
코 **74**–21
코 스프레이 **81**–23
코끼리 **135**–42
코끼리 코 **135**–47
코드 **9**–3
코막힘 **78**–7
코메디 **166**–10
코브라 **131**–40
코뿔소 **135**–29
코알라 곰 **135**–45
코요테 **134**–3
코치 **158**–2
코코야자 열매 **50**–22
코피가 나다 **78**–17
콘드비프 **53**–8
콘서트 **166**–6
콘센트 **44**–20, **151**–41
콘크리트 **149**–10
콘택트 렌즈 **81**–36
콜론 **113**–12
콜롱 **76**–5
콧수염 **23**–5
콩 **148**–3
콩류 **54**–26
쿠거 **134**–2
쿠바 인 **115**
쿠키 **54**–31

쿠키 판 **59**–27
쿠키 한 봉지 **56**–20
쿼터 **20**–4
퀘벡 **123**–5
퀴즈 쇼 **167**–23
크레용 **45**–21
크레인 **149**–7
크로셰 **163**–20
크로스컨트리 스킹 **160**–3
크로커스 **129**–25
크로코다일 **131**–37
크루넥 스웨터 **71**–26
크리스마스 **168**–18
크리스마스 트리 **168**–20
크림 그릇 **41**–13
큰 가지 **128**–3
큰 넙치 **53**–20
큰 손 **11**–2
큰 쇠망치 **149**–22
큰어치 **132**–7
클라리넷 **120**–4
클러치 **109**–45
클럽 **163**–26
클립보드 **143**–26
클립형 귀고리 **69**–38
키가 작은 **22**–18
키가 큰 **22**–16
키보드 **144**–7
키스하다 **33**–F
킹목사 암살 **115**
타다 **157**–W
타원 **118**–9
타이어 **108**–10
타이츠 **66**–11
타이프라이터 **142**–2
타이핑하다 **140**–M
타일 **43**–9
타임 클록 **146**–4
타자기 카트리지 **143**–31
타코 **60**–9
탁구 **159**–13
탁배원 **138**–38
탁상용 달력 **142**–6
탁아소 **94**–95
탁아소 직원 **94**–3
탄력 붕대 **83**–12
탄산음료수 **55**–52
탄산음료수 **60**–4
탄산음료수 6 개들이 팩 **56**–21
탄산음료수 한 병 **56**–13
탈 것 **152**–17
탈취제 **76**–4
탈취제를 사용하다 **76**–C
탑승 구역 **110**–6
탑승구 **110**–5
탑승권을 받으십시오 **111**–E
태산목 **128**–9
태양 **127**–10
태양 광선 차단제 **76**–6
태양 에너지 **126**–1
태어나다 **28**–A
태클하다 **156**–M
태평양 북서부 **123**–14
태평양 연안주 **123**–7
태평양 표준시 **17**–26
태풍 **103**–12

택시 **104**–18
택시 면허 **104**–22
택시 밖으로 **105**–5
택시 승차장 **104**–19
택시 안으로 **105**–4
택시 운전사 **104**–20
탬버린 **120**–19
터널을 통하여 **105**–11
터틀네크 스웨터 **64**–7
터틀넥 스웨터 **71**–28
턱끝 **74**–31
턱받이 **95**–8
턱수염 **23**–6
턱시도 **65**–28
턴테이블 **164**–12
테니스 **159**–14
테니스 라켓 **161**–2
테니스 코트 **153**–7
테니스화 **68**–22
테이프 덱 **108**–30
테입 **83**–5
텐트 **154**–10
텔레마케터 **139**–59
텔레비전 **42**–26, **164**–6
텔레비전 안테나 **38**–22
텔레비전 프로그램 **166**–3
텔레비전을 보다 **27**–S
텔컴 파우더 **76**–3
토글 볼트 **150**–33
토끼 **133**–1 **133**–13
토네이도 **103**–13
토마토 **51**–23
토성 **127**–4
토스터 **40**–7
토스트 **61**–3
토요일 **18**–7
토크 쇼 **167**–20
토큰 **104**–11
토하다 **78**–E
톱날 **150**–11
통(튜브) **56**–12
통역사 **138**–34
통장 **97**–5
통조림된 식품 **54**–4
통행금지 **107**–4
퇴근하다 **26**–M
퇴비 더미 **39**–10
투명 테이프 **143**–39
투바 **120**–14
투표하다 **116**–D
튀긴다 **58**–S
튜너 **164**–13
튤립 **129**–11
트랙 조명 **42**–3
트랙볼 **144**–15
트랙터 **148**–9
트럭 기사 **139**–61
트럭을 운전하다 **140**–E
트럼벳 **120**–13
트렁크 **109**–49
트레이 테이블 **110**–16
트레이닝 바지 **64**–15
트레이닝 윗도리 **64**–14
트레일러 **106**–17
트렌치 코트 **66**–20
트롬본 **120**–12

특대 **70**–5
특매가 **21**–3
특소 **70**–1
특송 우편 **96**–15
틀린 것을 고치세요 **7**–Z
티셔츠 **64**–12
티스푼 **63**–28
팀 **158**–3
팀 스포츠 **158**
팁을 놓다 **62**–J
파괴 행위 **100**–1
파도 **155**–6
파란색 **12**–1
파리 **132**–29
파스타 **61**–15
파스타 샐러드 **53**–15
파슬리 **51**–10
파운데이션 **77**–40
파이 **61**–21
파이 팬 **59**–28
파이프 **151**–16
파이프 렌치 **151**–42
파이프가 얼었다 **49**–19
파인애플 **50**–2
파일 폴더 **142**–11
파자마 **67**–4
파충류 **131**
파카 **66**–8
파티 **169**
파티를 계획하다 **169**–A
파파야 **50**–20
판독용 기호 **21**–4
판매대 **152**–23
판매세 **21**–7
판매원 **139**–50
판초 **66**–18
팔 **14**, **74**–9
팔꿈치 **74**–15
팔다 **21**–B
팔십 **14**
팔찌 **69**–35
패스트 푸드 **60**
패스트 푸드 식당 **90**–14
패스하다 **156**–H
패시파이어 (타월, 고무 젖꼭지 등) **95**–29
패턴 **73**–8
팩스기 **143**–23
팬 **40**–24, **158**–4
팬더 곰 **135**–41
팬에 기름칠을 한다 **58**–C
팬케이크 **61**–6
팬티스타킹 **67**–27
퍼레이드 **168**–2
퍼센트 **15**
퍼즐 **45**–22
페니 **20**–1
페달 **109**–47
페리 **104**–23
페이즐리 무늬 **70**–13
페이퍼 쉬레더 **143**–24
페이퍼 클립 **143**–44
페인트 **151**–20
페인트 롤러 **151**–46
페인트 브러시 **151**–47
페인트 팬 **151**–45
페인트칠하다 **149**–A

페트리 접시 **119**–6
펜 **3**–18
펜싱 **159**–5
펜치 **150**–7
펭귄 **132**–12
편안한 **30**–7
편의점 **90**–3
편지 **96**–2
편지를 타자치다 **142**–D
편지를 팩스로 보내다 **142**–B
평결을 내리다 **99**–E
평균 신장 **22**–17
평균 체중 **22**–21
평면도 **38**–1
평범한 블라우스 **71**–38
평상복 바지 **64**–8
평원 **117**–19
평일 **18**–12
평행 **118**–21
포도 **50**–1
포도나무 **128**–22
포도원 **148**–14
포도주 잔 **63**–20
포드 자동차 최초 모델 **114**
포스트 잇 노트 **143**–34
포옹하다 **33**–G
포유동물 **134**–**135**
포인세티아 **129**–23
포장 테이프 **143**–42
포장하는 사람 **146**–13
포켓볼 **159**–2
포크 **41**–21
포트 **144**–17
폭력 강도 **100**–5
폭발 **102**–4
폭포 **117**–2
폭행 **100**–7
폼 패드 **154**–13
표백제 **72**–8
표범 **135**–25, **135**–39
표준시간 **17**–32
표지판 **91**–29, **107**
푸딩 **61**–20
푸주한 **136**–11
풀 **143**–37, **162**–8
풀 뿌리개 **72**–12
풀오버 스웨터 **64**–11
프랑스, 스페인, 영국 탐험가들 **114**
프랑스와 인디언 전쟁 **115**
프런트 데스크 **145**–8
프런트 오피스 **146**–1
프레리 도그 **133**–22
프레리 프로빈스 **123**–3
프렌치 혼 **120**–15
프리웨이를 벗어나서 **105**–7
프리즈비 **159**–6, **161**–27
프리즘 **119**–20
프린터 **144**–12
프린트무늬 **70**–10
플라스틱 저장용기 **59**–3
플래시라이트 **151**–39
플랫폼 **104**–15
플러그 **164**–18
플런저 **151**–44
플로스 **77**–22
플로어 램프 **42**–15

플로피 디스크 144-5
플루트 120-3
플리마켓 152-22
피겨 스케이팅 160-5
피고 99-5
피고에게 언도를 내리다 99-F
피고측 변호사 99-4
피곤한 31-33
피라미드 118-13
피를 뽑다 85-G
피망 51-7
피부 75-51
피아노 120-16
피자 60-7
피컵하다 94-G
피크닉 153-D
피크닉 테이블 153-8
피크닉을 갖다 153-D
피팅 151-17
픽업 트럭 106-7
핀 155-2
핀 73-14
핀셋 83-2, 119-8
필름 165-26
필리핀 인 115
하늘색 12-3
하드디스크 드라이브 144-20
하드웨어 144
하마 135-43
하와이-알류트 표준시 17-24
하원 116-1
하원의원 116-2
하의용 슬립 67-23
하이비스커스 129-12
하이에나 135-31
하이킹 154-6
하이힐 68-17
하키 스틱 161-11
하트 163-29, 168-6
하현달 127-15
학교 5, 89-27
학교 종류 112
학교 횡단보도 107-13
학교등록 양식 4
학교를 다니기 시작하다 28-B
학교에서 공부하다 26-J
학생 2-3, 139-57
한 것을 점검하세요 7-Y
한국동란 115
한국인 115
한손잡이 나무 톱 150-4
한시 16-4
한시 사십분 16-12
한시 사십오분 16-13
한시 삼십분 16-10
한시 삼십오분 16-11
한시 십분 16-6
한시 십오분 16-7
한시 오분 16-5
한시 오십분 16-14
한시 오십오분 16-15
한시 이십분 16-8
한시 이십오분 16-9
할로윈 168-10
할머니 24-2
할아버지 24-3

합창 121-3
핫도그 60-6
항공 여행 111
항공 편지 96-13
항공권을 사십시오 111-A
항생연고제 83-9
항히스타민 연고제 83-10
해(년) 18-8
해가 비치는 10-6
해마 130-23, 131-32
해먹 39-2
해바라기 129-10
해변 117-10, 155
해변용 의자 155-14
해부 키트 119-7
해안 117-12
해왕성 127-2
해일 103-15
해충 구제인 49-21
해파리 130-14
핵소 150-5
핸드백 69-6
핸드백을 몸에 꼭 대십시오 101-C
핸드소 150-4
핸드트럭 146-11
핸들 108-26
햄 52-9
햄버거 60-1
햇볕에 탐 78-14
행복한 31-32
행상인 91-30
행성 127
향수 76-5
향수병에 걸린 31-21
허가받은 직업 간호사 87-24
허리 74-4
허리 보호 147-16
허리띠 73-3
허리케인 103-12
허벅지 74-16
허파 75-37
헌 신발 71-33
헐거운 바지 71-42
헐렁한 바지 71-42
헛간 148-11
헝가리 인 115
헝겊 기저귀 95-21
헤드폰 164-16
헤어 네트 147-18
헤어 드라이기 76-16
헤어 스프레이 76-12
헤어 클립 76-17
헤어스타일 묘사하기 23
헤어젤 76-11
헤지 울타리 39-1
헤지 울타리 깎는 가위 39-12
헬기 110-8
헬스클럽 89-21
혀 74-26
혀가자미필레 살 53-21
현관등 38-9
현금 20-13
현금 인출 97-D
현금 출납원 55-19
현미경 119-4
혈압계 84-12

혈압을 재디 85-B
혈액 검사 86-17
협곡 117-17
형 24-9
형수 24-15
혜성 127-25
호랑이 135-37
호리호리한 22-22
호밀빵 53-3
호박 51-13
호수 117-13
호스 39-9
호스테스 62-1
호주 125-6
호주머니 73-4
호출 단추 86-10
호출기 9-16
호텔 88-5, 145
호텔
호텔 도어맨 145-5
호흡 마스크 147-12
혹 135-51
혹서 10-15
혼 120-13
혼란된 31-27
홀 145-13
홈통 38-19
홍수 103-16
홍역 79-5
홍채 129-20
홍합 53-26, 130-17
화가 138-43
화난 31-29
화단의 잡초를 뽑으세요 39-A
화려한 블라우스 71-39
화면 2-2, 144-6, 152-12
화분 39-18
화산 폭발 103-14
화살 161-7
화상을 입다 82-H
화성 127-6
화요일 18-3
화장대 44-2
화장분 77-39
화장실 5-8
화장을 하다 77-P
화장지 43-15
화재 102-7
화초 128
화초 148-A
화초 39-19
화초 재배자 137-25
화폐 20
화학 119-2
환경미화원 139-51
환산율 15
환승 104-6
환자 84-3
환자를 보조하다 140-B
환자실 86
환자용 변기 86-13
활 161-6
활강 스킹 160-1
황새치 130-12
회계사 136-1
회교사원 89-23

회색 **12**–5
회의실 **145**–19
회전 카드 파일 **143**–17
회전의자 **143**–22
횡단 보도 **90**–8, **107**–10
후두염 **79**–4
후라이팬 **59**–5
후추통(식탁용) **41**–15
혹 **150**–34
혹단추 **73**–23
훈제 쇠고기 **53**–6
훈제 칠면조 **53**–4
휠체어 **80**–6
휠캡 **108**–9
휴가 **19**–46
휴대용 TV **164**–7
휴대용 라디오 **164**–2
흉곽 **75**–53
흉내놀이를 하다 **163**–G
흑설탕 4분의 1 컵 **57**–8
흔들다 **94**–H
흔들림을 경험하다 **111**–N
흔한 병 및 어린이 질병 **79**
흙손 **39**–14, **149**–12
흥미있는 책 **167**–30
흥분된 **31**–23
흰 개미 **49**–22
흰 빵 **53**–1
흰머리 **23**–13
흰색 **12**–14
히터 **108**–29
히프 **74**–5